ROUTLEDGE LIBRARY EDITIONS:
BUSINESS CYCLES

Volume 6

THE BIRTH OF THE BUSINESS CYCLE

THE BIRTH OF THE BUSINESS CYCLE

PHILIP MIROWSKI

LONDON AND NEW YORK

First published in 1985

This edition first published in 2015
by Routledge
2 Park Square, Milton Park, Abingdon, Oxon, OX14 4RN

and by Routledge
711 Third Avenue, New York, NY 10017

Routledge is an imprint of the Taylor & Francis Group, an informa business

© 1985 Philip Mirowski

All rights reserved. No part of this book may be reprinted or reproduced or utilised in any form or by any electronic, mechanical, or other means, now known or hereafter invented, including photocopying and recording, or in any information storage or retrieval system, without permission in writing from the publishers.

Trademark notice: Product or corporate names may be trademarks or registered trademarks, and are used only for identification and explanation without intent to infringe.

British Library Cataloguing in Publication Data
A catalogue record for this book is available from the British Library

ISBN: 978-1-138-85286-0 (Set)
eISBN: 978-1-315-71360-1 (Set)
ISBN: 978-1-138-85813-8 (Volume 6)
eISBN: 978-1-315-71818-7 (Volume 6)

Publisher's Note
The publisher has gone to great lengths to ensure the quality of this reprint but points out that some imperfections in the original copies may be apparent.

Disclaimer
The publisher has made every effort to trace copyright holders and would welcome correspondence from those they have been unable to trace.

THE BIRTH OF THE BUSINESS CYCLE

Philip Mirowski

Garland Publishing, Inc.
New York & London ★ 1985

Copyright © 1985 Philip Mirowski

All rights reserved

Library of Congress Cataloging-in-Publication Data

Mirowski, Philip, 1951–
   The birth of the business cycle.

    (British economic history)
  1. Business cycles—Great Britain—History.
2. Great Britain—Economic conditions. I. Title.
II. Series.
HB3783.M57   1985   338.5'42'0941   84-46008
ISBN 0-8240-6688-X

All volumes in this series are printed on acid-free,
250-year-life paper.

Printed in the United States of America

THE BIRTH OF THE BUSINESS CYCLE

PHILIP MIROWSKI

TABLE OF CONTENTS

Preface. iii

Chapter One: A Proposed Taxonomy of Thought About
 Macroeconomic Instability. 1

Chapter Two: Optimism and Oblivion in the Seventeenth
 Through the Nineteenth Centuries 13

Chapter Three: Twentieth Century Theories of
 Macroeconomic Instability. 33

Chapter Four: The Birth of the Business Cycle, Part I . .71

Chapter Five: From the Economics of Ceremonial Adequacy
 to the Economics of Cumulative Change. 89

Chapter Six: An Institutionalist Theory of the
 Business Cycle 127

Chapter Seven: The Birth of the Business Cycle,
 Part II. 159

Chapter Eight: The Rate of Profit in the Eighteenth
 Century. 173

Chapter Nine: A Chronology of Eighteenth Century
 British Instability. 215

PREFACE

This manuscript has undergone a number of revisions; yet, however much it has been altered, the author still gazes upon it with some hesitions and reservations as a work in progress. The first version was submitted to fulfill the requirements of a Ph.D. dissertation in economics at the University of Michigan in 1979. That was a lumbering and unwieldy manuscript, with one bound volume discussing economic theory and the other bound volume discussing English economic history, and very little in the way of integration of the two volumes. The next revision was begun in 1980, and before it came to an abrupt halt, it had managed to thoroughly recast the entire theoretical argument. Upon turning to the economic history, it soon became apparent that certain discrete elements of the narrative could be better presented in journal articles. One such original chapter concerning English share markets in the eighteenth century was published in the September 1981 issue of the Journal of Economic History as "The Rise (and Retreat) of a Market." Because of considerations about the general flow of the primary argument of the text, this original chapter has been omitted in this version, although the final chapter makes liberal use of data series described in that article. Instead, other historical explorations concerned with fixed capital and problems with the definition of the premodern economy have been liberally expanded. The offer of Garland Press to publish a version of the dissertation provided the impetus to attempt to weave all of the new material together into a single unit, but the reader should be warned that no attempt has been made to incorporate new theoretical developments in macroeconomics, nor to incorporate any of the very impressive further historical work done on the eighteenth century English macroeconomy since 1978.

If I were to indulge in a fatal predisposition and revise one more time, I would most certainly expand the chronology of 18th century business cycles to include new evidence on interest rates, bankruptcies, wages and the standard of living. I would also want to augment the institutionalist model of the business cycle to encompass considerations of value and price behaviors at a more fundamental level: although it was precisely this dissatisfaction which led to my more recent work on the relation of physics to economics, and in particular my forthcoming book More Heat Than Light.

I would particularly like to express my gratitude to Gavin Wright, my thesis chair at the University of Michigan. I still recall the foisting my latest enthusiasm upon his indulgent attention, be it Paul Feyerabend or some obscure Hungarian mathematical economist, or some convoluted attack upon neoclassical theory, and his patent attempts to follow my peripatetic trail. He paid me the greatest compliment a teacher may give to a student: he trusted me to do what I wanted. Also, I would like to thank the economics department of Tufts University for supporting the production of this manuscript, and Bill Zuber for his many lost weekends spent trying to render a sheaf of pastery paste-ups into a comprehensible typescript.

Medford, MA
March, 1985

CHAPTER ONE

A PROPOSED TAXONOMY OF THOUGHT ABOUT MACROECONOMIC INSTABILITY

There is no neutrally objective history of economic thought. There must always be some organized principles of selection, since no work can adequately summarize all thought even within a narrowly defined set of issues or controversies. The purpose of this first chapter is to explicitly prepare the way for our prospective journey by examining our chosen organizing principles. One way to introduce these principles of selection and organization is to first examine the parallel principles of other authors who have sought to outline the history of thought about macroeconomic instability.

The histories of cycle theories that have been written in the twentieth century usually start their narratives right after Adam Smith. From a perusal of these volumes, it seems that there have been two discrete periods in the history of economic analysis when an extended debate was aired amongst economists concerning the possibility and extent of macroeconomic instability. The first period began roughly with the publication of J.C.L. Simonde di Sismondi's Nouveaux Principes d'Économie Politique in 1819 and ended with the publication of John Staurt Mill's Principles of Political Economy in 1848; it has been dubbed the period of the 'general glut' controversy by succeeding historians. The second period commences in 1913 with the publication of both Albert Aftalion's Crises Périodiques de Surproduction and Wesley Clair Mitchell's Business Cycles and loses momentum during World War II. While certain important works in business cycle theory, such as those by Hobson and Juglar, were published between the two periods, these contributions were generally the work of outsiders to the economics profession. The first period ended with an internal consensus on the import of Say's Law; the second with a truce on the relations between "Mr. Keynes and the Classics."

There exist a goodly number of chronological histories of economic analysis concentrating primarily on theories of crisis and instability, so there is no need to reproduce their blow-by-blow accounts here. [1] A deficiency shared by all these volumes, however, is the lack of a unifying thread in the face of such a superabundance of ideas and criticisms. This in not to say that there have not been attempts by some authors to instill a little discipline into those inconsonant and unruly ideas. Alvin Hansen tried it twice: once in 1927 and a second time in 1951 after his conversion to Keynesianism. [2] The Hansen typology, version one, is absorbed more with any given theorist's attitude towards the phenomenon of capitalist instability than with the form and mechanics of his argument. Hansen (version one) postulates a three-way classification:

1. Capital

    a. the distribution of income

    b. roundabout production

2. Exchange

    a. errors and uncertainty

    b. speculation

3. Money

    a. credit and interest

    b. profit margins

Names get attached to each of the subheadings, but the walls of these particular boxes are impermeable; there is no sense that errors and uncertainty might be related to credit and interest, or that one can't do justice to profit margins without simultaneously taking into account roundabout production. Theories are treated as unreservedly antagonistic and immiscible. Hansen, version two, could not have been terribly happy with the end product of version one, if only because in the interim he had come to believe that the unifying gestalt had been supplied by Keynes. This conviction was evinced in the later book, especially in chapters 13 through 17, by a search through the classics for an references which might be interpreted as anticipation of the multiplier, liquidity preference, or the schedule of the marginal efficiency of capital. Predictably enough, many theorists disappear altogether from version two--Marx, for instance--while others, such as Malthus, gain disproportionate attention relative to version one.

Keynes himself, being a literate man, understood the importance of rewriting history in the interests of a good cause. His historical schema was a much simpler one: there were the Ricardians, who held sway over men's minds for over a century, and then there were the underworld dwellers, the "brave army of heretics," "Mandeville, Malthus, Gessell and

Hobson, constantly straining at the shackles of prevailing thought." Keynes' theoretical sympathies are conspicuous here, as he slights the more successful theorists in the same vein, such as Marx and Veblen. [3]

If only Malthus instead of Ricardo, had been the parent stem from which nineteenth century economics proceeded, what a much wiser and richer place the world would be today... Ricardo is investigating the theory of the distribution of the product in conditions of equilibrium, and Malthus is concerned with what determines the volume of output day by day in the real world. Malthus is dealing with the monetary economy in which we happen to live; Ricardo with the abstraction of a neutral money economy.

Again, attitudes seem to prevail over analysis as the lesson of history, since many of Keynes' actual theoretical choices--for one, his 'labor-embodied' measure of capital [4] --openly contradict Malthus' fundamental assumptions, and descend directly from the Ricardian tradition. In any event, the purpose of Keynes' historical foray was to provide an impressionistic backdrop to highlight his own theory. In this he was eminently successful.

Professor Haberler provides the most methodical and encyclopaedic history of instability theory in his Prosperity and Depression. [5] His main taxonomic divisions were:

1. Purely Monetary Theory (Hawtrey)

2. Overinvestment Theories

    a. Monetary (Austrians: Mises, Machlup, Von Hayek)
    b. Time structure of durables (Spiethoff, Tugan-Baranowsky)

3. Underconsumption Theories (Malthus, Sismondi, Hobson)

4. Psychological Theories (Keynes, Lavington)

5. Harvest Theories (Jevons)

6. Potpourri

    a. Errors (Pigou, Beveridge)
    b. Over-indebtedness (Fisher)

Haberler carries out the survey in the first section of the book in a meticulous and even-handed manner, expounding the various points of view and then providing reasoned criticism. A catalog is not a research program, however; a deficiency which Haberler must have felt, since he too capitulated to the Keynesian Revolution in later editions of the book. In the 1941 edition, he wrote, "It is now easy to see that any one of the various hypotheses concerning the causes of the downturn or the upturn of the business cycle which we have reviewed in the earlier chapters is compatible with, and can be expressed in terms of Mr. Keynes theoretical apparatus." [6] This, from the writer most critical of the 'apparatus' of the multiplier in the initial discussions of the General Theory! Ease in perception is expected to bear a heavy burden, since Haberler fails to elucidate the translations required to get from his categories to the marginal efficiency of capital, liquidity preference, etc.

While it is true that Haberler, Hansen or even Keynes himself did not draw with a precise brush the parallels between the Keynesian appartus and the opinions on instability that preceded them, is it not possible for us to shade in the necessary relief and draw the lines between these earlier taxonomies and his innovations of the consumption function, liquidity preference, and so on? While an extended examination of the Keynesian system must wait until Chapter 3, we shall not keep the reader in suspense until then. It seems, for a number of reasons, that all pre-existing ideas about economic instability cannot be reduced to some manifestation of a consumption function, and investment function, or some other Keynesian relation. To show this, we shall examine a specific historical instance from the life of Keynes, and state the more general objection to this program of organization of economic thought.

Keynes, as everyone is aware, made much of the claim that his theory was 'general', in that is subsumed previous thought as a special case. For example, in a collection of essays in honor of Irving Fisher, he wrote: "It seems, therefore, that orthodox theory requires (1) that there should be a state of definite and constant expectation and (2) that there should be a state of full employment. These limitations meant that it is a particular theory applicable only to certain conditions: and this is my justification for calling my own theory a general theory, of which the orthodox theory is a limiting case." [7]

Keynes personally believed that the dimensions of his 'generality' were those of shifting expectations and less-than-full employment: therefore, since most previous theorists tacitly assumed full employment and/or static expectations, their thought was reduced to a special case of his thought in that respect. But that is not the precise sense in which we usually think of one theory supplanting another because of greater generality. Complete generality would presuppose that every statement which was made in the obsolete framework can also be made in the superseding framework. This is the sense in which Haberler and Hansen think of Keynes' <u>General Theory:</u> if one wished to restate, let us say, Marx's concern over the macroeconomic implications of the falling rate of profit, one need only translate his obsolete jargon into the language of the marginal efficiency of capital in order to restate the concern in an <u>improved</u> and better understood form. Those who have, in the past, attempted to grapple with the meaning and intentions of 'obsolete' texts will perhaps sense the fallacy implicit here. It is relatively easy, in the history of any scientific discipline, to find conflicting scientific theories which are mutually incommensurable, even though they apparently deal with the 'same' subject matter. [8] The metaphor often used in this instance is the attempt to translate between two dissimilar languages. While it is true that with an adequate dictionary and a grasp of the respective grammars one <u>may</u> do a passible job of translation, knowledge of usage, connotations and experience in day-to-day communication within the framework of each respective language will certainly improve the quality of the translation. Whether this loss is felt to be severe will often depend upon the native language of the reader of the translation.

    This incommensurability is often present when the adherents of a subsequent theory turn their gaze back upon their forebears. One way this situation arises, which particularly interests us in the case of Keynes, is that some problems which demanded solution under the 'obsolete' system of thought are not solved within the context of the newer system, but are rather <u>dissolved</u> and removed from the domain of active inquiry. Some examples from disciplines other than economics are (a) the problem in Newtonian physics of the absolute velocity of the earth; (b) the problem of the trajectory of electrons in an interference pattern; and (c), the problem of whether incubi are capable of producing offspring or whether they require the seeds of men in order to do so. The first was 'dissolved' by the theory of relativity, which denies absolute velocities; the second 'dissolved' by quantum theory, which denies the existence of trajectories in interference patterns, and the third 'dissolved' by a shift in theology. [9] What was previously a problem is not explained away so much as it is ignored as being irrelevant or unlikely or unsuitable for discourse. This also happened in the 'Keynesian Revolution', and for this reason the Keynesian apparatus is <u>not</u> sufficiently broad framework for use in organizing preceding thought on macroeconomic instability.

    One instance of incommensurability was the continued controversy between Keynes and Friedrich von Hayek over the appropriate theoretical basis of macroeconomics. From the very beginning of their disagreement, Keynes continually pleaded a lack of understanding on his part and on Hayek's part. After a review by Hayek of Keynes' treatise, Keynes wrote in his notes, "He has not read my book with that measure of 'good will' which an author is entitled to expect of a reader. Until he can do so, he will not see what I mean or know whether I am right." [10] An exchange both of letters and of published comments ensued, after which Keynes wrote in desperation to Piero Sraffa and Richard Kahn, "What is the next move? I feel the abyss yawns.... Yet I can't help feeling that there is something interesting in it." [11] After a strongly worded broadside against Hayek by Sraffa in the Economic Journal, it appears all substantive direct communication ended. This frustration, when all is said and done, is the result of an incommensurability in their respective ideas which were not bridged by attempts at communication and creating a common 'dictionary'. Keynes felt he could ignore the 'Hayekians' because they seemed to always presume the existence of full employment equilibrium, whereas Hayek felt Keynes was ignoring the price-theoretic foundations of the then-paramount discipline of economics. Hayek was sure that the mere postulation of a multiplier presumed that demand for capital goods is derived from a demand for consumer goods, a proposition which he attacked in his work on the 'Ricardo Effect.' [12] Keynes, on the other hand, was sure Hayek was confusing the rate of interest with the marginal efficiency of capital. [13] What is of paramount importance for us, the heirs of Keynes (who triumphed) and not of Hayek (who lost) is not so much to decipher who was 'right' as to realize that rejection of the alternative meant a 'dissolving' of some previously important problems in the theory of macroeconomic instability.

The prime result of this particular confrontation is a loss of a certain tradition in capital theory - the Austrian school - which linked monetary phenomena, time, and capital in a vital way, because Keynes "felt that phenomena such as unemployment and movements of output could be explained on the basis of a model that used only some elementary principles of capital theory. Hayek fundamentally differed from Keynes on this point." [14] When the dust cleared, captial theory was not exactly banished from the theory of macroeconomic instability, but it was certainly diminished in importance, for the rather weak reason the Keynesian economics was supposedly the economics of the 'short run' in which capital could be taken as a datum. Long after this excuse was relevant, the use of production functions in Keynesian models kept this attitude alive.

We shall consider futher criticisms of the adoption of the Keynesian research program in Chapter 3, but for the present, we merely wish to highlinght the potential for incommensurability between the Keynesian perplex and the questions which motivated other theorists of macroeconomic instability, which in turn rules out the employment of the Keynesian apparatus in organizing the history of instability theory.

The question before us then becomes, "How should one pick and choose in trying to make sense of the theories of instability?" The compromise between an indiscriminate list of positions which the author happens to stumble across on the one hand, and the squeezing of every idea into a Procrustean bed of the concepts of a single school of thought on the other hand, would seem to be a conscious and consciencious framework which tries to be as removed as possible from any particular school. This framework would have to be so abstract that the thought of any school could be expressed within its orbit, and yet so specific that it focuses our attention on a finite set of issues. One way to summarize such an organizing principle is to conceive of theories of instability as being constructed in logical 'stages', even though this has not been the case historically. There are four 'stages' in our proposed schema:

1) First, conception of the macroeconomy as a unified 'system' which can be discussed as a discrete whole. As a consciousness of the expansion of the system is developed, it is then presumed that the component parts of the system must either all grow proportionately (such as outputs, population and the money supply) or remain fixed (such as the rate of interest or the velocity of money).

2) Increased sophistication with regard to the multiple determination of events, such that both the level and distribution of the component parts of the macroeconomic whole are determined simultaneously. In this stage, for example, it becomes clear that some determinant movement of components of the macroeconomy need not be proportional, but instead follow a more complicated scheme which then has feedbacks upon the level of activity as a whole. The major difference between this stage and the previous one is that 'Stage 1' theories picture disproportionate movements of macroeconomic components as being independent of the level (or rate of growth) of the macroeconomy as a whole, whereas 'Stage 2' theories are explicitly concerned with the fact that disproportionate movements of macroeconomic components will alter the rate of growth.

3) In this stage, the distinction between phenomena endogenous and exogenous to the macroeconomy (at least in the eyes of the school under consideration) are differentiated and made explicit. The hallmark of this stage is the explicit disavowal of the need by economists to explain certain phenomena, and yet these same specific phenomena may be appealed to as the 'cause' of macroeconomic fluctuations.

4) This is the most sophisticated stage, where the parameter/variable distinction ceases to be a dichotomy and instead becomes a continuum. The fixity of postulated relations are admitted to be only approximate, but instead of vitiating the analysis, further analytical devices are employed to deal with their continual metamorphosis.

The terminology of 'stages' should not mislead the reader into thinking that these innovations are strictly chronological in the history of macroeconomic theory. Instead, they display a logical order in that any subsequent stage can only be adequately incorporated into a theory if and only if the previous stage has already been clearly articulated within that same framework. Looking at it sequentially: first, one cannot have a developed theory of the simultaneous determination of the level and distribution of activity if one does not initially have an explanation of the proportional or disproportional movements in the components of the system. For example: many times dissatisfaction has been expressed with one-good growth models, since there are no prices or outputs in the conventional sense to be explained. All that is purportedly explained is the level of activity; but a level without specification of distribution and structure of an economy is rightly felt to be specious and trivial.

Secondly, an exogenous/endogenous distinction without a theory of the level and distribution of activity is also trivial. Let us say, for example, we think the weather affects the economy; and further, as economists, we cannot be held responsible for prediction and explanation of the weather. Further, we theoretically postulate that weather affects the economy specifically through agriculture as an imponderable which substantially alters the output of agricultural goods. If we only have a 'Stage 1' theory of the macroeconomy, this means that the growth of agricultural output is jolted into moving disproportionately with the rest of the economy; one would then postulate some sort of adjustment mechanism which would bring agriculture back into proportionate movement with other goods. However, the 'Stage 1' theory does not allow the 'jolts' to alter the movement of the economy as an aggregate--individual movements, as we have said, are there independent of macroeconomic movements. A very clear example of this 'Stage 1' thinking is the Marshallian notion of perfect competition, where the actions of the individual unit are <u>assumed</u> to be independent of the industry and thus the <u>economy</u> as a whole. In these cases, the endogenous/exogenous distinction is superfluous to macroeconomic theory, since there is no possible channel of causality leading from the exogenous shock, through the individual unit to the movement of the system as a whole.

Thirdly, the loosening of the parameter/variable distinction is largely ineffectual if there has not previously been an extended articulation of the previous stages. To see this, let us briefly examine one aspect of the macroeconomic thought of Thomas Malthus. In various places in his <u>Principles</u>, Malthus expressed concern that the 'indolence' of the working class acts as a drag upon the accumulation of capital. Now, this concern could be conceptualized in two very different ways. The first is that workers are inherently lazy and, if left to their own devices, will slacken off both in the intensity and quality of their work. This will cause the lines of endeavor that employ these lazy workers to not expand output as rapidly as the economy as a whole, and the economy will experience a disproportionality in the expansion of various lines of output. This is an incoherent Stage 1 theory as long as there is no specification of the interaction between this limping sector and the movement of the system as a whole. There is a second way in which this concern could be stated, which was not available to Malthus because the value theory he was groping towards and its lines of causality were not yet articulated. One could there interpret this indolence as an unwillingness to supply marginal labor unless there existed the incentive of a novel consumption commodity (or, in spatial terms, the market penetrates an area which was previously self-contained and non-monetized). In the marginalist framework, this could be expressed by a systematic alteration of the parameters of technology and tastes brought about by the introduction of a new commodity which itself would not need explanation by economists since it was exogenous to their chosen sphere of study. While Malthus did mention novel commodities as a possible counteracting force to indolence, he was incapable of including it as part of a macroeconomic theory because his theory was deficient in its development of Stages 2 and 3.

One major reason why these 'stages' of instability theory are not chronological is that progress in the development of a particular stage of theorizing may be forgotten or 'dissolved' in the process of the shift from one school of thought to another, in much the same way that Hayak's concerns over capital theory were 'dissolved' by the Keynesian Revolution. A striking example of this retrogression, which we will describe in the next chapter, is the supercession of the classical school of economics by the marginalist/subjectivist school. While it is true that many proponents of the classical school were also proponents of something like Say's Law (which is one simple restatement of Stage 1 theory), much progress had been made in the course of the 'general glut' controversy in clarifying the need for a Stage 2 component to macroeconomic theory. [15] The sophistication of these discussions was not sufficient to prevent them from being dissolved when the framework of discussion was shifted onto marginalist/subjectivist basis, at least until the advent of Keynes.

For the purposes of the present study, the proposed 'Stages' will provide a convenient taxonomy for study of the theory and history of macroeconomic instability. As such, it only provides a set of empty boxes in which we can sort various ideas, separated as much as possible from the exigencies and concerns of the particular school of thought we are examining at the moment. Again, perhaps the best way to display this neutrality is by offering various examples. Let us choose some specific school of thought, and then isolate the various Stages of instability theory as components at that school's thought. (These examples are merely to whet the reader's appetite, since the history of instability theory will be examined in detail in Chapters 2 and 3 below.)

What do the Stages look like in the neoclassical framework of economic theory? The first stage, as we have already indicated, corresponds to any neoclassical model in which Say's Law, or some approximation therunto, reigns as an operating principle. Say's Law states there can be no aggregate divergence of quantity demanded and quantity supplied, which is just a truism in the neoclassical system. Subsequent comentators [16] have divided up this concept into the finer gradations of Say's Equality, Say's Identity and Walras' Law, which state consecutively: the sum of the value of goods supplied <u>equals</u> the sum of the value of goods demanded; the sum of the value of goods supplied is identical with the sum of the respective goods demanded; and the sum of the values of goods supplied plus existing money equals the sum of the respective goods plus money demanded. In any of these forms, if the condition is thought to hold continuously, then there is no possibility of Stage 2 macroeconomics. This is the case, as Chapters 2 and 3 will attempt to document in detail, because any discrepancy between supply and demand in any one market is offset by an adjustment in a neighboring market without altering the aggregate sum total of product. Say's Law theorists called this a "disproportionality crisis": for instance, too many shoes being produced, which simultaneously must mean too few potatoes. In the 'short' run, some shoes go unsold and some potential demands for potatoes go unassuaged, but the effects of this disequilibrium upon the level of total product are thought to be transitory, so that when shoe and potato production are adjusted the total value of goods supplied is equal to the total value of goods demanded and both are equal to the previous total value of product. This situation may be summarized by saying that market adjustments are independent of the absolute level of output. Far from being an oversight of less sophisticated nineteenth century economists, this type of theory can still be found in most economic journals of the 1970's and 1980's. [17]

The level of sophistication is raised to Stage 2 when the realization is made explicit that the potential demand for the 'underproduced' potatoes may never be felt by the potato producers, especially if the shoe producers cut back on employment. This is the question of 'effective demand' which was the concern of Keynes. Stage 2 theories realize that market adjustments have feedbacks upon the aggregate level of 'income' which will, in turn, alter the whole configuration of supply and demand schedules. This feedback calls into question the conceptually necessary independence of demand and supply curves, and to a certain extent undermines the accepted price-theoretic conventions at the micro level. The full implications of an adequate Stage 2 theory within the neoclassical tradition is still a matter of debate and contention to this very day, as we shall discover in Chapter 3.

Stage 3 theories admit that there are certain imponderables which alter demand and supply schedules and yet are not expicitly considered in the conventional <u>ceteris paribus</u> conditions; that is, phenomena which do not come under the headings of income, endowments, tastes or technology. With the advent of econometrics (i.e., mathematical statistics applied to certain empirical problems in economics), these imponderables tended to be lumped together in an additive term at the end of the particular function under consideration, and called the 'error term'. It is an integral part of this innovation that these residual phenomena are not expected to be explained by economists qua economists. Carrying the logic but a step further, neoclassical economists such as Ragnar Frisch [18] proposed that if these random shocks impinged upon an essentially stable structure of mathematical relations, then it was possible that cycles would result. Note well that, in order for this innovation to be strictly logical, it is presumed that a Stage 2 theory already exists: 'random shocks' can only influence the level of macroeconomic activity or income if one first has a theory of the determinants of the levels of activity. If it were otherwise, random shocks would only cause temporary disproportionalities in equilibrium prices and outputs reminiscent of Say's Law. This explanation of macroeconomic instability is quite popular, as we shall discover in Chapter 3.

Finally, Stage 4 theories make their appearance in neoclassical economics as theories about systemic changes in the givens of the analysis, particularly changes in technological parameters associated with the name of Joseph Schumpeter [19], and changes in the parameters of taste, concisely summarized in an article by Luigi Pasinetti. [20] Once more, these explanations basically presume stages 1 through 3 are already analytically determined, especially the crucial analytical distinction between totally exogenous phenomena, which do not need to be explained or justified further, and determinate changes in parameters, which do need further justification. In the case of Schumpeter this is of paramount importance, since he is not altogether clear in his understanding of the fact that his Walrasian models cannot constitute a theory of the level of economic activity in and of themselves (Stage 2), and he does not provide a convincing explanation of his periodic waves of technological innovation which invites us to confuse them with totally exogenous accidents or shocks (Stage 3). If Schumpeter had clarified these issues, and if he had told a more plausible story about why epoch-making innovations were temporally 'bunched', his would have been a prime example of a neoclassical Stage 4 theory. A more concise example of a neoclassical Stage 4 theory can be found in an article by

Pasinetti called "Cyclical Fluctuations and Economic Growth". In it, Pasinetti simply accepts the multiplier-accelerator version of Keynesian theory (which we examine in detail in Chapter 3) and takes note of Frisch's hypothesis, which shows he is aware of Stages 1 through 3 in the previous history of macroeconomic theories. He then proposes a Stage 4 theory employing a neoclassical hypothesis about changes in consumer behavior known as Engel's Law, which states as income rises in the aggregate, consumers shift the bulk of their budget away from 'necessities' and towards 'luxury' items. Pasinetti proposes that this change in behavioral parameters, in conjunction with economic growth, causes structural changes in production which, in the presence of Stage 1 through 3 theories, results in continuous macroeconomic fluctuations.

In subsequent chapters, we will have occasion to refer to this 'Stages' framework, both as an organizing principle in discussions of the history of theories of macoreconomic instability, and as a guide in our own suggestions in the realm of theory and historical illustration. Returning to this theoretical touchstone from time to time will help to prevent us from 'dissolving' the work of our predecessors, at least in this one limited respect.

-13-

CHAPTER TWO

OPTIMISM AND OBLIVION IN THE SEVENTEENTH
THROUGH THE NINETEENTH CENTURIES

I. THE PRE-PARADIGM PAMPHLET LITERATURE

Written references to a state of 'decayed trade' can be found at least as early as the sixteenth century in England. It would be hasty to interpret such terms in the same light as their modern counterparts, however. "Trade" in early modern English pamphlets rarely referred to macroeconomic activity as a whole; in that era specific trades or sectors were the analytical units of the mercantilist writers. The tracts of Misselden, Malynes and Mun in the first half of the seventeenth century focused primarily on the international flows of specie and their impact on the international cloth trade. "Most commentators took it for granted that 'the want of money....is the first cause of the decay of trade'; and nearly all writers were concerned over the 'fearful effect that followeth the want of a convenient stock of money to maintain the prices, and to beat or maintain our home commerce.'" [1] The dearth or plentitude of money was thought to be a direct result of the rate of exchange between the pound and other currencies; reform involved various government policies to keep the monetary metals at home. If action were not forthcoming, 'overtrading' in cloth would result, which was commerce at a price which would prevent the ready sale of cloth on the continent.

Other seventeenth century writers chose agriculture as the sector of interest in explaining a localized decay of trade. William Petty is sometimes credited as the first political economist to mention business cycles, in his Treatise of Taxes and Contributions of 1662. The relevant passage mentions "....the medium of seven years, or rather of so many years as makes up the Cycle, within which Dearths and Plenties make their revolution, doth give the ordinary Rent of the Land in Corn." [2]

Again, the analysis stopped short with the landlord and the land; no links were forged with any idea of levels of activity as a whole. Indeed, the early Political Arithmeticians were busy simply making others aware that enumerations of economic phenomena should be of inherent interest to the state and to politically-minded citizens. To expect an intricate interplay of hypothesis and informed empiricism at this juncture is to presume much too organized an inquiry. Adequate tax revenues and an abundant population from which to recruit an army were sufficient goals. To each political objective corresponded a sector of the economy: these were the elemental quanta of analysis.

The first concern with trade in a larger sense coincided with the dawn of the eighteenth century. An indication of this broadened view can be discerned in the surviving records of Abraham Hill, an appointee to a royal commission created to look into the decay of trade in the late 1690's. [3] The commission was charged with its task on May 15, 1696 (old style calendar) and produced a series of reports up until March 22, 1700. Hill's notes reveal the preoccupations of the early Political Arithmeticians, including scattered statistics on the early distribution of imports and exports by nation, short annual time series of the numbers of brewers and victuallers in the early 1690's, estimates of population and counts of bound apprentices in the Weavers' Company. One gets the feeling that Hill, with his eclectic approach, almost would have felt at home in the NBER of Wesley Clair Mitchell. Nevertheless, when it came time to make a report in December 1697, the committee had to admit to a lack of a theoretical organizing principle in the aggregate:

> We have made Enquiries into the State of Trade in general from the year 1670 to the present time, and upon the best Calculations we can make by the Duties paid at the Custom House, we are on the Opinion that Trade in General did considerably increase from the end of the Dutch War in 1673 to anno 1668, when the late War began: But Trade being subject to many Accidents, and Variations; and all Accounts and Informations relating thereunto being liable to objection it does not appear in what proportion, or how much each trade has increased from year to year.

In the first half of the eighteenth century, references to the state of trade in a comprehensive sense appear with increasing frequency, although the measure or indicator of this state is never given much thought. Proposed remedies for perceived slumps begin appearing in the newpapers and Parliamentary debates of the day, which at least implicitly assumed some theoretical lines of causality. The <u>London Journal</u> of September 9, 1721 remarks, "We now see with pleasure that the Customs House Bills of Entry Goods Imported and Exported, which are published daily in print, begin to increase considerably, particularly with respect to the exports of our own woollen manufacture, great quantities of which are shipped for Portugal, Italy and Russia, but especially to Spain; People flatter themselves that when credit is a little better revived, Trade will consequently flourish...." And, again, on July 21, 1722, the <u>Journal</u>

reports, "Several Directors of the Bank conferred last week with the Treasury in relation to the Circulation of 1,900,000 pounds in Exchequer Bills, and we are told a considerable Progress is made in that Affair, which tis hoped will be a Means to revive publick Credit." [4] These references reflect the fascination that the concept of a 'Fund of Credit' held for writers in the period circa 1680-1725; a fascination that palled considerably when the massive losses from the South Sea bubble became apparent. It is striking that so early on credit looms large in explanations of instability, only to be totally submerged in later discussions.

Around 1750, there arose the initial outlines of what might be considered a Stage 1 theory of macroeconomic activity from a modern point of view. Earlier concerns about the causes of differential rates of interest on government securities were transmuted into the conviction that the economy-wide rate of profit was the key indicator of the robustness of trade. [5] As a corollary, any situation which threatened profits also threatened the aggregate level of trade, even though that situation might benefit other classes of citizens of the polity. As early as 1732 Pulteney argued in a debate in the Commons that "It is now a universal complaint in the Country that the high Wages given to Workmen is the chief Cause of the Decay of our Trade and Manufactures; our Business then is, to take all the Measures we can think of, to enable our Workmen to work for less Wages than they do at present." [6] As the distribution of class returns came to play an increasingly larger part in the theoretical and policy discussions of the later eighteenth century, we can discern both the origins of the Ricaridian system and its antipathetic mirror image, the underconsumptionist theories of the nineteenth century.

II. ADAM SMITH

Before there could be revival schools, the ill formed and amorphous wisdom of the pamphlet and the political debate had to be brought together in some formal consensus. It is from Adam Smith's Wealth of Nations that we date the inception of the discipline of economics because this book, more than any other eighteenth century work, performed this service. The Wealth of Nations was a particularly fertile source for later authors precisely because it was cast in the everyday terms of the newspaper and the public debate; at times analytical, at other times folksy and full of trivia and special pleading; and always containing at least two independent explanations for any given phenomenon. Its significance for the theory of economic instability was two-fold: it was the premier work to affirm the rate of profit in its place at the center stage of the pageant of economic progress; and it was the first work to import the agricultural notions of stocks and yields into the whole range of economic processes. As regards profits, Smith wrote, "It is the stock that is employed for the sake of profit, which puts in motion the greater part of the useful labor in any society. The plans and projects of the employers of stock regulate and direct all the most important operations of labor, and profit is the end proposed by all these plans and projects." The stress on the main index of well-being was shifted from employment as such to the levels of accumulated 'stock'; the measure of this stock was the measure of a nation's wealth. Smith's second innovation was to consider what this measurement might entail: "The whole expense of maintaining the fixed capital must evidently be excluded from the net revenue of society. Neither the materials necessary for supporting their useful machines and instruments of trade, their profitable buildings, etc., nor the produce of the labor necessary for fashioning those materials into proper form, can ever make any part of it." [7] Smith was oblivious to the fact that he was equating the welfare of the state with the welfare of the owner of 'stock'; the ideological implications of which were only to be drawn to their logical conclusions in the middle of the next century. Smith's synthesis thus contained within its structure the embryo of the 'general glut' controversy of the next 75 years. When Smith resolves all revenue, including all 'stock', into wages, rents and profits, he sets the stage for Malthusian underconsumptionism by suggesting that the whole exsisting produce of society is ultimately consumed by some individual. Simultaneously, by deprecating the role of money (the stock of money was to be subtracted from "the great wheel of commerce" in order to arrive at gross revenue,) and phrasing his discourse in terms of barter relations, he prepares the way for Say's Law and the Ricardian tradition. Most significantly, he popularizes the method of thinking about the economy as an entity greater than the sum of its parts, mainly through his concepts of the uniform rate of profit and the net revenue of society.

Smith, in his work, did not confront the problem of macroeconomic instability at any length, probably because he felt that the societal effect of the market could only be more salubrious than it already had been if only restraints on trade and other mercantilist policies could be nullified. He barely manages to mention any of the commercial crises previous to the 1770's, a strange oversight for one normally so garrulous when it came to historical minutae. As for theory, crises and slumps only attract his attention for one paragraph in the whole of the <u>Wealth of Nations</u>: "When the profits of trade happen to be greater than ordinary, overtrading becomes a general error both among great and small dealers....Sober men, whose projects have been disproportioned to their capitals, are likely to have neither wherewithal to buy money nor credit to borrow it, as prodigals whose expense has been disproportioned to their revenue." [8]

One of the many interesting aspects of this quote is its location in the <u>Wealth of Nations</u>. It does not make its appearance in Books I or II, the main locations of abstract theoretical discussion, but at the very beginning of Book IV, which contains both Smith's attack on the Mercantile System and the sections of his ideas which have contributed the most to his lasting fame: the insistence upon the natural progress of an economy free of government restraint and hinderance. What prompted this statement to be placed in this somewhat curious context?

The first reason for its location is Smith's characterization of the Mercantilists as believing that wealth consists of money in the form of specie or currency. If one accepted Mercantilist premises, then a theory of macroeconomic fluctuations follows directly: fluctuations in trade are both caused by and identical with fluctuations in the stock of money. As Smith writes, "No complaint is more common that that of a scarcity of money." This portrayal is not far from the mark during the eigtheenth century, as we have already seen. The unavailability of money is continually identified as a symptom and a cause of declining trade: but, it must be stressed, this lack of money includes a dearth of available <u>credit.</u> This shift in the definition of money creates a dissonance in Smith's discussion. Either credit extended always maintains a fixed proportion to specie, or else Mercantilists cannot be accused of believing only specie was wealth. Smith, in this as in so many instances of a potential logical hitch, simply suppresses the issue by implicitly assuming that the natural extent of credit is proportional to the volume of trade. It is true some intemperate individuals may overextend themselves; but when this is perceived by lenders (a heavy burden of perception which is not justified), they readjust their lending, and all must temporarily suffer because of the mistakes of the few. In this discussion, Smith still sees himself as refuting the Mercantilist doctrines. Previously, a dearth of credit was thought to have caused declining trade; in Smith, the mistakes of the prodigals in trying to expand trade too quickly leads to a shortage of credit and money. Far from being a refutation of previous thought, Smith, in actuality, merely begged a number of important issues: what determines the volume of credit? What determines the 'appropriate' rate of expansion? Did the Mercantilists really equate credit with wealth, or were they groping for some theoretical determinant of the extent of trade? Most importantly, if these prodigal individuals are fairly numerous, could not their continual disruption of trade impede the progress of the nation as a whole towards wealth?

It is this latter issue which provides the second rationale for the location of Smith's comment. If the unhindered spread of the division of labor and the market really did lead inexorably to economic progress, there remained the possible qualification that the spread of the market might develop its own internal barriers to further expansion in the form of gluts and stagnations. Smith's reaction to this potentially damaging qualification to his thesis of Book IV is to lay the responsibility for gluts at the feet of "improvident spendthrifts". However, there is another potential logical hitch here. If misguided individuals can by their actions periodically impede the orderly progress of the market, why should we believe that the government should adopt a minimal presence in the market? This question haunts Book IV, and is never confronted outside the single paragraph quoted above. The theoretical tension between progress and gluts was apparent to Smith's contemporaries: one of his more perceptive friends, David Hume, even tried to bring it to Smith's attention in a letter dated June 27, 1772: [9]

> We are here in a very melancholy Situation: Continual Bankruptcies, universal loss of Credit, and endless Suspicions...The Carron Company is reeling, which is one of the greatest Calamities of the whole; as they gave Employment to near 10,000 People. Do these Events any-wise effect your Theory? Or will it occasion the Revisal of any Chapters?

We do not possess Smith's answer to this letter, but we do possess the published version of <u>The Wealth of Nations</u>: The answer to Hume's inquiry was 'no'. The existence of 'gluts' and 'overtrading' was the Achilles heel of Smith's book, the phenomena capable of undermining his very thesis. Because of their threatening nature, the potential forms of macroeconomic instability were confined, at the very onset of the self-conscious discipline of economic, to an underworld of criticism and opposition.

III. THE GENERAL GLUT CONTROVERSY OF THE 1820'S

Between the 1770's and some time during the decade of the 1810's it seems any serious discussion of economic stability is totally absent from the recognized economic literature. A glib and superficial explanation of this phenomenon suggests that this was due to the fact that there were no perceptible macroeconomic fluctuations until the Napoleonic War period [10], but no one has ever bothered to substantiate that claim historically; and further, absence of this discussion from the literature specifically concerned with economics does not mean absence from the larger world of general periodicals. In England in the years 1793 and 1797, for example, there is concern expressed in the <u>Times</u>, the <u>Annual Register</u>, and other news periodicals over perceptions of flagging trade. Moreover, when we come to examine England's historical record in later chapters, we shall find some pronounced evidence of fluctuations, so the thesis that economic writers were merely following the dictates of their sense impressions must be rejected.

If this be so, then the question of why no one discusses the problems and potential for macroeconomic instability in this period becomes all the more curious. The authority of Smith's work may have played a significant role: David Ricardo, who succeeded Smith as the premier practitioner of political economy clearly inherited Smith's aversion to discussions of gluts and so forth. However, to cast the answer in these simplistic terms is to forget that inquiry into economic problems from the 1770's to the 1810's was not yet organized into a paradigm, and did not yet have committed practitioners in the sense we know today. The underdevelopment of economics as a science had two implications for our question above: first, there were no writers solely committed to logical criticism of Smith's work or to discussion of other 'economic' issues which arose; and secondly, since economists have come to trace their lineage directly from Smith to Ricardo, any generalist or journalist concerned with contemporary economic problems in a discursive way has been largely ignored in any history of economic thought.

It is a well known story that David Ricardo embarked upon his illustrious career as a political economist by reading <u>The Wealth of Nations</u> while on a vacation at Bath in 1799 and was encouraged to develop criticisms of certain errors he believed he had discovered in Smith. It is a characteristic sign of the developing orthodoxy that Ricardo did not number among Smith's errors or contradictions the one we have identified in the previous section of this chapter: the possibility of self-generated obstacles, or gluts which develop in the course of the spread of the market.

Ricardo's method of theorizing involved assuming the market equated prices to costs of production at the margin, and from there to describe the character of the resulting timeless (or, more precisely, period-specific) equilibrium. The aim and purpose of political economy for Ricardo was to ascertain these 'long run' equilibrium proportions between economic variables; and particularly, between wages, rents and profits. Growth, if it could be anything different from this equilibrium, must be a proportional change, with all the equilibrium relations maintained. (We ignore for the moment the increasing scarcity of fertile land, which provides the only element of nonlinearity in the Ricardian system.) In Ricardo there is scant awareness that there might be ongoing requirements of accumulation, which, if contradictory, would obstruct the continuing efficiency of the market. If, as Ricardo held, commodities purchased commodities, there could be no overall glut since the market always cleared. Ricardo understood that this assumption entailed a friction-less world, and felt, as do many economists today, that the unrealistic aspects of his model could be mitigated by introducing lags in reactions: [11]

> If wages are low, only one-half (of the output) may perhaps be given to the laborers. If high, three-fourths---but whether in the hands of the masters or of the men they would not have a different value...Mistakes may be made, and commodities not suited to the demand may be produced--of those there may be a glut; they may not sell at their usual price; but then this is owing to the mistake, and not to the want of demand for productions. For everything produced there must be a proprietor.

'Lags', 'frictions' and so forth are more modern and palatable terms for a much older idea: everything should hold some fixed proportion to everything else in the economy in its natural state; but periodically there are accidental divergences which are by their very nature transitory and independent of the level of aggregate activity. This is a very clear and distinct example of 'Stage 1' theories of macroeconomic instability. In Ricardo, that independence of the part and the whole is quite boldly stated, for instance, when he pronounces upon contemporary concerns over slumps in foreign trade: [12]

> An Increase of Demand is serviceable to a Country inasmuch as it procures for it a more extensive Market, and enables it to get a greater Quantity of Foreign Goods in Exchange for its own; but the Amount and Value of the Commodities produced, whether the Country possesses Foreign Trade or not, is always limited by the Amount of Capital Employed; and, therefore, Foreign Trade may alter the Description of Commodities produced, but cannot increase their aggregate Value.

Ricardo is perceptive in that he admits changes in demand must alter the list of physical commodities produced; however, in order to maintain the independence of the level of activity and spending behaviors, he must resort to holding the aggregate <u>value</u> of goods constant. This presumed constancy of <u>value</u> in the face of alternative spending behaviors also holds for the sub-aggregate known as Capital: [13]

> Credit, I think, is the Means which is alternatively transferred from one to another, to make use of Capital actually existing; it does not create Capital; it determines only by whom that Capital should be employed.

Capital determines the fixed annual value of the product of the nation, and that capital itself is a value fixed independently of its employment in the economy. Here, in a nutshell, we have a macroeocnomic theory which has persisted down to this very day, although its outward appearances have certainly altered over time. Keynes, much as he trumpeted the virtues of Malthus over Ricardo, was not totally immune to its influence. Modern writers, supposedly well-schooled in the pitfalls of Say's Law, also employ this framework regularly. We shall substantiate these claims in the next chapter, but for now it is sufficient to observe how Smith's suppression of certain theoretical problems was repeated and reified by Ricardo. The mechanisms of credit and money, which were identified by the pre-Smithian pamphlet literature as a primary source of instability, were labeled unimportant after the Bullion Report of 1810. Unemployment, it was claimed, was not due to any internal workings of the system, but was instead generally blamed on over-population. (The question which was begged, as Marx later pointed out, was that over-population occurred relative to a certain social structure, and not relative to some independently given state of nature.) In fact, the level of aggregate activity itself was left unexplained, even though this was coupled with a presumption that the existing state of economic organization would lead to 'progress'. On all fronts, theoretical innovations necessary to conceive of a Stage 2 macroeconomic theory were neutralized, one by one.

Ricardo, if anything, was a consistant theorist, and defended this conception of the economy both in print and in Parliament against a large audience of the skeptical. In his very first year (1819) as representative from the Irish pocket borough of Portarlington, he worked very hard for a resumption of cash payments and a return to convertability of notes into gold at a depreciated rate. His reason for supporting such a measure, other than his belief in the intrinsic importance of an invariable standard of value, was that an inconvertable paper currency encouraged overtrading---that is, 'mistakes'. But while money could cause distortions, it could not have any impact on production in the aggregate, so that the deflation implied in his conversion scheme could not be deleterious for the economy as a whole. Against numerous challenges by Lauderdale and others, Ricardo maitained the necessary equality between savings and investment and the reality of the assumption of full employment as a periodic state of affairs. [14]

Ricardo met formidable opposition in print in the works of Thomas Robert Malthus and, most effectively, J.C.L. Simonde di Sismondi, both referred to by later writers as leading members of the 'underconsumptionist' school. The reason for this appellation is best illuminated by Malthus' chapter on the 'Progress of Wealth' in his Principles: [15]

> The consumption and demand occasioned by the persons employed in productive labor can never alone furnish a motive to the accumulation and employment of capital; and with regard to the capitalists themselves, together with the landlords and other rich persons, they have, by the supposition, agreed to be parsimonious, and by depriving themselves of their usual conveniences and luxuries to save from their revenue and add to their capital. Under these circumstances, I would ask, how is it possible to suppose that the increased quantity of commodities, obtained by the increased number of productive laborers, should find purchasers, <u>without such a fall in price as would probably sink their value below the costs of production,</u> or, at least very greatly diminish both the power and the will to save.

The first sentence of the above quote begins to diverge from the Ricardian tradition by recognizing a form of disproportionality never before thought significant: that between consumption and investment. Ricardo could not accept that the issue be posed in this manner because there was no effective distinction in his labor embodied value theory between goods used for consumption and those for investment. [16] Use value was an analytical precondition which, once assured, played no active role in value determination. The operant categories for Ricardo were social classes, and not the mental contemplation of attributes. Malthus bent the Ricardian categories to his own uses by preserving the jargon but switching the value theory: he insisted on a 'labor commanded' value theory, wherein the amount of labor voluntarily traded determined equilibrium prices; this was a precursor to the later utility theories of value, since it was the act of choice in trading which governed exchange ratios. The second sentence of the above quote breaks with Ricardian conceptions completely, although Malthus possessed neither the acute insight nor the theoretical stamina to follow it up. Earlier, Sismondi had presented the matter succinctly. Rephrasing his objection in modern terms, the glut theorists did not question that the market would <u>clear</u> in period t (ideally: that is, at low enough prices); but they did question whether the resulting level of output could be maintained in period t+1 at those same equilibrium prices.

Note well that the two issues in the two sentences are conceptually distinct and separate, something Keynes overlooked when he was extolling Malthus' virtues to the detriment of Ricardo. Even if we accept Ricardo's value theoretic assumptions, his reasoning concerning output <u>over time</u> was deficient. His difficulty in thinking temporally is evident in his reply to Malthus' criticism: [17]

> It is quite true that commodities may exist in such abundance, compared with labor, as to make their value so to fall, estimated in labor, as not to afford any inducement to their future production. In that case labor will command a great quantity of commodities. It is this that Mr. Malthus subsequently decries. If Mr. Malthus means that there may be such a glut of commodities as to make them ruinously cheap in labor I agree with him, but this is only saying that labor is so high that it absorbs all that fund which ought to belong to profits, and therefore the capitalist will have no interest in continuing to accumulate. But what will be the situation of the laborer? Will that be miserable?

If there is no inducement to further production, what will happen in period t+1? Presumably the existing goods do not last forever. And, if there is no inducement to further production, where will the laborers get those wages to purchase that cornucopia of commodities? Perhaps the classical preoccupation with the stationary state accompanied by a zero profit rate becomes more comprehensible as an attempt to avoid this very problem.

Simplistic underconsumptionism, associated with Malthus on the right and Robert Owen and Rodbertus on the left, is merely a recognition of the possibility of disproportionality over time in the production of long- and short-lived goods: a gap between 'consumption' and total production is noticed and presumed to be disruptive. The error of the underconsumptionists (past and present) lies in their not realizing that investment, the effects of which extend over many time periods, <u>can</u> account for the gap. The underconsumptionists assume the purpose of production is consumption; workers are not allowed to consume all that they produce, so how can it be sold? If instead, the main purpose of production was profit--to accumulate--their problematic disappears, and a different theoretical query becomes germane: what determines the time distribution of accumulation (and therefore, the level of output)? This is the conceptual innovation which marks the second stage of the history of cycle theories: Problems of realization must deal with investment and the unique role of the business sector.

In the period of the general glut controversy, the insights of the underconsumptionists were not as much answered by the Ricardian orthodoxy as much as they were simply suppressed. Sismondi, the most perceptive and logical of the glut theorists, was the most vilified by the Ricardians. Torrens, McCulloch and Say all wrote articles attacking him in the decade of the 20's and Ricardo himself is reported to have accused Sismondi of being too much of a sentimentalist to be a good political economist. [18] J.B. Say was much more specific in isolating that quality of Sismondi which demanded refutation: "Why does he call for an inquiry into the laws which might oblige the entrepreneur to guarantee a living for the worker he employs? Such an inquiry would paralyze the spirit of enterprise. Merely the fear that the authorities might interfere with private contracts is a scourge and harmful to the wealth of a nation." [19] Sismondi responded to this half-logical attack as well he might with desperation: "...with all respect to the authority of the Pontiffs of the science, I could say, like Galileo, Eppur si Muove," [20] and Elie Halevy reports that he believed before he died that he had not made the slightest impression with his work. [21]

Contrary to certain neoclassical historians of thought, the general glut controversy of the 1820's was not settled through some compromise over the issues, with the only differences remaining in 'semantics'; there is instead an obvious degeneration in the quality of the debate over the next two decades, until by 1850 no recognized political economist diverges even a little from the orthodox doctrine of Stage 1 theory. The most striking and most familiar example of this degeneration can be found in the career of John Stuart Mill. His father, James Mill, was one of the early champions of what is now known as Say's Identity, so Mill Junior was subject to orthodox influence quite early. Yet, sometime in 1824-30, Mill wrote an article called, "The Influence of Consumption upon Production" which (a) acknowledged that the existence of money could obviate Say's Identity ; (b) observed that gluts were due to develop in lags between buying and selling, thus reintroducing temporal considerations into what had been an a-temporal argument; and, (c) stated an early anticipation of Walras' Law. Thus, during the decade of the 1820's J.S. Mill had been affected by the ferment in thought about macroeconomic instability. However, by the time Mill published his Principles in 1848, there is no longer any trace of the consideration of the above issues in his work and Say's Identity reigns supreme in political economy. Some authors, using evidence from Mill's correspondence, suggest the suppression of these issues was conscious, in order to forestall presenting the enemies of the established economic order with new ammunition for their diatribes. [22]

The reason we have spent so much time on what one might think were personal rather than scientific considerations during the general glut controversy is to stress a point which until now has been ignored: the controversy was not ended in consensus, but by mutual incomprehension and simple exhaustion. This is an instance of the 'incommensurability' we have described in the previous chapter: the participants in the debate were continually frustrated, never coming to believe that the other side was capable of understanding their position. This historical instance should accommodate us to the idea that controversies need not lead to understanding, but they can remain unresolved long after the heat of dissention. The proponents of Stage 1 disproportionality theories could not come to see the possibility of a Stage 2 theory of instability, because in part, the very possibility seemed to threaten the pillars of society. Once again, we return to the assertion that attitudes toward the concept of macroeconomic instability play as important a role in the development of those theories as do questions of logical development.

IV. THE PERIOD OF QUIESCENCE: 1850 TO THE TURN OF THE CENTURY

To say that discussions of macroeconomic instability were suppressed in the latter half of the nineteenth century is not to say they did not exist; it is merely to say they were not part of the recognized and structured discussion of the macroeconomy. The popular journalist D. Morier Evans wrote a series of narratives chronicling the financial crises of the 1850's and 1860's in England, with titles like Facts, Failures and Frauds and The History of the Commercial Crisis of 1847-48. Clement Juglar wrote the first edition of his Crises Commerciales Et De Leur Retour Periodique in 1860, beginning it with the rhetorical question, "If the theory of crises is so important, why is it still so obscure?" Max Wirth, perhaps less under the influence of the Ricardian School than the French or English, wrote his Geschichte Der Handelskrisen in the latter half of the 19th century, and the work went through many editions in his lifetime. It is true that all of these works share the attribute of a certain naive empiricism, scanning the history of the western European nations for various regularities in their macroeconomic experience, hoping that explanation will grow eventually out of observation. It is to this group, for example, that we owe the now ill-reputed notion that business cycles have a certain fixed periodicity. Their expositions are lacking in anything that could be graced with the name 'theory', to the point of even ignoring the advances made by the glut theorists of the 1820's. Yet they performed one very important service as an irritant: continually reminding the public that no matter what the political economists said, yes, it really did move erratically; and sometimes it just did not work at all.

However, there were theorists of macroeconomic instability who wrote during this period and who were quite sophisticated, and in the clear light of hindsight, anticipated much of the theoretical innovations of the twentieth century. But they were not recognized economic experts; they were moralists, gadflies, and socialist revolutionaries. Some have been totally forgotten, written out of histories of economic thought as part of the faceless mass of the undistinguished; while one has since become infamous. It is among this heterogeneous group that we find the disloyal opposition to the Stage 1 orthodoxy who kept the flame alive in this dreary period.

One of the moralists who have since been forgotten was John Lalor, who wrote a book called <u>Money and Morals</u> in 1852. Lalor explicitly placed his work in the traditions of Sismondi and Malthus, practically insuring the unpopularity of his work. Lalor's criticisms went straight to the heart of the orthodoxy; to their conceptions of money, credit and capital: "The conception of money capital existing independently, as a legally recognized transferable purchase power, exchangeable for, but never identical with, that specific capital which alone could exist in a state of barter--as a species of wealth capable of varying in amount, without any corresponding, or perhaps with opposite variations in that visible property which it commands, and, therefore, of having laws of its own--is a clue without which a current analysis of our complex and highly developed credit system is utterly impossible." [23] Of course, being a moralist, Lalor also made many observations thought to be put out of place in a treatise on political economy, which did not help the reception of his book. From our point of view, what is striking about his work is that it anticipates, almost in detail, much of the institutionalist attack on Stage 1 theory early in the twentieth century. We shall return to these points when we examine the work of Veblen in the next chapter.

A more famous antagonist of the orthodox school of economics was Karl Marx. Marx drew out the unsavory implications of the orthodox school's dependence upon the labor theory of value, and he ridiculed their lack of sophistication in ignoring the historical and social bases of market organization.

Most importantly, Marx in <u>Capital</u> and <u>Theories of Surplus Value</u> consolidated the nascent insights of the general glut theorists into his schemes of 'expanded reproduction': the first explicitly dynamic models and the first <u>explicit</u> Stage 2 models to be formulated in the history of economic analysis. The determinants of surplus value, and therefore investment, are spelled out; a dynamic equilibrium sequence of outputs is determined. The implicit assumption of a barter economy is also dropped: [24]

> When, for instance, the market is glutted by shoes or callicoes or wines or colonial products, does this perhaps mean that 4/6 of the nation have more than satisfied their needs in shoes, callicoes, etc?.....Would it not be simpler to say: Why do they not produce the shoes and callicoes for themselves?.....There is nothing to prevent all commodities from being superabundant on the market, and therefore falling below their price (i.e., cost of production). That is, all commodities, apart from money.

Marx was also the first to separate the time distribution of pecuniary accumulation from the time structure of physical technologies in the central chapters of Volume II of *Capital*. Most subsequent attention has been drawn to his theory of the secularly falling rate of profit and its attendant death-knell for capitalism, however. This is unfortunate, because in many ways Marx's theory of the falling rate is a preapprehension (and little more) of the fourth stage of instability theory, where the distinction between variables (such as levels of sectoral outputs) and parameters (such as the technological input/output coefficients and the wage bundle) becomes blurred. The theory of the falling rate of profit is a mechanism of socially induced technological change imposed upon an already 'complete' model: one that has unique, determinate solutions if the parameters were truly fixed. Since Marx's contemporaries were experiencing great difficulty comprehending the implications of the change in problematic (from the disproportionate satifaction of desires to the time distribution of the level of accumulation) for economic theory, they could have scarcely been expected to fathom the requisite logical steps necessary to arrive at the 'law' of the falling rate of profit. Again, we see that a fair comprehension of a previous stage of instability theory is a prerequisite for progress to the next stage.

Contrary to the Keynes' assertion, if only Marx, and not Malthus or Ricardo, had been the parent stem from which subsequent economic theory had developed, much needless confusion could have been avoided in the theory of macroeconomic fluctuations. Investment, meaning the accumulation of economic goods for the purpose of exacting a return, would have been the centerpiece of any model of growth; instead, we had to wait for Keynes before this variable was reinstated to its place of importance in orthodox economics. The key role of monetary phenomena in upsetting Say's Law and otner such logical proofs of the inherent stability of trade would have been a commonplace, making Robert Clower's contemporary reflections upon Keynesianism redundant. If Volume II of *Capital* had been studied more seriously, perhaps time would not have been treated so cavalierly by Marshall and his students. And, finally, there might have been a more balanced assessment of the interaction of mathematical models of production and exchange and the history of human institutions in the models and explanations of economies.

As is stood after Marx, no appreciable analytical progress was made in the theory of economic instability for the next half-century. Marx called the decade from 1820 to 1830 the great metaphysical period in English political economy; but with hindsight, the period 1860 to 1910 is much more deserving of that title. Under the sway of the then-novel 'marginalist' variant of subjectivist value theory, theories of macroeconomic instability receded into the imperceptible background. When confronted with the task of raising the level of the analysis from the individual good and the individual actor to the aggregate, the previously rigorous mathematical theorists became almost mystical, if not downright ethereal. Philip Wicksteed, normally one of the most critically intelligent of the tyro marginalists, exemplifies this tendency when he wrote about: [25]

> the paradoxical situation of general 'over-production' and 'glutted markets', accompanied by general want...But it is not really the abundance of things produced, or the abundent power of producing them, that causes the mischief, but the timidity and forelornness of those who weave the vast and intricate maze of promises, through confidence in which alone things can be moved from those who use them. For recurrent general depressions the only radical cure seems to be a raising of the intelligence and conscientiousness of both of the directors of industry and of the public.....Note, finally, that it is easy to exaggerate the magnitude of the material difference between prosperous and depressed times. The bulk of the business of the country goes on successfully all the time. It is only for a comparatively narrow margin that inflation and contraction succeed each other.

Such unabashed sophistry embarrassed some of the marginalists into coming up with a marginally less lame explanation of the plainly obvious commercial crises of the period. Ironically enough, the most noted attempt, William Stanley Jevons' sun-spot theory, has attained something of the historical status of a joke in the present-day economics profession. Yet in reading the original, one detects the pained tone of Jevons' search for a theory complimentary to his marginalst innovations, and the uncomfortable awareness of the ludicrousness of his position: [26]

> Assuming that variations of commercial credit and enterprise are essentially mental in their nature, must there not be external events to excite hopefulness at one time and disappointment and despondency at another?.....If the English money market is (N.B.) naturally fitted to swing or roll in periods of 10 to 11 years, comparatively slight variations in the goodness of harvests repeated at like intervals would suffice to produce those alternations of depression, activity, excitement and collapse which undoubtedly recu in well-marked succession.....I am aware that speculations of this kind may seem somewhat far-fetched and finely wrought; but financial collapses have recurred with such approach to regularity in the last 50 years that either this or some other explanation is needed.

Sometimes Jevons is credited with anticipating the econometric movement of the twentieth century because of his combination of empirical endeavors with theoretical work. Jevons' statistical work with respect to fluctuations provides us with an early case of the divergence between theory and practice of a positivistic philosophy of science which appeals to empirical quantification as the sole arbiter of final acceptance or rejection of hypotheses. His attempts to produce crude correlation coefficients between European grain price timeseries and sunspot occurrences failed the test of significance, and it is to his credit that he admitted it; but the attraction of his own theory was too powerful for him to accept such a setback. Towards the end of his life he thought he had found the sought-after correlations in the price series of the agricultural produce of 'tropical' regions such as India and China, leading him to lay the blame for fluctuations squarely at the feet of the heathen; certainly this was the substitution of two implausible intuitive leaps for a single significant correlation.

A more sympathetic reading of Jevons might suggest that his work with sunspots and harvests presaged our third analytical stage of instability theory, i.e., the 'random shocks' thesis or the distinction between exogeneity and endogeneity and their interaction in producing cycles. Jevons' hint that the economy is 'naturally fitted to swing or roll' would sound very modern to a contemporary rational expectations theorist. Although Jevons' work managed to anticipate much contemporary thought, this paricular idea that he constructed a Stage 3 theory would be ill-founded. Jevons and the other marginalists were deaf to the theoretical innovations of the glut theorists and the social underworld. they had little or no concern with how a unique sustainable level of output was set and maintained. Say's Law held that the market would ration incomes so that any adjustment would take place not at the level of aggregate production but within its internal compostition. From the standpoint of Walras' Law--that any excess quantity of goods supplied equalled the excess demand for money--overproduction of goods relative to money was simply a special case of disproportionality, albeit a case qualitatively no different from a disproportionality between the production of truffles and the production of caviar. Consequently <u>any</u> level of output could be maintained indefinitely, even (and for some theorists like Walras, especially) those that entailed a zero rate of profit. When Jevons wrote that the English money market was 'naturally fitted to swing or roll' in some given periodicity, he was contradicting his own marginalist theory of demand and supply which allowed no reason for the aggregate of output to move in any predictable pattern, although a combination of lagged reactions by actors and random or inexplicable 'shocks' could produce predictable fluctuations of <u>individual</u> prices and/or outputs. Therefore, orthodox economic theory remained stuck at the first primitive 'disproportionality' stage of instability theory. Assuredly, Jevons' sunspots qualified as random shocks, but because the only reaction allowed by the theory was a shuffle among sectoral outputs, there was no real conception of the 'propagation and impulse' problem, which had to wait for the discussions of Frisch and others in the 1930's. This stasis of late nineteenth century thought reiterates the necessarily sequential character of the stages in the theory of economic instability.

A word should be inserted here about the crop of monetary theories of instability which sprang up around the turn of the century. From the very beginning of the period of our short survey, economic writers had mentioned the effects of the state of credit upon the quality and quantity of trade. Even Ricardo, we recall, recommended a currency rigidly tied to the stock of gold in part to prevent extravagant expansions of credit. It seems fairly clear that at the same time most economists believed that money was essentially neutral, in that the rate of interest on loans was assumed to be brought into line with the physical rate of return on production, so that they were always equal. This formulation is made explicit in Walras' work, and, as we have already mentioned, a divergence from this norm is just another form of disproportionality. In fact, the works of Hawtrey and the early Irving Fisher can be read as increasingly sophisticated formulations of this disproportionality thesis, where the banking system is held to account for all the fluctuations in aggregate activity, although they are cast in terms of a given stationary level of output. [27] The lessons of the second, or 'realization crises' stage were reintroduced into monetary theory by Knut Wicksell around the turn of the century, although his influence was only felt in England twenty years later when his works began to be translated from the Swedish. He was, as Schumpeter wrote, the patron saint of those economists who renounced Say's Law. His canonization was the result of two innovations: the inscription of a demand curve for output as a whole, and his theory of the 'natural' and 'money' rates of interest. The first suggested a theory of an equilibirum level of aggregate output; the second postulated a degree of freedom of divergence from equilibrium. Notwithstanding, sainthood does not ensure infallibility, and there were many loose ends left in Wicksell's analysis: he was imprecise in his use of the concept of a demand curve for total output, since it was not clear what budget constraint was left to be held <u>ceteris paribus</u> in this schedule; alternatively, his distinction between the natural and money rate was weakened by the real rate being defined as Bohm-Bawerk's marginal productivity of roundabout processes, even though Wicksell himself had earlier pointed out that Bohm-Bawerk's measure of capital, the average period of production, will in general be a function of some exogenously given rate of interest. [28] However flawed Wicksell's analysis, he must be credited with bringing economic theory back to the second stage of instability theory, preparing the way for the second great internal discussion of business cycle theory.

So far four stages of instability theory have been postulated as an organizing principle of theoretical experience in history: Disproportionality, realization crises due to investment and monetary interactions, random shocks and systemic changes in parameters. The earliest <u>formal</u> explanations (starting with Smith and running through Ricardo and beyond) of economic disruption were posed as temporary divergences of production from some 'equilibrium' growth rate--Smith's 'overtrading', or Ricardo's disproportions--which, by their very nature were incapable of determining the actual rate of growth of the whole economy. In this conception, there can be 'overtrading' of shoes, but there cannot be overtrading in all produced goods. The next stage in instability theory had to be predicated on a theory of the level of output in general: that is, what level of output could be <u>realized and sustained</u> given the present configuration of economic variables. Any theory which purports to do this must consider the role of investment in the economy, and its manifestation as changes in the money values of businesses, the repositories and actualizers of investment. The 'general glut' controversy in England after the Napoleonic War period centered on this issue, but the force of Ricardo and Mill's authority drove the second stage of instability theory underground, outside of the formal economics profession. Marx, through a critical reading of

Ricardo combined with his contact with the French Utopian Socialist literature, was one of the very few theorists to systemize and develop this insight within the span of the following 100 years. The marginalists, isolated by their distaste for anything which was critical of the market, remained committed to notions of disproportionality and their other derivative explanations of economic disturbance. Jevons did anticipate some aspects of the third stage of instability theory (random shocks), but without the second stage (a theory of the level of output) such assertions had no context and therefore no serious theory resulted. It was only at the end of the period considered in this section, mainly through the work of Wicksell, that economic orthodoxy was brought back to a consideration of the second, realization crisis stage of instability theory. This deliberation ushered in a second fertile period of discussion, culminating in Keynes' General Theory. It is to this discussion and its aftermath that we now turn.

CHAPTER THREE

TWENTIETH CENTURY THEORIES OF MACROECONOMIC INSTABILITY

I. ORIGINS OF THE SECOND PERIOD OF INSTABILITY THEORY

"(In neoclassical economics)... the process is rated in terms of the equilibrium to which it tends or should tend, not conversely. The outcome of the process taken in its relation of equivalence within the system, is the point at which the inquiry comes to rest. It is not primarily the point of departure for an inquiry into what may follow. The science treats of a balanced system rather than a proliferation. In this lies its characteristic difference from the later evolutionary science."

--Thorstein Veblen
"Preconceptions of Economic Science"

After more than fifty years of resistance to the idea of some intrinsic source of macroeconomic instability, orthodox economists were not ready to dispose of old habits lightly. The theory of the level of aggregate activity could not enter through the front door of academic acceptability since it could not make it past the gate of Say's (or, more correctly, Walras') Law. What eventually happened was that the theory came in through the back door by donning the uniform of pure empiricism. This process was simultaneous and took place on many different fronts; no adequate history has yet been written of the second surge of the theory of capitalist instability. Such a history would fill a book in and of itself. In lieu of such an undertaking, a cursory outline is presented here, concentrating on the process within the economics profession in the United States and in England. The vantage point we shall adopt has the drawback of slighting the role of the non-academic scribblers, who provided a constant source of irritation and stimulation to the economic profession.

It is no exaggeration that Thorstein Veblen was the original back-door-man of academic economics. Veblen arrived at economics only after passing through philosophy and natural history and a failure to find teaching posts in these disciplines. He returned to graduate school in economics as a result of family pressure, after seven years of self-imposed exile in Minnesota. J. Lawrence Laughlin, a conservative economist of the period, conceived a liking for the moody, aging graduate student and took Veblen along with him to form the Department of Economics at the then-new University of Chicago. There Veblen began a long career of academic frustration; ironic for one whose name graced the masthead of the fledging Journal of Political Economy. Driven from Chicago to Stanford to Missouri and beyond (largely because of his public propensity to delight in the favors of young women, but also because of his indifferent pedagogy and unorthodox opinions), he left in his wake a trail of books and students whose loyalties to previous neoclassical theories were, at best, tenuous. Veblen's importance for our story is twofold: First, there is the attack on Utilitarian value theory which begins in The Theory of the Leisure Class (1899) and culminates in a 'theory' of business instability in The Theory of Business Enterprise (1904); and secondly, his influence on his most prominent student, Wesley Clair Mitchell.

The almost unrecognized version of Veblen's legacy as "bandwagon, snob and Veblen effects" in neoclassical price theory has obscured from view the abiding purpose of The Theory of the Leisure Class: to attack, both philosophically and anthropologically, any notion of value as resting upon 'utility'. This was done both in a static sense--conspicuous consumption, the dignity of predatory exploit, and the instinct of workmanship-- and in a more dynamic sense: "Social advance, especially as seen from the point of view of economic theory, consists in a continued progressive approach to an approximately exact 'adjustment of inner relations to outer relations'; but this adjustment is never definitively established, since the 'outer relations' are subject to constant changes as a consequence of the progressive change going on in the 'inner relations'." [1] One might be tempted to brush off this criticism as a trivial recognition that there are lags in behaviors and that the datum of given tastes can change, but this would miss the point of Veblen's work. He goes on to state that certain classes are more buffered from the winds of change than others, and that "the wealthy leisure class is in such a sheltered position with respect to the economic sources that make for change and readjustment. And it may be said that the forces which make for a readjustment of institutions are, in the last analysis, almost entirely of an economic nature."

Veblen expands his dynamic conception in The Theory of Business Enterprise. For the first time since Marx, he locates the direct responsibility for the business cycle in the behavior of the class whose function is the accumulation of capital. Thus he immediately short-circuits the confusion which besets the underconsumptionist discussions of crises, and escapes the marginalist concern with the individual and his/her wants (although, these concepts creep back in towards the end of the book). He brushes aside Walrasian gestalt with the brusque "men whose aim is not the increase of possessions do not go into business." He then continues to isolate the key determinant of accumulation in the pecuniary profit motive. Veblen was quite aware that any further disequilibirum theorizing would be stopped dead in its tracks by a 'Law of Distribution' which deduced rates of profit as outcomes of derived demands for producer goods which were in turn determined by 'felicific' demands for consumption. He explicitly completed his attack on marginalist theory in a review of J.B. Clark's Essentials of Economic Theory (1907): [2]

> Capital considered as a productive agent is substantially a capitalization of technological expedients and that a given capital invested in industrial equipment is measured by the portion of technological expedients whose usufruct the investment approprates. It would accordingly appear that the substantial core of all capital is immaterial wealth and that the material objects which are formally the subject of the capitalists' ownership are, by comparison, a transient and adventitious matter. . . If such a view were accepted, even with extreme reservations, Mr. Clark's scheme of the 'natural' distribution of incomes between captial and labor would 'go up into the air.'

When Veblen wrote, "The hedonistic postulates on which (Clark's) line of economic theory is built up are of a statical scope and character, and nothing but statical theory comes out of their development," he meant that any level of output and any level of accumulation was formally consistent with 'hedonistic' theory, so that no theory of the evolution of the economic system was possible. Veblen's path of escape from this straightjacket in The Theory of Business Enterprise was to ignore hedonistic pricing totally and talk solely in terms of aggregate levels of activity--anticipating Keynes by at least thirty years. Veblen takes the 'historical'definition of capital quite seriously, to the extent of ignoring the physical side of production for as much of the rest of the book. In this book Veblen locates the basic instability of modern capitalism in the disharmony between the engineer and his 'machine process' and the pecuniary business enterprise. The machine process standardizes everything in the course of capitalist expansion, both human and nonhuman, the result of which is a complex and interconnected system, capable of tremendous productivity, but also inherently vulnerable to disruption. (This aspect of Veblen's thought was later expanded during his flirtation with technocracy in his Engineers and the Price System). The pecuniary sphere of business, alternately, was motivated by monetary gain and not the indefinite expansion of goods. "It is, as a business proposition, a matter of indifference to the man of large affairs whether the disturbances which his transactions set up in the industrial system help or hinder the system at large, except in so far as he has ulterior strategic ends to serve." [3] Veblen's cycle consisted of an endemic divergence between the pecuniary return of the balance sheet and the social rate of growth of the machine process. [4] This notion of divergent rats of return, in a much less pessimistic mode, was also being explored by Wicksell at much the same time as an explanation of macroeconomic fluctuations. It was Wicksell's 'natural' and monetary interest rates, with their connotations of benign epiphenomena, rather than Veblen's pecuniary and machine processes, that became the parent stem of conventional macroeconomics in the subsequent half-century.

The rest of the <u>Theory of Business Enterprise</u> explored the motivations behind the pecuniary system's balance sheet disturbances. As befitted a writer in the era of the Robber Barons, Veblen was most interested in the consolidations of enterprises by financial mergers and the manipulation of balance sheet net worth through changes in leverage. He was one of the first economists (as opposed to businessmen) to stress that these actions were motivated by <u>pecuniary</u> gain which was not simply related to cornering the market for a good in scarce supply. "It is , of course, a trite commonplace that the earnings of any industrial business are a joint function of the rate of turnover and the volume of business. . . (the businessman's) means of increasing the magnitude of the turnover is a resort to credit and a close husbanding of his assets. . . Indebtedness in this way comes to serve much the same purpose, as regards the rate of earnings, as does a time-saving improvement in the processes of industry." [5] Veblen, no doubt under the influence of Marshall, relegates all the algebra supporting this contention to the footnotes. In Veblen's case this was a wise choice, since his algebra was as muddled as his wit was sharp. Let us recast his algebraic argument in somewhat different terms in order to illustrate his thought on capitalist finance.

Let P be profits net of interest paid, N be the balance sheet net worth, equal to assets minus liabilibities, A be balance sheet assets, L be the ratio of interest-bearing liabilities to assets and i be the rate of interest exacted on the liabilities. Assume, for the moment, that the assets of firms turn over once in the given time period, i.e., sales = assets, and that the only form of nonequity liabilities are interest-bearing debt. Net profits can then be expressed as the gross margin on sales, r, times assets minus interest costs, or:

$$P = rA - iLA$$

The rate of return on net worth is net profits divided by net worth:

$$\pi = \frac{P}{N} = \frac{rA - iLA}{N} = \frac{r - iL}{1 - L} \qquad (3.1)$$

With the rate of interest on debt given, the 'pecuniary' rate of return is a function of the margin on sales and the amount of leverage. The effects of leverage on the rate of return when the margin varies is displayed in Figure I. Firm A has no leverage: the value of its assets equals the value of its net worth. Firm B's leverage equals 1/2: its balance sheet is structured thus:

ASSETS	100	DEBT	50
		NET WORTH	50
	100		100

For Firm A, an increase in the gross margin by two percentage points means an increase in the rate of profit of two percentage points. For Firm B, an increase in the gross margin of two percentage points means an increase in the rate of profit of four percentage points. Leverage, therfore, acts as an amplifier of fluctuations in the rate of profit, in an upward direction at gross margins below the rate of interest. Two aspects of this simple model are worthy of special note: one, *ceteris parabis,* the amplifier is linear with respect to a varying gross margin; and two, if the rate of profit is assumed (by some mechanism) to be always brought into equality with the rate of interest, there can be no effect of leverage on the rate of profit. Further, the greater the leverage, the greater the amplification: increased L rotates line B in Figure I counterclockwise through the point (i,i).

Now, let us relax the assumption of a fixed flow of sales per unit time period. Let S be the ratio of sales to assets in any given time period. In that case, (3.1) may be rewritten:

$$\pi = \frac{rS - iL}{1 - L} \qquad (3.2)$$

The corresponding profit rates as a function of the sales/asset ratio are plotted in Figure II for our same two firms, this time assuming a fixed gross margin. Firm A, with no leverage, experiences a directly proportional rise

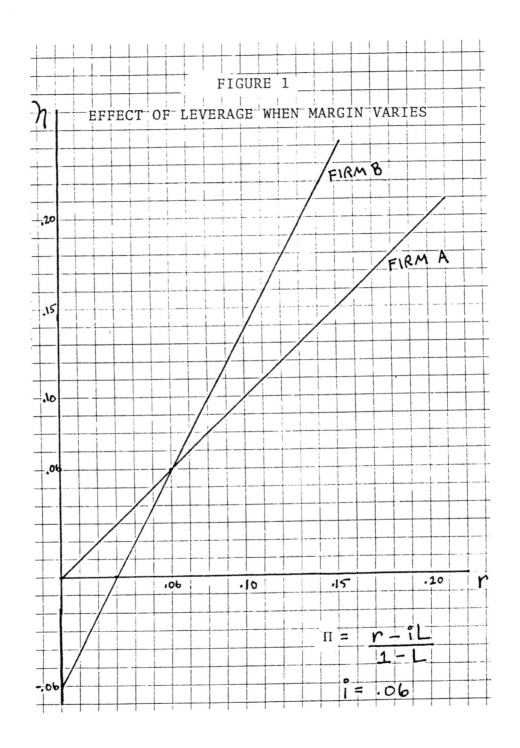

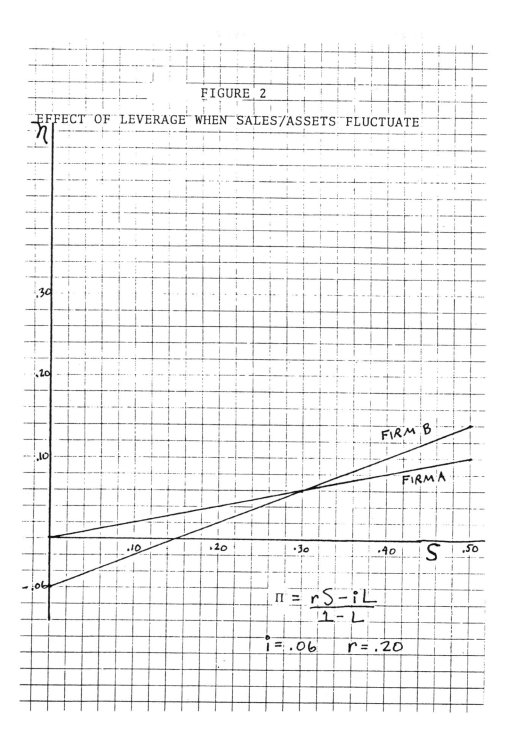

in the profit rate given an increase in the ratio of sales to assets; Firm B experiences a more-than-proportional rise given the same increase. Again, if the interest rate were somehow brought into equality with the rate of profit there would be no amplification, by rotating line B in a counterclockwise direction. In sum, increased leverage amplifies the effect of changes in the gross margin on the profit rate and the effect of changes in the sales/assets ratio.

These financial interactions may be combined in a more concise form by thinking of the profit rate on equity as being the product of a level (the net margin) and a velocity (turnover of sales per unit of net worth). This form of ratio analysis is familiar to anyone who has ever come within the influence of a business school as:

$$\pi = \frac{\text{net profit}}{\text{sales}} \cdot \frac{\text{sales}}{\text{net worth}} \qquad (3.3)$$

The first ratio in (3.3) is the net profit margin, while the second is the turnover velocity. If the net margin varies over time, a higher level of leverage will exaggerate movements in the profit rate. If sales per unit asset vary, a higher level of leverage will exaggerate its impact on the rate of profit. This second effect cannot be distinguished from the first equation (3.3) as it can in equation (3.2) because changes in leverage also alter the net margin by definition (that is, this margin is net of interest). Increased sales per unit asset (assets fixed) and increased leverage (sales and assets both increasing) both accelerate financial turnover, i.e., velocity of sales per unit net worth. Veblen did not delve much further than equation (3.1); thus he did not see that he left unexplained the level of aggregate activity--aggregate sales--and therefore did not develop a complete model of the business cycle. As it was, he simply believed the cycle was one of first increasing and then decreasing leverage, to the exclusion of all else. He was prevented from forging theoretical links between finance and the level of aggregate physical activity by taking the position that "borrowed funds do not increase the aggregate industrial equipment," a position he defended with statements which sound suspiciously like assumptions of full employment. [6] This quasi-neutrality of finance, really Say' Law in another garb, thwarted Veblen's attempted escape from the bounds of neoclassical doctrine. One might speculate that this contradiction accounts for his theories of "wasteful consumption" which were reversions to an unsophisticated underconsumptionist position in the last two chapters of Theory of Business Enterprise.

Veblen's work on business cycles made absolutely no impact on his colleagues [7], and, we might add, was also ignored in conventional histories of macoreconomic thought. Probably because of Vebeln's awareness of his growing isolation from mainstream economics, his later books became less and less concerned with economic theory writ small and more and more enthralled with the promise of a future technocratic elite of engineers. Veblen's economic thought might truly have been a fleeting flash in a dark landscape were it not for one of his illustrious students: Wesley Clair Mitchell.

Mitchell was one of the first students at the new University of Chicago, entering the school in 1892-3, just when Veblen was beginning his work on the theory of the leisure class. The two were temperamentally well-suited to each other; like Veblen, the young Mitchell chose to study both philosophy and economics; both were more concerned with the meta-implacations of economic theory than by Kuhnian 'normal-science' improvements in its existing structure. In later life, Mitchell wrote about this period in a letter to J.M. Clark: [8]

> Economic theory became a fascinating subject--the orthodox types particularly--when one began to take the mental operations of the theorists as the problem. . . Of course Veblen fitted perfectly into this set of notions. What drew me to him was his artistic side. . . There was a man who really could play with ideas! If one wanted to indulge in the game of spinning theories who could match his skill and humor? But if anything were needed to convince me that the standard procedure of orthodox economic could meet no scientific tests, it was that Veblen got nothing more certain by his dazzling performances with another set of premises.

Mitchell was a protege not only of Veblen but of Laughlin also; gold and silver monetary standards were burning questions of the day, and Laughlin guided Mitchell in that direction. His doctoral dissertation and much of his early published work concerned the history of greenbacks during the Civil War in the U.S.: thus Mitchell became known as a monetary theorist. He joined the faculty of the University of Chicago in 1900 and remained until 1903, when he took a position at the University of California. Veblen published the Theory of Business Enterprise in 1904. It is clear that Mitchell was present during the entire period in Velen's life when he was involved with the economic theory of instability.

An important point to note is that after 1908 and the publication of his second book, Mitchell was a respected member of the economics profession. In 1907 Mitchell lectured at Harvard, and was later tentatively approached regarding a position there. As he himself admitted in a letter to his fiancee, "Outwardly I live in the accredited academic fashion, and doubtless I have insensibly acquired through long association pedantic modes of expression." His writings possessed none of the sharp bite of a Veblen, and were preoccupied with the more immediate issues of the day. His historical work placed him in the forefront of those who felt that economics must rest on a much more empirical base, tethering previous theoretical flights of fancy closer to the earth. But sometimes the skepticism imbibed as an impressionable youth dies hard; dissatisfaction with previous monetary theories and his penchant for the collection of historical statistics led him increasingly to the subject of macroeconomic instability. As Mitchell later stated in his 1918 lectures on Veblen: "Crises, you do not find them included in a book like Alfred Marshall's Principles of Economics; but certainly you will find a considerable number of problems in the Theory of Business Enterprise which you do not find discussed in ordinary treatises." [9]

In 1913, Mitchell published a 600 page book entitled Business Cycles, which signalled the initiation of the second sustained discussion among economists of the potential instability of the capitalist system. Arthur Burns, speaking perhaps more from his personal experience than that of the profession as a whole, claimed that "No other work between Marshall's Principles and Keynes' General Theory has had as big an influence on the economic thought of the Western World." [10] Joseph Dorfman's assessment, although less hyperbolic (as evidenced by a lack of capitals on things Western) essentially agrees: "The test of a pioneering work lies in its ability to impose itself on currents of thought in such a way that it forces both present and future generations to face the problems it has exposed to view. . . the book sufficiently caught the trends of development in economic life to become a force in that development. In this sense, the theory of 'business cycles' was Mitchell's creation." [11] As if these glowing appraisals of Mitchell's work were not sufficient, we shall shortly carry the argument a little further: Mitchell's work was a necessary prerequisite for the favorable reception of Keynes' General Theory.

What did Mitchell's Business Cycles actually accomplish? First, in lieu of taking Veblen's critical route of directly attacking neoclassical theory in order to dispense with Walrasian/J.B. Clark price theory, Mitchell removed himself from its influence by attacking its rationalist epistemology: "There is slight hope of getting answers to these questions by a logical process of proving and criticizing the theories. For whatever the merits of ingenuity and consistency they may possess, these theories have slight value except as they give keener insight into the phenomena of business cycles. It is by a study of the fact which they purport to interpret that the theories must be tested." [12] Once he had rejected marginal productivity and utility theories, his organizing principle reads as if it were taken directly from Veblen: [13]

> Since the quest for money profits by business enterprises is the controlling factor among the economic activities of men who live in a money economy, the whole discussion must center about the prospect of profits...all the tables (of statistical data) and all the borrowed ideas were fitted into a framework provided by a study of economic organization today, which showed that the industrial process of making and the commercial process of distributing goods are both thoroughly subordinate to the process of making money.

But, unlike Veblen, he did not chastize preceding theorists for their deficiencies, nor did he presume to take full credit for his own scenario of the syncopated expansion of captial. Mitchell manages to mention Beveridge, Spiethoff, Lescure, Veblen, Sombart, Carver and Irving Fisher all in the same approving tones, insisting that each of these incompatible theorists had a piece of it right, but that no one had grasped the full picture. In fact, Mitchell's book is basically a catalogue, but a catalogue with a vengeance--no previous discussion of aggregate economic activity ran to six hundred pages of text with tables of timeseries of everything from agricultural prices to foreign wage rates. His 'theory', as summarized in Part III Chapter 5, is simply a chronology of the 'average' cycle: prices rise in certain phases and fall in others; 'tensions' appear in certain money markets at certain times; marginal returns fall in expansions; captialists become more or less 'timid'. One reason Mitchell's book was so popular was that he clothed the old microeconomic explanations in the garb of a more modern aggregate language. He concluded his discussion with some very practical recommendations, such as a thorough-going reorganization of the American banking system, countercyclical government expenditures, the stabilization of the price level, and the institution of a 'business barometer' to provide short-term forecasts to the business community. None of it was really novel, but somehow it had never been brought together in one place before, and never had it been written in such neutral tones of the disinterested economic technician.

Mitchell's impact on the profession did not consist solely of his treatise on business cycles. Mitchell's concerns coincided nicely with historical events in the same period; the two interacted in an ever-increasing spiral of activity. The onset of World War I, with the government's expanded involvement in the domestic economy, required increased collection and collation of the types of economic statistics that Mitchell dealt in. Moreover, Mitchell's ambivalent empiricism struck a sympathetic note with many members of the economics profession who were alienated in varying degrees from contemporary trends in economic theory. In 1920 Mitchell joined Malcolm Rorty, N.I. Stone and Edwin Gay (an economic historian) in founding the National Bureau of Economic Research. As Burns has written, "Most importantly, here was an experiment in democratic action, men of many shades of political opinion joining in the undramatic enterprise of viewing the factual findings of a technical staff." The aim of the Bureau was to research various indicators of aggregate activity, and, in substance, to reproduce and extend Mitchell's method in Business Cycles to the then-present in a more systematic manner. In 1920 the first topic of study chosen to receive NBER's support was an inquiry into the size of 'national income' and its distribution. The third study urged by Mitchell was "the subject of savings versus current consumption." No specific theoretical rationale motivated the choice of these variables: Mitchell's reasons for these particular choices were phrased in commonsensical everyday terms, such as if modern economic life was organized on the basis of making and spending individual money incomes, economic analysis should start from the fact. Irrespective of its humble origins, Mitchell's intuition was responsible for a veritable flood of NBER publications in the following fifteen years, including at least fifteen books specifically concerned with business cycles, and a number of works associated with the name of Simon Kuznets, which essentially defined national income accounts for future generations. The sharp downturn of 1921 gave added urgency (and therefore added support) to the work of the NBER. The first half of the Great Depression ratified that urgency and made Mitchell the public representative of the calm level-headed cadre of the economics profession occupied with the explanation of depressions, particularly after Irving Fisher became more and more the butt of ridicule. By the early 1930's, no English-speaking 'macroeconomist worth his or her salt could afford to be unfamiliar with Mitchell's work.

One of those economists was John Maynard Keynes. As early as December 1913, Keynes had asked Mitchell for an article on the then-new Federal Reserve Act for the Economic Journal, as one expert on money to another. Interest in each other's work continued, and Mitchell notes in his diary that during his tenure as Eastman Professor of Economic at Oxford (1930-32), he had both read Keynes' Treatise on Money carefully and had personal discussions with Keynes. [14] Later on in his term at Oxford, he held fortnightly conferences with Roy Harrod, Phelps-Brown and Bretherton on the subject of building a center of post-graduate empirical research at an English university. Mitchell engagingly writes in a letter to his wife that, "Presumably they turn to me for advice because they have eyes on the Rockefeller Foundation as a source of funds, and fondly believe that I may have some influence in that quarter." They were not far from the mark, because in 1944 when the application was finally submitted (with Keynes' name gracing the masthead) to set up a department of Applied Economics at Cambridge, Mitchell was chosen to read the text, and it seems he did expedite its acceptance. In the never-ending antiquarian quest for Keynes' intellectual ancestry, it is curious that Mitchell's contribution has been overlooked. [15] For it is clear that Mitchell broke some ground which made Keynes' triumph possible.

If one were to summarize Mitchell's intellectual legacy, it would be four-fold. First, by inventing the modern concept of a national income out of whole cloth, and then fleshing out the concept by providing actual numbers which purported to represent the idea, he created a new theoretical entity to be explained. If there had been no general impetus to think about 'income' or 'consumption' on a national scale, it seems safe to say that there would simply have been no multiplier and no marginal propensity to consume. [16] Walrasian economics, and to a lesser extent Marshallian economics, is at base inconsistent with such notions, a point to which we shall return later. Secondly, Mitchell inherited from Veblen a disdain for micro pricing theory. Many places in his lectures on Veblen in his Types of Economic Theory attest to Mitchell's ambivalence towards the marginal utilitarian value theory as having anything to add to the theory of the level of aggregate activity. [17] It is doubtful whether Keynes could have so easily ignored price theory in his General Theory if there were not respected precedents. Third, Veblen, and to a lesser extent Mitchell, shifted the portayal of the concerns of the actors doing the accumulation from purely physical productivity considerations to expectations and, most importantly, expected pecuniary profitability, paving the way for the Keynesian 'animal spirits'. Interestingly enough, Keynes' theoretical argument in his Treatise on Money was much more fundamentally concerned with amount of aggregate money profits in the economy; but this stress on profits was abandoned in the General Theory in exchange for a heavy dependence on the national income concept. Fourth, countercyclical government expenditures had been advocated by a respected economist more than twenty years prior to the General Theory. Patently, Keynes was not exploring the uncharted frontier.

II. KEYNES: CASSANDRA OR POLYANNA?

"What is it that makes the cleavage which thus divides us? On the one side are those who believe that the existing economic system is, in the long run, a self-adjusting system, though with creaks and groans and jerks, outside interference and mistakes... On the other side of the gulf are those who reject the idea that the existing economic system is, in any significant sense, self-adjusting."

--John Maynard Keynes, 1934

"...a world falling to pieces is ripe to drop Polyanna and take up Cassandra on the rebound..."

--Paul Samuelson, 1946

The period of the 1920's and the 1930's is a time of embarrassing riches for the theory of macroeconomic instability, embarrasing because nearly a half-century has elapsed since that period, and it is clear we have not yet fully digested the wealth of thought generated then. As yet, there is no history of economic thought of that time which does justice to both the many 'outsiders' to economics such as Hobson, Major Douglas, Foster and Catchings and Fredrick Soddy, as well as the growing ranks of 'insiders' who were becomoing convinced that something was wrong with the state of market theory. From widely divergent backgrounds, Mitchell, Gunnar Mydral, John Maurice Clark, Fredrick Mills, Alvin Hansen, Michal Kalecki, and Keynes himself were all insisting that in certain specific ways the system was not self-adjusting, at least in their most recent experience. One reason we have not as yet assimilated the views of all these men is that a curious thing occurred in the late 30's and early 40's, which we now call the Keynesian Revolution.

The 'Revolution' was a strikingly rapid spread of consensus throughout the neoclassical economics profession that Keynes had provided the theoretical underpinnings for a practical solution to the stagnation which beset the world economy in the 1930's. We have already seen that Mitchell in 1913 was advocating a regular government program of counter-cyclical expenditures. Both J.R. Davis for the U.S. and Howson and Winch for the U.K. have amply documented how 'pre-Keynesian' economists shared a fair consensus on 'Keynesian' remedies in the early 1930's. [18] As more and more economists came to see Keynes' General Theory as a justification for their previously held views, Keynes' star rose even higher in the firmament until he outshone all of the other authors we have mentioned. As we have also observed, the two major authorities on instability theories, Hansen and Haberler, revised their histories to state that Keynes had, indeed, finally fashioned the key which unlocked the conundrum of depressions. The speed and level of acceptance of Keynes' ideas, to the point of their being taught in introductory courses in economics twenty years after the book's publication, is relatively unprecedented in the history of economic thought.

However, such extreme notoriety has its costs; and the costs for economics were the the effective suppression of the other theorists we have mentioned, when their concepts did not easily complement those of Keynes. Among other things, this meant special emphasis placed on the Marshallian heritage, which employed the technique of <u>ceteris paribus</u> to deal with thorny problems in captial theory and the reconciliation of subjectivist value theory to cost-of-production theories of supply; it meant that the Austrian branch of neoclassical theory was considered unimportant or trivial; and it meant that Soddy's or Foster and Catchings' concern over profits and the disruptive role of finance were, from thenceforth, to be considered as the work of well-meaning cranks whose inchoate analysis was more than adequately subsumed under Keynes' apparatus. Another serious cost of widespread acceptance was that the economics profession had <u>not</u>, in general, changed its basic stance with regard to the question of the intrinsic stability of the capitalist economy; therefore, the accetance of Keynes meant that Keynes must be made acceptable. [19] The end result was a widespread concensus that most of the discussions of the 20's and 30's could be readily ignored and further, that Keynes really had very little new to say. It is our next concern to describe how this, our theoretical heritage, came to be.

Part of the hagiography which has affixed itself to Keynes has to do with the notion that the <u>General Theory</u> marked some sort of turing point in his <u>attitude</u> towards the general stability of the capitalist system (happening about the time of the quote which prefaces this section); but a more measured assessment shows that in this, as in so many other cases, the attitude towards instability preceded the actual analysis. In particular, the various reactions to suggestions in the <u>Treatise on Money</u> that the system was not essentially self-righting drew fire from respected members of the profession. As early as 1929, D. H. Robertson wrote that he could, "detect a flavour of Catchingism about the notion that 'profits' are normally not spent, and that 'incomes may fall short of the aggregate of sale-prices!'" [20] The only thing more threatening to a professional economist than being compared with a crank and an outsider was to be compared to the Great Bugaboo himself, which was the tactic of Hansen and Tout in their "Annual Review of Business Cycle Theory" in <u>Econometrica</u> of 1932, where they grouped Keynes' _Treatise_ with that other "learned but fallacious" work, Marx's _Capital_. Aspersions and insinuations such as these were generally sufficient to discipline most unorthodox economists, but Keynes' case was somewhat unique. He was already a well-esconced Cambridge don, already a name to be reckoned with: editor of the prestigious _Economic Journal_; author of the bestselling _Economic Consequences of the Peace_, which induced his publisher to give him carte blanche in that area; habitué of government circles; and principal tutor to some of the best economic minds of that generation. With the advantages of hindsight, we can now see that if this were to be a successful challenge to the Stage 1 thinking then prevalent in neoclassical economic theory, it would have to be made by someone with the unipeachable credentials of a Keynes. Of course, these sterling symbols of success have themselves become a problem for us, since for many it is inconceivable that someone so nourished by a paradigm might reject it near-totally. This incongruity, plus the general revisionism that follows in the wake of any momentuous thinker, have given birth to the continuing controversy over whether Keynes was a Cassandra or a Polyanna. This ambivalence, too, is a part of our theoretical heritage.

In order to assess Keynes' theory of the business cycle, it is first necessary to provide a short sketch of what Keynes did write in the _General Theory_. We shall start by presenting verbatim Keynes' definition of his key concept, the marginal efficiency of capital (MEC): "I define the MEC as being equal to that rate of discount which would make the present value of the series of annuities given by the returns expected from the capital asset during its life just equal to its current supply price." [21] The marginal efficiency of capital falls with increasing stocks of capital in the short period because supply price is _assumed_ to fall, because declining scarcity should reduce prices received. Investment is presumed to be carried out to the extent that the MEC falls to the level of the rate of interest, at which point it ceases.

The causal structure of Keynes' model, without his qualifications about feedbacks, is presented as a flow chart in Figure III. (All quantities are levels, except the interest rate). Keynes' first theoretical innovation was to make the rate of interest solely the outcome of an interaction between the supply and demand for 'hoards', or cash balances. Both these schedules were psychological propensities, which were functions of the rate of interest and the level of income. The inclusion of income as a functional argument makes the determination of income and the interest rate simultaneous, and not sequential, as in our schematic. But insofar as some central banking authority could satisfy greater or lesser liquidity preference and influence the rate of interest without undue exertion, this simultaneity would be a second-order effect, and seems to have been treated as such by Keynes. [22] With the interest rate thus set, in conjunction with the state of expectations as represented by the MEC, the level of investment was determined. It is interesting to note that, to a certain extent, this part of the model could accommodate conflicting micro expectations on the part of individual actors, since Keynes' definition of investment included changes in inventories. [23] At this stage another psychological law was postualted: "...men are disposed, as a rule and on the average, to increase their consumption as their income rises, but not by as much as their increase in income." In principle, this law could be used to fix the equilibrium distribution of output: "There is always a formula, relating the output of consumption goods which it pays to produce to the output of investment goods; and I have given attention to it in my book under the name of the Multiplier." [24]

The next step in the logic was a bit faltering, although it occupied all of Chapter 20 of the General Theory. A number of elasticities of output and employment with respect to effective demand appear in that section, although the gist is an assumption that to every level of effective demand there corresponds a unique distribution of the products of industries and their concomitant employments. Finally, Keynes specified that the price level was proportional to the wage rate divided by the marginal efficiency of labor, which was a marginal productivity condition derived from a production function times the volume of employment. [25]

This condition is the result of his assumption that "the rates of renumeration of different factors of production which enter into marginal cost all change in the same proportion as the wage unit." [26] This last step stands in sharp contrast to the usual Walrasian lines of causality, which first determine the level of employment and the real wage from the production function and the supply schedule of labor. Note that in both systems, however, the real wage rate equals the technologically determined marginal value product of labor in equilibrium.

Keynes was aware that a general macroeconomic theory should subsume cyclical phenomena as a special case. He wrote: "...the essential character of the Trade Cycle and, especially, the regularity of time sequence and duration which justifies us in calling it a cycle, is mainly due to the way in which the MEC fluctuates." [27] Recall that the schedule of the MEC is entirely a function of expectations of future income flows, and therefore is entirely a psychological phenomenon. (We noted in Chapter One that the early editions of Haberler's cycle compendium classed Keynes among the 'Psychological Theories' of the cycle).

Contemporaries of the General Theory did not initially know what to make of this compendium of aphorisms, ideosyncratic jargon and novel analytical mechanisms. The

FIGURE III: KEYNES' CAUSAL STRUCTURE

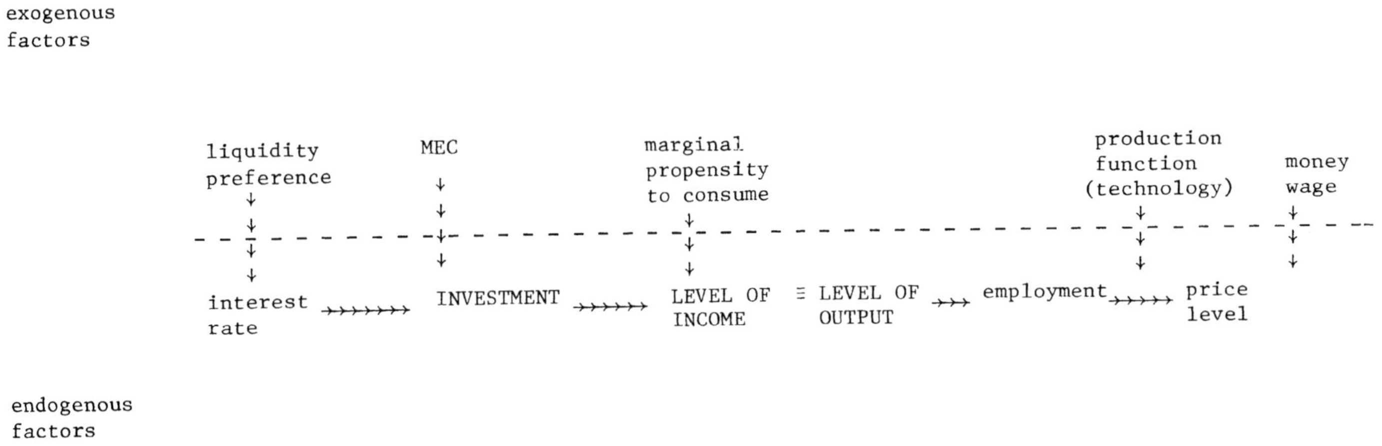

exogenous factors

liquidity preference → → → ⊢ → → MEC → → ⊢ → → marginal propensity to consume → → ⊢ → → production function (technology) → → ⊢ → → money wage → → ⊢ → →

interest rate →→→→→→ INVESTMENT →→→→→ LEVEL OF INCOME ≡ LEVEL OF OUTPUT →→→ employment →→→→ price level

endogenous factors

author believed that it showed the existing structures of consumption and investment were intrinsically unstable; and yet many a staunch neoclassical economist could not see that the underlying 'explanation' was all that different from that of Philip Wicksteed (which we quoted in the previous chapter): timidity, forlornness, mischief and ignorance; in a few words, deviant psychologies. There did seem to be some strains of thought with links to the past, most notably the underconsumptionist school: inadequate buying power was linked to consumption spending propensities, which reputedly become 'too low' in a prosperous country. There was an attack on conventional capital theory, in which could be discerned many of the same reservations previously voiced by Veblen; particularly in the insistence that capitalization of assets was not technologically or physically determined, but rather the function of some unstable behavioral propensitites having a close connection to the rate of interest. There were favorable mentions of Abbati, Major Douglas and Hobson. But whereas the earlier unorthodox theorists were unreservedly antagonistic towards orthodox theory, Keynes seemed to want a friendly sparring match played by Marquess of Queensbury rules. Sometimes he claimed that his analytics were the general case of which neoclassical theory was the special case; and yet, more than once, when backed into a ogical corner, he would suddenly become more 'orthodox' than his challenger. For example: when Hawtrey worries that Keynes' definition of the MEC cannot be as independent of liquidity preference as Keynes makes out (and thereby anticipates certain criticisms made of neoclassical captial theory thrity years later by Keynes' students), Keynes retorted: [28]

> "There are a number of passages where I seem to be more in the classical tradition than you are. Several of your criticisms of the practical applicability of the marginal theory of economics. There are, of course, some qualifications to this theory and some criticisms which can validly be made. But this is not a matter I could very well go into in this book. I am simply accepting the usual theory of the subject without attempting to refine on it."

Perhaps the orthodox economist of the 1930's may be forgiven his or her obtuseness in the face of the Keynesian Revolution, since they probably viewed neoclassical economics as needing some refinements, but sound in its basic premises, as Keynes sometimes appeared to do.

The question which confronts us, as opposed to Keynes' contemporaries, is what is the relation of Keynes' theory to neoclassical economics as we understand it? When Keynes was challenged to summarize his distinctive contribution, he wrote: [29]

> "The orthodox theory regards the MEC as setting the pace. But the MEC depends upon the price of capital assets; and since this price determines the rate of new investment, it is consistent in equilibrium with only one given level of money income... In a system in which the level of money income is capable of fluctuating, the orthodox theory is one equation short of what is required to give a solution. Undoubtedly the reason why the orthodox system has failed to discover this discrepancy is because it has always tacitly assumed that income is given, namely, at the level corresponding to the employment of all the available resources."

This corresponds to a criticism of what we have dubbed a 'Stage I' theory, where internal realignments of variables do not alter the level of activity of the whole. Stating this disagreement in this manner, however, did little to convince neoclassicists of the novelty of this insight, because they were already aware that the conventional ceteris paribus conditions were illegitimate: in the hands of a careful practioner, they were merely a matter of convenience in exposition. Keynes' innovation was appreciably more significant. Harrod (and later Hayek) saw that Keynes was indirectly undermining the very logic of the demand and supply functions. [30] Unfortunately, this was occuring at the same time Keynes was using an 'aggregate' demand curve and an 'aggregate' supply curve in order to facilitate explanation for those familiar with orthodox ways. Keynes' aggregate supply cure was a curious amalgam of psychological considerations and cost-of-production considerations mixed in unusual proportions. He employed them to explain the level of the aggregate product, and therefore the business cycle. His chronology of the cycle follows: [31]

> The disillusion comes because doubts suddenly arise concerning the reliability of the prospective yield, perhaps because the current yield shows signs of falling off, as the stock of newly produced durable goods steadily increases. If current costs of production are thought to be higher than they will be later on, that will be a further reason for a fall in the MEC. Once doubt begins it spreads rapidly. Thus at the outset of the slump there is probably much capital of which the MEC has become negligible or even negative. But the interval of time which will have to elapse

before the shortage of capital through use, decay and obsolescence cause a sufficiently obvious scarcity to increase the MEC may be a somewhat stable function of the average durability of capital in a given epoch.

Here, in a nutshell, we see Marshall's uneasy marriage of psychologically determined demand and technologically determined supply being reproduced. Sraffa, [32] in 1926, had revived Wicksteed's complaint that the demand and supply schedules for any particular commodity should be denominated in the same units in order to be inscribed on the same axis; in a pure Walrasian system this condition held since endowments were a datum and "the demand for my product reflects the desire of the other trader while the supply of my product reflects my desire." (Note well that this mode of theorizing implicitly assumes Say's Law). But when endowments are <u>not</u> given exogenously, and goods must be produced in time, the supply function no longer need be upward sloping. In fact, the Sraffa of 1960 carried this thought to its logical conclusion in his book <u>Production of Commodities by Means of Commodities</u>. If a firm is assured of purchasing however much of an input it desires at a price fixed independently of its own purchases, its own supply curve of output will be horizontal and <u>demand schedules (i.e., psychological considerations)</u> will not influence equilibrium price, only the quantities produced. In this sense, the Walrasian system is flawed at the very most fundamental level. Marshall, Keynes tutor, understood this, but attempted to save psychologistic value theories and their demand-determined pricing through the artifice of the theory of the firm. Marshall postulated the existence of a factor which was in fixed supply to the firm (thus resulting in 'diminishing returns' and a rising supply curve) but not fixed to the industry in the long run. This 'factor' was entrepreneurship. For Marshall, this innovation was quite salubrious, since it not only revived the system of demand-pricing but also provided a marginalist theory of income distribution which was linked, not to given endowments, but to the objectively 'scarce' factor in the process of production.

Keynes, while retaining much of the Marshallian spirit, relinquished most of its substance, and it was this parting of ways which led to the 'doubts' and 'disillusions' of the previous long quote. The upper turning point of the cycle comes, as we have seen, when investors lose their nerve. Now they may sense the chilling winds of change for no objective reason at all--and this would mean that the business cycle happens entirely in their heads, the implication being we should look to Freud (or, better yet, Jung) and entrepreneurial birth traumas for an explanation. On the other hand, their fear could be grounded in economic variables: that is, the yield on capital goods falls before the loss of nerve. Keynes argued for this latter possibility by linking the yield on capital goods to their scarcity: "...the only reason why an asset offers a prospect of yielding during its life services having an aggregate value greater than its initial supply price is because it is scarce." [33] A capital good may be 'scarce' for two reasons. Either there is not enough of it being produced to continue expansion at the expected rate, in which case it is simply a short-run 'bottleneck' and earns a temporary rent, or else prices are demand-determined due to the existence of a fixed factor. If Keynes took the former position, his 'General Theory' would be reduced to the special case where rigidities cause some systematic divergence from equilibrium; here his theory would be no different from the Ricardian strain of disproportionality theories we have examined in Chapter Two. Alternatively, if Keynes took the latter position, the equilibrium level of output would be detemined by the interaction of supply and demand in the market for the 'fixed' factor, irrespective of liquidity preference, the multiplier, and all the rest of the Keynesian paraphenalia. Taking all of this into account, we see that Keynes' story of the cycle contradicts the rest of his model in the General Theory. Either the rate of return is set entirely by the level of investment, which in turn is only a function of 'animal spirits' (in conjunction with the psychology of liquidity preference), or the rate of return is set in the market for the fixed factor and then investment reacts to this rate. Given a utility/psychologistic theory of value, both stories cannot hold simultaneously, unless the 'animal spirits' are tamed into the short-run mistakes of psychological perception which are continually brought back into line with a Walrasian general equilibrium. This mode of reconciliation sums up the innovations of American Keynesianism after Keynes' death.

Of course, an alternative solution would be to dispense with neoclassical theory and its psychological foundations of price theory altogether, and effectively leave the MEC unexplained. This, in fact, is what the preponderance of the General Theory does, although it is not made explicit because it would have meant total rejection of orthodox economics. Harrod, after reading an early draft of the General Theory, warned against precisely that: [34]

> "(The General Theory's) effectiveness is diminished if you try to eradicate very deep-rooted habits of thought unnecessarily. One of these is supply and demand analysis. I am not merely thinking of the aged and fossilized, but of the younger generation who have been thinking perhaps only for a few years but very hard about these topics. It is doing great violence to their

fundamental groundwork of thought, if you tell them that two independent demand and supply functions won't jointly determine price and quantity. Tell them that there may be more than one solution. Tell them that we don't know the supply function. Tell them that the <u>ceteris paribus</u> clause is inadmissable and that we can discover more important functional relationships governing price and quantity in this case which render the supply and demand analysis nugatory. But don't impugn that analysis itself."

However much posturing went on about courting controversey and 'raising a dust', it appears Keynes took this advice to heart. Keynesian economics had been presented and taught <u>as if</u> it were entirely consistent with Marshallian, and later Walrasian, microeconomic theory, even though its author was aware that this might not be true. Far from being an insignificant point of doctrine, this is probably the critical flaw of Keynesian economics. It has led to a tiresome and persistent controversy down to the present day concerning the appropriate microfoundations of macroeconomics. [35] It also is the taproot of the various internal inconsistencies which exfoliate throughtout Keynes' analytical structure.

One of these inconsistencies was identified by Bertil Ohlin directly after the publication of the <u>General Theory</u> in and article which Keynes, as editor of the <u>Economic Journal</u>, refused to publish. Ohlin noticed that Keynes rejected the marginal analysis of the demand for labor, and yet uses marginal value productivity in his explanation of the MEC. As if this lack of symmetry in theory were not perplexing enough, Ohlin also notes that when Keynes does speak of marginal products, they are in terms of marginal physical units, even though Wicksell had earlier called this procedure of accounting for capital into serious question. [36] An alteration of capital at the margin does not involve lopping off a chunk of iron from a machine; rather, it means altering the value magnitude of a large collection of objects aggregated at their prices. Since any alteration of purchases can potentially influence all other prices, the augmentation or dimunition of capital at the margin is no easy matter: these problems have come to be known as 'Wicksell effects'. Although Keynes was somewhat familiar with the writings of Wicksell, he had not absorbed these lessons, as we can witness from Keynes' description of the business cycle quoted above. The psychology of doubts and disillusions causes the downturn, but the upturn is caused by the "<u>use, decay and obsolescence</u>" of capital objects over time: that is, by their physical melting away until they are scarce. Here Keynes makes the explicit error which Ohlin had isolated: less physical objects do not necessarily mean less 'capital' in value terms. Keynes could not pursue this potential contradiction because of his ambivalence toward Marshallian price theory: he would contradict his own theory of the level of output if supply curves generally sloped upward; and yet he could not bring himself to deny the neoclassical theory of demand-pricing, since he himself depended heavily upon 'psychological propensities' to drive his analysis. As it stood, he opted to explain the downturn by psychology and the upturn by physical phenomena, as if they only came into play at those specific disjunct times, an artificial <u>ceteris paribus</u> condition which was never made explicit.

Keynes' selective use of arguments having to do with physical capital objects leads us to another inconsistency in his analysis: his supression of the dimension of time in his theory. More than once Keynes was quite vague when it came to the issue of whether the multiplier was instantaneous, or if it took some finite but rather long period of time to work its way through the system. Most of the <u>General Theory</u> was written as though the multiplier created the savings which were needed to accompany new investment instantaneously, and this confused many economists, particularly because Keynes' <u>Treatise</u> had denied that this was the case, but also because the main analytical point made by outsiders such as Foster and Catchings and Soddy was that the time distribution of savings and investment had no reason to coincide. Keynes waved these objections aside by insisting he was just working in terms of an arbitrary time unit in which his equality held by definition, [37] much as Marshall dealt with the 'short period' and the 'long period'. In spite of that, there were other occasions when he seemed to be saying that the quantities of saving and investment could diverge, at least in some 'short period'. [38] This confusion appears to arise from a rather late change of mind on the part of Keynes, which he alludes to in his lecture notes of 1937: [39]

"Those who are old enough and attended in 1931-32 may remember a contraption of formulas of processes of all sorts of lengths depending on technical factors with income emerging at a given date corresponding to input at an earlier date. My distinction then was between input and output. I would lecture on this at considerable length and at one time it occupied several chapters of my book. But I discarded it partly because it was frightfully complicated and really had no sense to it, but mainly because there was no determinate time unit...When one is dealing with <u>aggregates</u>, aggregate effective demand at time A has no corresponding aggregate income at time B."

There Keynes admits that there is no determinate time unit in analysis because he believes there is no relation between expectations and plans at one date and the realized results at a later date. This conviction dates back to his early work on the theory of probability distributions. This conviction also undoubtedly accounts for his hostility toward Austrian economic theory, about which he once wrote, "God knows what the Austrians mean by 'period of production.' Nothing, in my opinion." [40] Therefore, it is irrelevant to ask whether the multiplier is simultaneous or not, because Keynes dismissed the question through avoidance of any treatment of time in most of the General Theory.

We write 'most', and not 'all', because Keynes could not escape making some reference to time when dealing with the business cycle. We can observe this by once more returning to his chronology of the cycle. The time which elapses between the downturn and the upturn is, he states, "a function of the average durability of capital in a given epoch." Again, this is in conflict with his Marshallian underpinnings and with the timeless analysis of the remainder of the General Theory, as Ohlin so perceptively noticed. [41] If Keynes were consistent in making his case, he would have maintained that the time patterns of capital were variable instead of fixed; and further, that they, too, were functions of psychological propensities and changing price relations. This avenue of escape was closed to him because of his uneasy relation to neoclassical price theory. [42]

The Keynesian abdication from coming to grips with time in aggregate economic theory has had deleterious repercussions in the interim between the General Theory and the present day. It has been fashionable to 'explain' the apparent tension between Keynesian macroeconomics and neo-Walrasian microeconomics by insisting that the former is the "economics of the short run", while the latter is the configuration of long run equilibrium. As the reader may have begun to perceive, nothing could be further from the truth. This faulty division of the anaylsis into separate boxes obscures the fact that Keynesian economics and neoclassical price theory have points of serious contention which cannot be reconciled without drastic revision of one or the other's foundations. It ignores that Walrasian general equilibrium is a Stage 1 theory, while Keynes explicitly was dealing with Stage 2 concepts. It also tries to impute a time frame to a work which is devoid of a time frame, and which ran into serious logical problems when a time frame was required. And finally, it papers over Keynes' hostility to Walrasian equilibria as possessing any practical relevance, which is perhaps most forcefully stated by one of his best-remembered aphorisms: "In the long run we are all dead." What can this mean, but that such long run/short run distinctions are, at best, empty intellectual exercises if the long run is never attained?

A third inconsistency in Keynes' work also arises from an implicit interconnection between the 'demand' and 'supply' sides of the analysis, and is linked to the absence of time in the analysis. Keynes believed the fatal weakness of what he termed 'classical' theory was the fact that the interest rate, and monetary relations in general, were portrayed as passive; they would always adjust in reaction to any change in the underlying real factors. He felt that his liberation from this conception came with the severance of the determination of the interest rate from real factors, and the location of that determination within the sphere of the supply and demand for cash balances, which he termed 'liquidity preferences'. This proved a curious choice for a number of reasons. First, it ignored a voluminous literature in monetary theory which questioned the very construction of a demand curve for money as inconsistent with the utilitarian theory of value. [43] Secondly, his stress on specifically <u>cash</u> holdings led him to downplay any independent status of <u>finance</u> in his analysis. This odd dichotomy came to light only after the publication of the <u>Genereal Theory</u>, in an exchange with Robertson and the <u>Swedish school</u>. Initially, Keynes accused Ohlin and the Swedish school of being inadvertently 'classical' because their concern over the net supply of new credit was identical with the older concern over net current savings, and, therefore, they believed the interest rate equilibrated savings and investment. The error was, in fact, Keynes', and not the Swedes', since they never insisted current saving was identical to new credit; they believed the two diverged fairly regularly. What concerned the Swedes was instead how new net investment was <u>financed</u> if it took place prior to any concommitant increase in income. As we have seen previously, as long as Keynes suppressed the time structure of spending and income, this question appeared meaningless within his framework: that is, Swedish theory and Keynesian economics were incommensurable on this point.

When Ohlin resisted the suggestion that he be lumped together with the classical economists, Keynes made one more attempt to come to terms with Swedish analysis in his article "Alternative Theories of the Rate of Interest" in the 1937 <u>Economic Journal</u>. He admitted there that funds may be required for investment <u>prior</u> to the corresponding saving, and that these funds might be obtained either by issuing financial instruments or else through the good graces of a bank. He then goes on to write: [44]

> "...unless the banking system is prepared to augment the supply of money, lack of finance may prove an important obstacle to more than a certain amount of investment decisions being on the tapis at the same time. But 'finance' has nothing to do with saving. At the 'financial' stage of the proceedings no net saving has taken place on

anyone's part, just as there has been no net investment. 'Finance' and 'commitments to finance' are mere credit and debit book entries, which allow entrepreneurs to go ahead with assurance...Credit, in the sense of 'finance', looks after a flow of investment. It is a revolving fund which can be used over and over again. It does not absorb or exhaust any resources."

This position takes Keynes' denial of the time structure of inputs and outputs one step further: he admits that time may elapse between investment considerations and the savings that they give rise to, but he goes on to insist these time lapses are inconsequential for the process as a whole, because they are bridged by 'finance', this 'revolving fund' which he maintains is 'self-liquidating' for the community as a whole. Thus he feels justified in his opinion that there is no time structure for the multiplier because finance obviates any effects it might have. Since this is not immediately obvious or plausible to an economist steeped in the controversies of the 1930's--Hayek, Robertson, Hawtrey, Fisher, Major Douglas and a host of others were concentrating on credit as a disruptive force in capitalism-- Keynes further justifies his position by appealing to the fact that credit is merely a ledger entry, offset by a corresponding entry in the other column.

Whenever a beleaguered theorist resorts to a truism in order to shore up a dubious proposition, we should become even more skeptical. In this particular case, skepticism is more than warranted. The 'truism' that someone's asset is someone else's liability, and that in the aggregate they both cancel out, is faulty precisely because it abstracts from the passage of time. At any point in time, the entries on the left- and right-hand sides of the ledger do cancel: but that has nothing to do with the determination of the level of economic activity. The ability to shift the distribution of flows _in_ time is the crux of the matter. Neoclassical theorists assume that the 'returns' are fixed by technology, or else are exogenous givens prior to the analysis; so to take more of the flow now in 'consumption' means having less flow for later. However, if the force and rationale of the economic system resides in accumulation and the increase of production, and not consumption, then to lay claim to more of a flow now means having more flow over the whole future horizon <u>if the processes of production and finance are functioning smoothly</u>.

In fact, Keynes' treatment of finance presents an interesting contrast with his treatment of the quantity theory of money. He rightly insisted that the quantity theory was deficient because it assumed money was neutral with respect to the real economy; a deficiency he then counteracted with his theory of liquidity preference and its relation to investment. Yet, in order to restrict liquidity preference specifically to the demand for and supply of cash balances, he found it necessary to maintain that 'finance' (i.e., credit) was neutral with respect to the real economy, something even many neoclassical economists had not espoused at the time. He was willing to assume this neutrality to the point of writing, "I am unable to see that changes in the schedule of the MEC have any obvious or predictable effect on the liquidity function." [45] This would mean that there were no possible feedbacks between changes in determinants of the rate of return and the demand for "money".

One can only speculate that Keynes' desire to dissociate himself from the 'money cranks', whom were to be found everywhere in the 1930's, led him to adopt such a strong position concerning the neutrality of finance. Further elaborations of his theory in later years only confirmed this bias. For example, Keynes in the September 1939 Economic Journal chose to respond to some econometric work done by Jan Tinbergen, at least in part because the interest rate, a key variable in the Keynesian system, did not fare well in Tinbergen's investment equations. As a response to this bit of empirical disconfirmation, Keynes suggested a re-specification of the investment function to include the difference between the rate of profit on costs and the rate of interest on loans, with the proviso that the rate of interest would always tend to equal the rate of profit. The reader will recall from the previous section of this chapter that the presumed equality between the interest rate and the rate of profit is a sufficient condition to rule out any effects of credit upon the rate of return: that is, it is tantamount to the assumption of the neutrality of finance.

The major pitfall which snared Keynes was his stated desire to remove the interest rate from all of its classical equilibrating roles. He was so determined to deny the interest rate had much influence on saving that he ended up advocating the neutrality of finance. He was so detemined to deny that the interest rate acted to bring investment into line with saving that he never provided a plausible theory of investment demand. Instead of questioning the meaning of those aggregative demand and supply schedules directly, he shifted their arguments around into other demand and supply schedules. These loose ends in his theory were not harmless, but led directly to the two major weaknesses in Keynesian economics today: the lack of concern with how government deficits are financed, and the lack of any plausible theory of inflation. If finance and credit were felt to be neutral, then Keynesians would not expect there to be major feedback effects from the continual debt finance of government deficits, essentially because liquidity preference is supposed to be relatively independent of the MEC. Insofar as Keynes had abjured the Swedish concern over finance and the price level and, furthermore, had retained Marshallian price theory without exploring its consistency with his aggregative theory, there was no solid foundation upon which to build a theory of inflation and deflation. These weaknesses have recently provided the rallying point for the anti-Keynesian reaction, which we shall survey in the rest of this chapter, along with the demise of the second great discussion of macroeconomic instability.

In summary, the perception of Keynes as a Cassandra or a Polyanna depends upon the stance of the observer. From the viewpoint of a Paul Sammuelson in 1946, confident that the economic system was intrinsically stable when supplemented by a few appropriate Keynesian nudges, Keynes was a Cassandra whose warnings of potential misfortune had to be calmly evaluated: and of course, Sammuelson's Principles text became the vehicle. But then there were the other theorists, more pessimistic, who were left behind in the new rush of confidence. Michal Kalecki in a prophetic paper warned that politics could obviate most attempts to apply the Keynesian tonic. The 'outsiders' concern with money and credit became passé and even embarrassing. Academic Marxists questioned the Keynesian reliance on neoclassical concepts. To this ragtag collection of economists, Keynes looked more like a Polyanna, who insisted things were getting better and better every day and in every way. The opinions of this latter group were theoretically insignificant, nevertheless, because the triumph of the Keynesian Revolution had effectively stilled the debate over theories of instability of the capitalist economy.

III. THE AFTERMATH

With the onset of World War II and the ensuing quarter century boom, the theory of aggregate instability practically faded from sight. It was displaced by discussion of the various components of the Keynesian model and their 'microeconomic' bases--that is, their relation to Walrasian general equilibrium theory. In the interests of brevity, we propose to divide the discussion of these tendencies into problems in the theory of investment and income, the multiplier-accelerator model and problems with the large econometric simultaneous models.

We have described in the last section how Keynes left a legacy of two theories of investment: one, an 'animal spirits' theory, where inherently unpredictable expectations were controlled by the interest rate and an equally unpredictable liquidity preference; and the other, a theory of declining physical marginal productivity ruled by a factor fixed from the point of view of the firm. The latter theory was elaborated by many neoclassical economists, most notably by Dale Jorgenson, and has been largely incorporated into the large econometric models discussed below. The attraction of this sort of model has had to do with the fact that it involves constrained maximization at the firm level, thus being compatible with the Walrasian world view. On the whole, these models have added little or nothing to the theory of macroeconomic instability since they have placed such a heavy emphasis on the production function. The result was the optimum level of output was always determinate, irrespective of the level of effective demand, because physical returns were fixed. Later doctrinal controversies involving the theory of capital exposed the logical fallacy in this line of thought: physical returns at the micro level cannot conceptually determine the rate of profit. The implications of this recent criticism for instability theory are explored in the next chapter.

The 'animal spirits' model, needless to say, was not felt to be a rigorous specification for econometric testing or for the new image of the economist as technician of macroeconomic stability. Early attempts at building econometric models of investment with a focus on the interest rate were found to be disappointing. A short time after the publication of the General Theory, many economists realized that they could bypass the animal spirits theory completely by linking investment to changes in the level of aggregate output, and thereby produce cycles in income in a simple two-equation model. In this manner, one could still claim to be a 'Keynesian', while simultaneously satisfying the predilection for a mechanically deterministic model. The mechanism by which this was accomplished was the accelerator, promulgated in an article by Samuelson [46], although antecedents of the concept could be found in the work of J. M. Clark and Alvin Hansen. Expectations were replaced by observable investment behavior: investment was postulated to move in some fixed relation as regards changes in national income. Harrod, Fellner and others were quick to suggest that use of the accelerator was essentially the same thing as presuming a normal physical relation between capital stock and national income, or output in equilibrium growth. Expectations in a certain sense were reduced to technology, or at least the postulate of rationality could enforce the conformity. [47] From this innovation Samuelson derived a second order difference equation in national income which might produce cycles given some plausible values for the parameters involved--here we shall call them the acceleration coefficient and proportional marginal propensity to save. As Samuelson recognized, it is the nature of difference equations to produce continued and unabated oscillation only when the parameters have a very particular configuration; that is, when the roots of the characteristic equation lie on the unit circle. Otherwise, various configurations of the roots will lead either to damping or explosive behavior. Samuelson pointed out that from the Keynesian point of view, the most economically credible patterns of the parameters would lead to damping and convergent behavior. This finding concerning stability was a major step in the homogenization of Keynes, since this limitation meant there was no market phenomenon which caused chronic and intrinsic instability.

It seems the full import of this statement was not immediately clear, since the multiplier-accelerator became, and still is, the most commonly found textbook explanation of the business cycle. [48] Also intriguing is the fact that no textbook bothers to estimate any of these simple relationships, even though such prudent circumspection is nowhere equally in evidence for that equally nebulous relation, the production function. If we postulate the usual textbook model of the two relation system:

$$Y_t = I_t/s + Z/s \qquad (3.4)$$

$$I_t = v(Y_{t-1} - Y_{t-2}) \qquad (3.5)$$

where s is the marginal propensity to save, v is the acceleration coefficient, and Z is the constant of the savings function. Substituting, we arrive at the reduced form equation:

$$Y_t = v/s\ (Y_{t-1} - Y_{t-2}) + Z/s \qquad (3.6)$$

The reasons that estimates of the parameters Z/s and v/s are never included in textbook expositions are, we suggest, two: one, that in this particular version of the multiplier-accelerator model (but not the original Samuelson version) the point estimates of the coefficients of equation 3.6 on income lagged once and income lagged twice should be equal in absolute value (which apparently is never the case); and two, it seems that the exigencies of statistical estimation thwart any attempt to discover if the system is stable or unstable.

The second criticism is much more substantial, and deserves a much more technical exposition than the style in which the author has opted to cast this text. For our present purposes of summarizing the history of theories of economic instability, we need only survey the implications of the econometric problem. If we may borrow the language of the econometricians, there is only a very low probability that present econometric techniques will ever identify 'unstable' or 'explosive' roots in an appropriately specified linear model. The irony of the situation is that the multiplier-accelerator model is popular as a didactic device precisely because the coefficients of the solution of the difference equation have an economic interpretation and thus would seem to lend themselves quite readily to empirical stability analysis. But this 'empiricism' is a sham, since this definition of 'instability' is effectively ruled out of bounds by statisitical theory before the anaylsis starts.

If the question of macroeconomic stability within the context of the mulitiplier-accelerator model is substantively untestable, then why has it become the de facto explanation of the cycle in the classroom? It certainly is not an intuitive idea that investment is a simple function of the level of output, or its rate of change. One might suggest that it acts as a parable: business cycle theory after Keynes, such as it is, means deducing a reduced-form difference equation in national income, or perhaps some other variable of interest, and then examining the resulting econometrically estimated characteristic roots. The accelerator provides a paradigmatic example of technique, showing that if one ties the level of something to the rate of change of something else in an interdependent system, fluctuations are sure to result. Appreciation of technique obscures the fact that there is no theoretical motivation for the functional form or for believing the results of the estimation. Admittedly (one would assure the critical student) a simple consumption function coupled with an equally simplistic acceleration principle ignores most of the phenomena which the economists thought important in the analysis of business cycles. In principle, one would intone reassuringly, we certainly should include those considerations in a more general model.

This appears to be the line taken by Hicks in his influential book in the 1950's, A Contribution to the Theory of the Trade Cycle. Hicks traced the origins of this attitude concerning technique back to Frisch's seminal article on "Propagation and Impulse Problems" in 1934, which showed that ". . . the acceleration principle established an analogy between economic fluctuations and the 'waves' which are so elaborately studied in physics; thus a vast amount of knowledge and technique acquired for other purposes by applied mathematicians and physicists suddenly became relevant to the economic problem." [49]

One of the lessons quickly assimilated from the applied mathematicians was that a linear difference equation, of any order, will in the limit converge either to a constant or to an expotential growth curve (with the exception of a certain improbable knife-edge configuration of coefficients). Neither of these situations resembled the course of an economy of which anyone was aware. Hick's innovation was to introduce quasi-nonlinearity into the familiar multiplier-accelerator (M-A) model by a continuous revision of the intial conditions of the difference equations, which he called 'Floors' and 'Ceilings'. Hicks' Ceiling was dubbed Full Employment, although one could have as well called it the Ultima Thule, since it was merely a trend line imposed with scant theoretical rationale, other than the exorcism of unseemly problems of pure exponential growth. (A recurrent theme among these M-A models is their dogged disregard for the physical and social conditions of production except when a trend line is needed to mitigate the grossly mechanical operations of the mathematics; at which point 'technology' and 'bottlenecks' materialize out of nowhere.) Hicks' Floor was a continuing dose of Autonomous (read "unexplainable") Investment. The system was kept in motion by a difference equation in national income which was presumed to have explosive parameters. As we have suggested, this would be well-nigh impossible to verify empirically. Quite inexplicably, this book ratified the M-A model as <u>the</u> explanation of cycle for the next twenty years. A spate of articles followed employing the same basic framework accompanied by innumberable "ratchets," "switches," "floors" and "ceilings"--all quite devoid of any new theoretical ideas.

It should be mentioned that the specifically <u>mechanical</u> problems of the M-A models were recognized extremely early by Richard Goodwin, in a series of papers published in the early 1950's. [50] He suggested that the output of the M-A model would resemble known timeseries of national income, if one were willing to make either of two adjustments: 1) make the multipliter nonlinear; or 2) expose the system with damping coefficients to a continual stream of random shocks. He also pointed out that the same mathematics of the M-A model could produce fluctuations about a stationary level or problem-free steady growth (which, formally, is the same as the Harrod-Domar model), but it was incapable of producing both results simultaneously. As a possible rebuttal to these criticisms, he fashioned various nonlinear M-A with a 'technological progress' trend term superimposed. While in one sense, M-A models acheived the height of elegance in Goodwin's work, they also reached a new peak of self-absorption with technique, numbing the mind with mixed difference-differential equations which could only be solved analytically by graphical integration (if at all), proliferating phase diagrams, etc. Although Goodwin himself was not an econometrician, the exercises he described were the ultimate in <u>Gedanken</u> experiment, fitting a curve to any conceivable set of points. What was sorely lacking in his work was a commitment to explain why the nonlinearities were necessary from the viewpoint of economic theory, and not solely that of mathematical technique.

While Goodwin chose the first of his two proposed methods of remedying the mechanical problems of M-A models, a much larger number of economists became enamoured of the second solution. The advent of high speed computers and the resulting ease of linear regression analysis encouraged the widespread fitting of least-squares equations to various theoretical macroeconomic relations, including the naive M-A models. The act of fitting these equations divides the variance of the dependent variable into a deterministic part and a stochastic 'error' component. Once it was realized that, in general, the deterministic part of the M-A models would evince damping characteristic roots (both because they were linear and because statistical techniques forced them to be so), it was only a matter of time before econometricians began to maintain that the cyclical paths of capitalist economies were due to random shocks (which were the same as their least-squares residuals) impinging upon the stable macroeconomic relationships. The 'theory' behind this assertion was intuitive: there are phenomena exogenous to economic behavior (and economic theories) which feed into behavioral relations. Those exogenous factors which loomed large in behavior were often included as explanatory variables, but the number of exogenous phenomena was great, and many of these individually independent 'disturbances' was deemed normally distributed by some variant of the Central Limit Theorem, and would end up in the error term of the regression equation. When introduced into the damping deterministic difference equation, these random shocks produce a dependent variable which fluctuated indefinitely without damping. The econometricians cited Slutsky [51] as an early pioneer in these sorts of explanations.

At this juncture, the theory of business cycles and macroeconomic theory proper parted ways, at least among American economists. The econometricians became the guardians of cycle theory, such as there was left, while the pure theorists left all notions of instability behind. Starting with Hicks' article on "Mr. Keynes and the Classics," the Keynesian system was refurbished from the ground up and had become compatible with the neoclassical worldview. Hicks represented the Keynesian concerns over liquidity preference and its repercussions on investment by expanding the system to three equations: the expanded multiplier, $S=S(Y,r)$, where r is the rate of interest, Y the level of nominal income, and S aggregate savings; the investment equations, $I=I(Y,r)$; and liquidity preference equation, $M=L(Y,r)$, where M is the exogenously given stock of money. Imposing the equilibrium equation of savings and investment, the first two expressions were equated and plotted in (Y,r) space, resulting in a schedule which sloped downwards, if certain partial derivatives were held to their 'correct' signs. The plot of the third equation in the same space was assumed to slope upwards, intersecting with the other schedule at a single point, mimicking the familiar demand and supply schedules. The Hicks Hansen IS-LM model was later elaborated through the addition of a 'labor market' in which both employment and (in the absence of rigidities) the real wage rate were determined--in the very anti-Keynesian sequence of being prior to levels of aggregate income and the interest rate. [52] The 'neoclassical synthesis' was capped by the addition of the 'real balance effect,' in which a changing price level helps equilibrate investment through its effects on the holdings of money balances, and through the 'Phillips curve,' which relates money wage changes to past levels of the unemployment rate. As sectoral equations multiplied, the question of instability got lost in the shuffle, since each new addition to the IS-LM framework guaranteed by its functioning that the only true equilibrium level of aggregate activity would be that characterizing full employment (in the absense of those pesky rigidities of wages). Perhaps this is why naive M-A models have proved so tenacious as the textbook explanation of cycles: when all the components of the neoclassical synthesis are taken into account, there is no possiblity of having an integrated cycle theory. (One should perhaps qualify this statement by noting the arbitrary practice of lagging any number of variables in the preordained functional forms.)

In a sense, the econometricians went on the offensive, starting in the late 1950's. First one, then ever-increasing numbers of economists maintained that the burgeoning macro-econometric models encompassed the state of the art Keynesian theory. The result was felt to be a real advance in cycle theory, and from the point of view of our 'stages of instability theory,' it was. Dating from Jevons and even earlier, theorists had blamed the weather and other imponderables for disrupting the delicate balance of equilibrium; but they were incapable of clearly specifying the extent of these disruptions, since they had no theory of the level of output. (In our schema, stage 3 was impossible without stage 2.) Once such a theory was in hand, it became for the first time possible to specify the paths of response to random shocks and empirically see if they could bear the blame for the cycle. An important initial attempt at this sort of analysis was performed by the Adelmans in their simulation runs of the Klein-Goldberger model. [53]

The Klein-Goldberger model was non-linear and therefore held little prospect of being reduced to an analytically solvable difference equation in national income, so the Adelmans chose simulation techniques in order to pose the question of the cycle-generating capability of the deterministic part of the model. As we have now come to expect, the system as a whole was damping, and therefore endogenous cycles could not be traced to the theoretical structure. Moreover, the model produced only weak and unrealistic oscillations if random shocks were added to the exogenous variables, but gave believable (by some very <u>ad hoc</u> NBER standards) oscillations in GNP if white noise was tacked on to the end of every equation. (As an interesting sidelight, the Adelmans judged both the long and short interest rate equations too implausible to simulate in their original K-G form, and so they arbitrarily set the short rate at 2.5% and the long rate at 3.5% <u>for the duration of the simulation run.</u> Such actions betray an over-zealous belief that equations of the M-A form are the only possible explanation of macroeconomic instability. Would Keynes have recognized this model of the trade cycle? To some, the failure of the 'Keynesian' theory to account for cycles was discomfitting; yet for most the structure/shock distinction was ideaologically congenial, since instability or fluctuation could not be traced to the economic system per se.

The Adelmans' article signalled a flood of similar experiments. [54] Over time, the discussion of cyclical fluctuations in the context of large econometric models became more statistically sophisticated. Instead of plotting the simulation output and categorizing them along NBER lines, the output series were subjected to spectral analysis to test for the existence of cycles of fixed frequencies in an explicit manner. Later, E.P. Howrey outlined a method of deriving the analytic solution of a system of stochastic linear difference equations, thereby bypassing simulation techniques alotether. [55] By solving for the characteristic roots of the multi-equation econometric model, one could definitively answer to question of whether the theoretical specifications of those large-scale models acted as an amplifier for the random shocks impinging upon its (necessarily) stable structure.

The culmination of the work springing from this econometric ebullience was a conference sponsored by NBER in late 1969 at Harvard on econometric models of cyclical behavior, later represented by a two-volume compendium of papers there presented. [56] The staging of the conference was a tribute to the consensus about the subordinate place of business cycle theory with respect to macroeconometrics, since the theory and the econometric models were rarely distinguished in the works of the participants. The results of this staggering amount of work using the most advanced large scale econmetric models up to that time were, frankly, disappointing. The conclusions, in a nutshell, were: a) all the models examined were dynamically stable when treated as deterministic systems--in theory they do not produce cycles, and b) the models all produced series with spectral peaks which clustered around the average duration of cycles in the NBER typology when those models were exposed to serially correlated shocks, both within and across equations. Did this latter result provide evidence for the hypothesis that cyclical fluctuations are the outcome of stochastic disturbances impinging on a dynamically stable response-mechanism? (Was Slutsky correct?) Not quite.

The only participant of the conference who applied the recently developed analytical techniques (to not simulate but rather derive the theoretical implied spectra directly from the model) was Howrey [57] in his study of the Wharton model. He first confirmed theoretically that the deterministic model was stable by extracting the characteristic roots of the linearized version and showing the effects of the one pair of complex roots were swamped by the contribution of larger positive real roots. Secondly, he examined the implied spectra of the output of the model and concluded the model's lag structure did not impart the kind of smoothing required to convert a sequence of random shocks into cyclical fluctuations of the random variables. Thus the classcial Frischian impulse-response mechanism was called into question <u>as an explanation</u>.

The glaring dependence of all the models on serially correlated shocks to produce cycles left some uneasy with the rapidly shrinking economic content of these models: [58]

> It should be emphasized that broadening the class of shocks to include perturbations in exogenous variables--and to allow for serial correlation in the disturbances to equations and exogenous variables--diminishes the role of the model structure as cycle-maker. If the real roots dominate the cyclical ones and the lag structure does not convert serially independent random shocks into cycles in the endogenous variables, the model structure becomes simply a multiplier mechanism for amplifying shocks of any kind. There is still an impulse-response mechanism, but the cycles are inherent in the impulses rather than in the responses.

Thus, in the late 1960's, a sort of schizophrenic attitude took root in the economics profession. To outsiders and students, a brave and self-assured facade was maintained whereby the large econometric models were held to embody the best that macrotheory had to offer; and what macrotheory had to offer was the homily that the economy was inherently stable. Internally, some practitioners realized that their retreat to autocorrelated "shocks" was rapidly removing all explanation of macroeconomic stability outside of the purview of economics. We have suggested in the first chapter that a necessary stage in business cycle theory is the endogenous/exogenous distinction, the separation of society into that which economists profess to explain and that for which they abdicate responsibility. In this case, the sheer amount of phenomena falling outside the boundaries of 'economics' was a source of anxiety with regards to the research program implied by this kind of 'economics.' What reassurance could be gained from knowing the economy was 'stable' if the economy was being defined as a small, passive (and ultimately insignificant for the question of stability) fraction of social existence? What is a 'stable economy', if all macroeconomic fluctuation comes from outside the 'economy'?

The disenchantment of some economists with the big econometric models, if we have dated it correctly, came at a crucial time: just before the worst recession in the United States since the Great Depression of the 1930's. The coincidence of widespread unemployment and rampant inflation chilled any cozy public image of the economist as a self-assured technician, and made parts of the textbook IS-LM analysis embarrassing to teach in introductory courses. Further, one of the linch pins of the neoclassical synthesis--the production function--came under increasingly sharp theoretical attack. [59] Many believe that this criticism alone would have been sufficient to undermine the 'neoclassical synthesis' and most econometric work, since both depend very heavily on marginalist theories of distribution. Finally, those who were rankled by the blind neglect of monetary phenomena in orthodox macrotheory found a literate and coherent champion with the publication of Axel Leijonhufvud's <u>On Keynesian Economics and the Economic of Keynes</u>. Clearly, no matter what the political stripe, many were rife with discontent over received macroeconomics in the 1970's. As Minsky has written, twenty-five years of study of the <u>General Theory</u> has led to the belief that Keynesian models are either trivial, incomplete, inconsistent or indistinguishable in their results from older quantity-theory models. [60]

CHAPTER FOUR

THE BIRTH OF THE BUSINESS CYCLE, PART I

History and Economic Theory

Up until now, this volume has been concerned with what Gunnar Myrdal once called immanent 'criticism', where theories are traced historically and expanded upon until the reader becomes gradually aware that there are certain recurrent flaws and ambiguities in their internal logic. Once the author has coaxed the reader into this mind frame, it is comparatively easy to produce catharsis by suggesting that if we were only to fix this, that and the other thing through the juggling and revision of previous theory, we would arrive at the summum bonum, the correct theory. While this tension and subsequent release is good form from an aesthetic standpoint, the present author has come to believe that this method of argument is deficient, and may even be part of our present impediment in the understanding the causes of macroeconomic instability. The reason immanent criticism alone is misleading is that the process of theorizing is left without a context, carried on as if a void; and this is especially true when it comes to theories of macroeconomic instability.

For instance, has it yet occured to the reader to wonder why there were only two fruitful discussions of macroeconomic instability in history, or why they happened when they did, or why it seems we are now in a period which, as yet, has no novel contribution to make to those discussions? These questions have certainly accompanied the author in the course of his reading. These are larger questions of consciousness of macroeoconomic instability, as opposed to its abstract discussion. There are questions of how we come to know what we know: questions which cannot be dealt with adequately employing the methodology of implicit criticism. Nonetheless, these questions are not a waste of time if they can help us break out of a frustrating reprise of consideration and reconsideration of previous theory. In this chapter we propose to attempt a history of the consciousness of business cycles which will complement, yet also distance us from conventional theory.

There is a rather impressionistic generalization which can be made concerning the timing and content of theories of macroeconomic instability. It seems that a necessary precondition for a serious discussion of instability is the existence of a group of economists predisposed to believe in the fundamental instability of the capitalist system <u>before</u> they have elaborated their analysis. This was certainly true of Sismondi, Marx, Veblen and Keynes, to name only the most illustrious thinkers. One possible hinderance to present discussions is the lack of such a tradition, with Western economists continually professing belief in the stability of the economy without any adequate justification.

There is another generalization to be made about the timing and content of these theories. The dominant theme of the new theories of any era seems to arise directly out of some set of contemporary experiences. The first general glut controversy coincided with the pronounced crises of the later Napoleonic and post-Napoleonic War period, which coupled obvious over capacity on the part of war-related industries with a swelling army of workers pressing for an augmentation of inadequate wages. These experiences were transmitted into concerns over whether a 'glut'--i.e., excessive inventories and capacity--could be general, and over the possible inadequacy of wages to purchase the mass of produced goods. Marx appears to have been heavily influenced by the Chartist movement and the agitation for the Ten Hours Bill, in which he saw evidence that for "the first time...in broad daylight the political economy of the middle class succumbed to the political economy of the working class." [1] Not only did he interpret this as verification of his central thesis of class conflict, but it also informed his more specific theoretical notion of surplus value as actual embodied labor hours denied the laborer, with its resultant implications for further accumulation and growth. Veblen wrote in response to the excesses of the era of the Robber Barons and the Gilded Age, and the financial crises in the US in the 1890's. The journalists had personified the Captains of Industry; it merely remained for Veblen to draw out the implications of their sabotage of industrial production processes. And finally, how much of the spread of the Rational Expectations school can be explained simply by the painfully fresh remembrances of dislocations caused by the OPEC cartel (i.e., random shocks) and accelerating inflation in the face of faltering production? The list could go on and on [2]; but our purpose is not to painstakingly locate each theorist in his experiential matrix. Our project is rather to become sensitive to how this quite understandable reaction to perceived events in our respective lifetimes has shaped our thinking in ways which we have not fully understood.

One effective way to jar our complacency is to attempt the following: let us take the most current explanations of business cycles, and attempt to transport them back two centuries or so. For example, the Rational Expectations approach: Does the efficient markets hypothesis deny that speculation in corporate shares 'caused' the South Sea

Bubble of 1718-1720? Or another instance, the Left Post-Keynesian approach: did class struggles over the share of total income in any sense 'cause' the crash of 1825? Was it the multiplier-accelerator in conjunction with random shocks which brought about the extended slump of the mid-1780's?

These questions would never be answered as much as they would be avoided, I should expect. The superficial excuse would be that there was not enough 'good data' surviving from those periods; but that would be a red herring drawn across our path, since the paucity of empirical data rarely prevents any theoretical structure from being used as a preliminary explanation of some interesting phenomenon. A more substantive response would be that these theories are not applicable to those situations, because the market structures conceived of as supporting these theories did not exist in a well-developed state two centuries ago. Contemplation of this response for a few moments will reveal a certain cognitive dissonance in this position. In what way, precisely, are the theories we have surveyed in the last two chapters specific to certain market structures, institutions or historical epochs? Or, more to the point, when and where do these theories apply, and when are they obviated by circumstances? If, as we have suggested, theories tend to grow out of the significient experiences of the eras in which they were conceived, do they then become hothouse plants, unable to survive the succession of seasons and the transition to a different epoch?

A not unrealistic definition of a rigorous economic theory would seem to include a specification of the appropriate time frame and insitutional structure within which the construction is supposed to operate. However, there seems to be a philosophical bias against this form of rigor in economics, which probably derives from an earlier logical positivist disdain of 'historicism'. This position conventionally holds that there are no scientific historical explanations *per se*, but rather only general explanations of specific historical events. [3] A popularized version of this bias usually consists of some invidious comparison of economics with physics, such as 'truly scientific laws remain operative in all situations, such as the law of gravity'. This has led to an admiration for theories which purport to be 'general' in the sense that they have no time horizon or reference at all; an a-temporal bias evident in the widespread lack of specification of institutional and temporal boundaries in the modern models surveyed in the preceeding chapter. This sought-after quality of generality acts as a drug upon the clarity of economic thought in the following manner: initially there appears a noteworthy set of economic events not anticipated by the previous sets of theories. The first inclination is to tinker with the existing theories; or if we are lucky, along comes a Veblen or a Keynes to offer a somewhat novel analysis. This process continues and the economics discipline peripatetically focuses first on this aspect, then that aspect of the economic process; in the course of events 'dissolving' or simply forgetting the insights of a previous phase. Each succeeding phase is touted as being a general theory; when in fact it is the very opposite of being general, since theories rapidly are made anachronistic with each new shift of attention; almost with the same speed that new model cars can replace their 'outdated' predecessors. We arrive at the point where any attempt to apply modern theories of instability to relatively remote historical circumstances produces embarrassment, since directly or indirectly it exposes this contradiction in the a-historical ideal of generality.

Economic theorists, because they are never forced to confront the issue of historical applicability, have not been made aware of this contradiction; but practicing economic historians have recently stumbled upon it. Specifically, the study of the Great Depression of the 1930's has again come into vogue, largely because confidence in the continued uninterrupted growth of the US has faded. In the course of events, one mainstream economic historian decided to apply the contemporary textbook IS-LM model to that historical instance, as one would reasonably have expected him to do, and he found that the conventional framework cannot explain the initial downturn or its severity. [4] This failure is more than a little unnerving, since it suggests IS-LM is adequate in practice for the present, but can't even be seriously employed to explain the period within which it was originally conceived. The economic historian is then brought face-to-face with a fundamental theoretical issue: when does the 'IS-LM world' start? Are the origins of this world co-temporary with the origins of the theory? Does the theory precede the appropriate circumstances? (That is, are economists generally visionaries?) Or are economists laggard, assimilating explanations after some experience?

If and when these questions are sidestepped, a great opportunity is foregone: an opportunity for the practice of history to critique the practice of economic theory. For if it is true that economists generally have neglected the specification of the temporal and institutional boundaries of their explanations, it could be a significant source of confusion in present discussions. Therefore, to pose the question of, say, "when does the business cycle begin?" is not simply an antiquarian quest or a historian's ploy to organize reams of colorless data, but a theoretical program to journey to the center of our unspoken presuppostions about macroeconomic instability.

A search of the literature reveals that economists and economic historians do possess presuppositions about the temporal appearance of the business cycle, even though it is never a matter of explicit or extensive concern. In the next section some of these representative predispositions are sampled in order to further develop our history of the consciousness of macroeconomic instability.

On the Etiology of Instability

"It is a well-accepted and commonplace fact that the business cycle is a modern phenomenon--a product of the modern economic order with its technical condition and legal institutions."

--Alvin Hansen, Business Cycle Theory

"Every statistical time-series can be analyzed, by purely mechanical methods, into trend and cycle; it is a natural human way of thinking, applicable, in a rough way, to non-numerical data also. Why should we not treat the Economic History of the World as a single process--a process that (at least so far) has a recognizable trend? Even the rise and decline of civilizations can find a place among the cycles that are imposed on it."

--Sir John Hicks, A Theory of Economic History

The fortunes of trade have always been erratic. If mere disturbance of trade comes under the rubric of the business cycle, then the business cycle is as old as human society.
Evidently, many people believe this to be the case. One poular history of business crises maintains that a Mediterranean-wide depression existed in the Roman world in 33 A.D., and that it was this, as well as the compelling wisdom of the Judean carpenter, which encouraged the rapid spread of Christian beliefs. [5] Others cite the paralyzing plagues which swept Medieval Europe in the mid-sixth and mid-ninth centuries as examples of cyclical business activity. The few scattered statistics which survive from early Rennaissance Europe clearly show marked fluctuations in international trade. Carus-Wilson's compilation of early English export records portray both raw wool exports and cloth exports moving fitfully about differing trends, with apparent troughs in 1435/6, 1464/5, 1504/5 and 1521-3. [6] As we approach the present day, we find certain historians pinpointing financial disturbances rooted in governmental defaults on loans as examples of the ubiquity of the business cycle in the past. [7] Manifestly, if the essence of the business cycles is disturbance of trade, then a history of macroeconomic fluctuation would have to date from Biblical times.

The immediate objection to treating all unsettled phenomena as evidence of a business cycle has been stated by Irving Fisher, in his own inimitable fashion, as early as 1925: [8]

"Of course, if by the business cycle is meant merely the satistical fact that business does fluctuate above and below its average trend, there is no denying the existence of a cycle--and not only in business but in any statistical series whatsoever...weather conditions necessarily fluctuate about their own mean; so does luck at Monte Carlo. Must we speak of...'the weather cycle' and the 'Monte Carlo cycle'?"

The observation that something fluctuates is an ineffectual statement, and lacks any meaning or interpretation without some implicit or explicit correlative theory. In particular, some form of theory is a prerequisite for applying the same label to an economic phenomenon in 1973 and 1523. The statements of economists and historians when discoursing on macroeconomic history are revealing in this respect. Even if they only mean to finesse the issue, their remarks confront the foundations of their economic doctrine with broad sweeps of history in a way that is largely discouraged in the 'normal science' functioning of both disciplines. To see this, let us sample the range of these confrontations.

The most ingenuous level of discourse can be found in textbooks and other similar contexts, where it is asserted that on the one hand there are pre-modern fluctuations, and on the other hand there is the modern business cycle. For instance, Robert Heilbroner writes in the poular text The Worldly Philosophers, "When (Adam) Smith lived and wrote, there had not yet been a recognizable phenomenon which might be called a 'business cycle'." [9] No footnotes or citations are given; nor is any supporting evidence offered. Businessmen also partake of the folklore, and exhort each other in the same terms: "Although there have always been cycles of some sort in every phase of human activity, the business cycle as we now know it is of comparatively recent origin. It is not very long since almost all manufactured goods were made to order by industrial craftsman and delivered by them direct to the ultimate consumers. Supply and demand, therefore, were in close touch with each other and there was little excuse or reason for any maladjustment between the two." [10] One can almost feel supply and demand snuggling blissful and innocent in those days Before the Fall. Historians have played no little part in the dissemination of this folklore: "Fluctuations in the seventeenth and eighteenth centuries were shorter and came to an end more abruptly than those of the nineteenth century. They were dominated to a considerable extent by harvest fluctuations associated with the vagaries of climatic conditions and therefore do not bear much resemblance to those rooted in a mature industrial economy." [11]

Again, this statement is presented without any further documentation or amplification. Patently, we must know what it is we are talking about before we insist that whatever-it-is was not around 250 years ago. The above statements presume a shared agreement on the meaning of 'modern business cycle' which does not exist among economic theorists or historians. As evidence of this basic indeterminancy, we pass in the next section on to a number of authors maintaining a somewhat higher degree of sophistication than the foregoing.

Three Common Definitions of the Premodern Economy

It seems there are three common definitions of the premodern economy. The first of these three associates the advent of the modern business cycle with the advent of physical machines employed in the process of production. Mikael Tugan-Baranowski started his history of crises in England with the year 1825 because: "Le second quart du XIX siècle a donc vu de nouvelles formes économiques refouler énergiquement les anciennes. La substitution de la grande production à la petite et de la machine au travail à la main a amené un accroissement énorme de la productivité du travail." [12] A more recent economic historian echoes this sentiment: "Even were comprehensive statistical series to be discovered it is unlikely that anything like the modern trade cycle would be found operating in the early seventeenth century economy. The extremes of commercial paralysis regularly alternating with periods of hectic expansion, which run through the history of the nineteenth century, seem to be associated with the growth of capital goods industries and the factory system. A marked feature of non-agricultural occupations in the period under discussion was, however, the relative unimportance of fixed capital." [13]

There appear to be three steps to this argument. First, the _differentia specifica_ of the modern cycle is held to reside in the employment of time-phased processes in the production of economic goods. Secondly, the characteristic that designates the boundary between the modern age and antiquity is an unambiguous quantum jump in the use of those extended time-phased processes. Third, it is concluded that there is a distinctively modern cycle, the idiosyncracies of which arise from these time-phased properties of the widespread employment of fixed capital. From our survey of contemporary macroeconomic thought above, we know that the first step of the argument is on weak ground, since most recent theory has ignored time-phased production altogether as a root cause of business cycles. In fact, such concerns have not prominently been discussed since the writings of Marx and Bohm-Bawerk on 'roundabout' production. (This neglects the more recent work of Hayek, which is not discussed at all.) The next step in the syllogism, which involves empirical work on the prevelence of fixed capital in the premodern period, is based on a surprisingly scanty literature, which is called into question in Chapter Eight below. [14] A case is therein made that if fixed and circulating capital (under the same definitions of these terms employed in this literature) are reckoned in purely monetary terms, there is no empirical evidence that the ratio of fixed to circulating capital today is any greater than it was in eighteenth century England. Finally, the concept of capital itself is much more problematic than the unpretentious ideas of big machines or lumpy investments would suggest, which betrays a lack of familiarity with recent capital theory on the part of this group of authors.

A second group of authors generally associates the watershed with some aspect of the incipient organization of credit institutions, although they do not all agree on its theoretical import. There seem to be two variants of this position. The first variant asserts that early crises were premodern because they were confined to manias of financial speculation and credit expansion by the foolhardy, the neophyte and the misled. [15] Curiously enough, Marx is included in this group, although in general he was the economist most conscientious about the historical bases of his theoretical categories. Towards the very end of his Theories of Surplus Value, Marx offers the very cryptic remark: "Adam Smith did not yet know the phenomenon of over-production, and crises resulting from over-production. What he knew were only credit and money crises, which automatically appear, along with credit and the banking system." [16] This statment appears in the context of criticism of Say's Law (which he shows is couched in barter terms and abstracts from money) which makes the remark all the more odd. Nowhere in Theories of Surplus Value does Marx elaborate on what he means by 'only credit and money crises'. In lieu of any adequate explanation, we can only remind the reader that the monetary aspects of Marxian economics were perhaps the most undeveloped parts of his system at the time of his death.

The second variant of the second definition orchestrates a financial overture as heralding the brave new era, although this concept is as dissonant in the context of their systems of economics as the denial of its importance was in the Marxian system. Wesley Clair Mitchell called the disturbances that followed the institutionalization of credit "more modern in character", but he quickly qualifies this judgement by adding, "Though such episodes may fairly be called financial crises, they differ from their recent counterparts both in affecting only a few trades and in depending directly upon war or the fiscal embarrassments of governments. Even in the eighteenth century most English crises arose from other than business sources." [17] Mitchell does not mention any specific cases. Such equivocation about causation and origins was an outgrowth of the fact that Mitchell did not adhere to any fixed theoretical stance in his work, as we have suggested in chapter three. Because of this, the only question of historical watershed that Mitchell ever confronted squarely was one of the empirical availability of statistical timeseries. Joseph Schumpeter, another of this group, was only marginally more consistent with regard to this question. To set the bounds of his inquiry in his Business Cycles, he wrote: "Capitalism is that form of private property economy in which innovations are carried out by means of borrowed money, which in general, though not by any logical necessity, implies credit creation." This would imply, Schumpeter admits, dating the genesis of modern cycles as far back as the late twelfth or early thirteenth centuries for southern Europe. Yet when it comes to treating this theoretical mandate seriously, Schumpeter, like his predecessors, balks. He writes, "...it is also clear that the spectacular crises of the seventeenth and eighteenth centuries link up more plausibly with wars and other noncyclical catastrophes than those of a later time." [18] Nowhere is any evidence of the timing of these premodern cycles provided. Once more we are confronted with an abdication of responsibility when it comes to supporting the contention that the seventeenth and eighteenth centuries somehow do not matter. This equivocation reveals a lack of theoretical guidance as to what we should be looking for. Neither Mitchell nor Schumpeter had a well-articulated theory of money and finance and their relation to instability; yet being historically literate, they had to face the fact that the preponderance of contemporary evidence from the seventeenth and eighteenth centuries points to credit and finance as the major disruptive factor. Moreover, both tend to date their cycles by crises which, they realize, were credit and financial crises. This may also explain Marx's cryptic comment: no one aware of history in such acute depth could pass off the South Sea Bubble or the Law system as an event not worthy of some note. The result was to sweep this particular contradiction between theory and history under the rug by lumping together the eighteenth century and the obscure murky times of antiquity. As we approach the present, this becomes the conventional wisdom, handed down from textbook to textbook, [19] with no further critical thought. Presumably this stems from the fact that conventional economic theory has since strayed even farther from the idea that credit has any effect on the macroeconomy. [20] As long as finance plays such an insignificant role in macro theory, it is impossible to argue that financial institutions mark the watershed between pre-capitalistic and capitalistic formations.

There is a third group of authors which defined modernity as periodic regularity in fluctuations, without delving further into their substance or cause. Reckoning in this manner, the more fixed the periodicity of the fluctuations and the more this periodicity resembles some ideal periodicity (which ranges between authors between 7 and 20 years, when the 'long swings' take over), then the more modern the economy. [21] This is often coupled with the contention that earlier fluctuations were merely due to wars and harvest fluctuations. [22] In this view, premodern instability can be explained by associating a crises with a specific historical event, which itself is non-cyclical. Mechanical periodicities rule the discussion obscuring the fact that this group possesses no underlying theory of the cycle.

The simple equation of modernity and periodicity will not hold up on either logical or empirical grounds. The only logical conception which could motivate this 'story' would be picturing the economy as a stable, rigid black box upon which random shocks impinge. One would then expect that ouputs from the process would exhibit discernible fixed periodicities. This conception most nearly corresponds to the Rational Expectations school of macroeconomic thought. Some adherents of this school could argue (although I am aware of no actual instance of this) that the defining characteristic of the premodern economy was its spottiness and lack of integration, in which case it could not act as a stable black box process. The problem with assuming this stance is that it presumes the theory would tell us what specifically it was about the economy that was spotty or irregular, or what structures or institutions were missing in premodern times. But this is precisely what it is incapable of doing. Nothing is explicitly assumed about the actual social and institutional structure of the economy in this world-view. In fact, this is what the 'periodicity' group means to avoid: a specific institutional definition of the premodern economy. If the only human artifact dealt with by the theory is the 'market', then we are driven back to Phoenecia and before to find the birth of the business cycle. [23] There can be no logical case that fluctuations in the eighteenth century were premodern, based solely upon the commencement of a fixed periodicity in some arbitrary indicator.

Moreover, periodicities are often in the eye of the beholder. Jevons, with his sunspot theory, thought he had found the fixed dicennial periodicity as far back as the 1670's, at least initially. But when he learned a bit more about the actual periodicity of sunspots, which were somewhat different from those he had expected, he effortlessly reinterpreted the data to fit the new scheme of periodicities. Partly, this was because his theory did not tell him which indicator was the crucial vehicle of fluctuation, so he simply switched timeseries. [24] Hunting for periodicities, like hunting for the Snark, is a quest without description or map.

A Digression Concerning Wars and Harvest Failures in the Context of Walrasian General Equilibrium

The authors surveyed in the previous section strove to identify the great divide in macroeconomic history without the concerted aid of economic theory, which was their collective downfall. We shall observe that this certainly is true in the case of statements about wars and harvest fluctuations in their relation to the historical macroeconomy. Although this work does not directly address the question of the great macroeconomic divide, it is very germane to the common observation that all premodern fluctuations were the result of wars and/or harvest failures.

The first bit of conventional wisdom proffered when discussing theories of the interrelation of agriculture and the macroeconomy is that there is an "undisputed correlation between the state of the harvest and the state of trade." [25] A.H. John and T.S. Ashton [26] have argued that good harvests in eighteenth and early nineteenth century England caused low prices which were a boost to industrial demand and thus macroeconomic expansion, while J.D. Chambers and G. Mingay [27] have insisted that those very same low prices in a largely agricultural economy produced distress and acted as a drag on economic expansion. The only empirical study of which I am aware (by V. Timoshenko) examined the state of the harvest and the macroeconomy in the United States between 1866 and 1920 and concludes, "A low ratio of agricultural to industrial prices generally precedes, or is coincident with, a business revival; a high ratio very often occurs during periods of great prosperity or financial stringency and precedes, or is coincident with, a recession." [28] If one detects a degree of tautology in the fact that a low terms of trade ratio may characterize either a recession or a boom, one is not too far from comprehending the 'conclusions' of this study. Timoshenko was hampered both by the lack of any single measure of aggregate activity with which to compare the terms of trade, and the absence of appropriate statistical techniques which would corroborate or call into question his conclusion. In fact, all of the above-mentioned authors generally shy away from any theoretical measure of aggregate activity. A quick examination of the literature calls into question the prevalent notion that harvest conditions and aggregate activity are clearly and directly related, as in a simple correlation. They may still be related by some more roundabout process, but in order to assess that possibility, a more structured theoretical framework must be introduced.

This is what the Walrasian adherents claim to do. Through the intermediation of a theory of pricing and resource allocation, neoclassical analysis attempts to trace the paths of reaction to an initial dislocation, such as a harvest failure. It was, therefore, a foregone conclusion that an economist would step in to the historians' fray and attempt to settle the issue. This was in fact done by R. Ippolito in a 1975 article. [29]

Ippolito reinterprets the question as follows: what additional amount of non-agricultural goods could be purchased at the new level of productivity (that is, the change in harvest condition), holding the consumption of agricultural goods constant. In casting the problem in this form, he approximates the construct of a compensated demand curve employed frequently in neoclassical demand theory. As a first approximation, Ippolito treats the problem as an exercise in partial equilibrium analysis, where a horizontal supply curve of agricultural goods is shifted by harvest conditions, which in turn shifts a conventional down-ward sloping demand curve due to a change in disposable resources. The horizontal supply curve is patently counter-factual (for example, it rules out the influx of imported wheat at higher prices), but is necessary from Ippolito's point of view because he has no empirical information on shifts in the quantity of output supplied: with a horizontal supply schedule, a percentage shift in harvest is identical to a percentage shift in realized price. Given his assumptions, the resources available for the purchase of either a greater amount of agricultural goods or of purchases of non-agricultural goods is equal to the share of agriculture in the total product times the percentage change in price, if the share of agriculture is constant (another counterfactual assumption in the face of independently fluctuating agricultural output). Add to this some behavioral elasticities of demand for agriculture taken from the twentieth century, and he thus arrives at some estimates of the magnitude of the change in purchases of industrial goods due to changes in harvest conditions. In this first approximation, Ippolito finds relatively small changes in industrial demand, given the magnitude of agricultural price changes from 1730 and 1750. In his second approximation, he allows agricultural goods to be an input in industrial production (as characterized by a smooth substitution Cobb Douglas production function), so that relative price shifts might also influence industrial prices indirectly. This elaboration results in predicted shifts in industrial demand indistinguishable from zero. If we were to believe Ippolito, changing harvest conditions made no appreciable difference to the functioning of the eighteenth century English macroeconomy.

Ippolito's conclusions do not follow from his analysis because any Walrasian general equilibrium system with appreciable substitution in consumption and production, coupled with an auctioneer who prevents disequilibrium trades, is the embodiment of Say's Law. Any shock to the system is immediately compensated for, and full employment (or previous level of employment) is preserved. Unfortunately, there is no theory of the aggregate level of output here, nor on the level of aggregate 'demand'. If Ippolito had realized this, he could have dispensed with his supply and demand curves. The only potential for changes in the level of aggregate activity would be the case where substitution was lacking in most of the system--general equilibrium with rigidities. A consistent neoclassicist could not point to harvest failure as an important source of pre-modern business cycles; the 'cause' could only have been the rigidities, which are assumed, not historically motivated.

There is another lesson to be drawn from Ippolito's article. For a neoclassical economist to maintain that harvest fluctuations were the cause of premodern cycles, he or she is implicitly assuming that Walrasian theory is equally applicable to pre- and post-modern conditions. But in that case, what precisely is it that sets apart the premodern economy from today's conditions? There is a contradiction here: early fluctuations are all due to acts of God and Nature, but there is no theoretical difference between today and 250 years ago. [30]

We find the same confusion when neo-Walrasians turn their attention to the impact of war upon the macroeconomy. An earlier vintage of economic historian had a tendency to maintain that eighteenth century wars either had a minor, or somewhat beneficial impact upon capitalist growth. [31] When the 'new' economic historians came to engage in their penchant for correcting their elders, they began imposing a general equilibrium model upon the historical event. The result was the same as in the case of harvest fluctuations: the level of aggregate activity was implicitly fixed, so any statements about the impact of war on macroeconomic fluctuations were unfounded, at best. [32]

As a consequence, we must be wary of the neoclassical economist when he or she shrugs off the macroeconomic fluctuations of the eighteenth (and nineteenth) centuries as 'merely wars and harvest failures'. There is at present, no articulated theory of what historical circumstance separates modern from premodern conditions. (There is, however, an inarticulate awareness of the outlines of a neoclassical theory of history, which we shall briefly survey in the next section.) The appeal to wars and harvest failures derives from a tendency to discount any economic history before the twentieth century as relevant to present conditions (which in turn conflicts with the 'timeless' neoclassical epistemology).

Some Theorists in Search of an Auctioneer

The distinction between modern and premodern economic structures, which seems to be taken for granted by most writers, becomes less and less substantial the more and more it is examined. This unsubstantiated belief, as has been hinted in previous sections, is the fault of the economic theory, and not the facts. Neoclassical theory entertains the existence of no historical artifact except the abstract market, and therefore cannot differentiate between historical epochs, except between those where the market is absent and those where it is present. [33] Strictly speaking, as long as the market is historically present, then the earliest fluctuations and the 1973-5 downturn are generically similar, in that their <u>ultimate</u> causes can be described in the same theoretical manner. As long as one adheres to neoclassical value theory, this seems to be the only logical conclusion of a search for the origins of the business cycle.

Although I can cite no explicit statement of this position from the neoclassical viewpoint, I predict that such a statement is on the horizon. In particular, a few perceptive neoclassical economists--Sir John Hicks and Robert Clower--have already laid the foundation for what, I am sure, will eventually become the conventional explanation of historical macroeconomic instability. It remains only for an avid avatar of the new economic history to hear the distant drummer and lead the troops.

Hicks initiated this reinterpretation of the pageant of economic events with his book, <u>The Theory of Economic History</u>. While in many ways lacking historical substance, it is the first consistent attempt to make economic history and economic theory congruent since the work of the American Institutionalists. Although the name of Walras is not mentioned in the book, it is clearly both a tribute to and justification of the Walrasian world view. For, if we are to look for an institutional artifact in the Walrasian schema which could be traced through history, what could it be but the 'auctioneer'? "There is a transformation which is antecedent to Marx's Rise of Capitalism, and which, in terms of more recent economics, looks like being even more fundamental. This is the Rise of the Market, the Rise of the Exchange Economy. It takes us back to a much earlier stage of History." [34]

<u>The Theory of Economic History</u> attempts to locate the motive force in The Rise of the Market in the persona of the merchant. In the process, law, politics, the state, agriculture, and all production processes are reduced to effervescences of the ideal activity of individual trades. "The distinction between the pure trader, who buys to resell, to resell what is physically the same as what he had

bought, and the artisan or 'producer' (Hicks' quotation marks-PM) who works on the things he has bought, so as to resell them in a different form, is often regarded as fundamental; but economically, and even socially, it is not a fundamental as it looks. It is a technological, not an economic distinction." [35] Hicks even tries to escape the Walrasian dilemma of ownership (and therefore the human institution of the state) necessarily preceding the existence of the market by imagining merchants historically enforcing their own rules of conduct de facto and de novo; and how else, but through the free give-and-take of competitive trades in the market. As history, this is a travesty of the facts; but as a story, it is the most internally coherent construct since Marx portrayed the historical movement from one mode of production to another as an economic dialectic revealed through dialectical materialism. For Hicks, the postulated Rise of the Merchant is the auctioneer finally personified, the missing historical link which concretely explains how prices are set in 'perfect competition'; how the 'market' spreads; how institutions comprising the organization of groups can be explained as resulting from the interactions of individuals. He writes, "The evolution of the institutions of the Mercantile Economy is largely a matter of finding ways of diminishing risks." Human history is reduced to the history of the individual's act of constrained maximization.

If this were all there were to the neoclassical saga, we would pay it no further heed in this book. But it has not been Hicks, but rather Robert Clower who has drawn out the implications of this account for the theory of macroeconomic history. It was Clower who pinpointed the location of the Walrasian inability to adequately deal with disequilibria as residing in the conventional role of the auctioneer. More recently, Clower has been arguing for the replacement of the auctioneer by a 'trade coordinator' who keeps inventories and sets prices: again, essentially the persona of the merchant. By combining this concern with the Hicksean story, the neoclassical theory of instability can potentially take on a historical dimension: "We can imagine coordination failures to occur from time to time because individual agents develop an irrational passion for cash rather than goods and services. But such failures--commercial crises, as they might be called by a student of eighteenth and nineteenth century economic history-- would surely be short-lived, for real balance effects would operate with a vengeance in this kind of commodity money world." [36] In this scenario, premodern trading organization is defined by the holding of long-lived goods by trading specialists: gold, and other physical stores of value. Clower believes that the time dimension of stocks does not, in itself, harbor the potential instability: Thus his invocation of 'real balance effects' in that remote land of eighteenth and nineteenth centuries.

In Clower's view, in some not quite clearly specified way, the modern trade specialist is qualitatively different. He or she deals in a non-physical 'money' which is more susceptible to violent instability and which may not possess a self-correcting character. Here the all-important historical role of the merchant/trade specialist comes into play: "Sustained and serious coordination failures might occur because insolvency of trade specialists would temporarily eliminate from the economy market homeostats that are essential for effective coordination of the notional economic plans of individual agents." Modern instability is due to a weakness in the hub of the wheel; premodern instability, less serious, is due to some irrational lapse by inexperienced or hypersensitive trade specialists. Through it all, Walrasian theory, by nature a-historical, is applied to all history which possesses a market. No longer Horatio Alger, but rather Willy Loman becomes the central protagonist in the story of business cycles in the modern period.

Obviously this history (and a reasonable amount of the theory) has yet to be written. Clower's belief that the eighteenth and nineteenth centuries possessed only commodity monies, or that they were in the financial Dark Ages is patently mistaken, as we shall argue below. It would take an historian with a firmer grasp of the rise of finance to take the Hicks/Clower hint and turn it into operational history. We do not choose to do so here, for theoretical reasons developed here and in the subsequent chapter. The aim of this little exercise in histographic prediction is instead to show that history is infinitely pliable in the hands of a creative theoretician. It is not that neoclassical theory cannot potentially be shaped into a historical narrative; it is rather that the story can only take certain forms when controlled by the theory. The stories which we have surveyed in the first three sections of this chapter are inconsistent with the economic theories held by their exponents. Periodicities, credit and fixed captial are not important parts of the Walrasian <u>gestalt</u>. If there is to be a consistent historical examination of instability from a neoclassical standpoint, it must be from the vantage of the auctioneer and the market: this is the Hicks/Clower insight.

What is Modern About the Modern Economy?

Without being too precise about it, everyone who has given some measured reflection to economics believes there is a modern economic system; however, when pressed to elaborate, many or most are at a loss to express what the essence of that statement is. We have seen a few attempts, having to do with the prevalence of fixed capital, the existence of financial and credit institutions, and the existence of fixed periodicities in some economic indicator; but without exception these all falter on logical grounds because they have no conceptual link to the theoretical systems endorsed by the various individuals. Insofar as any of these individuals work within the neoclassical tradition, they are restricted theoretically to the level of institutional and temporal specification present in neo-Walrasian theory. The level of institutional specification in neoclassical theory is nearly nil, because it is predicated only upon the prior existence of a 'market' of unspecified proportions and characteristics. It is interesting to note that here our concern over the theory of macroeconomic instability and our interest in historical specification converge, since it is specifically this lack of insitutional content which is the major stumbling block in both of these inquires. Without specifying how the market functions, we can neither explain 'market failure' nor locate the market in history.

It is true that there are some neoclassical economists who have taken note of this very fundamental flaw in their theory: some names that come to mind are Martin Shubik, Douglas North, and Svetozar Pejovich. [37] They have been quite inventive in suggesting some methods of augmenting conventional neoclassical theory: Shubik, employing game theoretic techniques, and North and others employing Marshall's Principles of Continuity, which can be roughly paraphrased as "anything which can be varied within an arbitrary length of time will be subject to change as a result of individual optimization decisions." Unhappily, most of this inventive effort has been for nought, for the very simple reason that the neoclassical concept of accounting for insitutional parameters is to make them subject to the control of the market: one can see this still leaves the institutional structure of the market unexplained, and further, effectively inexplicable. Since we as yet have no theory of how the market functions, then what structures organize the 'meta-market' which allows us to purchase more or less of various forms of organization, including the market? Who enforces these virtual 'trades'? And who sets the price of the price of the 'market'? Basically, neoclassicists persist in holding dear two diametrically opposed objectives: one, to make everything which was exogenous endogenous; and two, to cast all theory in the form of a constrained maximization problem on the part of psychologically atomistic individuals. A moment's reflection will reveal that doing both is an impossibility. Recall that the hallmark of a stage three theory of macro instability was the capability of identifying what was exogenous from the point of view of economic theory. Neoclassical economics, because of its lack of institutional specification, lacks this logical capability. [38]

Neoclassicism, by striving for the 'generality' of physics in extending its analysis over all human history, does justice to no period, including our own. It is this generality, this idea that a good explanation should not depend upon the specifics of any place or time period, which must be relinquished if we are to crack our double conundrum of an adequate theory of macroeconomic instability and adequate historical specificity of the boundaries of economic analysis. In this respect, we can look to the earlier theorists of macroeconomic instability such as Marx and Veblen, who had no fear of suggesting that their analysis was only valid for a particular time period and a particular configuration of events.

It is the very notion of an 'economic model' which requires revision. In this day and age, an economist understands a 'model' to be the extention of the conventional paradigm of the maximization of some quantum subject to fixed constraints to some novel situation; one then employs the appropriate mathematics to arrive at determinate result; and, if one has an empirical bent, one might employ statistical methods to identify the magnitude of certain crucial parameters (such as constants in production function or demand curves). Individualistic contrained maximization has no institutional/historical content; therefore, an institutionalist theory will appear to lack such a model. This will not be the case if we instead expand our notion of a model to include any logical apparatus which can organize the four stages of instability theory outlined in chapter one. Such a revised model can still perform other conventional functions: for instance, identifying key macroeconomic indicators and important theoretical variables and constants, and the organization of a taxonomy of causes of instability. In any event, it cannot claim to be 'general', since there is no such thing as institutional generality.

In pursuit of such a revised model, we now turn to examine various components of conventional economic theory, in order to become aware of their a-historical and anti-institutional biases.

CHAPTER FIVE

FROM THE ECONOMICS OF CEREMONIAL ADEQUACY TO THE ECONOMICS OF CUMULATIVE CHANGE

> "...the Walrasian model does not capture any of the market failures macroeconomists have been concerned with for forty-five years. The argument must thus be about appropriate models of the whole economy, and that strikes me as largely a theoretical problem."
>
> --Frank Hahn, "Monetarism and Economic Theory"

The moment has arrived in this work where criticism can give way to the suggestion of the outlines of an alternative theory. To sense the lack of historical and insitutional content in our present modes of analysis is an important first step. On the path to an institutional theory, but it is only a first step, a vague dissatisfaction which lacks a focus. Just because those economists and historians who have suggested modernity be gauged by credit institutions, the prevalence of fixed capital or fixed periodicities have based their cases on faulty premises, it does not mean that they were necessarily wrong--it only means they have not developed sufficient reasoning to convince us that it might be so. To develop a theory of macroeconomic instability with an explicit historical content, we must have some idea of how our present concepts and predispositions result in a lack of historical/institutional reference; and, in many cases, how they rule out the potential for unstable results prior to any analysis. If we consciously choose theoretical terms which make room for instability, then we shall not repeatedly find ourselves returning to a cul-de-sac: say, the way the neo-Walrasians keep finding that 'involuntary unemployment' in their scheme can only result from abitrarily rigidified price adjustment schemes or deviant psychologies.

In pursuit of this objective, we propose to examine the following fundamental concepts of any economic theory, with an eye towards their revision:

a. Value

b. Time

c. Capital

d. Income

e. The rate of profit

f. The firm and finance

Under each heading, the present conventions will be outlined, possible impediments to instability theory will be identified, and then an alternative position will be suggested.

a. Value Theory

Intone 'value theory' near a Western economist, and he or she will probably hear 'price theory'. There is one other conventional usage of the word 'value': value judgements. The latter is used to mean what people think or believe about phenomena, as opposed to what simply exists. These beliefs are generally measured along an axis of 'goodness' or 'badness', approval or disapproval. Interestingly enough, both usages converge for the neoclassical economist. The individual, according to neoclassical theory, ranks everything he or she sees along some ordinates of approval, and then trades with other individuals in a market in order to get things which command higher approval in their view, the result of which (through an instrumentality not clearly envisioned) are stable trading ratios, or 'prices'.

There is a different meaning of value in economics; this is the sense it will be used in this work. In this usage, value theory is the underlying metaphysics of economics, and because of this, it rules economic epistemology. In this sense of the term, neoclassical economics possesses a value theory separate from, but governing its price theory. In the last century, this usage of 'value' was much more widespread: Mill could write, "Almost every speculation respecting the economical interests of a society thus constitued implied some theory of Value. The smallest error on the subject infects with corresponding error all our other conclusions; and anything vague or misty in our conception of it creates confusion and uncertainty in everything else." Wieser wrote, "Value is the essence of things in economics." [1] Before we consider the implications of this notion of value for cycle models, it may be interesting to review how value theory came to be reduced to price theory in the West.

Adam Smith, as befits his role as pioneer, avoided much subtlety and controversy in moral philosophy by originally dividing all value into the dichotomy of 'use' and 'exchange'. 'Use-value' in classical economics became a residual catch-all, employed to beg the question of the motive forces of exchange: since the market somehow expanded use-values, it spread in space and time, bringing with it the division of labor, further exchange, and eventually the imputation of class incomes. Later writers were quick to notice a latent inconsistency in that Ricardian theory postulated one underlying motive (use-value) for the spread of exchange, and a separate motive force to determine equilibrium exchange (embodied labor hours). There seemed to be two potential paths to make the 'why' and the 'how' consistent. The first was to make all ideas of value correspond to psychological appeal, and the second was to consolidate an intrinsic metaphysic of value. Samuel Baily first advocated the former; Karl Marx first advocated the latter.

Baily instituted the formal reduction of value to price in 1825 (a year of a great crash, as we shall see) by stating three postulates: (a) Value is an effect produced in the mind; (b) Value is similar to distance in that it did not exist as an absolute quantity but as a comparison; (c) absolute magnitudes could not explain relations of exchange since they themselves did not require exchange to pre-exist them. [2] It is easy to see that Baily is making metaphysical statements: statements about how the world is structured, about what it is important to know in order to discuss the world, and an implied epistemology concerning what in the world it is possible to know. We recognize this same theory of value in Walras, and in neoclassical price theory. Some neoclassicists maintained that this use-value could be measured in cardinal 'utils' or some other imaginary psychological quanta, but were unable to sense the dissonance this evoked relative to their underlying metaphysics. In the Baily-Walras-Debreu theory of value, the psychology of the individual is the unit of analysis, but it is itself inherently unobservable. This is why value judgements are so irrelevant in neoclassicism, while observable price-value is the overriding concern. Economics, in this view, is the science of observable relations between things which are caused by the unobservable preferences and tastes of individuals.

Any theory of value cannot help but color the whole approach to any particular problem. One example of this has already been discussed in a cursory fashion: as long as each good possessed as an endowment is part of the data of neoclassical analysis, supply curves can be readily handled as inverted demand curves: i.e., offer curves, or curves of disutility involved in giving up some goods. In our view, the drawback to this type of analysis is that it takes both the level and distribution of output as givens. As Sraffa has clearly shown, if production by numerous individuals at prices parametric to their actions and some further observable relation between goods called 'technology' are postulated, and levels of output are arbitrarily set, then equilibrium prices have no room to be determined by tastes. This is a contradiction in neoclassical value theory per se. To bring psychology back into production, it is necessary that some good which enters into all productive activities be scarce: that is, that there be an increasing disutility in making more of the good, just as in the simpler model there was increasing disutility in giving up part of the endowment. In the final analysis, the theory of value determines what is to be acceptable as an explanation.

Marx took the other route of postulating an inherent trait of goods as the ultimate determinant of their value, although his 'socially necessary' embodied abstract labor time is also unobservable. Marx evaded Ricardo's inconsistency by postulating a different motive force for the spread of exchange; not the psychological assuasion of wants, but the drive to reproduce and expand the total of labor embodied in goods through the process of accumulation. This drive itself derived from the need to sustain class positions and power: social relations. The individual in this vision is much less significant, while the level of output and its distribution are the interesting questions; prices are clearly secondary. Economics, in this view, is the science of observable relations between people which are caused by the unobservable properties of things.

Granted that there are at least two very different value theories in economic thought; what is the importance of value theory for models of economic instability?

i. Value theory, through its epistemological imperatives, informs an analysis of which phenomena can be treated as exogenous; that is, what it is not necessary to explain, or what is of secondary interest from the vantage point of the economist. We have already witnessed the crucial role exogeneity plays in cycle analysis. Also, if one accepts that there is a certain modicum of tautology in every movement from assumptions to conclusions, value theory contains, in embryo, the answer to the question that it asks. Example: what ultimately causes business cycles in Marxian theory? Social class conflict of the labor time embodied in goods. What ultimately causes business cycles in neoclassical theory? Psychological misperceptions due to lack of information, rigidites, etc.

We have attempted to highlight the fact that the preeminent instability theorists of the twentieth century all repudiated neoclassical value theory to a greater or lesser extent: Veblen because of his evolutionary economics, Mitchell because of epistemological considerations, Keynes because of his respect for uncertainty. It seems this repudiation was necessary in order to generate a novel answer to the question of the causes of instability.

ii. Value theory identifies the ultimate unit of value, which can in no conceivable situation be valueless. Relative prices can be expressed in any value theoretic system by individual ratios between physical units, which is unwieldy in a many-goods world. They can also be expressed by normalizing all those physical ratios to a single good in the denominator, called the numeraire. The choice of numeraire is not arbitrary, contrary to what is written in many neoclassical textbooks. In neoclassical analysis, the good chosen as numeraire must be psychologically prized by at least one individual at all times; while in Marxian analysis the good must be continually produced by a positive amount of abstract labor time as a necessary requirement for expansion of the system. Thus the meta-unit of value must always be expressed through the numeraire. Because of this value theory cannot be sloughed off as an arbitrary numeraire problem.

iii. The concept of growth can only be rigorously expressed through the basic unit, unless the model is cast in terms of a one-good world or if the whole economy is taken to expand in the same proportion. That is, only if output can be unambiguously ranked along the ordinal value index can there seriously be said to be more of anything.

iv. The less are the number of things or relations that are held fixed in the analysis, the more crucial becomes the value-theoretic content of the phenomena of change. For example, in neoclassical analysis, if we are concerned with an isolated commodity in the short run, it seems relatively harmless to take spot supply and endowments of actors as given, and have price determined by psychological considerations. If instead we are concerned with a lone commodity in the 'long period', it seems permissable to take the distribution of incomes as a datum. But if we wish to make statements about the course of the whole economy over time, we must deal with ultimate causes, which depend on value theoretic assumptions. Obviously, the theory of aggregate cycles and instability is the one area of economic inquiry which is most dependent upon value theory. The solution, proposed by the Walrasian General Equilibrium with Rigidities school, of freezing many economic variables to produce cycles is a manifestation of that school's unwillingness to face up to its own value theory; that unwillingness grows from the uneasiness (not shared by the Rational Expectations school) concerning the fact that all unemployment is voluntary in a Walrasian system, because 'voluntary' is a psychological value concept, and all value-psychology is presumeably already contained in the given utility functions.

v. The economic concept of equilibrium derives from and is conditional upon the underlying value theory. The idea of equilibrium was borrowed from physics; many of the physical connotations of being 'at rest' were subsequently imported wholesale into economic ideology. To maintain that equilibrium is some sort of value-neutral concept implying a lack of change is obviously inadequate as theory: what is so crucial to the functioning of a society that it should not change? In fact, this is not the real meaning of equilibrium in economic theory. Instead, it appears to mean that the value-determinants of the system are consistent, given a certain configuration of events. For example: in neoclassical theory, the intersection of demand and supply schedules means that the psychological dispositions of the relevant actors are in synchrony given the reigning configuration of prices and quantities. In Marxian theory equilibrium means the smooth and unhindered equalized rate of accumulation of embodied labor values by a class of capitalists.

The important point here is that the concept of equilibrium can vary so drastically across value regimes that there may be no possibility of translation. In particular, some argue that recent economists have been so vague about 'equilibrium' that they have held contradictory notions to be true simultaneously.

Garegnani has elaborated this argument in a recent paper [3] which states that neoclassical value theory cannot support a 'center-of-gravity' notion of equilibrium growth, which is defined as the exaction of a uniform rate of profit on costs in all sectors of production. While using the same word, neoclassicals have shifted the connotation to 'short-period' equilibria, which are essentially devoid of economic meaning for the theory of instability, since their only definition is the rapid sequential solution of a large number of felicific calculations based on data which are themselves changing rapidly. Between each fleeting rest point and the one that follows it there is nothing in common and nothing fixed. For our purposes, we shall note it is very difficult to have a theory of the cycle if there is no center about which to cycle.

vi. The very conception of economic value up until the recent past has been largely responsible for the a-historical and a-institutional character of economic theory. Both existing value theories (the labor theory of value and the neoclassical subjectivist theory) have been concerned to trace the foundations of value to some supposedly 'natural' state of affairs. Marx assumes that the full product of the laborer belongs to the laborer in some a priori sense, whereas the neoclassical economist insists that the unhindered operation of the market will distribute to individuals what they actually psychologically want within the limitations of their initial endowment. This is what Veblen refered to as 'ceremonial adequacy': that some desired state of affairs is dubbed 'natural', and that all subsequent behavior is rated with respect to this abstract ideal. In these two cases, the ideal, while politically sanguine for the respective groups, is so very abstract that it is devoid of any historical application.

The appeal to a natural state where underlying value determinants are expressed transparently is another manifestation of the desire for a 'general' theory independent of any historical or institutional circumstances. Institutionalist theory has persistently resisted this temptation to anchor value in some prior and immutable state of affairs outside of economics proper. The value determinants of objects are themselves socially malleable, and therefore historically contingent. [4]

vii. The final contribution of value theory to the concept of macroeconomic instability is the implicit notion of a 'conservation of value' law in economic theory. For instance, Marx argues that surplus must be created in the production process, because embodied labor is neither gained nor lost in the act of trading. This is a conservation law, similar to the law of conservation of mass and energy, which allows for the account of ingress and egress to be balanced. Early defenses of Say's Law were cast in similar terms: the value of inputs was held identically equal to the value of outputs in the aggregate; so supply created its own equivalent demand. Later marginal productivity theorems are only minor variations on this theme.

These implicit conservation laws have in practice militated against a logical theory of business cycles. All conservation laws are of the form: "Quantum X is independent of Transformations A through N." Essentially economic conservation laws state that the quantum of value is independent of the trading activities of the actors, or the level of the value of output is independent of their activities. This is nothing other than a restatement of Stage 1 theorizing: all adjustments happen within the system while the level of activity remains uneffected. Thus, whenever these types of conservation laws are invoked, they block all progress beyond a Stage 1 theory. [5] This is most pronounced in the case of very simple models, where abstraction from trading, money, time and many goods is effectively translated into the independence of these phenomena vis-a-vis the level of activity determined within the model.

Considerations (i) through (vii) demand that we reject the two major value theoretic traditions in Western economic. Still, our alternative must have some epistemological base, which means it must have some sort of value theory as a guide. Here we shall opt to combine the work of John R. Commons with recent economic anthropology and neo-Marxian economics to develop a "historical theory of value." This value theory will be relevant to a single mode of production: that organization of production and distribution known as 'capitalism'. From Commons we take the idea that definitions of value are largely juridical, since the very concept of a transaction is a legal construct of recent vintage. [6] Therefore, we immediately know that this is not a value theory which holds abstractly through all time and space; it must have a well-specified historical context. The ultimate unit of value will be a fixed basket of the basic commodities prevalent in the chosen historical era; equilibrium will be defined as the smooth accumulation of a portion of that basket and the consequent expansion of a legally defined going concern known as a 'firm'; and the only assumed conservation law will be that legislated in the particular era (example: all dollars are legally equivalent in trades). In the historical theory of value, there is no 'natural' state of affairs which can act as a benchmark for the analysis. The philosophical foundation of this theory of value is that "man defines himself". Economics controlled by the historical theory of value is the science of the observable relations among institutions which are caused by the unobservable power relations between person and person.

b. Time

One of the more advanced textbooks in capital theory will serve to demonstrate the palpable unease with which economic theorists gaze upon illimitable, never-resting Time: "Capital theory as we know it has scarcely begun to come to grips with the issues posed by time. Inadequate though a model is that treats time just as it treats space, economists have proved willing to work within the confines of such models for a long time." [7] The 'willingness' alluded to has made itself manifest in the neoclassical system by an enlarged preference set or utility function defined over all 't': time, like position, color, smell and texture, is treated as just another attribute of goods which is subject to approval or disapproval. One possesses 'time preference' just as one possesses 'sweetness preference' or 'woodwinds preference'; yet it has not been the custom to treat these three 'goods' symmetrically. For in the neoclassical system, 'time preference' is the attribute which distinguishes the worker from the capitalist, while 'sweetness preference' will merely make it more or less difficult to keep one's weight in harness as one ages.

There is a thin line between the treatment of time as an attribute and time as a good in neoclassical theory. The present habit of including a separate time variable in neoclassical utility functions is the best example of this fundamental confusion. [8] The fact that no one else has objected shows that time is a nebulous variable in economic analysis. Perhaps no one would object if 'length' or 'mass' were included as explicit arguments in utility functions along with other goods which possessed these properties. This 'innovation' is even more problematic than one might initially think, however, since one can at least buy long, massive objects if one is delighted by the prospect, but one cannot buy an extra hour of one's lifetime. (St. Thomas

Aquinas objected to the taking of usury since time was a gift given equally to all by God.) A neoclassicist might aver that his rational economic man will buy more time for himself if offered a high enough hourly wage, but this is the same confusion over again, since the object of the transaction in question is freedom from the necessity for the sale of labor power, not time. This freedom has a time dimension, just as it also possesses a 'sweetness' dimension and a 'woodwinds' dimension.

Another misleading statement which is rooted in this confusion is something to the effect that 'time is scarce,' or 'that there are only twenty-four hours in a day.' Labor time becomes the one 'scarce' good which circumvents the Sraffan challenge and assures demand-pricing of commodities. Nicholas Georgescu-Roegen parodies this line of thought by asking, "Would the fact that there are one million microns in one meter make space more plentiful?" [9] While 'scarce time' is a metaphor which may capture some of our intimations of mortality, it is hardly rigorous economic analysis. One cannot buy time; one can only occupy time in chosen activities. Time cannot be hoarded into a stock. Time denominates a stock.

Sir John Hicks, in Capital and Time, [10] states that there are two prevalent ways of incorporating time formally into economic analysis, but in fact we would like to suggest that there are three: the sectoral disintegration method, the Von Neumann method, and the perfect certainty method. The first and last have been known to lapse into the erroneous equation of time with goods we have just discussed, but all supress the phenomenon of time in production to a greater or lesser extent. Let us consider each of the methods in sequence.

The sectoral disintegration method consists of associating different time-durations of production with conceptually separate 'sectors' or 'industries': a 'consumption good' and a 'capital good'. The multiplier-accelerator in its most familiar guises is a sectoral disintegration model, since it depends upon the existence of an identifiable 'investment' sector which does not have the same characteristics of the consumption good sector. The problems of the sectoral disintegration approach in relation to instability theory may be grasped by considering a textbook introduction to the simple accelerator, $I(t) = v(Y(t-1) - Y(t-2))$: "It is convenient to divide the flow of time into discrete 'periods,' but at the present stage of the argument this is merely a matter of exposition and the duration of the 'period' may be defined arbitrarily...If investment projects require a certain minimum time to complete, however, the duration of the 'period' must not be less than this minimum." [11]

Even in a two-good model, what is the meaning of the length of an investment project? It is the length of time one input is physically present in the production process, or some weighted average of these durations, or the time from which the first ground is broken for a new plant until the first unit of product rolls off the assembly line, or is it the time from which the money is invested until it is returned to the investor (or the time the good is exchanged for money)? The duration of the chosen period is functionally arbitrary, because there is no theoretical guidance as to what it must be. Such arbitrary freedom is not trivial or harmless, moreover, when it is used to further arbitrarily juggle some unruly parameters:

> "(In the simple accelerator) The expression 'v' measures the normal ratio between a stock of capital at a point in time and the flow of output over a period of time. In order to give a numerical value to v it is therefore necessary to specify the period over which the flow of output is to be measured...The version of the acceleration principle at present under discussion is not plausible unless the duration of the periods t, t-1, etc., is very short. Hence the value of v appropriate in the present context will be correspondingly high." [12]

It might be thought that this was a forgivable momentary lapse, for after all, the theoretical sophistication of the textbook audience would not be very high. On the contrary, the arbitrary manipulation of time subscripts has been cited again and again in the literature on sectoral disintegration models, but the warnings have fallen on deaf ears. Ott [13] showed that the confusion of the acceleration coefficient and the technical marginal capital/output ratio was the result of some implicit theorizing about the timing of variables. Kennedy [14] carried the criticism much further, showing that most two-sector models employing neoclassical production functions treated time a-symmetrically as between prices and quantities, and that making the implicit lags in production functions explicit would lead to the collapse of the duality of prices and quantities. As a very limited and simple example of the profound implication of supressing time in economic analysis, consider the investment function $I(t)=v(\dot{Y}(t))$. If this is taken to mean $I(t)=v(Y(t)-Y(t-1))$, the unspoken assumption is that investment undertaken in period t will make possible a rise of output in the same period. If instead it is interpreted to mean $I(t)=v(Y(t+1)-Y(t))$, then investment produces a rise in output in the succeeding period; although this could hardly be thought of solely as a <u>behavioral</u> equation, except under conditions of perfect certainty, which would themselves rule out the possibility of a business cycle. Adding the 'definitions' I=S and S=sY and substituting, we arrive at $Y(t)=(v/(v-s))Y(t-1)$ in the first case, and $Y(t+1)=((v+s)/v)Y(t)$ in the second case. In the first case v must be greater than s to make economic sense, which explains the motivation behind juggling the length of the time period. But the real reason v must be so large is the implicit assumption that investment produces output in the same period: i.e., there is no 'physical' constraint on the expansion of output in the time domain. The second case does not have this problem, but makes no sense because it rules out the possibility of a business cycle. No further progress can be made in cracking this theoretical chesnut as long as time is treated as arbitrary sequence. The problem is not circumvented by casting the analysis in continuous time, either, since continuous time analysis involves the sequential dating of individual inputs and outputs, which the method of sectoral disintegration was created to avoid. The sectoral disintegration method obscures the problem of long-lived goods in economic analysis, the problem it was supposed to have solved.

The second category, the Von Neumann method, postulates that each 'firm' lasts only one infinitesimally long period. The Von Neumann method overadjusts for all the problems of the sectoral disintegration approach: it shrinks the relevant time period very small and specifies in fixed relation the amount of progressively infinitesimally older inputs that are required to produce a unit of final output. While the construction is mathematically tractable, it unfortunately makes little or no economic sense. It is rare that a production process requires its long-lived inputs to be a certain specific age in order to be functional. It presumes, moreover, that all fixed capital goods in place are re-evaluated continually by a market, even if no market can exist for them--for example, the drill press which cannot be moved intact once it is in place, or the assembly line which can only produce a highly specific model of a good. This presumed efficiency of the market of course precludes any theory of instability. Von Neumann imported this formally elegant though impracticable solution from the realm of physics, where it had earlier attracted criticisms of a similar sort. To quote one physicist: [15]

> ...the basis of the whole theory is the infinitesimal interval ds, which is supposed to be given. Once given, the mathematics follows. But in a physical world, ds is not given, but must be found by physical operations, and these operations involve measurements of time with clocks whose construction is not specified.

The 'clock' for our purposes is the frequent and efficient re-evaluation of capital by the market, and like the physicist's imaginary clocks, no concern is spared for how the clock works.

The third category, which Hicks does not mention, is the pure general equilibrium approach we characterized at the beginning of this section, where time is treated unflinchingly like space. To quote a classic text: " A good at a certain date and the same good at a later date are different economic objects, and the specification of the date at which it will be available is essential...A commodity is therefore defined by a specification of all its physical characteristics, of its availability date, and of its availability location. As soon as one of these three factors changes, a different commodity results." [16] Note that even here the specification of the time period is arbitrary: the shorter the time period measure, the more commodities there are to be dealt with. The difference between the general equilibrium and Von Neumann approaches is that the latter at least tries to describe a system which moves through time, albeit in an artificial way, while the former must include all time from Adam to eternity in one monstrous constrained maximization calculation. [17]

Each method supressed the time axis in formal analysis: by trying to make duration coincide with industrial classification in the sectoral disintegration approach, by transforming tiny age gradations into distinct goods in the Von Neumann approach, and by making time a quality characteristic in the Walrasian general equilibrium approach. It is astonishing that almost no one wishes to include the time dimension explicitly in the model, which would seem to be the obvious solution. Stocks would then unambiguously have the dimensionality of a physical quantity multiplied by a time variable.

It goes without saying that the ability of a theory to be historically specific depends crucially upon an adequate treatment of time. Time in the sectoral disintegration and Von Neumann approaches is indifferent to origin, and has no other characteristics to differentiate 1720 from 1920. Time in the Walrasian general equilibrium approach can't even elapse, because with the auctioneer or with perfect certainty the present has no differentiation from the future. Attempts to simulate the passage of time by attaching calculable probabilities to goods at various dates implicitly rules out the possibility of 'disasters', which really means time has no fixed landmarks, no 'points of no return'. [18] The suppression of the time axis is the bulwark of the supression of historical content in economic theory. Without an explicit accounting for time, theoretical entities have no context within which they can persist, and without persistence there can be no cogent concept of change.

In an institutionalist economics, time as duration and time as the unfolding of history are treated separately. First, the unit of time cannot be arbitrarily specified, but must itself be an institutional datum. If it so happens that the economic units of the society largely denominate their flows and re-evaluate their stocks accounts once a year, then a year is the institutional time unit of the analysis. Secondly, all stocks will be measured by the multiplication of a physcial unit flow and a time duration:

STOCK OF 'Z' = (UNITS OF FLOW 'Z') X (DURATION OF TIME IN 'YEARS' IN WHICH FLOW 'Z' IS PRESENT WITHIN THE BOUNDS OF THE PARTICULAR PROCESS)

This will serve to remind us that stocks have a quantity dimension <u>and</u> a time dimension, and that the magnitude of a stock may also be altered along its time axis, as well as through physical accumulation or decumulation. Thirdly, one method of acknowledging the passage of historical time is to realize that the quantum of the stock of Z changes with every re-evaluation of either the physical dimension or the time dimension. We shall argue shortly that the time component of stocks is itself a function of historical time, which allows for an indication of historical change. This variety of economic thought conceives of change as a determinate movement of the parameters of a situation, rather than the mechanical output of a rigid function, such as the conventional difference equations of post-Keynesian econometrics.

This latter concept of historically evolving time parameters will play a central role in our institutional theory of cycles. In it, we shall define 'the rate of turnover' as the reciprocal of the time duration parameter of a stock. Say a specific machine is present in the production process of hats for ten years until it becomes 'rubbish'. (This duration may be thought of as the mean of a distribution of actual machine lifetimes.) The rate of turnover of that machine in hat production is the 1/10; this turnover being an indicator of the speed with which this particular machine moves through the economy. Now in historical time, this speed of movement will itself change, due to various social economic and technical factors. The alteration of these factors, and thus historical change, can in part be captured by tracing the movements of turnover parameters through history.

c. Capital

The theory of business cycles and the theory of capital are inseparable, two aspects of the same idea in a capitalist era. It is conventionally accepted that fluctuations in the level of economic activity are caused in the first instance by fluctuations in investment in production activities. Increments of net investment are held to be additions to the stock of aggregate 'capital'. This capital has not been too meticulously defined in the recent past, as economists are becoming increasingly aware.

Curiously, the theory of business cycles has been relatively immune from this onslaught of criticism, since, as we have seen, contemporary economists have persisted in writing accelerator models as functions of some desired aggregate capital stock.

There were hints that the definitions of the terms 'I' and 'K' were the weak points of the accelerator practically from its inception. Even before Joan Robinson's seminal article on the production function and the theory of capital, a survey of the investment literature concluded, "It is not easy to find a rationale for the accelerator principle." [19] There were problems with basic concepts: no one had suggested how to identify net induced investment and differentiate it from autonomous investment. J.M. Clark and others attempted to clear up the concept by insisting that the accelerator principle would only operate at full capacity, for otherwise, increased demand could be met by extending production without additional 'investment', at least in fixed capital (Here the suppression of time dimensions again rears its ugly head). But, as Knox reminds us, "The terms 'capacity' and 'surplus capacity' are much bandied about in discussions of the accelerator principle, but they are not defined." Even more damning than the charge of vagueness was the implicit contradiction in the idea that the rise in output must precede rise in investment for the accelerator to work: but how could output rise if everyone were operating at full capacity? The accelerator purports to be that which it is not: a theory of the timing of investment.

The confusion over the accelerator was symptomatic of deeper underlying weakness in the theory of capital. Since Mitchell's time theorists of the business cycle have recognized the level of capacity utilization as one of the crucial variables in predicting turning points; yet the theoretical rationale has been neglected up till the present. The macro-econometricians have been known to use indices of capacity utilization in their production functions, such as those put out by the Federal Reserve Board, as ad hoc 'adjustments' to the capital stock. Participants at a recent conference on business cycles condemned this technique: "This practice occurs in spite of the fact that an optimizing firm with a Cobb-Douglas production function always uses all of its capital and that no microtheory leading to any aggregate production function with utilization-adjusted capital has been put forward." [20]

The participants neglected to mention that neoclassical constrained maximization is inconsistent with anything but 100% plant utilization because of the usual capital malleability assumptions of the smooth quasi-concave production function. One might then think that capacity utilization could easily be introduced through the artifice of 'vintage' capital model of the 'putty-clay' sort, but the flaw is much more fundamental than that. [21] There exists a literature in the neoclassical tradition which tries to subsume the capacity utilization decision under the conventional constrained maximization framework. This literature first divides 'idleness' into intended and unintended components; it then further divides the intended component into excess capacity due to anticipated demand fluctuations and/or growth, and intended idleness due to temporal fluctuation in input costs. [22] The optimization calculation takes place at the firm level, where the data of the calculation include <u>exogenously given</u> growth and variance of output demand and the time patterns of input prices. (Examples sometimes given of the latter information include things like night-shift pay differentials, 'free' light during the day, 'free' warmth during the summer, and so on. One of these authors summarizes these notions as the 'fact' that "...people like to work normal hours while capital equipment has no time preferences." Machines themselves may have no preferences, but their owners are systematically forced to 'prefer' certain time patterns of production, as we shall argue in below.) This microeconomic literature has no logical power in the context of an explanation of macroeconomic instability for two reasons. The first is that levels of saleable output must be given as data in order for the optimization calculation to take place; but the level of output will itself be a function of economy wide levels of capacity utilization. Far from being a harmless example of partial equilibrium analysis, it is in fact Say's Law revealed in a more modern guise: to pretend a firm could calculate some optimum is to tacitly assume that the possibility of equilibrium is indifferent to the level of output. This is <u>the</u> Walrasian vice. The second failing of this literature is the presumption that some optimum distribution of 'incomes' can be determined by output demands and a given technology, and that it is solely these tastes and technology which detemrine the time fluctuations of input prices. If the marginalist theory of input price determination were faulty in these respects, then the rest of the utilization literature would lose all logical foundation. Recent Cambridge controversies in capital theory have called the neoclassical determination of input prices into serious question.

It has been recognized as a result of the Cambridge capital debates (which are adequately summarized in the Harcourt references) that the neoclassical treatment depends crucially upon the 'unobtrusive postulate' that any change in an economic system brought about by a fall in the profit rate must increase the equilibrium ratio of capital to labor, 'capital' being here the value of physical production goods in terms of some unit of consumption goods. The Cambridge criticism has shown that there is no necessary inverse relationship between the rate of profit and the value of capital; this point has been more or less conceded by the neoclassicals. [23] The implications of this concession are more far-reaching than have been appreciated. One immediate implication is that the capacity utilization decision cannot be posed as a constrained extremum problem, the heart and soul of neoclassical economics.

A homelectic maxim concerning business cycles is that a recession creates the conditions for the ensuing revival by re-evaluating capital and therefore improving the prospect of profitability, encouraging investment, and so on. The crucial step in this argument is the re-evaluation of capital; as a result of the Cambridge criticism it is also the theoretically weakest link in the chain of argument. Incongruously, the Post-Keynesian school seems to have spared its mentor in this respect: in Chapter Three we have witnessed that he was as uninhibited in his use of the unobtrusive postulate as any modern-day 'Bastard Keynesian". Keynes specified that the marginal efficiency of capital--the discount rate which equated expected lifetime returns with supply price--must fall with accumulation because of a rising supply price, and compared his theory favorably with Irving Fisher's 'rate of return over cost'. [24] Some maintain that Keynes' theoretical consistency would be preserved through confining the analysis to the short-short-run, which perpetuates the improbity with respect to the analysis of time which we have described in the previous section. Perhaps the reason that the Post Keynesian school up till now resisted posing any explicit model of investment is that the inconsistency in capital theory would then be traced back to their own shores.

A theory of macroeconomic instability which employs a 'well-behaved' neoclassical production function (which is the unobtrusive postulate incarnate) is an untenable theoretical practice, once the theoretical debates of the 60's and 70's are taken to heart. The neoclassical 'well-behaved' production function obstructs and vitiates the modeling of many cyclically important phenomena because of its lack of the following properties: the separate social determination of the distribution of titles to the ownership of property, the variance of capacity utilization, the alteration of the time structures of production, the dual nature of capital as a fund of money and a collection of physical objects used in production, and the distinction between social relations and technology. Worst of all, most attempts to justify the usual neoclassical equilibrium must assume as a corollary full employment, which is obviously self-defeating in an attempt to model macroeconomic instability. [25]

How then must we account for capital, the central concept in a capitalist era? Institutional economic theory must attempt to embody as much social content as possible in the notion of 'capital', which makes accounting for its many facets difficult. If capital were a fixed eternal object, having a simple physical existence such as is assumed in neoclassical theory, then there would be but one quantum of capital at one time and place. A method of introducing greater diversity into the concept of capital, is to first admit that there is more than one manifestation of capital at any particular historical location. For simplicity, let us first split capital into the two components which seem to give economic theorists the most trouble: the physical aspect, and the financial aspect.

The physical aspect of capital is what most persons think of as capital goods. It is a disparate collection of objects which are used in production processes to give use to further commodities. It is necessary to be quite specific as to the boundaries of the processes of production, because otherwise it is easy to slip into the notion that <u>all</u> objects are capital of one sort or another, whence capital becomes so all-encompassing that it loses any theoretical significance. [26]

Since physical capital is a collection of disparate items, how should we account for it at the level of the whole economy? In the 'price of production' framework, this is done by making a list of each object within a particular production process: say, one hat equals so many yards of felt, so much thread, so much ribbon, so much labor, and so forth. Next, we attach time parameters to each of these objects in the manner described in the previous section, in order to denominate the stock of these materials present in the production process. This list of physical stocks is the physical aspect of capital. For purposes of aggregation and comparison, these various items are associated with a 'price of production', which is the set of prices which would reign in the economy if prices were set strictly to cover current costs plus a provision for expansion of value at a uniform rate for the whole economy. [27] These prices of production are not the prices we should expect to actually see in any economy, in part because they assume a perfect equilibrium of expansion which would rule out any macroeconomic instability, <u>a priori</u>, and in part because they ignore any role of finance and money in the setting of prices. They are only an analytical convenience: employing prices of production, we can compare the physical capital of a country at two different dates, and thus speak concisely of a rate of growth of accumulation in an economy. Thus the physical side of capital is measured in these artificial units of prices of production.

Some useful aspects of thinking of the physical manifestation of capital in this manner is that the problem of the relation of capacity utilization to the accelerator is solved, and the injection of legal and social relations into the 'pure' theory of capital is made explicit. To take the first issue, capacity utilization of this form of capital is no longer measured as some percentage of maximum capacity, but is instead measured by the magnitude of the weighted average of the physical turnover parameters of the process. For instance, if it takes felt, a machine and labor to make hats, and their respective rates of turnover in hat production are 4, 1/10, and 5, then the rate of capacity in the hat production process is some appropriately weighted average of those three numbers. Thus changes in capacity utilization are rated as changes in the speed with which component objects move through the structure of production. Recalling that the stock of capital is the product of a flow of objects times the reciprocal of their rates of turnover, then it becomes apparent that <u>changes in capacity utilization change the aggregate magnitude of physical capital</u>. This has been the crucial error in all treatments of capacity utilization prior to the present: the quantum of capital has been treated as though it were independent of the mode and extent of its utilization: yet another 'unobtrusive postulate', and another implicit prop of 'Stage 1' theorizing.

This theoretical innovation also explains why plants persistently operate below 'maximum' capacity, while further new investment takes place: plainly, there is no fixed maximum of plant capacity utilization. Capacity is a function of all the rates of turnover, which includes labor, inventories, and works in progress. An assembly line may be able to move at a certain rapid rate, but will not do so as long as it is constrained by the rate of which labor will work, or the number of shifts run around the clock, or the rate at which materials are available. It is impossible for an individual firm to subject these quanta to a constrained maximization calculation, since physical turnovers are determined in part at a social and macroeconomic level. Firms generally operate at a target rate of physical turnover, which when persistently exceeded due to growth of the market, leads the firm to invest in a new plant. Therefore, unlike neoclassical analysis, this conception of capital can encompass an accelerator theory of investment with rises in output and sales <u>prior</u> to the addition of new capacity.

However, if that is all this newer conception of physical <u>capital</u> could accomplish, it would still not be an <u>institutional</u> theory. But a further consideration of the notion of physical turnover shows that these parameters embody the historical and institutional content of abstract capital. Take, for example, the rate of physical turnover of labor in the production of hats. The speed at which labor turns over in the production process is a function of the intensity of the work and the social conventions of the workplace. The rate at which hats are made in the laborer's home is different from the rate under the supervision of the factory: thus capital is different under a putting-out system and under factory organization. Further, the rate of laboring per time unit differs between a system where there is one day-shift of work, and a system where shifts of laborers work in the same production process round the clock. The presence or absence of shift work is an historical phenomenon, conditioned by the social relations, of the time period. Finally, strikes, slowdowns, soldiering and Taylorism are all historical evidence of the state of class relations in the workplace, and they all are predominant influences on the rate of physical turnover of labor. Here is a method of the analytical incorporation of the insight of the Left Post-Keynesian school regarding the effect of class antagonism upon macroeconomic variables. Therefore, the parameters of the physical turnover of capital do triple duty in the institutionalist theory of capital: they indicate capacity, are conditional upon the historical relations of production in the workplace, and are a function of the level of class antagonism in the particular era. The reader may notice that paramters is not really an appropriate name for these measures, since they change with the passage of historical time. Rather than there being a dichotomy between parameters and variables, there is a continuum: and it is this continuum of fixity which will allow for a Stage 4 theory of macroeconomic instability.

So much for the 'physical' aspect of an institutionalist theory of capital. There is another aspect of capital which, while seemingly conceptually separate, co-exists simultaneously with capital as a collection of disparate physical objects: this is capital as a homogenous sum of money, capital as a fund of value. The financial manifestation of capital is not located in the process of production as much as it is in the firm, the main unit of capitalist organization. Within the firm, financial capital is organized into the catefories of the balance sheet: various assets, liabilities, and forms of equity. Net changes in these quantities are identified in the income statement and cash flow accounts of the firm. All of these manifestations of financial capital are not indifferent to historical and institutional location, because the structure of accounting practices and the legal structure of the firm are themselves historically specific.

In an institutionalist theory of capital, the financial aspect is analytically represented in a separate yet parallel manner. This idea is a direct descendant of Thorstein Veblen's work in The Theory of Business Enterprise, where "the earnings of any industrial business are a joint function of the rate of turnover and the volume of business." Recent convention equates the firm's capital with its net worth, but this omits assets which are financed by liabilities. In fact, the reason a single figure for net worth is an inadequate analytical representation of financial captial is because it ignores the time dimension. In institutionalist theory, the stock of net worth is the product of the magnitude of assets and liabilities and the duration of time the various financial assets and liabilities reside within the firm. This conception of capital allows us to attribute a separate rate of turnover to financial capital as well as the rate attributed to physical capital. The measure of the rate of financial turnover is the reciprocal of the duration of the presence of a certain asset or liability in the firm. For example, a ten year loan has a rate of turnover of 1/10, whereas if inventories tend to stay in the firm for three months, they have an annual rate of turnover of 4. The aggregate financial turnover of the firm is the weighted average of the turnover of assets minus liabilities. However, since all flows are denominated in money terms, this financial turnover is equivalent to the net cash flow of the firm per year divided by its net worth; or

$$\sum_i \left[\frac{ASSET_i}{NET\ WORTH} \times (RECIPROCAL\ OF\ DURATION\ OF\ ASSET\ i) \right] \text{MINUS}$$

$$\sum_j \left[\frac{LIABILITY_j}{NET\ WORTH} \times (RECIPROCAL\ OF\ DURATION\ OF\ LIABILITY\ j) \right] \text{EQUALS}$$

$$\frac{ASSET\ FLOWS\ PER\ YEAR\ --\ LIABILITY\ FLOWS\ PER\ YEAR}{NET\ WORTH}$$

Aggregate financial turnover is the same as the ratio of net cash flow to net worth, or more plainly, the time in 'years' it takes one monetary unit of net worth to return to the firm in the form of its net cash flow.

We shall argue shortly that financial turnover performs the parallel analytical function of physical turnover in institutionalist theory. It is a parameter of the system, and yet it is altered by specific historical events. For example, it may already be apparent that the level of financial turnover is a function of the level of leverage, or debt-equity ratios in the economy. In the section on the firm and finance below, it will be maintained that the extent of leverage is largely institutionally determined. The rate of financial turnover is also a function of the level of concentration in the economy, since mergers, holding companies, trusts and so forth are promulgated in order to alter the balance sheets of firms. Finally, changes in the very legal structure of firms can alter the rate of financial turnover in the economy. All of these historical and institutional phenomena are subsumed under this dialectical concept of capital.

d. Income

In the course of the evolution of conventional macroeconomics, it has become standard practice to use aggregate concepts without once considering what they do and do not mean. The prime example is the mirror image of capital, called 'income'. Nearly every contemporary macroeconomist writes 'Y' on a blackboard without a moment's theoretical justification. The fact that the house is built on sand is most often concealed by a tedious preceding section on National Income Accounts filled with recitations of endless taxonomic categories which themselves lack theoretical justification. Since everyone knows what their own check looks like on payday, such bravado usually goes unchallenged; and, after all, economics is an abstract science. Yet in twentieth century the theory of income has been something of a <u>fait accompli</u>: ask what income is, and you will be shown a number.

The origins of the notion of theoretical income can be traced back to the Physiocrats' <u>produit net</u>. In their agricultural conception of the economy, seed is both investment and end-product, returned in the unchanging rhythms of the agricultural year, and it is obvious that one receives back, in general, more crop than is needed for replacement seed and food to support the year's labor. Net product is this surplus. The meaning of net product is much less clear when one imports these agricultural metaphors into other sectors of the economy, as Adam Smith did with his 'gross' and 'net' revenue. The concern with the concept of income, both individual and social, originated in the eighteenth century: surviving accounts and accounting textbooks were structured, in the period before 1700, for the sole purpose of keeping a consistent record of asset transactions and historians of accountancy have found no evidence of our contemporary concern with periodic income reports. [28] By the eighteenth century larger firms had worked out some conventions by which they could gauge the health of trade to their own satisfaction, but cost accounting was not consistent with any particular definition of surplus other than positive realized cash flow. For example, time-phased payments were often posted on a cash basis: that is, when the actual currency entered or left the firm's coffers, and not when the costs or benefits were incurred. The individual or corporate income in the eighteenth century was more of a cash-flow concept based, we might add, squarely in the tangible reality of money.

The idea of social or national income was instituted and promoted by the imposition of national taxation on earnings in the late eighteenth and early nineteenth centuries. When Pitt instituted his war taxes in 1799, many people for the first time had to disclose an 'income', which was a profound and novel experience for those unaccustomed to think in the government's terms. Government had moved from predatory exactions on particular individuals in earliest times to taxing specific things, such as land, or the objects of excise; now it proposed to tax the cash flow of certain <u>classes</u> of individuals. This was represented in the second war tax by the five schedules: A, which was aimed at those who garnished rents; B, on farmers' produce of land; C, on the interest received by holders of government funds; D, on the profits of trade and commerce; and E, on the salaries of people who held official pensions, offices or stipends. [29] The process of standardizing the cash flows of certain functional classes of economic agents suggests the possibilities of certain regularities in those flows; it was only a short intuitive leap to add the components together to get a 'national income'.

Economic theory had little or no influence on the process. One author wrote in 1938, "No evidence has been discussed which would lead one to suspect that the Inland Revenue definition of income has ever been seriously questioned by British students." [30] Alfred Marshall, Pigou, and others accepted it basically because they had no theory of the aggregate level of activity, and so could not complain that some important aggregate was being overlooked or misconceptualized by the government.

Historically, the British income tax was repealed at the end of the Napoleonic Wars, but was reintroduced in 1842. The state-imposed definition was still evolving, however, since there was no allowance by the tax code for the depreciation of physical holding until 1873; what finally carried the day was not economic reasoning, but business pressure to gain preferential treatment. Income, as we know it, was imposed upon economic theory by events, and not vice versa.

At the beginning of the twentieth century, Irving Fisher attempted to reconcile the business and popular uses of 'income' with neoclassical value theory. He stated that the only income that theoretically mattered was 'psychic' income; but alas, "Even the individual who experienced them (the psychic events) cannot weigh and measure them directly." [31] Fisher effectively ignored this insurmountable problem and equated 'consumption' of the services of goods to income. Investment was only postponed consumption, so "spending and investing differ only in degree, depending on the length of time elapsing between the expenditure and the enjoyment," and all wages, rents and profits were really the same analytic thing, time-phased receipts of various terms of postponed consumption. Investment is not part of the period's income in Fisher's system. Capital is a residual valuation problem once the rate of interest and the time stream of satisfaction are known. Causality flows:

physical capital goods → flows of services → income values → interest rate
income values ↓ capital values

Although the Fisherine system is still taught in economics, it was recognized quite early that its attempted reconciliation of neoclassical rigor and popular usage was a failure. Corporations and nations could not have an income in the Fisherine world because they could not experience psychic enjoyment. Consumption, upon which the definition of income was based, was not itself defined. Contrary to Fisher's assertions, his system and double-entry bookkeeping were incompatible because the businessman determines income as a residual, where Fisher deemed equity the residual. A point that is frequently overlooked is that the Fisherine micro system contradicts orthodox macroeconomics: $Y=C$, not $Y=C+I$, as some would have it. Yet, we must remind the reader, Fisher's theory of capital and interest is taught as being complementary to the Keynesian system, and as a theoretical justification for national income accounting.

Hick's dictum in <u>Value and Capital</u> that income is "the maximum value which an individual can consume during a week, and still expect to be as well off at the end of the week as he was at the beginning" has inexplicably become the last word on the income concept in theoretical economics. (One invariably sees this cited in accounting texts as what economists believe.) Inexplicably, because Hicks wrote on the previous page: [32]

> I do not believe that they (the concepts Income, Saving, Depreciation, and Investment) are suitable tools for any analysis which aims at logical precision. There is far too much equivocating in their meaning, equivocation which cannot be removed by the most painstaking effort. At bottom, they are not logical categories at all; they are rough approximations, used by businessmen to steer themselves through the bewildering changes of situation which confront them.

Hicks makes it sound as though the businessman thought the whole scheme up <u>de novo</u>, where in fact it was primarily imposed from the outside by institutional constraints.

Why is income not a suitable tool? Just look at the definition: "Individual', 'consume', 'expect', 'well off'. Time is arbitrary; everything is psychological; it presumes perfect certainty or else it is incapable of being known. Further, this quicksilver concept cannot be aggregated over individuals who intrinsically cannot compare their psychic states, and whose expectations are most probably contradictory and thus doomed to disappointment. Yet this aggregate measure is purportedly to be used to gauge levels of disequilibrium aggregate activity.

Can the reader hear the creaks and groans of the procrustean bed? Henry Simmons did in 1938: "traditional theory is concerned primarily not with <u>Einkommen</u> but with

Ertrag-- the pricing of goods and productive services. Its acquaintance with Einkommen is tenuous, implicit and largely incidental." [33] This judgment was was passed thirty years before Clower made a similar point about the Walrasian system: incomes are assumed, not explained.

Keynes was aware of these sort of controversies when he wrote the General Theory. Nonetheless, Keynes approached the concept by backing away from it. "The concepts of output as a whole and its price level are not required in this context (of aggregate analysis), since we have no need of an absolute measure of current aggregate output, such as would enable us to compare its amount with the amount which would result from the association of a different capital equipment with a different quantity of employment." [34] Yet ten pages hence he produces a definition of aggregate income, supposedly identical to aggregate output, as equal to total sales minus user costs. User cost was in turn defined as the change in value of capital equipment plus stocks of unfinished goods plus inventories over the period minus maintainance and physical inputs purchased from other entrepreneurs, all evaluated in the instance when equipment was not used to produce any output. User cost does not coincide with any known accounting conventions [35], and was found so opaque and counter-intuitive by Keynesians that no attention has been paid to it since. This is noteworthy because existing national income accounts do not derive from or represent Keynes' chosen analytical tools.

Keynes stared the problem of income in the face and then ignored it, even though it was the focal point of his general theory. He denied needing a measure of aggregate output in order to bypass the muddle of capital theory, and insisted that his aggregate income did not encompass exactly the same set of problems. He left unexplored the empirical historical basis of the income concept. Aggregate consumption, the alpha and omega of the Keynesian system, also drew a blank: "Expenditure on consumption during any period must mean the value of goods sold to consumers during that period, which throws us back to the question of what is meant by a consumer-purchaser. Any reasonable definition of the line between consumer-purchasers and investor purchasers will serve equally well, provided it is consistently applied." [36]

Keynes careless attitude towards the fundamentals of income and consumption was unfortunate for a number of reasons. First, it restricted the major theoretical terms in his system to abstract constructs which had no pre-existing historical reference. This has led to the incongruous situation where historians now feel they must fabricate retrospective national income accounts out of whole cloth in order to even discuss macroeconomic history. Secondly, in elevating 'consumption' and the consumption function to the central place in his system made it seem as if he were adopting neoclassical value theory; an ambiguity leading to problems already discussed above in Chapter Three. Thirdly, by stressing consumption and income, he in effect removed the spotlight from the determinants of investment and accumulation, the phenomena which every major theorist preceding him had identified as the critical variables in macroeconomic instability. And finally, Keynes' use of 'consumption' held more than a hint that his sympathies resided with the earlier school of underconsumptionist theorists, which was in fact true, given his championing of Malthus over Ricardo. However, to espouse an underconsumptionist bias acted to thwart his attempt to build a Stage 2 theory. To work in terms of 'consumption' in neoclassical value theory means a choice to invest less now, because <u>investment is simply postponed consumption</u>. Any change in investment would be met by an equal and off setting change in consumption, leaving the total quantum of flow unchanged, and leaving the analyst back in the land of disproportionality and Stage 1 theories. The very terms 'consumption' and 'income' contain biases which make it difficult to construct a theory of macroeconomic instability.

Despite the fact that its terms were undefined and riddled with ambiguities, the Keynesian system had an indispensable ally in the campaign to defeat the 'classics': Simon Kuznets' national income accounts. In the early 1920's, long before Keynes felt the need to reason in these aggregates, Wesley Mitchell and the NBER decided, for essentially non-theoretical reasons, to generate statistics on national income. The numbers were waiting there by the time the <u>General Theory</u> burst on the scene; Keynes used them in the book, even though they had little relation to his theoretical concepts. The theoretical motivation behind the numbers was more Smith than Keynes: "net national product or national income is the value of product specifically attributable to labor, capital and entrepreneurial ability." [37] Kuznets was quite frank about the weaknesses of his rationale: "For those not intimately acquainted with this type of work it is difficult to realize the degree to which estimates of national income have been and must be affected by implicit value judgements." He admitted that what was included was arbitrary: both theft and capital gains were excluded on the grounds of being 'unproductive' (a Smithian distinction); gross returns from human 'services' (i.e., wages) were added to the net return from the use of capital without any possible justification; business balance sheet estimates of capital consumption were accepted at face value. Business accounting conventions were not followed consistently, but higgledy-piggledy: keeping some here, abandoning others there. Time-phased production was not treated consistently: for one arbitrary group of industries production was defined on an accrual basis--that is, as costs occured--while for another group cash market basis was employed. Even a clean concept like 'net' got tangled:

Kuznets admitted that what was net depended on how big the unit of analysis was: if the atom of analysis is the individual person, then wages are intermediate goods and should be excluded from income. This is the neoclassical case. But the final irony, which Kuznets does not highlight, is that much of the raw data which is the grist for national income accounts estimates comes from income tax data. Things have not much changed since the late nineteenth century, when it was that the economists uncritically accepted the Inland Revenue definition of income. If anything, things have degenerated, since even the tax code definition is not rigidly adhered to, but instead, national income is now a hodgepodge of business, governmental and theoretic concepts which satisfy no one because they mean no particular thing.

All very well and good (here huffs the economic statistician), but any time one gets one's hands dirty in real world data one does not come out smelling like a rose. Compromises must always be made, it is true. But there is a confusion here which can be traced back to neoclassical value theory. Irving Fisher was the only economist to confront the income concept squarely: if one adheres to neoclassical theory, then all value is psychic value, so the only precise income concept can be psychic income. Psychic income arises in the process of consumption, which is made manifest as the flow of consumption. The difference between income and capital is just a distinction as to the time location of consumption relative to the 'now'. There are some puzzles left to be worked through concerning the interest rate: these were the sorts of problems Fisher felt moved and shook the economic world. Of course, no aggregation is possible, unless we assume every individual is identical, anticipates the same things, etc.

Simultaneously there is another income concept, the one that has been continually imposed from outside of the economics profession, mainly by the government in its never-ending quest for taxation. This is the concept which associates cash flows with social classes of people: 'laborers' get wages, 'capitalists' get interest. All are treated differently by the government. Certain classes are thought only to consume--their entire cash flow is called income. Other classes provide employment--most of their cash flow is called amortization, capital gains, etc. The actual proportions depend upon the extent of the benign attitude of the government towards the employer classes. The same individual may receive in practice workman's and renter's and capitalist's 'incomes' at the same time; that is not the point. This income is a naturally aggregative concept; aggregation does not take place over individuals but over abstract social classes. The government taxes each class category separately and distinctly.

Modern economics has not reconciled these two very different concepts, and flips back and forth between the two as if they were equivalent. There have been signs that something might be amiss, but they are largely ignored. For instance, how should the purchase of a refrigerator be handled? For Irving Fisher, a refrigerator is a pure investment from which the buyer derives a flow of 'services' which would be treated as an imputed income. But recall that the flow of investment that the refrigerator represents would never be included in the national income accounts as consumption, if those accounts were defined to be consistent with neoclassical theory. Yet the purchase of a refrigerator is a cash flow that the government deems taxable as a 'consumption' good. So instead, a compromise is worked out, and the refrigerator is called a 'consumer durable'; that class of people who do not exact a profit return on their time-phased holdings. The distinction between consumption and investment falls between two stools, adhering neither to the 'felicific income' concept, nor to the 'class income' concept.

The problem is that there are more lines of causality here than one analytic variable can represent; and the historical class dimension of cash flows have been down played. We need separate variables for:
  i. the time distribution of physical production
  ii. the time distribution of money flows
  iii. economic demarcation of distinct social classes

The seemingly harmless assumption that 'workers' don't save out of wages forwarded to them prior to the production process is the attempt by the Post-Keynesian school to collapse these three dimensions into one variable; and it fails just as surely as the neoclassical aggregate. Social categories cannot do yeoman service for all these variables without some loss of historical social context. Workers are defined to be people who prefer not to save in neoclassical theory. The Post-Keynesian school seems not to be aware that is espouses the same position.

Physical stocks are things present in the process of production for specific time durations. 'Placements' are societal titles to contractual money flows, which possess distinct time durations. Contrary to Irving Fisher, the latter are a function of interest rates, while the former are functions of the physical rate of growth. The American Institutionalist school were keen on this distinction: "The technology of production of materials yields output regardless of who owns or employs it. Rights of property convert it into income." [38] 'Classes' are defined by the reigning rules concerning rights to property, which includes title to control over the labor time of others. If we were quite serious about the concept of income, it would only measure net expansion: claims to machines and people. But income is never the same concept from one historical period to the next, since the claims to rights are always changing, as are the people (is an hour of labor today the same as an hour in 1729?) and the machines (the economic problem of measuring technical progress). Besides, who would wish to maintain that neoclassical income was a measure of economic progress if it were plain that its main component of increase was the unprecedented rise in the world's population? Income is a useless measuring rod for a consistent theory of capitalist instability.

If the reader retains a conviction that there is some objective phenomenon called income which can be maximized from a purely technological point of view, let him or her consider the fact that productive efficiency does not and cannot abstract from a value theory because there must be a clear and distinct universal standard of comparison. Quoting Sen, "...the entire approach is based on two underlying assumptions, viz. a.) a watertight partitioning of the components of each activity into the production of desirable commodities and the using-up of inputs, which is treated as a negative contribution, and b.) confining the valuation problem to a class of rules...which depends upon the institutional set-up in question." [39] It is a trite but true observation that efficiency is relative: An oversight that does no small harm in the present, and great damage to the past.

e. The Rate of Profit

If one were compelled to judge the relative importance of analytic variables in macroeconomics from the amount of care and attention which economists lavish upon them one would, I think, have to rank aggregate national income first, probably followed by the level of the stock of money. The rate of profit would rank somewhere down near the bottom of the list, along with the mortality rate of the population and the number of bankruptcies per capita. Recently I spoke to a quantitative economic historian who had compiled a vast amount of balance sheet and profit data from late nineteenth century England; what, I enquired, was the average rate of profit in ballpark figures? He replied that it hadn't occured to him to bother to calculate it. He opined that the rate of profit on equity would not be a very meaningful number.

Of course, from within a certain context, he was correct. The rate of profit in the neoclassical system is superfluous, a residuum. In the conventional Walrasian system the rate of profit is zero in full equilibrium with perfect competition. [40] The existence of profit is the result of a rent in this theory: either a monopoly rent, or some good in temporarily scarce supply; it is a sign of disequilibrium. Joseph Schumpeter built a theory of business cycles based upon this single idea: bunched innovations increase productivity and initially monopoly rents accrue to the innovators, leading to a period of expansion and vitality. When the innovations peter out, the market eventually dissipates the rents and the period of disequilibrium draws to a close with a return to a zero profit rate. As history, this was a marginal improvement over pure Walras, but Schumpeter had difficulty convincing others that innovations arrayed themselves in neat fixed cycles with names like Kondratieff, Juglar and Kitchen, and little more attention has been paid to such notions.

Manifestly, businessmen think they are making profits, and they think they are doing it all the time. There has been some theoretical effort to reconcile this fact with their underlying Walrasian value thoery: the most prominent being Frank Knight's <u>Risk, Uncertainty and Profit</u>. Knight openly asserted that his work was "an inquiry into the causes of the failure of ideal competition to be fully realized in fact." [41] Profits, he wrote, were a non-contractual residual left over after the entrepreneur hires the other requisites of production and pays them at contractual rates. Risk is presented by the fluctuation of returns due to calculable probabilities, and can be arbitraged away in the market by insurance and borrowing: therefore, interest is a non-profit component, a return to risk. Uncertainty, on the other hand, is inherently uncalculable; the outcome of uncertainty is profit or loss. Ownership is irrelevant to profit, since it is a return to entrepreneurial ability. In fact, Knight attacked the Holy Trinity of the factors land, labor and capital as an anachronism from immediate post-feudal Europe. In his view all returns except the residual due to uncertainty were <u>all</u> returns to invested capital, 'human' or otherwise. The 'human capital' school of contemporary labor economics has simply carried out the original mandate of Knight in this respect. [42]

Knight's story about profits has became esconced in the canon of economists' venerable tales, even though the analysis was long ago found wanting. For if Knight was correct, profits would be intrinsically and inherently incomprehensible and unpredictable. (Knight thought they would probably be negative in the aggregate). There could be no empirical regularities of profit by definition. [43] Since no one would be persuaded to take economists seriously if they insisted that economic phenomena important to the conduct of business were innately unexplainable, the economics profession dropped Knight's analytics. However, they have surreptitiously retained the ideologically agreeable part of his parable.

Modern neoclassical economics has pursued the following research program with respect to the concept of profit: make a list of all the explicit costs of production, then examine the surplus over and above these costs. Create some imputed costs of production, and then attribute the above surpluses to these costs, thus wiping out any 'non-functional' surplus. Finally, point to the Walrasian zero-profit condition and reaffirm the faith that, in full tranquil eqilibrium, profits will be zero. What has happened is some slight of hand: 'pure' economic profit has been defined away, so that the zero-profit condition remains inviolate.

In practice, there are as many imputed costs as there are apologies for the status quo, which best explains why profit theory is held in such ill repute. In the face of such a plethora of 'costs', one can only wend one's way through the thickets by making a list of the various manifestations of profit:

- a. earnings (wages of management)
- b. differential earnings of management (i.e., disequilibrium rents)
- c. monopoly gains
- d. 'marginal productivity' of 'capital'
- e. differential time preference for consumption (i.e., Fisherian interest)
- f. reward for abstinence (a slight variation on (e))
- g. gain from successful risk-bearing
- h. gain from successful uncertainty-bearing (Knight)
- i. residual claimant gains due to luck

If I have missed any of the more popular ones, I must apologize, but there is no recognized authority on these matters. The prospective student is invariably presented with a random selection from this list when he or she first encounters economics, [44] and then hears or reads no more on the subject throughout undergraduate and graduate education and beyond.

This is not the place to subject each individual 'explanation' to critical scrutiny; but it may be instructive to briefly extend the criticism of earlier sections in order to indicate some broad outlines of discontent. Perhaps the most favored explanation of profits is the idea that it is a return for the bearing of risks. (This, even though the most respected neoclassical theorist of risk, Kenneth Arrow, calls this a 'recondite' notion). In this parable, streams of revenue are technologically determined, but in a stochastic manner, so that associated with each technological process is a variance over time. Investors passively face these prospects with varying degrees of taste for 'risk' (variance) aversion. Prices of investments are set such that higher variance streams are priced less due to general distaste for the prospect.

First, let us assess the import of this theory for a larger theory of macroeconomic instability. The variance of revenue streams <u>must</u> be independent of the actors' investments for <u>this</u> scheme to produce a determinate outcome. Yet the independent existence of the variance of returns to capital belies the whole notion of a business cycle <u>due</u> to the changing level of investment.

Neoclassicists <u>assume</u> the variance of a crucial component of 'income', when the object is to describe its function determinants. This is yet another instance of the pervasive influence of Say's Law in neoclassical economics. The only cycle which could arise in this view would be the result of a shift over time in the distribution of portfolios due to psychological motivations, which is made manifest through a changing aggregate variance of profit. As in other parts of neoclassical capital theory, disequilibrium trades are banished from consciousness.

Risk theory is poor macro theory, but it is quite efficacious as ideology. Those that take chances and win are the owners of the means of production, while those that lose or are too timid to try are the workers of the world. This particular ideology has always had a poor empirical grounding. People who do not employ others are hardly ever recipients of wage differentials attributable to contractual returns with higher variances. In fact empirical evidence shows, on the contrary, that it is the unionized sector which obtains both lower variance and higher mean wage streams. Seasonal and tertiary sector jobs are notorious both for low pay and instability of tenure. Further, recent work shows that employers shift a good deal of the variance of their own cash flow streams on to their workers through layoffs, overtime, etc.; the market does not generally arbitrage this risk into higher wage rates, but lower ones. [45]

One might try to bypass this objection by insisting that risk is only experienced in relation to non-contractual claims, but this mistakes risk for uncertainty. Moreover, what this in fact means is that risk is a class concept, a return to those located in a particular contractual nexus within the production process. <u>Ipso facto</u>, this theory of profits is thinly disguised apologetics.

The foundation of profit theory on differential time preference can be rejected out of hand as being useless in a theory of macroeconomic instability on the grounds covered in the section on 'time' above. Further, some economists believe that any theory of a stable equalized rate of profit is incompatible with the 'temporary equilibrium' method of the Walrasian theorists, [46] a position we shall not attempt to summarize here. It will suffice to note that consistency with the value-theoretic stance, the meaning of equilibrium and the explicit incorporation of time all impel us to search for a different rationale for the rate of profit.

From an institutional viewpoint, the rate of profit is the key indicator of the state of the macroeconomy, because it is the rate of accumulation in long-period tranquil equilibrium. The institutions of capital exist in order to expand; profits are the measure of that expansion. To prevent confusion, we should specify that there is a 'real' rate of growth and a 'financial' rate of profit, and that the two can diverge. The real rate is equal to the rate of physical accumulation; but even at the firm level the measurement of accumulation is a comparison of a disparate set of items, so we must keep in mind the problem of the specification of relative prices of production and their determination as part of the theory of the real rate of growth. The financial rate of profit presents a different problem: it is a ratio of money units to money units, so we are not concerned with the aggregation problem as we are with the real rate. Instead, the financial rate of profit is the outcome of accounting conventions and the institutional context of generalized accumulation. We shall discuss the real rate in the remainder of this section, and the financial rate of profit in the next section of this chapter.

In the institutional value-theoretic scheme, the physical rate of growth is equalized across all sectors in equilibrium. It is competition which effects this equalization, but not the competition of neoclassical theory: [47]

> (In neoclassical theory)...competition was a feature of the day to day operation of markets; here it is a feature of long-run investment plans. Here it is not necessary that there should be a perfectly elastic demand for the output of each seller in each market at each moment of time; it is necessary that there should be no limitation on access, given time, to any market, so that an equal rate of expected profit on investment tends to be established throughout the systems.

The real rate is equalized through the mechanism of investment in physical accumulation, and not through the price system per se. For instance: let us picture a sector of the economy which produces a basic good in the Sraffian sense: a good which is required directly or indirectly by other industries as a prerequisite for their expansion. Suppose the physical rate of growth in this mature industry is above the average equalized rate. This industry will then eventually experience a falling off in sales, as the rest of the system cannot absorb that volume of its products. First the financial rate of profit will fall in that sector because of inventory accumulation. As a consequence investors will wish to place their pecuniary funds in sectors with higher rates of financial profit, which will in turn encourage increased physical accumulation in these sectors. Meanwhile, increased inventories, excess capacity and lowered financial profit rates will discourage physical accumulation in the original sector. Eventually, there is a tendency towards an equalized rate of physical accumulation.

To understand that the concept of competition employed is palpably different from the neoclassical approach, one need only consider the phenomenon of monopoly under the two theoretical regimes. In the neoclassical schema, the existence of monopolies can be an explanation for the existence of profit, but it vitiates any assumption that the rate of profit be equalized. In the institutional scheme, profits exist irrespective of the existence of monopoly; while physical monopolies can influence the financial rate of profit through the restriction of output, to do so indefinitely would cripple the expansion of the whole system. Today's monopolies are not physical monoplies for the most part, but financial monopolies, dependent upon institutional claims to the ownership of the 'firm'. The existence of a financial monopoly may slow down the adjustment time of the system as a whole to equilibrium; it does not inherently prevent the equalization of the physical rate of accumulation. On the contrary, some economists would argue that the increasing concentration of capitalist financial organization acts to increase this kind of competition in the economy rather that reduce it because multi-product conglomerates can more easily equate the rate of physical investment between sectors, since a large number of sectors are now encompassed by the firm's pecuniary boundaries. [48]

To summarize: in the institutional conception of the economic world the physical rate of accumulation, and not some hybrid notion of income, is the key variable to be explained in the macroeconomy. This is because an institutionalist does not see the system as being run for the felicific benefit of the actors, directly or by some invisible hand; the system exists for the sake of accumulation of 'profit'. It is this accumulation which calls the tune to which the players must spin; not the actors' tastes or preferences.

f. Finance and the Status of the Firm

Neoclassical theory asserts the insignificance of aggregate profits in two ways: the first, as we have seen is to define it away as an inconsequential residual; and the second, here considered, is to maintain that even if it were on analytic consequence, its empirical representation in business accounts is either economically meaningless or economically unimportant. After such an epistemological onslaught, it is no wonder that most economists gaze upon profits with something akin to existential nausea.

The group of writers who consider business accounts meaningless usually hold one opinion in common: that some marginal productivity notion of profits is correct, and that accountants, through sheer perversity (if they are not feeling generous towards other academic disciplines) or technical difficulty (if they are generous), refuse to keep truthful records. One of the more generous souls is Sir John Hicks, who argues that because the whole system depends on beliefs and expectations, it is <u>ex ante</u> and not <u>ex post</u> profits which inhabit the economists' models. Accounting definitions can be nothing but <u>ex post</u>, the outcome of surprises and disappointments, windfalls and shortfalls; therefore while accounts do represent real phenomena, their value is nugatory for the economist.

A much less generous soul is Oscar Morgenstern, who accuses accountants of not heeding the probabilistic nature of the world. [49] He complains that "the contacts between economic theory and accounting theory and practice are far thinner than one would like," but leaves the impression that accountants should have humbly approached economists for advice long ago. Morgenstern has two complaints about accountancy: that inventories, etc., are not carried on the books at their 'true' prices; and that balance sheets add up values of varying degrees of certainty. Morgenstern assumes that accountants know what the 'true' prices are, and persist in maintaining stocks at historical costs out of anachronistic habit or custom. Likewise, he wonders why accountants do not attach probabilities to the values of various assets and liabilities: cash on hand would bear a probability of one, inventories could be realized with a probability of .8, goodwill with an even lesser probability, and so on. Morgenstern ends this disquisition by suggesting that these two revisions in accounting practice would produce balance sheets more consistent with techniques of aggregation, subject to the proviso that the individual firm's probabilities were independent of other firms.

These strands of thought share a very Platonic epistemology. There are, they say, ideals in men's minds which are--or, in their case, should be--only approximated by men's words and deeds. It is taken for granted that the economists' theoretical ideals are also those of the accountant. Never mind that there are both practical and theoretical problems in choosing which prices should be used (during an inflation or otherwise) or specifying a two digit figure representing time preference which inhabits the inner recesses of the entrepreneurial mind, or the sheer absurdity of assuming that one firm's probability of realizing its goodwill account in independent of all other firms' (Say's Law again); these are not worries of the neoclassical economist. Never mind that economists cannot agree among themselves what capital is, or how it should be measured. Accountants should recognize the superiority of the neoclassical economists' theoretical framework.

There is a more sophisticated objection to the empirical content of business accounts among economists. It involves the argument that the mode of keeping business accounts is neutral with respect to significant economic variables because the market conveys adequate information to all parties irrespective of bookeeping categories. This contention consists of two sequential steps: the 'efficient markets' hypothesis and the Modigliani-Miller theorem.

The efficient markets hypothesis asserts that market prices, and share placement prices in particular, fully reflect the available information concerning that firm and the impact of that information on expected income streams. Previously we have intimated that economists have not often been very clear as to what this impact should be. It has been shown that under certain restrictive assumptions a weak implication of neoclassical price theory is that sequential price changes in an efficient market should be independent: a time series of prices from such a market should have the characteristics of a random walk. [50] Recent empirical work has revealed almost no serial correlation of stock prices in a wide range of environments, and this is interpreted as support for the efficient markets hypothesis. [51] Other types of tests have been devised, but they do not derive from implications of neoclassical models per se, but simply seek to test if the direction and timing of price changes correlates with new information about the balance sheet status of the firm.

The Modigliani-Miller (MM) theorem employs the efficient markets hypothesis in the strong sense as one of its assumptions: that the market value of the firm is equal to its future stream of physical returns capitalized at the appropriate rate of return for that class of firms. (The 'assumption' is really a circular definition, but let us ignore that.) The two results of the MM theorem relevant to our purposes are: "the market value of the firm depends only on its real earning power and on the market capitalization rate for pure equity streams of its class, and not at all upon the particular mix of security types that characterize its formal structure"; and "common shares in levered corporations in the same class have higher expected yields than those in less levered corporations in the same class--a differential which can be thought of as compensation for the greater 'riskiness' attached to levered shares." [52] In plainer words, the amount of leverage in the economy has no repercussions of the financial valuation of share placements (equated with 'capital' in this view) and therefore on the firm because investors will, through arbitrage, match the corporate leverage in their own portfolios. In the absence of differential taxation of interest and dividends, the mode of accountancy or finance makes no appreciable difference to the macroeconomy. MM would therefore rule out anything like Veblen's antipathy between movements in the physical sphere of production and the financial machinations of the owners.

Burton Malkiel summarizes the logic behind the MM theorems: [53]

"The MM proposition is simply an assertion that two firms with the identical earnings stream cannot sell for two different values in the market because one packages its claims in a different manner...MM argue that then assertions is equivalent to the proposition that in a perfect market a dairy farmer cannot earn more for the milk he produces by skimming off some of the butterfat and selling it separately. It is true, of course, that butterfat sells for more per unit weight than whole milk. Nevertheless, the advantage the dairy farmer might get by selling relatively expensive butterfat is lost because the residual product he has left to market is skim milk, which is not worth as much as whole milk, per unit weight. What the dairy farmer gains by selling high priced butterfat is <u>exactly</u> offset by the lower revenue he receives from his sales of skim milk."

Here, in one compact place, we can observe the confluence of all of the theoretical predispositions in neoclassical economics which militate against a logical theory of macroeconomic instability. First, the market is assumed <u>a priori</u> to function perfectly: this is neither proved nor motivated. Second, all adjustments happen <u>immediately</u>: that is, all passage of time is abstracted away. This absence of time in a particularly flagrant abuse of logic, since the 'good' being bought and sold in the market for share placements is a timephased stream of returns, which MM represent as a single-valued variable 'X', which possess no time dimension. Third, the idea that any gain is exactly offset by movements in market prices is nothing but a restatement of a conservation law: the sum total of value is independent of any financial activities on the part of the firm. These types of conservation laws are nothing but restatements of Stage 1 theories of the macroeconomy. This is another piece of fairly persuasive evidence that neoclassicists are incapable of advancing beyond Stage 1 theories of the macroeconomy. Fourth, when MM consider 'risk', they mean increased variance, but do not mean risk of disaster, which is the commonplace notion of risk. More than once it has been pointed out that if there is even a minor possibility of bankruptcy, the MM theorem breaks down. [54] There is nothing particularly deep in this observation: <u>MM assume</u> the stream of returns is independent of the firm's actions, but this can't be true if the firm does so many wrong things that its earnings stream disappears. Further, the certainty-equivalent method rules out 'disaster' by assumption, in any event. [55] Fifth, the financial market is presumed to efficiently transmit all relevant information in the form of market prices; but what if the information from the real markets is about 'false trades' rather than market clearing quantities? Then the efficient markets hypothesis is stating that the market accuracy transmits false and misleading signals. [56] Sixth, the whole MM discussion takes place from the viewpoint of the shareholder, and not the firm itself. In neoclassical theory, it is the individual who is all important, and not the firm. To see that this must be so, consider the MM-style firm which faces a prospectively risky investment. By defintion, the firm cannot 'roll' its own homemade leverage in order to reduce its risk, unlike the shareholder of the firm. In what sense, then, is finance 'irrelevant'?

The MM theorem, and the conventional disdain for finance in economic theory in general, is a simple corollary of the structure of neoclassical theory. As Vickers so aptly puts it, "It would appear that analytical nihilism is triumphant! Apparently, in the theory of the structure of the firm there is no longer any need for any firm at all." [57] The legal structure of the firm, its method of finance, increasing concentration and mode of organization are all irrelevant in the face of an all-powerful market which efficiently expresses the desires of atomistic individuals. To quote a prominent neoclassical macroeconomist, "If business behavior is taken to be competitive, the business sector simply traces out the efficient envelope of available technology in response to demand shifts. The distinction between business and households becomes the distinction between 'nature' and 'tastes' on which identification in the supply-demand paradigm rests." [58] One could not be much more blunt about it than that. The firm is simply its production function, which in turn is a purely 'natural' datum. The business sector is not active, but functionally passive, shaped and controlled by a market which is not described, but simply asserted to be effective. The efficiency of the market leads to all sorts of 'separation theorems': production, investment decisions, the structure of finance and trade are all independent of one another. The firm as an historical entity is superfluous in this whole process. This, in fact, is why neoclassical specialists in industrial organization have continuously been frustrated in their quest to find some solid rationale for the theory of the firm. [59] At the risk of being repetitive, it is palpably clear that there is no room for institutions in neoclassical economic theory.

The institutionalist theory of macroeconomics avoids all of these pitfalls by starting from the fact that the firm is the central economic institution in a capitalist era, and changes in its form and function are the underlying cause of changes in the economy. Instead of the neoclassical penchant for assuming that the market functions like a black box, institutionalist theory sees the success or failure of the market as an institution derived directly from the efficacy of the firm as an institution. Since the firm gauges its own progress by the rate of profit, we, also, track the movements of the rate of profit as our prime macroeconomic indicator. If there is a major innovation in the firm structure--say, the rise of the corporate form--then the institutionalist must alter the whole theory of macroeconomic instability to make it coeval with the historical period under examination. The firm is another of those parameters of economic theory that change with the passage of historical time, largely because the firm can attain its goals either by sticking to the rules of the game or by influencing institutional change on its own behalf: that is, the firm is a major locus of power in a capitalist society. [60] It is quite possible that these rule changes are crucial to an understanding of the institutionalist theory of macroeconomic instability.

CHAPTER SIX

AN INSTITUTIONALIST THEORY OF THE BUSINESS CYCLE

Why the 'Birth of the Business Cycle'?

If the author has made a credible case in the previous chapters, it would appear that our present understanding of macroeconomic dynamics is in a sorry state, but that the various components of alternatives are lying about here and there in certain neglected works, particularly those works by institutionalist theorists. Part of the forgotten heritage of these institutionalists is that no economic theory can be general in the sense of being a-historical. If we are to take these strictures seriously, and not merely repeat them as platitudes, then it becomes impossible to simply lay out a model of the macroeconomy and call it <u>the</u> general theory of (fill in the blank). Instead, the correct path to macroeconomic theory is to first demarcate the historical era and institutional framework of interest, identify the crucial institutional phenomena which define the macroeconomy, and then construct the theory.

The question then becomes: where should we start? The temptation is immediately to start with 'now.' After all, 'now' is what we personally know best; moreover, the problems of the present are always pressing, and our interest is predominantly occupied by what we should do next, under the rather colorless title of 'policy'. Further, since science is also a social process, there are very strong incentives to concern oneself with present policy: grants, publishing outlets, government positions, consultantships and so forth. Regardless of these very impelling considerations, I would like to argue that this process of theory construction should begin in the past, and preferably, the somewhat distant past. The reasons for this choice are not immediate nor apparent, and therefore they deserve some elaboration.

After all is said and done, there is an uncomplicated, seemingly commonsense rebuttal to the economist seeking to explain macroeconomic instability in some logical manner. What is the use, goes this rebuttal, of expending all that effort and imagination in searching for the root causes of instability, when all you have to do is look around you: the economic system does not break down in any dramatic manner, goods are produced, incomes are distributed, goods are sold, people get by. Bluntly, the market may not work 'well' according to various criteria, but ultimately, it does work. Why, therefore, persist in this quest to explain instability? (A corollary to this position is the obverse in times of trouble: say from 1930 to 1933 or thereabouts, maintaining that nothing works.) We have already observed this predisposition to believe the 'economic system' is fundamentally sound on the part of many economists.

The flaw of this commonsense position is not that we may hold differing subjective opinions over what works and what does not, but rather that the mere statement of the premise makes the result a forgone conclusion. When someone says 'the market works' they generally are thinking of the market as a single institution or as an isolated mode of social organization. However effective the market, it plainly does not produce the results that are generally attributed to it on its own. Another insight of the institutionalist writers is that the economic system is an interlocking and symbiotic set of institutions, of which the market is a limited, albeit significant, subset. Much of chapters four and five were devoted to substantiating the claim that neoclassical economics is incapable of capturing the institutional framework outside of the market, and therefore incapable of even framing the question of the efficiency of the market in any comprehensive manner.

It is precisely because the market is imbedded in its larger institutional and historical framework that it is a mistake to immediately set to work theorizing about our own era. The market as a strong social organizing principle has been present in economic life for at least three centuries, and within that time a number of other social institutions have evolved which support, oppose or presuppose the operation of the market. It follows that the present stability of instability of the market is not due to its intrinsic nature as much as it is due to this complement of symbiotic social institutions. More specifically, the last century has witnessed an increasing tempo of conscious political intervention in market operation, which must certainly be taken into account in any assessment of market stability. Therefore, the project of explaining macroeconomic fluctuations becomes more complex and more conditional upon what has previously elapsed with the passage of historical time.

Since the evolution and proliferation of relevant institutions creates problems of increasing complexity for the theorist of macroeconomic fluctuations, one possible research program is to consciously choose an historical period where these modern institutions are only present in a rudimentary state, or where some of the more recent innovations are absent. Playing out the logic of this suggestion, the very start of the research program should then coincide with the very origins of the phenomena under review and revision: in our case, the birth of the modern business cycle.

The disadvantages of this program are obvious: data is poor or non-existent, collective memories fade, and historiography tends to lose resolution as we delve deeper into the past. But let us compare these drawbacks to the advantages of such a program. First, there are quantitatively fewer modern institutional variables to account for, since much social organization of the market arises in reaction to market operation. The theory can start in relative simplicity, to be later augmented with further complicating historical phenomena. Secondly, by locating the study of instability in the past, we can maintain a more detached perspective upon much of the contention which arises from the politically charged nature of the question of instability when applied to present circumstances. Further, we may avoid some of the faddism which has beset theories of macroeconomic instability in the past. Third, especially by searching for the origins of modern instability, we are looking at a society in transition from one mode of organization to another. The historical record of a period of transition can actually help us to identify the institutions and variables important to a theory, because records will stress phenomena which the actors situated within the period find disturbing, threatening, or curious: that is, new. All in all, these specific motivations act to encourage discussion and contemplation, qualities which appear to be at a premium in the era of economists as advisors, power brokers and advocates. The rise of the economics profession itself is one more complicating institutional macroeconomic innovation of comparitively recent origin. For these reasons, this work chooses to confine its research project to the origins of the phenomena under discussion, the birth of the business cycle.

A Definition of the Modern Economy

A search for origins presumes that we know what it is we are looking for. Since chapter four documented the fact that there is no agreement on this issue, it would be helpful to be clear from the outset about what is modern about the modern economy. We propose five main characteristics of the modern economy:

1) the sale of human labor power by the laborer on the same basis as other market commodities to:

2) a legal and financial entity called the firm, which is defined by its accounts and its legal rights, and which exists to facilitate the accumulation of profit through:

3) concious and concerted control over the organization and physical turnover of material production, and through:

4) manipulation of the balance sheet and cash flow variables which constitute the firm:

5) which in the presence of interfirm and intrafirm market competition bring about a tendency for and equalized rate of firm expansion, or to put it differently, an equalized rate of profit.

It is the contention of this work that this bundle of attributes, sufficiently fleshed out by institutional particulars, constitutes the modern macroeconomy. The absence of <u>any one or more</u> of these attributes defines the premodern economy; in which case a separate and distinct theoretical framework would be needed to discuss "the economy" or "macroeconomic fluctuations."

The preceeding collection of attributes are not unrelated. Historically the latter four have evolved directly from the first institution as the development of imperatives arising from the organization of wage labor. The exsitence of wage labor as something other than a sporadic phenomenon presumes the prior existence of an institutionally defined surplus. This surplus may take many forms in different institutional contexts, but in the modern world the surplus arising from production (as opposed to rents gained from non-reproducable items) takes the form of <u>profit</u>. The fundamental motive behind the employment of <u>wage</u> labor is the accumulation of this profit. The remaining four characteristics of the modern economy revolve around the mechanisms of profit accumulation.

Wage labor presumes the expendability of any individual human personality in the process of production, because production is always presumed to be a 'going concern', which is immortal as long as it continues to operate within its own working rules. [1] Since human beings are not immortal, they are replaced by other human beings through the wage labor contract. In very early times, the locus of accumulation of profit was an individual person, but this raises the same problem vis-a-vis production as the role of the individual laborer, since entrepreneurs are no more immortal than laborers. At first the locus of accumulation was shifted to the entrepreneur's family, but this was unsatisfactory, because there was no dependable guarantee of a going concern. This problem was eventually averted through the development of the institution of the firm. The firm is the manifestation of the going concern, because it is the locus of accumulation, whereas the entrepreneurs are the adjuncts crucial to its operation, yet individually expendable. In this way of thinking the firm is the mirror image of the wage labor contract.

The existence of both wage labor and the firm presumes some mechanisms of control by the firm over the physical processes of production. Some of these potential control mechanisms, such as choice of technology and production lines, are totally within the purview of the firm. Other control mechanisms involving the relations between the laborer and the firm are in part dependent upon the social and legal framework within which the firm must operate. Since the accumulation happens through time, one of the major control mechanisms of the firm has to do with its rate of productive activities. Certain of these rates are given by the technology of the era: these are the gross 'material' boundaries within which the firm must work. Within these boundaries, there is appreciable room for alteration in the speed of production of surplus: through control of the physical activities of the laborer, the regularity of the work of the laborer, and the larger rate of capacity utilization of plant structure. Only in the modern economy does the firm both possess the awareness of these latter capabilities and the institutional framework within which to alter them. The awareness arises from the concept of a measured uniform linear 'time', itself an institutional innovation tied to the previous concept of the purchase of human labor separate from actual purchase of the organic being. The institutional framework derives from legal notions of the wage labor transaction and from social convention: for example, the ability to hire willing workers seven days a week between the hours of midnight and 8 A.M. The manipulation of rates of physical turnover is intimately tied to the prior development of the wage labor relation.

Once the regimen of time pervades the physical production relations of the firm, it becomes apparent that the financial structure of the firm must also become subject to the law of the clock. Because the firm is the fundamental unit of accumulation, it must be made comparable to all other firms with respect to its rate of accumulation. Quantitatively, this means that firms are rated according to their expansion in money units per unit of uniform time. Accelerated accumulation can result from increased physical turnover or increased financial turnover, the latter meaning a faster circuit of each unit of value invested through the marketplace. This is merely a restatement of the truism that a low markup can be offset by high turnover.

Historically, just as physical turnover was constrained by social and institutional conventions, so too was financial turnover. Not only did comprehensive and relatively standardized financial accounts have to be kept, but they had to be kept in such a form that their significance would not be lost upon the record-keeper. In order to be able to gauge financial turnover, certain accounting conventions had to be first developed, such as strict periodicity in the casting up of the accounts; the distinction between the entity of the firm and the indentity of the owners; the distinction between the firm as a continuously changing sum of value and the sums of money which pass through the firm; the distinction between stocks and flows generally; and some special treatment of debts and other time bargains. As these tasks of record keeping become more and more onerous for the owner of the firm, a separate type of wage laborer was created to assume the burden, and the profession of accountancy was born. In fact, the creation of the accountant is the extension of the logic of wage labor to the firm itself, because the keeping of useful records demands regularity and supervision in the same manner as the control of physical turnover in the actual production process. Since these characteristics define wage labor, these functions were separated from the role of ownership so that they too could become subject to the law of the clock.

Finally, if the market is to allocate surplus across lines of endeavor, not only is it necessary to possess comprehensive firm records, but also an appropriate institutional structure which allows investments to move among firms in search of the maximum return. This is a restatement of the classical notion of competition, where the movement of money capital among processes and firms assures that there is a tendency for the equalization of the rate of profit. In order for this to happen, there must be recognized channels for the flow of finance: a functioning market in firm placements, some sort of banking structure, legal assurances for negotiability of debts and placements, and, of course, evidence that these structures are actually used.

Thus, we have a sketchy list of particulars which constitute the rudimentary institutional framework of the modern economy. However, we cannot come to grasp why these particular characteristics are embodied in particular historical practices until we see how they operate and interact in the context of institutional economic theory.

An Institutional Model of the Business Cycle

Let us assess the five components of the modern economy in the order in which they were introduced in the previous section. First, there is the existence of wage labor. Perhaps the major intellectual hurdle of our age which economists must perennially face is the question of the appropriate method of modelling the wage and the wage-labor relation. The use of the production function coupled with the marginal productivity conditions was the method employed in many previous cases, but considerations outlined in previous chapters have rendered that approach untenable. The Post-Keynesians, with reference back to the classical economists, have suggested that distribution must be treated as logically prior to any operation of the market mechanism, which has in practice led them to posit both the level of the wage in value terms and the composition of the wage in commodity terms to be exogenously given prior to the analysis. Clearly this is an unsatisfactory state of affairs; but the reason it is an unsatisfactory method is that many particular institutional considerations are thereby passed over. Given that our present model is not meant to be a self-contained explanation, we shall employ the Post-Keynesian method, keeping in mind that it must be further complicated as the analysis becomes more elaborate.

In the simplest possible conception, the wage can be pictured as the passage of some proportion of total output to the laborers. It is common practice in Sraffian/Post-Keynesian models to write the physical technology of production as a matrix of flow requirements of inputs, which includes as a separate row the wage bundle of physical commodities which the worker 'purchases'. We shall imitate this practice, with some amendments, in writing a matrix A:

$$A = \begin{array}{c} \text{Production} \\ \text{Processes} \\ \\ \\ \text{Wage} \end{array} \left[\begin{array}{cccc} \overset{\text{Physical}}{\underset{\text{Inputs}}{}} & & & \overset{\text{Labor}}{\underset{\text{Input}}{}} \\ a_{11} & a_{12} \cdots & & a_{1m} \\ a_{21} \cdot & \cdots & & \cdot a_{2m} \\ \cdot & \cdot & & \cdot \\ \hline a_{m1} & a_{m2} & \cdots & 0 \end{array} \right] \quad (6.1)$$

Patently, any time the wage is not received in barter terms, but rather in _money_, then the composition of the wage in our matrix may change. Also, the implication of the zero in the bottom right-hand corner of the matrix is that there is no flow of labor which the laborers themselves require in order to reproduce their own labor. In one obvious sense, this is not true, since this ignores the vital role of familial organization and what has been perhaps infelicitously called 'home production'. However, it does capture one very important aspect of the modern economic system present at its origins: at least initially, there is a clear bifurcation between the reproduction of output and the reproduction of the laborer. In this situation, the laborer is quite explicitly expendable: both because of the impersonality of the wage labor contract vis-a-vis the immortality of the 'going concern', but also because at the birth of capitalism the labor supply is recruited from the pre-capitalist sector in times of labor shortage. For both of these reasons, the fledgling modern sector is able to relinquish all responsibility for the reproduction of the laborer, which means that the conditions of the reproduction of the laborer have no effect upon the operation of the modern sector: thus, the zero in the matrix. Certainly, as the market penetrates and transforms the pre-modern sector, this situation is mitigated; at which point, the specification of our matrix would have to change.

The second component of the modern economy to be incorporated into the model is the presence of the firm. The firm is defined by its financial manifestations: its balance sheet, its income statement, and its ledgers. The simplest conception of a firm portrays it as a sum of value; the object of the operation of a firm is to expand that sum of value. This rate of expansion is summarized in the firm's rate of profit, which is defined as the flow of profit net of all costs divided by the accounting value of the firm (its net worth or equity). We must be quite specific about this at the outset, since there is much confusion in the existing literature among the ratio of profit to net worth, the ratio of profit to assets, and the rate of interest. As we shall argue shortly, these ratios are quite separate; and to collapse all three into a single ratio prevents the construction of a significant segment of business cycle theory. Firm rates of profit will be expressed as follows:

$$\text{Firm n: } \pi_n = Z_n/N_n \qquad (6.2)$$

where Z is net profit, and N is the net worth of the appropriate firm.

The third component of the modern economy is the concerted organization of the rate of physical turnover within the process of production. Physical turnover time is defined as the length of time a particular input must be present in the confines of the production process in order to produce one unit of output. The <u>rate</u> of physical turnover is defined as the reciprocal of the physical turnover time of the input. Since both are defined as time duration per time unit, the magnitude of these quanta are directly conditional upon the choice of the unit of measure time.

For example, suppose in the production of knives the 2/10 of a knife required for the production of a single knife (i.e., one knife as input is fully used up in the production of five knives) must present in the process for approximately 2.2 time units. This would be due to the fact that the processes involved in the making of knives required the use of a knife with an average useful life of 2.2 time units. The rate of physical turnover of knife inputs in the knife-making process would then be 1/2.2, or approximately .455 per time unit. Moreover, suppose the 1/10 of a knife required for the production of a single unit of cloth only had to be present in the production process for approximately .42 time units. Then the <u>rate</u> of physical turnover of knife inputs in cloth production would be much faster, at 1/.42 =2.38 per time unit. Note that the same physical input will have different rates of physical turnover when employed in different lines of production. Each physical input, although homogeneous in physical substance, is tagged with a unique temporal identity in each different production process.

In our example, let us give every input its temporal 'tag' in each process of production. These tags can also be arrayed in the form of a matrix, as follows:

$$T = [\tau_{ij}]$$

$$= \begin{array}{c} \\ \text{Production} \\ \text{Processes} \\ \\ \\ \text{Wage} \end{array} \begin{array}{c} \text{Length of time} \\ \text{physical input is} \\ \text{present in production} \\ \left[\begin{array}{cccccc} \tau_{11} & \tau_{12} & \cdots & \cdots & \cdots & \tau_{1m} \\ \tau_{21} & \cdots & \cdots & \cdots & \cdots & \tau_{2m} \\ & & & & & \vdots \\ \hline \tau_{m1} & \tau_{m2} & \cdots & \cdots & \cdots & 0 \end{array} \right. \end{array} \begin{array}{c} \text{Required} \\ \text{labor} \\ \text{presence} \\ \\ \\ \\ \\ \end{array} \quad (6.3)$$

The last column tells us how long the contractual unit of labor must be present to produce one unit of output: For example, 1.26 time units in the production of a knife, and .84 time units in the production of a unit of cloth. There is the possibility of some confusion here, since conventional specification of labor inputs are often single-valued functions of a time variable: say, so many manhours of labor per unit output. The unspoken implication of this choice is that if it takes more manhours of labor to make the same unit output, then the increased 'inputs' require an increased wage compensation. It was one of the great contributions of Marxian economics to recognize that this was not in general the case, and that the contractual wage relation simply assured the presence of the worker in the production process, but did not insure the magnitude of effort within production. In Marxian economics, this concept is summarized in the crucial distinction between 'labor' (that is, the actual effort) and 'labor power' (the contractual presence of the worker and the potential subordination relationship). In institutional economics, this same insight is captured in the distinction between the number of contractual labor units required to produce a unit of the good in question and the length of time those laborers are present in the production process to produce a single unit. In our example, it only takes one-tenth of a contractual laborer to produce a single knife, but given the state of both technical and social relations within the workplace, that laborer must be present for 1.26 time periods for the result to emerge (or, to state it differently, one laborer produces ten knives in 1.26 time periods). If, for instance, it happened there were some institutional change which allowed an intensification of work process within the context of the same physical technology in the production of knives, the physical turnover time would fall below 1.26, while the contractual labor requirement of 1/10 would remain the same. In this manner, the mathematics is capable of summarizing the state of social relations within the workplace: a clear improvement over the absence in neoclassical economics of any historical social specificity.

Another advantage which derives from this conception of physical turnover is that the concept of capacity utilization is not measured as some proportion of maximum output, but rather as a weighted average of all of the physical turnover times in the particular production process. Hence, capacity is pictured not on a relative but on an absolute scale of operation. To see this, imagine a situation in the production of knives where there is a fall in usage of capacity. Less knives are being produced per time period, so the average lifetime of inputs per unit output rise in the process, and physical turnover time lengthen: say, the turnover time of knives rises to 4.2, and the turnover time of cloth to .63. Any weighted sum (with strictly positive weights) of all the turnover times in knife production will rise, which indicates that the intensity of employment of inputs has decreased. Since there are no absolute boundaries to the periods within which turnover times can vary, there is no scale of capacity which runs from zero to 100%, but only a continuum of potential rates of turnover.

The incorporation of physical turnover times may also shed some light upon a phenomenon after discussed in economic theory under the rubric of 'returns to scale'. In neoclassical economic theory, the maintainance of the artifice of demand-determined pricing requires some assumptions concerning the technological effect of the expansion of output both at the firm level and the level of the industry. [2] The justification for the assumed regularities is always phrased in terms of some 'indivisibilities' and 'lumpiness' or some particular relation between 'fixed' and 'variable' costs due to the physical characteristics of particular inputs. [3] However, since consideration of the time dimension has generally been supressed in modern neoclassical economics, little thought has been expended upon what form these indivisibilities might assume. In fact, the conventional examples given of industries with increasing returns to scale, such as hydroelectric power generation or assembly-line production, all imply the employment of some inputs with very long physical turnover time relative to the other inputs in that process. Could it be that the neoclassical concern with returns to scale is nothing more than the supressed time axis of production making a surreptitious reappearance in the form of arbitrary assumptions about scale? If this is so, than returns to scale must also be a function of all the social and institutional forces which we have suggested impinge upon physical turnover. Further, although we shall be employing linear model of production in this work, it in no way implies 'constant returns to scale', as has often been maintained by advocates of neoclassical production functions. This model is <u>more general</u> than the neoclassical production function in <u>its ability</u> to treat matters of scale, as well as social and institutional considerations.

Given that we have specified both the required amounts of inputs and their time distribution within the process of production, we have implicitly defined the physical stocks accumulated in the course of production. A stock is defined as the flow quantity of physical inputs present in the production process multiplied by the appropriate physical turnover time. [4] In our present example, the stock of knives in knife production would be $(.2) \times (2.2) = \overline{.44}$ knife per unit output, whereas under the same condition the stock of cloth in knife production would be $(.2) \times (.21) = .042$ cloth per unit output. We can develop a stock matrix for the whole economy by individually multiplying each flow input requirement in expression (6.1) by its corresponding physical turnover time (6.3):

$$B = A \otimes T = [a_{ij} \cdot \tau_{ij}]$$

$$= \begin{bmatrix} a_{11} \cdot \tau_{11} & a_{12} \cdot \tau_{12} & \cdots & a_{1m} \cdot \tau_{1m} \\ a_{21} \cdot \tau_{21} & \cdots & \cdots & a_{2m} \cdot \tau_{2m} \\ \vdots & & & \vdots \\ a_{m1} \cdot \tau_{m1} & \cdots & \cdots & 0 \end{bmatrix} \quad (6.4)$$

Note that depreciation is already implicitly included in the definition of the stock through the specification of the expected average life of the good, so that there is no need for a separate specification of a depreciation rate. However, if the economy is to grow, then expanding production of goods requires inputs to be proportioned so that both present productive capacity is maintained and some future output must cover replacement of inputs plus some proportionate growth rate in the economy's stock of productive goods, or:

$$x = Ax + \lambda Bx \quad (6.5)$$

where x is the vector of goods in the economy, the A matrix is the array of flow input requirements corresponding to our expression (6.1), and the B matrix is the array of stocks present in the production process corresponding to our expression (6.4).

The fourth component of the modern economy is the ability possessed by firms to alter their balance sheet and cash flow variables in pursuit of higher profit, which is tantamount to altering the firm rate of financial turnover. Much of the foundation of the institutionalist theory of financial turnover derives from Veblen's <u>Theory of Business Enterprise</u>, which was summarized above in chapter three. We shall attempt to capture his insights by rewriting the expression (6.2) for the rate of profit of each firm as :

$$\pi = Z/N = \frac{r(S/A) - i(L/A)}{1 - L/A}$$

$$\pi = [r \cdot (S/N)] - i\left(\ell/1-\ell\right) \qquad (6.6)$$

where
- Z = firm net profit
- N = firm net worth
- A = total firm assets
- L = total firm liabilities
- r = profit margin on sales gross of interest charges
- S = firm sales
- ℓ = L/A or rate of firm leverage
- S/N = firm financial turnover = Υ
- i = the rate of interest

Thus the profit rate of the firm is a function of its gross sales margin, its financial turnover and its degree of leverage in its balance sheet. While all three variables are not strickly independent, they do have different determinations in the institutionalist theory of the business cycle.

The gross sales margin is largely a function of the level of price competition faced by the individual firm. Firms which face very little competition, due either to isolation or institutional protection mechanisms, are able to exact a relatively high margin or sales. Firms which are situated in a market where price competition is a feasible strategy will find that gross margins will be driven to relatively lower levels.

The level of firm financial turnover Υ is both a macroeconomic and an institutional phenomenon. It is a function of macroeconomic conditions, since sharp unanticipated movements in sales will initially be made manifest as a reduction in the amount of sales to which a unit of investment generally gives rise. But more fundamentally, one major way institutionalist theory differs from neoclassical economic theory is that it does not portray the magnitude of firm net worth as the outcome of a large number of optimization decisions on the part of the firm's owners. It instead suggests that the ratio of firm sales to firm net worth is itself an institutional datum, a function of the institutional structures which define the firm: thus, the value of net worth is adjusted by the firm in order to remain within the rough boundaries of financial turnover dictated by the institutional context. The level of financial turnover is then partially endogenous, in that it depends upon the action of other firms, and partially exogenous, in that it is determined by the institutional structures of the firm. In this manner, financial turnover plays much the same role in the theory of the firm that physical turnover plays in the theory of physical production relations: it summarizes the state of institutional innovation in a quantitative measure.

Financial turnover gauges the ability of firms in general to control their various pecuniary inflows and outflows and thus subordinate those flows to their main objective of realizing profit. It is conventional wisdom that money which lies dormant is money not garnishing a return; and, the less 'dormant' the money, the greater the return. From the point of view of the individual firm, money has a 'velocity', although the meaning here is not the same as in the quantity theory of money. Velocity for the firm means the rapidity with which invested funds can complete their circuit through the marketplace and return to the firm; this velocity has to do with the capacity to realize profit. Whereas all firms would prefer to push their financial turnover to infinity, they are prevented from doing so by two considerations: (a) it would take the concerted co-operation of all firms, and would therefore contradict any existence of market competition; and (b) firms with higher-than-average financial turnovers are perceived as having higher variance in their rate of profit and therefore higher risk of failure. Thus the existence of a regime of competition and the potential for failure which it implies acts to keep firm rates of financial turnover within a relatively narrow range at any point in time.

An examination of the third component of the profit rate can elucidate how this process is supposed to occur. All of the firms in a particular institutional setting start with some roughly similar rates of financial turnover Υ. Some of the more aggressive firms would like to increase their profit rate by increasing their financial turnover, but they are constrained in doing so by the growth of the economy as a whole and by their present market share. The firm could change their situation by altering these constraints, mainly through an increased rate of investment. However, in order to increase the rate of investment, some inflow of funds must be increased, and the most common method of achieving this goal is for the firm to borrow the required funds. This increased level of liabilities in relation to the assets of the firm is known as increased leverage. This leverage is a two-edge sword, in that it allows the firm to shift the distribution of its money in flows nearer to the present, but at the same time it increases the firm's obligations which possess a time structure independent of the level of activity of the firm. If the rate of interest on these loans is less than the firm's existing rate of profit, and if the firm is successful in increasing its sales, then the result of this strategy will be an extended financial turnover (i.e., more sales relative to the same net worth) and a higher rate of profit. On the other hand, if the new investment cannot be translated into increased sales, the level of financial turnover will remain constant and the rate of profit will fall, subjecting the firm to possible risk of failure.

In the institutional theory of the macro-economy, this continuous pressure on the part of some firms to increase their financial turnover through increased leverage is taken as a given. If some firms manage to be persistently successful at this tactic, it will act to increase the institutional average level of financial turnover in the whole economy. If the tactic fails, largely because of fluctuations in the macroeconomy, these overextended firms are wiped out and the overall average level of financial turnover falls. This suggests that we expect the longterm evolutionary trend of financial turnover to be rising, as firms manage to institute a higher amount of leverage as the institutional norm, as well as to innovate new financial arrangements which minimize the amount of pecuniary investment required to give rise to a unit of sales.

We observed in chapter 5 that many economic theories have made attempts to avoid some logical contradiction in their treatment of the passage of time by arbitrarily altering the unit of time in the analysis: the von Neumann treatment of capital being an extreme example. In institutional economics, this option is explicitly foreclosed beforehand, because the time unit of the analysis is itself explicitly institutional. The unit of time against which both our parameters of physical turnover and financial turnover are measured is the average time interval between the firms' casting up of their accounts. The reason for this is that the firm must be able to act upon its perception of these critical quantities, and therefore the shortest period actively employed in the reevaluation of information defines the time frame of our analysis.

The fifth component of the institutional model of macroeconomic instability is the expression of the tendency towards any equalized rate of profit. This result can be expressed as an equilibrium condition that each individual firm's rate of profit will be equalized, and that this equalized global rate of profit holds some stable relation to the rate of accumulation in the physical economy. The most straightforward candidate for the equilibrium condition would be:

$$\pi_1 = \pi_2 = \pi_n = \lambda$$

This specification is not adequate for an institutional theory of the economy, however, because it presumes that the business sector will expand at the same rate as stocks are accumulated in the <u>whole society</u>, and of course, this need not be true. Even in our simple example, the economy is also defined to include the household/laborer sector, which also accumulates some stocks of physical goods. In a more complicated model, stocks of goods may also be present in any pre-modern economic sectors which may play an important role in the functioning of the overall economy even though they are not owned and controlled by firms. These considerations suggest that not all physical stocks are accumulated in the business sector: or, in different words, the aggregate of firms is not identical with the economy as a whole.

A more complex model could explore the possible intricacies of the relationship between the accumulation of business stocks and stocks in other sectors of the economy, but to simplify matters here we will assume there is a fixed proportional relationship between business stock accumulation and total accumulation. If business accumulate 'α' of all incremental additions to stocks, then our equilibrium condition becomes:

$$\pi_1 = \pi_2 = \pi_n = \alpha \lambda \qquad (6.7)$$

The parameter 'α' can be interpreted in such a way as to underscore the fact that institutionalist models of the economy are historically contingent, and therefore resist abstraction away from underlying institutional structures. Compare the equilibrium condition (6.7) with the conventional equilibrium condition in neo-Keynesian growth theory:

$$g = s\pi$$

where g is interpreted to be the growth rate of the accumulation of capital, s the rate of saving out of profits, and the rate of profit. [5]

This neo-Keynesian condition is generally derived from some interpretation of Keynesian equilibrium where aggregate voluntary savings must equal aggregate voluntary investment. The difficulties created by the Keynesian view of the world have been discussed in chapters three and five above: the measurement and significance of capital is suppressed; income, savings and consumption are inadequately defined concepts; the role of pecuniary relationships is not adequately separated and distinguished from that of the physical relationships; dividing social classes up according to their savings propensities does not capture the critical nuances of an economic system predicated upon institutional and class distinctions; and temporal relationships are obscured. The proposed equilibrium condition (6.7), while superficially similar to the Keynesian savings/investment identity, avoids all of its problems by not collapsing the origin of flows and their final destination into a single equation. Instead, it expresses the <u>consistency</u> of a large array of physical and social relations of reproduction with the accounting behavior of firms and their role in the larger economic society.

Therefore, equation (6.7) defines an institutional alternative to the conventional macroeconomic concept of 'saving'. The only meaning of 'savings' in institutional economics is that of a transfer of current physical resources to the business sector for use in whatever manner it sees fit. This transfer may come out of current production of the business sector or from other sectors, either voluntarily or involuntarily. From this vantage point, savings is not thought of as an exogenous behavioral propensity, but rather as a gross flow crossing analytical boundaries which separate capitalist firms from the rest of economic society. A society in which capitalist market organization occupies a very small niche will exhibit very weak claims upon the accumulation of economic stocks--in other words, α will be very small. Conversely, a society in which market organization has come to penetrate many facets of life will exhibit a relatively large value of the parameter α. Hence, equilibrium itself is historically contingent, in that it is conditional upon the level of development of market organization. Because of this, α could be dubbed the 'market penetration parameter'.

Full Equilibrium and the Four Stages of the Theory of Macroeconomic Instability

Any theory of macroeconomic instability consists of a well-defined specification of problem-free growth (or 'equilibrium') and an orderly taxonomy of potential modes of divergence from the problem-free state. The function of the four 'stages' of macroeconomic theory outlined in chapter one above will be to provide the framework of our (hopefully) orderly taxonomy. These stages, which are little more than steps along the path of increased complexity and sophistication are: (1) simple proportional expansion without feedback and hysteresis, (2) explicit feedback between the past values of sub-units of the economy and present rates of expansion of the whole, (3) the development of the rationale for an explicit dichotomy between exogenous and endogenous phenomena, and (4) the transformation of the parameter/variable dichotomy into a continuum.

If we substitute expression (6.6) into expression (6.8), we find that for each firm equilibrium requires that:

$$\gamma_\alpha = (1/\alpha) \{[r \cdot \Upsilon] - i(\ell/1-\ell)\} = \lambda \qquad (6.9)$$

This states that all of the financial relationships which constitute the rate of profit of the firm--the profit margin, the rate of financial turnover, the extent of leverage and the interest rate--must be consistent with the historical extent of the penetration of the market in society and rate to which that society is accumulating physical stocks. If λ, the rate of stock accumulation, could potentially assume any numerical value, then it would be a trivial matter to bring rates of profit into line with rates of physical accumulation. The fundamental problem, however, is that rates of physical accumulation are constrained by the exsisting physical and social relations of production, as well as immediate past levels of sectoral output. These constraints are summarized by the myriad considerations which constitute the model written as expression (6.5).

Suppose that the historical situation provided us with values for all the variables on the left-hand side of (6.9); given further the technology and social relations of (6.5), we could solve for levels of output which would produce the implied level of λ. But when we impose the further restrictions (as part of the further <u>definition</u> of equilibrium) that the feasible values of $\overline{\lambda \text{ must}}$ be positive—contracting economies are ruled out—and that λ must be continuously sustainable—that is, the economy should be able to reproduce that rate of growth indefinitely—then the permissable range of values of λ is reduced to a single number, which may not necessarily correspond to the rate warranted by the other variables in (6.9). Although we shall avoid Harrod's conception of the 'warrented' and 'natural' rates of growth, there are some similarities in this procedure. First we explore the separate determinants of the rates of exapansion; then we note that there are no simple mechanisms to act to bring the different rates of accumulation into conformity; and then, finally, we shall explore the dynamics of feedback between the varying rates, which may result in a conception of 'quasi-stability'.

Let us sketch a proof of the existence and uniqueness of the rate of expansion of a physical economy like that of (6.5) which corresponds to our expanded notion of equilibrium. Letting $\mu = (1/\lambda)$, we can rewrite equation (6.5) as:

$$x = \lambda(I-A)^{-1}Bx$$
$$\mu Ix = (I-A)^{-1}Bx$$
$$0 = ((I-a)^{-1}B - \mu I)$$

Each element of A, and therefore B, is greater than or equal to zero by definition. If A is 'productive' (that is, one gets back more output than one must use as input of any particular good), then the matrix (I-A) has a strictly positive diagonal and semi-negative off-diagonal elements. The 'productive' condition [6] is sufficient to insure that (I-A) is non-singular and that $(I-A)^{-1} > 0$. It is then apparent that $(I-A)^{-1}B$ is also a non-negative matrix. One further assumption we shall make is that the matrix $(I-A)^{-1}B$ is indecomposable: that is, we assume that at least one input is used either directly or indirectly in all production processes. Since labor is included in the matricies A and B, this assumption is fairly straightforward. Given these assumptions, the Frobenius theorems [7] state that: a matrix $(I-A)^{-1}B$ has a dominant characteristic root μ^* which is real and positive, and associated with μ^* there is a characteristic vector $x^*>0$. All other characteristic roots of $(I-A)^{-1}B$ will be less than or equal to μ^* in modulus. If any element of $(I-A)^{-1}B$ rises, than μ^* also rises. The scalar μ^* will be called the Frobenius root of $(I-A)^{-1}B$.

The Frobenius theorems for nonnegative indecomposable square matricies are often interpreted in the economic literature as existence proofs for a nonnegative set of equilibrium prices and outputs corresponding to a balanced rate of physical accumulation λ^* in the context of linear production models. [8] In the case of this particular model, the Frobenius theorems also directly relate changes in the turnover times τ_{ij} to changes in the warranted balanced rate of physical accumulation. If the time any individual good is required to be present in any single production process is reduced, it reduces the maximal eigenvalue μ^* and therefore raises the warranted rate of physical accumulation λ^*.

Thus we have shown that an eqilibrium rate of expansion of the physical model (6.5) exists, and it is unique. We have also developed some comparative static results that any phenomenon which speeds physical turnover raises this equilibrium rate, be it increased intensity of the labor process, increased capacity utilization, or any other phenomenon commonly confused with economies of scale. Veblen's antinomy between the industrial and pecuniary processes is expressed in this model by the substitution of λ^* on the right hand side of (6.9), as the rate of expansion warranted by the situation within the production process. Tranquil and unproblematic growth would require that profit margins, rates of financial turnover and leverage all adjust to this warranted rate. If our discussion of the determinants of these variables is accurate, then there exists no simple feedback mechanism which will bring this situation about; and, indeed, there are structural pressures to cause endemic divergence. Competition may act to drive the profit margin below its warranted value. Pressures to increase leverage and financial turnover may drive these variables above their warranted values. Further market penetration may render all of the existing values of all three variables inappropriate for equilibrium expansion. Sharp fluctuations of interest rates, which we provisionally treat as given in this system, may also disrupt tranquil equilibrium. It would seem that full tranquil equilibrium would be a fortuitous and unusual event.

If full equilibrium is unlikely, what does the actual operation of the system look like? Armed with our definition of full equilibrium as a benchmark for comparison, we can now inquire into the nature of macroeconomic instability.

STAGE ONE: DISPROPORTIONALITY

Stage one theories are distinguished by their tendency to portray the disequilibrium movements of component variables as exactly offsetting one another so that the 'fundamental' determinants of the aggregate level of activity remain unaltered. These rudimentary theories decouple the disequilibrium time paths of particular variables from the time path of the economy as a whole. The condition that the full tranquil eqilibrium path of the economy be independent of fluctuations of output is extremely stringent, although this stringency is only mode manifest in a model which allows many possible feedbacks of that sort.

In our present model, constancy of the full equilibrium path requires the following conditions: Output in period t must be completely determined by output levels in period t-1; and this 'stationarity' of the economic structure can only mean that there is no role for inventory accumulation in any production process. Further, there can be no response of capacity utilization or physical turnover to changes in output level. Firms cannot alter their balance sheets or financial turnover in any manner in response to output fluctuations. Finally, the extent of market penetration of the society cannot be influenced by fluctuations in output. A mechanistic economy, which is the only kind of economy which can be described by difference equations, is a gaggle of zombies; or more aptly, it is a set of billiard balls colliding on a level surface. It is this conception which has prompted much of the opposition to orthodox macroeconomic theories which we have surveyed in previous chapters.

It is surprizing that one can still derive output fluctuations from such a restrictive set of assumptions; but then, neoclassical economists have been doing it for years. An example would be a difference equation derived from our production model such as:

$$x(t) = (I-A)^{-1} Bx(t-1) \qquad (6.10)$$

Suppose the vector of outputs in period t-1 diverges from the balanced growth path, perhaps due to some 'shock' to the system. In period t the output of some industries rises, while that in others falls. Aggregate output and employment can either rise or fall, depending upon the underlying method of aggregation. (This by itself may suggest why GNP is such a misleading macroeconomic indicator.) Eventually, in the absence of further 'shocks', all sectors converge to the uniform overall growth rate of output of $1/\lambda* = \mu*$, with the speed of convergence depending upon the spectral characteristics of the matrix $(I-A)^{-1}B$. Output and employment fluctuations leave no lasting imprint upon the economy: it is in this sense that they are decoupled from the fundamental determinants of economic growth.

Stage one theories are homilies about Discomfort in Paradise: some ill-defined exogenous 'disturbances' impinging upon a theoretical structure which functions as a homeostatic device for righting all wrongs. This conception is embodied in the mathematics of difference/differential equations, which divides the analysis into unexplained 'initial conditions' and the passive mechanical response to those conditions. There is no real fear in Paradise, and that is why there are no changes of inventories, capacity utilization, etc, etc. Stage one theories are rather banal representatives of the nature of the economic process. Nevertheless, a Stage one portrayal of the economy is a necessary prerequisite for an acceptable theory of macroeconomic instability, because one must have a clear idea of success before one begins to define failure.

STAGE TWO: ENDOGENOUS ALTERATION OF FULL EQUILIBRIUM

A stage two theory introduces history into the timeless mechanisms of the preceding model by endowing the actors with an independent ability to act. The clearest discussion of the difference between these two classes of models has been provided by David Levine's work on the theory of markets. [9] He demonstrates that both classical and Walrasian economics portray the market as realizing a result which is already fully determined prior to the economic process. The 'natural' fundamentals are the true determinants of prices and outputs, so there is no role for the firm, other than to passively ratify those pre-existing conditions. This is illustrated by the activities of firms in our stage one model in (6.10): There they are supernumeraries.

Levine suggests that one way to escape this straightjacket it to deny that markets are even potentially capable of organizing production: [10]

> ...consider the production requisites of the firm. To the extent that these are made up exclusively of circulating capital, the productive life of the firm is essentially consistent with the market forms implied in the idea of market clearing price...To subject the market in [long-lived] plant and equipment to the conditioning of market-clearing price would be tantamount to making the depreciation and retrieval of value invested largely accidental...

In this view, firms exist in order to resist a regimen of market-clearing prices, and to transform the market in such a manner such that they survive the vagaries of market fluctuations. It is impossible to capture this aspect of firms in a model which does not consider the passage of time and evolutionary processes, because the firm exists to transcend the 'fundamental' determinants of growth. A model could begin to convey this vision of how an economy works by allowing firms to change the equilibrium level of activity through the process of responding to macroeconomic fluctuations. For the purposes of illustration rather than exhaustive enumeration of these types of phenomena, we shall briefly discuss two analytical models built upon the foundations already laid out: an augmented investment multiplier/accelerator, and an inventory/capacity utilization adjustor.

In order to expand the model, let Π be a vector of individual firm profit rates $\pi_1 \ldots \pi_{m-1}$. Let us then rewrite the output adjustment equation (6.10) as mediated by some function of past firm profit rates:

$$x(t) = f(\Pi(t-1))(I-A)^{-1}Bx(t-1) \qquad (6.11)$$

This version of the model resembles most convetional multiplier/accelerator models in that investment is keyed to immediate past realizations, and tends to 'overshoot' levels of production warranted by those past realizations. The extent of this divergence will of course depend upon the behavior implied by the function f, but that is not the issue here. First, unless the function f converges to the identity matrix as profit rates become uniform, then the system has no stable equilibrium growth rate. Secondly, and more importantly, if <u>any</u> of the determinants of the firm profit rates are made partial functions of past production (so that finance and production become interdependent), the system develops the tendency to wander off any tranquil growth path. It is in this way that finance and prices enter into macroeconomic determination; but there are no means by which they can convey sufficient information to direct investment back towards the previous configuration of full equilibrium. To put it a different way, there is no market which can act to coordinate financial and physical turnover through the instrumentality of a static market-clearing equilibrium. This illustrates Levine's contention that it would be suicide for a firm to passively accept market-clearing prices. Instead it must resort to the transformation of its temporal conditions of production and finance in order to persist and grow. The problem for the firm, however, is that survival of the individual firm is not identical to survival of the macroeconomy.

This consideration leads us to the second amendment of the model. A firm is not constrained to blindly follow the dictates of its current technology and current flow of sales. When confronted with an unexpected contraction of its market, most firms initially try to stabilize price by building up stocks of inventories and lowering capacity utilization. Both of these phenomena make their appearance in this model as a <u>lengthening</u> of the duration of time which inputs reside in the production process; i.e., the τ_{ij}, terms in the T martix increase in magnitude. As we have demonstrated above, any increase in the turnover times monotonically reduces the full equilibrium growth rate of the economy. The result of this behavior is that <u>there is no longer any technologically determined benchmark of equilibrium growth</u>. It is the dilemma of all capitalist adjustment policies that what is rational from the viewpoint of the individual firm is not rational from the vantage of the system as a whole (and <u>vice versa</u>). This is the Achille's heel of the conviction that prices in markets convey sufficient appropriate information to coordinate activity.

For the purposes of illustration, suppose that there is some regular behavioral reaction function on the part of firms which encompasses the response to sharp divergences of sales from trend:

$$\tau_{ij}(t) = g(dx_i(t-1)/dt) \qquad (6.12)$$

$$\frac{dg}{dx} < 0 \qquad \frac{d^2g}{dx^2} < 0$$

The economic intuition behind this function g is that sales fluctuations are met initially by changes in capacity utilization and inventory accumulation in the opposite directions, but that more extreme or extended divergences from trend are coped with through other means. Such behavior makes the coefficients of the B matrix endogenous, which in turn results in fluctuations of the equilibrium growth rate $\lambda *$ in the same direction as the divergence from the previous trend. The second derivative of the function g prevents the system from careening from infinite growth to infinite contraction, but the system can no longer be said to have a technologically determined equilibrium growth path. Instead, it wobbles in a non-mechanical manner within a corridor [11] defined by the function g, in conjunction with the other determinants of fluctuation which we have already surveyed. Combining (6.11) and (6.12), we arrive at a model where financial variables and output are determined siumultaneously (defining sales as output minus inventory accumulation), and yet there is no exogenously determined equilibrium path to which firms passively correspond.

Rather than perceiving the fact that this system cannot be 'solved' for some unique, optimal equilibrium growth path as a drawback, institutional economic theory should display such results as the logical position of a school of thought which consciously rejects the ahistorical and reductionist predispositions of neoclassical economics. `Models' in this context, do not serve the same tasks of explanation because 'explanation' itself is paradigm-specific. [13] In this particular case, many of the parameters of the model represent combinations of social and physical considerations: the τ_{ij}, for instance, measure the lifetime of goods in production, but that duration in turn is the outcome of decisions about inventory accumulation, capacity utilization the intensity of the work process and other social relations. There is no single efficient or optimal method of production because there is no 'natural' maximum. The actors in this drama write their own scripts.

STAGE THREE: ENDOGENEITY AND EXOGENEITY

The main function of an articulated distinction between exogeneity and endogeneity of phenomena in a well-developed economic model is to postulate why a system, once it gets into equlilibrium, is eventually thrust out of it again. We have observed this theoretical mandate in discussions in chapter three of econometricians who appeal to the random shocks appended to their equations in order to explain divergences from equilibrium. For such econometricians, the world is divided into a mechanistic (endogenous) 'economy', and the rest of the world, which according to some appeal to the central limit theorem posses certain (exogenous) stochastic properties. These shocks are the only thing which prevent the time path of the economic variables from assuming stable equilibrium positions. Fluctuations are explained by the inherently unexplainable.

It would seem a better idea to redefine the role of exogenous phenomena as influences impinging upon the macroeconomy which fall outside of the projct of developing a _model_ of macroeconomic instability, but do not exist beyond the pale of explanation by economists. Mathematical models, by their very nature, have great difficulty in explaining change and innovation. [14] Nonreversible and unique events which constitute the march of history should be included in explanations of macroeconomic instability, but with the understanding that the techniques employed in those explanations should be those of historian rather than those of the physicist.

An illustration of this reconceptualization of the exogenous/endogenous distinction can be sketched with the help of our present model. The model takes the institution of the frim as fixed and given. The rule structures that govern the meaning of firm ownership, the content and significance of accounts, the legal claims to assets and liabilities, the relations of power and hierarchy in the workplace, and so much else are exogenous in the sense that they cannot be modelled with difference equations, but they clearly can influence macroeconomic stability. The rise of unions, for instance, alters both the wage bundle and the average intensity of the work process, which in turn alter the coefficients of the A and B matricies. Unions would not exist without capitalism, but they can hardly be said to be determinate results of that organizational form.

In our model, the values of our physical turnover parameters τ cannot be understood in mathematical isolation. The level of the τ's in any given country, is the product of innumerable social and historical forces. One such social innovation was the invention of adequate indoor lighting (mainly gas lights) which allowed round-the-clock utilization of industrial buildings and concommitant large-scale production machinery. Another was the decline of "Saint Monday" in England in the nineteenth century: the gradual abolition of a social institution of absenteeism from industrial work patterns. [15] Both are examples of a speeding up of physical turnover through time, but as in the case of financial turnover, there have also been counter-tendencies. In fact, the element of class struggle within the boundaries of the workplace is simultaneously captured by this turnover time variable. 'Soldiering', waves of strike activity, unions' contractual arrangements about conditions of work, and a host of other phenomena are institutions which lengthen average turnover time, offsetting the drift of the evolution of Western social structures towards more 'efficient' and 'rational' workplaces. In the face of these conflicting trends, the average level of physical turnover must be determined from its historical preconditions.

Again, in parallel with financial turnover time, if the exact level of physical turnover were purely insititutional, it would be a rare coincidence that sustained growth were ever achieved in the history of capitalist expansion. A degree of freedom in turnover in the physical sphere is achieved by the behavior of entrepreneurs in varying their capacity utilization of plant and equipment. It will be recalled we suggested that, under a neoclassical regime, it makes no rational sense to vary capacity utilization, especially when recent captial theory debates have been taken into account. Conversely, in the model we are proposing, the ability to vary capacity utilization, in combination with the ability to alter the financial leverage of the firm, is the primary reason why capitalist macroeconomic growth has been as stable as it has been historically. These behaviors offset to a certain degree the gross imbalances between institutional turnover parameters, technological possiblities and markups constrained by inter-capitalist competition. It is through these behaviors that the social relations of the turnover times move more often than not in relative harmony, constrained to remain within the corridor of quasi-stability discussed in the last section.

One should not be lulled by words like 'harmony' or 'stability' into believing that these mechanisms of growth lead to anything necessarily like socially desirable ends, however. Imagine, for a moment, the tranquil equilibrium of an ecomony given a technology, the markup, and the existing institutions of financial turnover. Suppose because of the absence of worker militance or the existence of social movements like "Taylorism", the institutionally determined average physical turnover rates were much more rapid than the implied equilibrium rate. Entrepreneurs, faced with ever-growing stocks of unsold inverntories, lay off workers and reduce capacity utilization in an effort to bring physical turnover in line with the other parameters of the system. Here we have what seems to be an ailing economy: workers unemployed, plant lying idle, and investment drooping because of disappointing financial rates of profit. A perfect capital market with perfectly divisible machines and perfectly mobile investment would make no difference in this situation: there would still be less than full employment, because of the historically determined levels of average turnover. The 'quasi-stability' of which we write involves the macroeconomic compatibility of real and financial accumulation, and not the welfare of the individual actors swept up in the system.

This conception of exogenous explanation reverses the usual procedure in 'cliometrics': here the historical research is an indispensable part of the model, rather than the employing of the model to explain the "history". [16] A prime illustration of this redefinition of the role of exogeneity is demonstrated in our treatment of the ratio of sales to equity at the level of the firm, which we have identified, after Veblen, as the index of the rate of financial turnover Υ. We have outlined a number of ways a firm might alter the character of its cash flows in order to increase its short-run profit rate. The constraints on these actions are quite fluid: they involve the willingness of other sectors to change both the level and time-pattern of liabilities; the relative ease in contracting new debt; the shifting nature of the balance sheet as a convention and its function of relating net worth to cash flows. Many of these activities appear immediately to set into motion counterbalancing forces. New debt increases liabilities in the future. A sharp increase in the profit rate is supposedly followed by a commensurate increase in balance sheet equity, bringing the profit rate back down. Undoubtedly it is the short-run and apparently self-correcting nature of these transactions and conventions which lead most contemporary economic theorists to overlook finance entirely as a source of macroeconomic disturbance. This is often stated as the truism that someone's asset is someone else's liability, and that in the aggregate these must cancel out. Even Keynes, the archtypical financier/rentier, gave tremendous weight to the demand and supply for money as currency, but denied the function of money as finance. The <u>General Theory</u>, so dependent of investment and its return for its construction, paid precious little theoretical attention to how the investment and the return were determined from the capitalist's point of view. When subsequently pressed on this point, he wrote in a rebuttal in the Economic Journal: [17]

> ...finance is essentially a revolving fund. It employs no savings. It is, for the community as a whle, only a bookkeeping transaction. As soon as it is 'used' in the sense of being expended, the lack of liqi=uidity is automatically made good and the readiness to become unliquid is available to be used over again. Finance covering the interregnum is, to use a phrase employed by bankers in a more limited context, necessarily 'self-liquidating' for the community taken as a whole.

The reason Keynes and so many other economic theorists ignore the financial sphere is that they are inevitably abstracting from the passage of time in their models. At any point in time, the entries on the left- and right-hand sides of the ledger do cancel: that is not the point. The ability to shift the distribution of flows in time is the crux of the matter. Most theorists assume the 'returns' are fixed by technology, the hand of God, or by more imaginative means; to take more of the flow now in 'consumption' means having less flow later. But if the force and rationale of the system resides in accumulation and the increase of production, and not consumption, then to lay claim to more of a flow now means having more over all time if the processes of production and finance are functioning smoothly.

Neoclassical theory in general, and Modigliani-Miller type theses in particular, assert that there can be no divergence of financial flows from physical flows. In this way, neoclassical predilections actively hinder the study of finance as a potential source of capitalist instability. Even if one accepts that there exists a full complement of spot and futures markets which eventually force net cash flow into line with the value of net physical product there is no market, real or imagined, which can operate along the time dimension of stocks to equate the values of the stock of financial equity to the stock of physical holdings valued at equilibrium prices. To put it another way, there is no market in physical and financial turnover, since they cannot be traded, one for another. Actual markets can only deal in flows, by definition.

How, then, is the economic system kept from an ever-divergent path from equilibrium? In the sphere of finance, the answer revolves around the pecuniary institutions of capitalist ownership and the existence of leverage as a contrivance which adjusts turnover. In our model, we have deduced that the value of financial equity must move in a fixed relationship with the level of activity in tranquil equilibrium. Yet we have also assumed that there is continual extra-market pressure to increase the amount of claims on financial flows. These claims are legal titles, the nature of which are contingent upon historical precedent and political power. Changes in these claims are changes in the amount of net worth <u>per unit</u> cash flow. It is the role of financial institutions in causing this species of macroeconomic fluctuation, which is conceptualized as exogenous. [18]

The significance of financial institutions may best be motivated by a short detour through history. Table 1 presents condensed balance sheet and income statement information from the U.S. manufacturing sector over the last forty years. When the highly erratic rate of profit is broken down into its markup and turnover components, certain regularities become apparent. The Great Depression was characterized by a massive deterioration in the rate of financial turnover, which was only revived through the onset of World War Two and the government largesse of war finance. Until 1970, the rate of turnover was strikingly stable. This stability was maintained through growth cycle and recession, through changing market conditions and rates of growth, and through fluctuating market prices. This pattern suggests, at least to the author, that the rate of financial turnover Υ is not as much a market phenomenon as it is an institutional one.

The institutions controlling financial claims are myriad, and have a long history of development. Some of these institutions, such as limited liability, tiered debt, goodwill accounts, insurance, and the whole ongoing evolution of banking practices with regards to industrial finance, act to increase the normal or average level of sales per unit net worth. Other institutions, such as preference shares, trusts, holding companies, 'splits' and most governmental regulation of accounting equity tend to reduce the average level of sales per unit net worth. The tension arises between groups who wish to increase cash flows given the <u>status quo</u> and those groups who press for increased claims to existing flows. The legal evolution of contract law in various countries plays a large role in the determination of financial turnover, although the direction of the influence is conditional on the strength of the groups influencing legal innovation. Some of these institutions are quite old; while others are much more recent. The spread of preference shares in England from 1770 to 1850 or the coming of limited liability in the mid-nineteenth century started as <u>pis aller</u> of groups desperate for a new source of liquidity, but rapidly mushroomed into legal forms which had an immense impact on the financial rate of profit in these periods. A more recent example is provided in Table II by Japan, the capitalist <u>Wunderkind</u> of the post war period. Japan, unlike

TABLE I

MANUFACTURING SECTOR AGGREGATE BALANCE SHEETS AND INCOME STATEMENTS, FROM IRS RETURNS, 1931 - 1970

Year	Net Profits Before Tax	Net Worth	Sales & Oth. Rec.	Markup	Υ Financial Turnover	π Profit Rate %
1931	-218	38369	39472	neg	1.02	-.5
1932	-1039	35428	28878	neg	.81	-2.9
1933	355	34914	31682	1.1	.90	1.0
1934	1387	38131	40581	3.4	1.06	3.6
1935	2494	37611	47473	5.2	1.26	6.6
1936	3636	38467	55378	6.5	1.43	9.4
1937	3686	41239	61560	5.9	1.49	8.9
1938	1615	41260	50489	3.1	1.22	3.9
1939	3571	42438	57603	6.1	1.35	8.4
1940	5313	44163	66246	8.0	1.50	12.0
1941	10310	48398	91606	11.2	1.89	21.3
1942	13554	55071	117895	11.4	2.14	24.6
1943	16428	60688	144560	11.3	2.38	27.0
1944	14754	63070	152673	9.6	2.42	23.3
1945	10179	64150	140155	7.2	2.18	15.8
1946	11508	67589	137087	8.3	2.02	17.0
1947	16477	76674	178173	9.2	2.32	21.4
1948	17985	84083	198260	9.0	2.35	21.3
1949	14158	88885	185285	7.6	2.08	15.9
1950	23608	97041	218272	10.8	2.25	24.3
1951	24697	104725	252956	9.7	2.41	23.5
1952	20228	109497	258969	7.8	2.36	18.4
1953	21290	113814	278495	7.6	2.44	18.7
1954	18194	119903	264966	6.8	2.20	15.1
1955	25816	130993	303211	8.5	2.31	19.7
1956	24504	138988	316697	7.7	2.27	17.6
1975	22677	146275	330749	6.8	2.26	15.5
1958	18424	154850	326940	5.6	2.11	11.8
1959	25026	161890	363157	6.8	2.24	15.4
1960	22200	169069	371093	5.9	2.19	13.1
1961	22538	176516	377580	5.9	2.13	12.7
1962	25386	n.a.	407865	6.2	*2.20	*13.6
1963	28825	193461	429507	6.7	2.22	14.9
1964	32552	205362	464820	7.0	2.26	15.8
1965	39509	221578	514719	7.6	2.32	17.8
1966	43490	237229	571009	7.6	2.40	18.3
1967	39486	258509	590822	6.6	2.28	15.2
1968	43560	276766	648965	6.7	2.34	15.7
1969	40386	304196	710084	5.6	2.33	13.2
1970	30456	313684	722911	4.2	2.30	9.7

n.a.: not available.
*Estimates by interpolation by author. 1931-1933 are derived from a separate sample and benchmarked to 1934.
Source: U.S. Historical Statistics; 1957 edit., p. 582; supplement and 1976 edition.

TABLE 2

JAPANESE MANUFACTURING SECTOR FINANCIAL RATIOS

Year	Markup	Turnover Υ	Profit Rate π
1954	5.4	2.7	14.2
1955	5.0	2.8	14.2
1956	6.4	3.3	21.3
1957	6.0	3.3	20.0
1958	4.8	2.8	13.7
1959	6.5	3.2	21.3
1960	7.2	3.5	25.6
1961	n.a.	n.a.	n.a.
1962	5.2	2.9	15.2
1963	5.8	3.1	18.4
1964	5.2	3.2	17.0
1965	4.2	3.3	14.0
1966	5.3	3.7	20.0
1967	6.0	4.3	25.9
1968	5.8	4.5	26.4
1969	6.1	4.8	29.4
1970	5.4	4.8	26.1
1971	3.7	4.5	16.9
1972	4.5	4.7	21.4
1973	5.9	5.6	33.3
1974	3.3	6.0	19.9

n.a.: Not available to author.

Source: Nihon Ginko (Bank of Japan Research Dept.), Financial Statements of Main Industrial Corporations, various issues; calculated from consoldiated balance sheets of a varying sample of corporations.

the US, has recently been sympathetic to a very close financial working relationship between banking and manufacturing concerns, coupled with an avowed openness to flexibility with respect to financial innovation. [19] The result has been a secular rise in the rate of financial turnover, barely restrained by recessions, to a level higher than that in any other Western conutry investigated. This institutional difference between Japan and the US has produced widely differing rates of profit in the two countries, and therefore very different rates of growth.

The most plausible intrepretation of these diverse cases is that the average or normal value of equity per unit cash flow in the economy is exogenous to our mathematical model and is a product of the evolution of financial institutions in the particular historical cultural environment. The absolute rate cannot be predicted as the outcome of a constrained maximization calculation, although we can identify the direction a particular innovation may have on the existing rate. A severe debt-deflation, such as occured in the 1930's, which drastically reduces the value of net worth in response to a sharp abatement of cash flow, may also be thought of as another of these institutional innovations, having to do with bankruptcy laws instead of institutions built around 'going concerns'.

The fundamental long-run character of the turnover relation is very important to the theory of business cycles. Gross value of net worth will fluctuate with cash flow in the short run, but the average rate of financial turnover will move much more slowly in reaction to changing circumstances. Financial innovation is characterized by appreciable inertia, which carries the macroeconomy further from sequential equilibrium growth rates. The nature of this innovation varies between nations, making equalization of the rate of profit, and therefore of rates of growth, very unlikely. The international disproportionalities will exacerbate fluctuations in sales, especially in countries heavily dependent on foreign trade. Institutional pressures are relatively slow to percolate through the balance sheets of the economy, by which time objective conditions in the real sector may have changed. It is the differential turnover times in the real and financial spheres and the relative speeds of reaction of these rates of turnover which are the loci of capitalist disequilibrium which we identify with the aid of our revised concept of exogeneity.

If financial turnover were solely institutional, it would then be difficult to see how capitalist economies ever managed to experience sustained growth. The situation of the individual capitalist unit, or firm, is not without some leeway. When Veblen identified volitional changes in leverage as driving a wedge between the real and financial spheres, he viewed it as being purely disruptive of growth. Contrary to Veblen, we would like to suggest that small changes in leverage are the primary reaction mechanism available to the individual unit when it is faced with disequilibrium rates of turnover. We therefore divide movements in financial turnover into long-run institutional changes and short-run balance sheet changes amenable to mathematical description.

STAGE FOUR: THE PARAMETER/VARIABLE CONTINUUM

Stage four theories have been a rarity in economic thought, mainly because economists have been unwilling to admit that there is very little that remains constant about human society over time. The predisposition to mimic the natural sciences, with their fundamental postulates of the constancy of natural law, has precluded economists from admitting that most of their parameters are not constant over time.

A theory of instability must recognize that, once the distinction is made between exogenous and endogenous phenomena, there are certain endogenous movements of the system which operate outside of the time frame of the actors in the model. Because these changes move relatively slowly, they can be included in a model as parameters, which nonetheless are altered in value over long periods of time. In this construction, the model which we have developed in previous sections has no actual parameters, but only variables of differeing speeds of endogenous change. In the model at hand, a large number of parameters have already been designated as possessing this historical character. To recapitulate the list, they are: the market penetration parameter α, the technological flow parameters a_{ij}, the labor intensity paramters τ_{im}, the own-labor parameter a_{mm}, and the wage stock paramters τ_{mi}. Each of these classes of relationships are transformed by the expansion of the capitalist system and influence its stability.

The clearest examples of a stage four theory of instability would be one dependent upon the market penetration parameter. It is an often unconscious assumption that any economic model referes only to a capitalist mode of production, thus implicitly ignoring the simultaneous co-existence of non-capitalist modes, often even situated cheek-by-jowl within the same national or geographic entity. This unconscious process of abstraction is detrimental to a theory of macroeconomic instability, because the interaction of the capitalist and noncapitalist spheres may introduce a structural source of disturbance to the capitalist sphere. This source could be the relationship between developed or underdeveloped countries, or between the sphere of domestic production and that of the monetized economy, or between the urban sphere and the self-sufficient hinterland. The market penetration parameter and own labor input parameter are attempts to incorporate such considerations explicitly into the model. We expect the magnitude of both parameters to rise in trend as the capitalist system expands into both external and internal social spheres which were previously organized along different lines. This expansion, which is merely a corollary of capitalist growth, has a feedback effect upon future sustainable rates of growth, thus reinforcing the institutionalist insight that social systems must exhibit hysteresis, and that no system can ever precisely exhibit the same behavior twice.

The primary conclusion of this entire discussion is that an institutionalist theory has absolutely no prior expectation of "stable", "balanced", "vonNeumann ray", "turnpike" growth. The theory of growth and the theory of instability are two sides of the same coin. This theory reverses the conventional problematic of discussions of the macroeconomy. Instead of inquiring how it is that law-governed economies periodically diverge from their natural intrinsic stability, an institutionalist theory asks how is it that such a non-teleological and loosely interrelated system managed historically to achieve the growth which it did. The purpose of the model is to suggest certain potential answers to this question. For example, perhaps the output and capcity adjustment behavior of firms in a certain early historical period acted to encourage stability. Alternatively, perhaps the historical movements of certain stage four parameters, although causally independent, acted fortuitously to cancel out each others' tendency to push the system away from a moderate sustainable rate of growth. Perhaps, rather, certain exogenous social innovations were induced in reaction to percieved instability. While the model can suggest many potential reasons why growth has been sustained over three centuries of capitalist organization, the story can only be fully constituted through an historical narrative.

CHAPTER SEVEN

THE BIRTH OF THE BUSINESS CYCLE, PART II

What kind of economy does the model in chapter six describe? The five main characteristics are (1) the sale of human labor by the owner on the same basis as other commodities to (2) a financial entity called a firm and defined by its balance sheet, for the purpose of the accumulation of profit through (3) control of the organization and time structure of physical production and (4) manipulation of balance sheet and cash flow variables under the firm's control; and (5) the tendency of interfirm and intrafirm competition to bring about an equalized financial rate of profit on the money value of firms. It is the contention of this chapter that this bundle of attributes, sufficiently fleshed out by institutional particulars, heralds the historical manifestation of the modern macroeconomy. The absence of any one or more of these attributes defines the premodern economy; in which case a separate and distinct framework is needed to theoretically discuss 'economics'.

These characteristics may serve to locate the modern economy in time and space. Institutions which embody these characteristics start in localized enclaves and only eventually spread across whole continents. A fully cohesive theory of macroeconomic instability would search out these enclaves, irrespective of national borders, and treat them as individual instances of the same process. Unfortunately, due to chauvinism and linguistic barriers, most histories are confined by national boundaries. This obstacle, in part, confines this study to enclaves within one set of national boundaries: those of England and Scotland; although a survey of institutional innovation would reveal that parallel developments could be found in other parts of northwestern Europe. By concentrating on a national history, however, we may become quite specific about the timing of the arrival of the postulated institutional framework. Specifically, the birth of the business cycle may be located in England soon after the Glorious Revolution, in the late seventeenth or early eighteenth century.

The presence of a wage-earning class of substantial size in the England of 1688 is a fact accepted by many economic historians. We possess a contemporary estimate of the relative distribution of classes in that year thanks to Gregory King's <u>Natural and Political Observations</u>. The proportion of families compromising each social group were: [1]

cottagers & paupers	29%
laboring people & seamen	30%
merchants & shopkeepers	4%
farmers	11%
freeholders	13%
military	3%
artisans & handicrafts	4%
aristocracy, gentlemen, etc.	6%

Realizing that most cottagers and paupers were landless agricultural wage labor, at least seasonally, at least half of all families had participated in the wage system directly by this period. [2] But within England the wage system was concentrated in certain areas, such as the counties circling and south of London, the midlands, and parts of southern Scotland and the Teeside; these will provide us with most of our examples of the new economic structures.

The conscious pursuit of profit presumes both the existence of the means and the awareness of the quest. The change in economic mentality in the late seventeenth century has been noted by both political philosophers and the institutionalist school of economics. Thorstein Veblen traced the modern notion of business property back to the confrontation of two contrary ideas: the first, the customary authority of medieval times, which portrayed property rights as mere stewardship linked to near-immutable status relations; and the second, the natural right doctrine of appropriated property as the result of expended labor. Veblen saw the substitution of the latter for the former reach its climax in England in the controversy between Sir Robert Filmer and John Locke in the revolution of 1688. "The free workmen, master of his own motions and with discretion as to what he would turn his efforts to, if anything, had by Locke's time, become an habitual fact in the life of the English community to such a degree that free labor was accepted as the fundamental factor in all human economy, and as the presumptive original fact in industry." [3] We should recall that this 'freedom' was not that of actual whim, but a presumptive freedom on the part of the legal structure. Veblen seemed to think that the existence of this wage-labor force in the last decade of the seventeenth century had transformed habitual modes of thought: "Under the agrarian-manorial regime of the Middle Ages, it was not felt that the wealth of the large owners must, as a matter of course, increase by virtue of the continued employment of what they already had in hand....Particularly, it was not the sense of the men of the time that wealth so employed must increase at any stated, 'ordinary' rate per time unit....In industrial pursuits, profits apparently came to figure as a regular and ordinary incident only when the industries came to be carried on a mercantile basis by relatively large employers working with hired labor." [4]

The intellectual hurdle that had to be cleared before the implications of the altered mode of consciousness could run their course was the widespread disbelief that economic activity was something other than a zero-sum game. A characteristic dogma of premodern society was that trade and industry were inherently sterile, a dogma which was preserved well into the eighteenth century, embodied in the economic theories of the Physiocrats. Most statements of this belief employed agricultural metaphors, and had an ancient lineage. The medieval scholastics depreciated trade because money could have no natural offspring; Locke simply asserted the contraposition of the metaphor, in his comparison of money with land. [5] A recent historian of seventeenth century economic thought observes a shift from the static goal of punitive trade to the dynamic possibilities of expansion in the rash of pamphleteering which reached maturity in the 1690's, thus transforming commerce from a program into a process. [6] Part of this distinction involved the corollary that domestic trades were not sterile and therefore accumulation was natural. Offshoots from this branch of reasoning were traditional <u>laissez-faire</u>, as well as the idea that the pecuniary gains of trade were inevitable and could be legislated against only at the peril of the polity; and the conviction that the poor must be gainfully employed--that is, producing a surplus. It is this intellectual ferment of the later seventeenth century to which we owe these tenacious ideas.

The metaphor of growth of the economy is not the only intellectual transformation which preceded the institutional framework of the modern macroeconomy. Growth, either natural or manipulated, must have an explicit time dimension. As a matter of fact, 'time' itself must be transmuted from biological time into clock time. In various precapitalist economies for which there are reasonable ethnological descriptions, work and non-work seem to be difficult to distinguish; technique and ritual are interchangeable. Work tends to be collectively defined, and therefore measured by biological rhythms: the diurnal cycle, the seasons, the harvest year, weather cycles and the like. In such a society the seventeenth century English proverb that "everybody's work is nobody's work" would make no sense, because such distinctions were rarely made. [7] In societies where labor is segregated from the rest of human experience, the work of the individual is both imposed and measured by another individual; while the indulgence in biological rhythms becomes the province of those who do not have to 'work' (as Veblen maintained in his theory of the leisure class). [8]

This imposition of a 'measured time' by one individual upon another presumes a shared concept of measurement. It was only in the seventeenth century that such 'objective' time became a reality. Mechanically, the clock dates from the mid-fourteenth century, [9] but before the application of the pendulum in the mid-seventeenth century, these clocks would lose an hour a day and were gravely affected by atmospheric conditions; they were also vulnerably fragile and immobile. From 1650 on improvements multiplied, and with the invention of the spiral balance spring in 1675, portable watches achieved an essentially modern level of functional precision. Notably, by 1680 England attained European pre-eminence in the line of watchmaking. [10]

The temptation to view the historical timing and location of this development as a portent of things to come is impossible to resist. The English watch was a "dark mill grinding in the night" for many reasons. It was the one valuable possession pawned in times of difficulty. It was an intimation of the form of the coming technology of industrialization: the measured transfer of power by serrated gears. It was the paradigm and the metaphor of order, which in English thought was rapidly imported into all aspects of reality, to the point where the Newtonian clockwork threatened to engross the whole universe. But most importantly, it defined labor by both an internal and external clock, the minutes of which ticked off the relative speeds of accumulation.

A thorough history of the creation of a time sensibility remains to be written; the prolegomenon has been provided by E.P. Thompson's seminal article on "Time, Work-Discipline and Industrial Capitalism". [11] With the division of existence into own-time and employer's-time, disagreement over elapsed intervals of these quantities became problematic. Paid labor initially has too many dimensions of tasks--quantities, qualities, vagaries of environment or input, circumstances due to employer's activities--to be measured by any other convention then the lowest common denominator: an hour of the employees's existence. The latitude which the employee enjoys in this less-than-precise relationship is, in the language of the theory developed in chapter six the archetype of the problem of physical turnover for the employer. In part, it was dealt with by the institution of piece-wages, and in part it was dealt with by the supervision of external clocks. An example from 1700 is provided by the Law Books of the Crowley Iron Works, which proscribe timesheets, time-keepers, fines for loitering and encouragements for informers. [12] By the mid-eighteenth century, this form of organization seems to have become widespread in every workshop not personally supervised by the owner directly. A prominent instance is the Wedgewood potteries, where workers were not allowed to wander at will under pain of fines, were forced to be punctual and work fixed hours, even though the technology in no way demanded this rigidity in the function of production. It is entertaining to read of Wedgewood's complaints about the habits of various well-known artists commissioned to decorate some of Wedgewood's wares: the artist class of society, socially encouraged to indulge in whim and biological rhythms, proved to be incompatible with the new form of organization. In the end, the taskmaster was personnified in the ever-present machine: "The most prominent feature of Etruria was the bell, and the next--the clock." [13]

Systems of labor-time control in production were well developed by the end of the eighteenth century. Firms like Boulton & Watt instituted 'Proposed Standard Times' for activities such as the boring of cylinders and the centering and turning of pistons and covers. Ingenious methods of enforcing these times were developed, such as the perversion of the journeyman system: here the firm would contract with a foreman under piecework provisions to supervise a group of men in production, but the foreman would sub-contract with the men at a fixed hourly wage. In this case the foreman had personal incentive to drive the men and quicken the pace of the work, since he received the differential between the piece rates and the wages, over his own wage. Schemes such as these were "...an excellent incentive for speeding up the work. The foreman would be willing to agree to a somewhat low figure...since he would pocket all the gains obtained through speedier work. The other workmen...would realize only later that through this new system, although their money wages remained the same, the speed, intensity and regularity of their work was considerably altered." [14] One would only add that the gains did not accrue solely to the foreman. Speedup in general increased the physical rate of profit.

Interestingly, time was the new idol. A significant change in the late seventeenth century was that the clock was also made interal, or as Wedgewood wrote, "...to make such machines of the Men as carrot err." Clocks and religion unite in exhorting regularity in the 1670's: "A wise and well skilled Christian should bring his matters into such order, that every ordinary duty should know his place, and all should be...as the parts of a Clock or other Engine, which must be all conjunct, and each right placed..." [15] Schools took up the cadence: "Observe exchange-time, look to your markets...there are nicks of time, in which, if your actions fall, they may set you forward apace: seasons of doing and receiving good last not always." [16] Later, the very name 'Methodism' would preach the husbandry of time. The saying that time is money dates from this era. All of this concern appears to have had the purpose of breaking down the resistance to the measured hour, and to convince laborers to eschew schemes to circumvent the clock. It marked the beginning of concerted control of physical turnover in the workplace through the influence of conscious and unconscious behavior. William Petty set the tone when he wrote that it would be better to "bring the Stones at Stonehenge to Tower Hill" than to allow workers to lose their faculty for working.

There are elements of physical turnover other than the control of the worker's rhythm in the workplace. The utilization of capacity and the control of inventories are the other critical instruments available to the capitalist enabling the adjustment of the rate of expansion. Evidence on the awareness of this fact is hard to come by, since information on these mundane problems of organization seems even less fascinating to business historians than questions of factory discipline. Still, glimmers of awareness shine through in the various letters of managers, as well as boards of directors resolutions and directives, such as that of the General Court of the Carron Company in 1764: "...to be extremely cautious to avoid every oncost expense that is not absolutely necessary for the accomodation of the present works. To keep our dead Stock of materials, and goods of every kind as low as we can with safety and lessen the expense of every particular as much as we can with prudence." [17] More explicitly, Josiah Wedgewood understood that the discipline of the clock extended beyond the worker: "...these expenses (of fixed equipment and plant) move like clockwork, and are much the same whether the quantity of goods be large or small, you will see the vast consequences of making the greatest quantity possible in the given time." [18] Before 1700, Ambrose Crowley kept very close records of all the materials in possession of workers, as well as general stock ledgers, partly to protect himself from embezzlement (which may be viewed from our perspective as a variable portion of the real wage), but also to shorten the time stocks lay idle within the confines of his factory.

Lest we think that all control over physical turnover is a matter of relations between the individual employer and the individual workman, it will do well to remember that it is also closely related to the interactions of the employer and working classes. A strike, or concerted industrial sabotage (such as Luddism) is a mass effort by workers to slow physical turnover to a crawl and thereby reduce the rate of profit. In this respect, the eighteenth century marks the incipient realization on both sides of the power of this tactic and its implications. Before the infamous Combination Acts of 1799-1800, there were over 40 acts of Parliment restricting specific types of workmen's organizations. But in general, all workmen's combinations were treated by employers as criminal offenses (with the support of the local justices) well before the law ever recognized them as such. In the late seventeenth century, there is evidence of combinations for the purpose of strikes for higher wages among wool-combers and miners which resulted in riots and the intervention of the military. [19]

If there is one common thread running through all the histories of businesses of this period, it is the rampant fear of combinations and industrial disputes. [20] Although in many ways an inchoate and spontaneous development, the existence of labor resistance in the late seventeenth and early eighteenth centuries represents the final component of the modern development of the structure of physical turnover: time becomes an object of struggle in the workplace.

So far attention has been upon the time dimension of the accumulation process, and its various manifestations located in the late seventeenth and eighteenth centuries. But accumulation of wealth has two salient aspects: one, the rate per standardized time unit, and two, the vehicle of accumulation. To underscore this distinction, let us consider two words often used interchangeably: factory, and firm. Physical turnover is the province of the factory; yet the firm and factory are not coterminous. Under modern conditions, a firm may have no relation to the factory; it may not have much physical presence at all. Because that is the case, we must instead discover the defining characteristics of the modern firm in its financial dimensions. Specifically, the unit of accumulation, the firm, is defined by its monetary components: that is, the items of the balance sheet. In this sense, the firm is the quintessence of pure value, whose purpose is merely to expand. The modern firm is not a real person, nor is it identified with any particular human being. The only two quantitative characteristics all of these units have in common are money value and objective time; all other characteristics being peculiar to institutional situation and circumstance. Because of this, all firms are only quantitatively comparable as an expansion of money units per unit time: that is, the rate of profit on balance sheet equity.

This financial incarnation, the firm, is often dated back to medieval Italian forms of the organization of trade: the <u>commenda</u>, the <u>collegantia</u>, and especially the <u>compagna</u>. Postan has made a case for finding these forms in England in the fifteenth century in substance, if not in name. [21] These units were not strictly modern, however, because they were inextricably tied to a specific person, or more rarely, persons; the only <u>raison d'etre</u> for such an organization was the projection of a distinct task which a single man could not conceivably carry to fruition alone. Quite often they were dissolved when the original task was completed; and if not, the withdrawal of a partner dispersed the enterprise. The structure of these forms was quite complementary to the medieval notion of trade as a punitive enterprise. The implementation of the English joint stock company in the mid-sixteenth century was a step towards the modern concept of the firm, in that shares became partially transferrable. [22] However, the property rights of the shareholder were in an extremely confused state, with doubts rampant about who, if anyone, was actually liable for the company's debts, or who held the claims on its profits and holdings. It was only after 1600 that English companies came to regard their 'capital' as permanent: shares were no longer cashed in at the end of a task or person's life, but could only be redeemed for money in the marketplace. [23] In London, by 1680 there was continuous trading, involving fairly uncomplicated procedures, of the shares of the big joint stock companies, and a visible and accessible marketplace for any other shares. [24] By the 1690's, regular share lists were published in order to keep potential investors abreast of developments. [25] Again we witness the significance of the last decade of the seventeenth century in England. It is from that date that we are able to allude to the modern firm as a sum of disembodied money seeking expansion.

There were two obstacles which had to be circumvented in the seventeenth century in order for the firm to take solid root. First, the political fear of _imperium in imperio_ had to be overcome, as it became obvious that a successful joint stock wielded much power, and tended to develop a system of hierarchy similar to a parliamentary government. [26] This prejudice was palliated through the extensive personal interconnections of early joint stocks with government dignitaries, and through these companies assuming quasi-governmental duties, such as the provision of public finance and the organization of political support groups. Second, the suspicions concerning the nature and functions of a spectral entity not identified with any particular human being had to be assuaged. It was often maintained, well into the eighteenth century, that anything a joint stock could do, an individual could do better. [27] It took a process of trial and error to discover that the advantages were largely financial and that the modern corporation was "a device which permitted investors to reap the rewards of success but pass the price of failure onto their creditors," or more precisely, to shift flows of accumulation over time in their own favor. [28]

Once a firm took on the character of a disembodied sum of money, it bacame possible to apply the discipline of the clock to money itself in a direct manner. This involved the discovery that money could potentially make more money without the intercession of actual production. Earlier financiers had had experience with government securities and their vagaries, but the seventeenth century saw the extension of pure finance into the 'private' sphere. "...By 1630, then, most of the elements of a speculative terminal market in shares were already present in the Amsterdam Bourse. Speculators commonly shold shares which they did not possess at the time of their sale, and surpluses were settled up on _rescontre_. This only became a regular feature in the second half of the seventeenth century." [29] The time bargain is a special case of the alteration of financial turnover, where small sums of money equity are made, through balance sheet alterations, to initiate even larger flows of monetary bargains. The English were quick to copy this innovation in the field of finance, for it is clear that time bargains were widely understood and contracted for by the last decade of the seventeenth century in London. [30]

Another important component of financial turnover is the use of leverage in the balance sheet. The German Historicist school of economists would often associate the exaction of interest as evidence of a capitalist mentality, while more recent historians have found instances of the disguised exaction of contractual interest (such as the 'dry exchange') extending back well into medieval times. [31] Part of this reinterpretation of the historical record has been to suggest there was no substantial difference between modern and pre-modern loan finance, which is certainly an overreaction to previous historiography. For as Lawrence Stone has written, "Money will never become freely or cheaply available in a society which nourishes a strong moral prejudice against the taking of interest at all--as distinct from the objection to the taking of extortionate interest." [32]

Even more importantly, the logistical support of the state is required if debts are to become freely transferrable and accompanied by some legal assurance of the property rights of the creditor. Prohibitions against the exaction of all interest were repealed in England in 1545 (37 Henry VIII c. 9), but guarantees of negotiability and assignability had to wait a hundred years or more: for example, it was only in the seventeenth century in England that the death of a debtor did not negate the rights of the creditor. By the 1680's in England, a broad range of the pamphlet literature argues for the need and necessity of legal securities of debt in order for trade to flourish. [33] The legal fiction of a perpetual capital required the parallel fiction of the perpetual obligation. The development of the inland bill of exchange after 1600 provided a standardized legal instrument with which to create credit, but English common law only recognized the negotiability of notes in 1704 with the passage of the Promissory Notes Act. [34] Upon these and similar assurances, bill brokerage and other manifestations of an active trade in promissory instruments spread rapidly through western Europe.

To discover whether these mechanisms for speeding financial turnover were consciously employed in the eighteenth century is a much more difficult task than tracing parallel developments in physical turnover in the workplace. Partly, one might suspect that the historical literature is thin in this area because conventional economic theory has not been accustomed to giving much credence to the concept of speculation. Another modern bias which hinders the historical quest is the belief that eighteenth century accounting practices were so faulty and haphazard that contemporaries were incapable of making any rational calculations at all, much less realizing that financial manipulations could lead to an augmented profti rate. The first of these objections was addressed in chapter five; the second objection will be examined in the following chapter. In the interim, it is sufficient to note that all of the institutional foundations were essentially in place in England by the turn of the century, so that both finance and production could potentially be controlled in both their temporal and extensive dimensions by the fledgling firm.

Recalling the earlier unfounded definitions of the premodern economy, it is not the use of machinery or credit per se which characterizes the modern economic world. Likewise, the 'rise of the factory' and the 'Industrial Revolution' are not the macroeconomic metastases which usher us into the singularities of modern economic organization. Much of this picture of the world is a leftover from Weberian ideas about the dawn of capitalism as a process of 'rationalization': work discipline is a problem of 'education'; the use of machines and the economic benefits of the 'division of labor' require this discipline and regularity; the ability to operate on large scale, for some reason, is considered to be a significant achievement; and the adoption of double-entry bookkeeping causes a rationalization of the investment process. Pollard, for one, thinks that the "genesis of modern management" must be dated some time after 1750, because it was only then that large-scale industry was carried on between four walls, employing a labor force disciplined by 'economic' sanctions and a bookkeeping system with a 'rational' notion of capital. [35] The problem with this scenario is that it portrays industrialization as a necessary outcome of a technological imperative: a determinism more rigid than Marx's historical materialism.

From our vantage point, a more congenial scenario of the rise of the factory (but not the firm) has been proposed by Stephen Marglin. [36] He points out that in many of the early factories, there were no immediate technological imperatives demanding the chosen form of organization. Smith's motives for the division of labor (increasing dexderity, the saving of time in passing from one task to the next, and induced innovation) really only imply separation of tasks, and not specialization in a factory. Marglin then asks, wherein did the advantages of factory organization lie? The answer was in the process of the discipline of the labor force, since the transformation of the individual producer into a wage laborer took place before either the form of machinery ordained that production processes must be in coordinated sequence, or that equipment was prohibitively expensive. Technological change, far from being a determinant, was itself determined in its bias, since the preference for minutely specialized and sequentially linked production led entrepreneurs to organize and develop those types of processes.

The main weak point in Marglin's case was his inability to explain why, if there were no initial technological advantage to the factory, it spread with such rapidity and force as the prefered mode of organization of manufacture, and continues to do so down to the present day. The answer, from within the context of our own framework, is that the organization of the factory is more 'efficient' in a very specific sense, and that the institutional structure of the firm insures that superiority.

The _lacuna_ in Marglin's argument is that he never asks: 'efficient' from whose point of view? From our survey of the control of time in physical production, the late seventeenth and early eighteenth century innovations in labor discipline were more efficient in that they accelerated turnover: more work was exacted per unit time period. One would not expect artisans to impose the same discipline upon themselves, because they valued their ability, as 'freeborn Englishmen', to indulge in biological work rhythms. [37] Accelerated turnover would only be perceived as an advantage by someone outside of the production process, but who depended upon the pace of that process to exact returns; i.e., the capitalist. The acceleration of physical turnover through the imposition of work discipline presumes a prior split betwen a laboring and a profit-garnishing class. Once the split has occured, pecuniary returns are undeniably higher in the clock-organized mode of production.

The superiority of this 'capitalist' organization rests not only in the structure of the factory, but also in the structure of the firm. It has often been noted in economic history that part of the process of the formation of a wage labor force is the assumption of debts by either small independent cottage producers or quasi-independent laborers. In both these cases the debts are rarely made good, and the independent actor is drawn into the wage labor nexus through a generally futile attempt to free himself of the obligation. In the seventeenth and eighteenth centuries, workers who might potentially be transients in the factory were tied there by a somewhat insidious catch-22: wages were paid irregularly and often extremely late, with lags up to six months not uncommon; or else wages were not paid when natural conditions or shortages of raw materials halted production. To tide them over, workmen went into debt to their employer; and then repetition of these conditions made it impossible to escape the factory, and further debt. [38] This is evidence of the modern firm using its superior capacities to control financial turnover, and thereby bring about the physical conditions for further expansion. By delaying wages, the firm accelerated its cash flow at the expense of the workers. It is as if the seller had to pay interest on trade credit, instead of the buyer. By its privileged access to trade credit and its ability to manipulate its balance sheet, the firm had a distinct advantage over the organic person in this respect. Because of the creation of the institutions of financial and physical turnover control, the capitalist form of organization gained ascendancy over those forms that preceded it.

To recap: the existence of wage labor led to the conception and implementation of objective time as well as the creation of a vehicle of accumulation, the firm, separate and distinct from the human actors who execute actual tasks. The construction of objective time in the workplace first manifested itself in the discipline of workers, and later in the extension of the concept of increasing physical turnover in the production process as a whole. The construct of the firm was also brought under the discipline of the clock by developing methods, such as the increase of leverage in the balance sheet, to increase flows of money per unit money stock. [39] The facility in manipulating money flows was used to compromise other previous forms of the organization of production and supercede them, reinforcing the institutions of physical turnover and creating the conditions for rapid expansion of capitalist organization. The transition to the modern macroeconomy was not technologically determined, but a social process which involved the working-out of the implications of wage labor.

Therefore, we have developed the institutional characteristics of our model enumerated at the beginning of this section from the postulated historical existence of wage labor, except for the last: the equalization of the rate of profit. The equalization should arise from the fact that, since the firm is a sum of money, its expansion is able to be compared with that other firms, and relative freedom of transfer of ownership should result in a tendency for all firms to expand at the same rate. Because of the theoretical confusion over the meaning of the rate of profit outlined in chapter five, there has been very little historical work done on this issue. As a consequence, we shall defer the discussion of the final institutional element of the model to the next chapter.

In conclusion, we have made a case that most of the specifically modern institutions defining the modern macroeconomy can be found in England at the turn of the eighteenth century. If this is true, then it makes sense for a history of modern macroeconomic instability to commence its search in the eighteenth century. Further impetus is lent to this decision by the fact that, although trade had obviously fluctuated sharply in the seventeenth century, [40] there was qualitative change in the character of disturbance in the last two decades: "...between the crises of 1682 and 1696-7, there is an interesting phenomenon which affects the position of the two groups--those engaged in foreign and home trades respectively--in a different manner in each case. Until the crisis of 1682 each previous disturbance of this kind produced an appreciable effect on practically every company in existence at the time. In the same way the effects of the crises from 1685 to 1688 may be traced on companies concerned chiefly in the home trade, while those whose business lay abroad were unaffected." [41] This suggests the incipient potential for endogenous disturbance, and not just exogenous shocks. Further, it is recognized that the 'bubble' of the years 1693-5 constituted the first English boom in company formations, [42] a propitious sign of the nascent development of the firm. We shall therefore date our study of instability in England from 1690.

CHAPTER EIGHT

THE RATE OF PROFIT IN THE EIGHTEENTH CENTURY

Profits and Economic History

It seems odd that although histories of wages, both real and nominal, occupy much space on the shelves and reading lists on economic historians, histories of profits command nowhere near commensurate attention. Admittedly, there is a tradition of reporting profits (usually in appendices) in business histories of particular firms; but even these--and they are not plentiful-- rarely subject to any sort of analysis, their only purpose to redound to the greater glory of the entrepreneur(s) whose portrait is inevitably the goal of such histories. Again, there exist histories tracing the vagaries of various interest rates over long stretches of time, but these manage to resist any empirical attempt to relate such changes to any specific profit movements.

One can't help but wonder how this state of affairs came about, especially when one considers that in the England of roughly 1750-1850 the rate of profit had become theoretically central in the budding science of political economy. G.S.L. Tucker has ably shown how earlier concerns with the determinants of the rate of interest on money loans were transmuted by the classical economists into the credo that the rate of return on investment in production was the key to economic progress. [1] This belief, while having undergone many metamorphoses since then, still commands the respect of many, if not most, economists. If theory and history interact, then historical neglect must be a result of more than mere indifference.

At first glance, one might suggest that wages are historically more accessible than profit data, and thus more conveniently extracted from the manuscript record. Indeed, eighteenth century pamphleteers sometimes carried on vicious verbose warfare over whether a particular trade or joint-stock experienced excessive rates of profit, supposedly with both parties having access to the same records. Adam Smith wrote, "Profit is so very fluctuating that the person who carries on a particular trade cannot always tell you himself what is the average of his annual profit." [2] Modern writers often interpret this indeterminacy as the result of deficient accounting procedures. One purpose of this chapter is to inquire if there might be a germ of truth in this criticism.

As might be expected, the modern view of eighteenth century accounting practices is shaped by the context in which interest in the historical record arose. In this instance the impetus came from the German historical school of economic theory, associated particularly with the name of Werner Sombart. In Der Moderne Kapitalismus, Sombart endowed double-entry bookkeeping with the power to separate organic needs from the pure desire for accumulation and to promote economic rationality through the meticulous categorization of information. He wrote, "The very concept of capital is derived from this way of looking at things; one can say that capital, as a category, did not exist before double-entry bookkeeping." [3] Professor B.S. Yamey has since pointed out in a series of articles that all the functions Sombart attributed to double-entry techniques could have equally well been realized with single entry accounts, and that rationality did not depend upon a single form of record-keeping. [4]

Yamey's redefinition of historians' attitudes towards early modern accounts was even more fundamental, however, as he began to call into question the very adequacy of surviving early accounts in measuring proprietor's equity or income. More recently, several authors have pinpointed what they have seen as the significant lacunae of seventeenth and eighteenth century accounting practice: [5]

1) Domestic and private accounts were haphazardly intermingled. For example, Sir Charles Peers, a merchant involved with trade with Malaga and a director of the Bank of England, recorded in his profit and loss account the loss of some forks, spoons and candlesticks which had been left behind in Malaga. [6]

2) Many times books were not closed with a fixed periodicity. Instead, to save the trouble of starting another folio, many accounts were balanced only when a page was filled.

3) Income and expenditure accounts were sometimes posted on a cash basis: That is, money flows were recorded only when realized. This results in a violation of the Golden Rule of accounting to always match costs to revenues.

4) Depreciation charges were quite often ignored, or else posted haphazardly. As an illustration, the Million Bank (actually not a bank but an early eighteenth century investment trust dealing primarily in government annuities), having made no allowances for the eventual termination of the annuities, carried them on their books at full face value for more than 60 years. Suddenly, in 1765, it was decided to write down the value of the total holding from eighteen to fourteen years' purchase,

involving a shrinkage of assets by more than 116,00 pounds in one year. [7]

5) In the case of many proprietorships, profits were not explicitly tallied prior to investment expenditures out of surplus, so if the proprietor(s) did not periodically re-evaluate their holdings or withdraw funds from the business, no written record exists of the proprietors' income.

6) The structure and timing of borrowing can cause the rate of return to be over- or under-estimated. A striking example of this kind of tinkering was uncovered by R.H. Campbell in his history of the powerful Scottish concern, the Carron Company. Joseph Stainton, the manager of Carron, wrote to his brother Henry in London and

"suggested that the sums written off in the two previous years be brought back as debts to the particular accounts and be written off gradually. This Stainton thought, would keep the undivided profits intact, which he considered most important. Therefore, 37,449 pounds were to be brought back to the accounts, and with this the loss of 7,682 pounds on the previous half-year converted into a profit of 5,417 pounds and the inventories reduced by 24,053 pounds. This method, Joseph Stainton told Henry, 'does not alter our present half-years' balance a whit in the main from what we intended it'." [8]

Any of these alterations cause formidable practical problems in assessing any particular company's books. Yet confronted with these admittedly tough questions of interpretation of the historical record, one might still expect to find some reconstruction of accounts by historians. (Campbell's careful work with the Carron Company is a positive instance.) The task may be tedious and extensively complicated by the need to reinterpret the various closing accounts, but equally difficult studies in the areas of slavery and historical demography (to name only two) have been tackled by economic historians. We have already argued that profits should occupy a pre-eminent position in the hierarchy of economic indicators. It seems the history of profits have been neglected not only because the task was difficult, but more importantly because contemporaries deem it conceptually irrelevant for understanding capitalism in the early modern period.

The crystallization of this point of view occured in two influencial articles by Sidney Pollard in the early 1960's. In a study of the accounting practices of some late eighteenth and early nineteenth century firms, he wrote: [9]

"Very few of these firms showed in their accounting practices an understanding of the meaning of the concept of capital, particularly fixed capital, as postulated by the 'classical' scheme. Their practices were characterized by two main heresies: the treatment of capital as auxilliary to entrepreneurship instead of the central motive force behind firms, and the confusion between capital and revenue...there was no clear-cut attempt to adapt accounting practice to the notion of capital as generalized, depersonalized property, seeking the highest returns irrespective of its concrete embodiment, as postulated by economic theory."

A later article reinforced the point by stressing that early firms, even those engaged in heavy manufacture, had very small ratios of fixed to circulating capital, and therefore could not be expected to have evolved complex notions of rates of return on roundabout processes because they did not need them. [10] As these articles represented the only thinking done in this field, we were left with the opinion among historians that the classical long-period variables, and specifically the rate of profit, were and are superfluous to any understanding of movements in the eighteenth century macroeconomy.

The six accounting 'errors' in our list become more comprehensible when we perceive that they fall under three headings: improper time distributions of income and expenditure; a confusion of the person and the business; and distortions resulting from wilful financial manipulation of accounts. Pollard makes no analytical contribution to these objections; he simply supplies an interpretation as to why they are evident in the eighteenth century, an interpretation amenable to the neoclassical gestalt. This gestalt, already discussed in detail, theoretically expects no single equilibrium rate of profit once roundabout processes and price expectations become important considerations in producing for the market (and, certainly, all factors being rewarded in proportion to their scarce marginal productivities). Pollard has projected this theoretical sequence back upon historical events. His interpretation consists of two observations: we now understand capital, and by implication, its accounting demands better than eighteenth century businessmen, and that is because they had very little fixed capital to contend with, compared to more modern conditions. We should like to question in detail Pollard's observations.

FIXED CAPITAL IN THE HISTORY OF ECONOMIC DOCTRINE

The first author of a narrative history of capital accumulation and the first recognized theorist of capital accumulation were one and the same: we are referring, of course, to Adam Smith. In The Wealth of Nations, we are presented with the vision of a nation's two-fold path of prosperity. A nation may increase the number of its productively employed laborers, or it may increase the productive power of its previously employed laborers. The former occurs through the instrumentality of an increase in capital, by which Smith means an increase in the fund of resources advanced to sustain labor during the act of production. The latter is brought about by a furthering of the division of labor, which is primarily a social activity, and by the "addition and improvement to those machines and instruments which facilitate and abridge labor." This last method of increasing the annual produce of a nation also involves capital accumulation, but the object of this accumulation diverges from the nature of a fund forwarded specifically to labor; and so Smith felt he must elaborate further upon this dual aspect of capital. Stock, said Smith, can be resolved into the categories of fixed capital and circulating capital. The distinction between the two was not an issue of the relative durability of objects, as the modern reader might be tempted to think; rather, the distinction consisted of whether the object afforded a profit without or with "circulating or changing masters."

In this definition, a certain quantum of corn is properly fixed capital, since in its travels from the granary to the ground and back again, it does not leave the orbit of the individual owner. This conception was integral to Smith's vision of the two-fold path to improvement, since the first mode of expanding productive laborers in order to increase the annual product demanded the advance of a greater circulating capital, whereas the second mode of the addition and improvement of instruments which facilitate and abridge labor demanded a greater fixed capital. Thus the tracing of the relative and absolute movements of fixed and circulating capital, in conjunction with the spread of the social divisions of labor, was tantamount to recording the history of the progress of a nation on its road to prosperity for Smith.

The theorists of capital immediately following Smith conceived of value as consisting of labor time, and so for them, capital was congealed evidence of past expenditures of labor time. As one consequence of this shift in value premises, the concepts of fixed and circulating capital became altered in meaning. They now denoted the relative durability of objects within the process of production. The reason behind this alteration was that, in the context of a system of labor values, the labor time embodied in the instruments of production itself has a collateral time dimension; and it was logically necessary to account for its duration in the process of transferring that labor time from captial-object to product-object. As Marx stressed by way of definition: [11]

> We have seen in general that all capital value is constantly in circulation, and that in this sense all capital is circulation capital. But the circulation of the portion of capital which we are now studying is peculiar. In the first place it does not circulate in its use form, but it is merely its value that circulates, and this takes place gradually, piecemeal, in proportion as it passes from it to the product, which circulates as a commodity....It is this peculiarity which gives to this portion of constant capital the form of fixed capital.

This altered conception was not entirely divorced from that of Smith, in that capital was still differentiated into value which remained within the orbit of the capitalist and value which traversed the larger circuit of capital, but now this analytical distinction was no longer identical with the distinction between "fixed" and "circulating" capital. Also, like Smith, the record of the accumulation and differentiation of fixed and circulating capital was still a major theoretical benchmark of any conceivable economic history. In particular, fixed capital (conceived of as duration of use) was thought to be an index of the progress of accumulation: [12] "As the magnitude of the value and the durability of the applied fixed capital develop with the development of the capitalist mode of production, the lifetime of industry and industrial capital lengthens in each particular field of investment to a period of many years, say of ten years on an average."

It might seem that it would only have been a few short intuitive leaps from the theoretician of capital to the historian of capital once this formulation was achieved, but in practice the leaps were never made because of certain theoretical problems with the labor value concept vis-à-vis empiricism. Capital, for Marx, had many more dimensions than the simple axis of durability; some examples were the concept of "social necessity" as an average of labors expended, the distinction between physical durability and turnover in the sphere of circulation, the distortion of the price axis relative to labor values, and the variety of social relations in the workplace. Once all of these considerations were brought together, the problem of the form of an empirical narrative of the accumulation of capital along any single axis became essentially intractable, in that a serious examination of any one dimension demands a rigorous account of all other influences. The continuing controversy about the transformation of labor values into the realm of money prices is but one aspect of this inherent intractability; the realistic determination of the "socially necessary" expenditure of effort is another. Apparently the history of the accumulation of capital from a labor theoretic point of view remains unwritten because the issues and their relation to empiricism as conceived therein are too overwhelmingly complex.

Another major school of economists which succeeded the labor theorists reacted against both the previous value theoretic basis and against the intractability of a many-faceted "capital." The marginalist school anchored value in certain presumed psychological propinquities, and then slowly confronted the question of the implications of this value-theoretic shift for the definition of capital. The earliest reaction, on the part of Walras, Jevons and the Austrians, was to focus on the time dimension as the definitive characteristic of capital. This conscious act of abstraction from all the previously suggested attributes of capital can be seen clearly in Jevons' writings: [13] "I would say, then, in the most general manner, that whatever improvements in the supply of commodities lengthen the average interval between the moment when labor was exerted and its ultimate result or purpose accomplished, such improvements depend upon the use of capital. Whenever we overlook the irrelevant complication introduced by the division of labor and the frequency of exchange, all employments of capital resolve themselves into the fact of time elapsing between the beginning and the end of industry." It is interesting to note that, as Marx retained certain elements of Smith, the marginalists at first retained some vestige of the labor-value orientation, in that both Jevons and the Austrians identified the endpoints of this abstract duration as the initial application of <u>labor</u> and the final enjoyment of the good in the end process of consumption.

It was not long before the adherents of the marginalist school realized that this particular definition of capital was discordant with the posited psychologistic theory of value. Böhm-Bawerk uncomfortably sensed this in a few isolated instances in his work: for example, in one place he argues against what he believed to be erroneous fiction that goods preserve their <u>economic</u> identity over time [14]; in another he admits that a last-minute change in psychological intentions with regard to the consumption of goods may alter instantaneously the quantum of capital present in the economy. [15] These qualifications suggest that the duration of an economic good's existence is not an "objective" or independent fact, but rather an epiphenomenon conditional upon the shifting psychological predispositions of the populace. If this were true, the duration of a good's existence could hardly be isolated as the fundamental characteristic which distinguishes it as capital <u>per se</u>. In a logically consistent treatment of capital from the stance of the marginalist school, duration is merely one characteristic of a good among many, subject as are all other characteristics to psychological approval or disapproval. Characteristics such as temporal location, color, texture, spatial location and so forth are all of the same epistemic significance to the average rational individual. This realization has led contemporary marginalists to deny that duration is the essential characteristic of capital; the standard operating practice is to treat time in the same analytic manner as one treats space.

Where is the narrative historian of capital accumulation left by this recent change in the understanding of capital? Among the theorists there is no consistent answer; and further, some merely compound the confusion. As an example, within the confines of the same aritcle, J.R. Hicks insists on the economic irrelevance of the physical identity of capital (as is sensible within the marginalist framework), and simultaneously also insists on the crucial historical role of fixed capital (in the physical sense of the labor theorists) in the genesis of the capital concept and capitalism itself: [16] "The Classical schema, as we have seen, began with trade and was extended to agriculture; so long as stocks and works in progress were the main part of the manufacturers' physical assets it could be extended, in much the same way, to manufacture also. But, when a large part of his capital became <u>fixed</u> in plant and machinery, a candidate had appeared for factor status..." Hicks confuses Smith and the labor theorists, but also confuses the labor theorists with his own neo-Walrasian tradition. If capital writ modern is in no way necessarily linked to the character of long-lived goods, then the large-scale adoption of long-lived production goods in a transition period dubbed "the Industrial Revolution" should have only minor theoretical significance.

Frank Fetter understood the logical implications of marginalist value theory for the economic historian as early as 1930: [17]

> The terms fixed and circulating capital are distorted expressions of the truth that various kinds and various portions of investments are more or less readily salable, confused with the technological truth that various physical agents are more or less durable in nature. The definition of capital determines in turn the meaning more or less vaguely attached to such phrases as the capitalistic age. Some see in capitalism essentially the use of labor saving machines; this is a technological conception of capitalism. Others, more eclectic, see in capitalism

essentially the wage system where the employer owns all the physical agents. But consistently with the (marginalist) value concept capitalism is merely the price system, the commercial exchanging organization of industry, where valuations, incomes and property take on financial expression.

One financial school of thought much less familiar to modern economists, the American Institutionalists, also stressed the financial rather than the physicalist aspect in their definition of capital; but they differed from the marginalists in that they demoted the market to one of many consciously constructed social mechanisms, and proposed a Darwinian natural selection in place of a utilitarian basis for their theory of value. To quote John Commons, one major proponent of the school: [18] "modern capital is not capital in the physical sense....It is nor corporeal property, but it is incorporeal and intangible property. Its name is 'assets'....We must distinguish between titles of ownership and substance of ownership." Their value theory led them to examine the legal structures of economic relationships, and particularly, the manifestation of capital as corporate accounting quantities.

Of course, from this excessively brief survey of the relation of the notion of fixed capital to the various paradigms which have made use of the concept, one should not conclude either that these distinctions were as clear-cut as we have made out, or that defintions followed each other chronologically with lock-step certainty. At any point in time, some theorists were not in agreement about the meaning of the term "fixed captial," at least in part because the term was employed without explicit definition. Yet there are two things which are important to notice from our present perspective: (a) the term "fixed capital" can only be defined within the context of a specific school of economics, and therefore cannot be employed with impunity without first assuming something about the character of the audience; and (b) with the sole exception of the contemporary marginalist school of economics, the track record of the accumulation of fixed capital relative to circulating capital was the primary index of the economic progress of a nation. We now turn to the impact of these two observations upon recent historiography.

FIXED CAPITAL IN ECONOMIC HISTORY

Almost every major economic theorist concerned with the role of capital in economic growth believed that capital was becoming more fixed over time, with the exception of the modern neoclassical (or general equilibrium) school, which remains silent on this issue. This silence does not prevent working neoclassical macro- and micro-economists from harboring in this belief, as we observed earlier in this chapter. Why does the belief in this "parable" persist? What does existing empirical work have to say about the trend in the fixity of capital?

The modern consensus of historians may be paraphrased as follows: in the Industrial Revolution, firms' requirements for fixed captial were relatively small (largely for technological reasons), with most of their investments tied up in circulating capital. Because firms' investments were relatively liquid, they had little need of long-term financial markets; and further, for the same reason they functioned quite well without more modern forms of business organization and finance such as the joint-stock company, and modern double-entry accounting techniques. Therefore, even though many skeletal institutions of the capital market might exist prematurely, there was no pressing need for them.

This interpretation, with minor variants, has come to be conventional textbook wisdom in contemporary economic history. This consensus essentially can be traced to an article by Sidney Pollard in the early 1960's. The Pollard article has maintained that, "Between the days of the earliest large-scale industrial enterprises of which details exist and the first half of the eighteenth century, the ratio of fixed to circulating capital had altered hardly at all." [19] Pollard, both in this article and in later work, drew out the implications concerning the irrelevance of long-term finance and the absence of modern accounting as arising directly from this fundamental fact of the relative unimportance of fixed capital in the early modern economy. He then suggests that the period usually identified as the "Industrial Revolution" did experience a rise in the ratio of fixed to circulating capital, but that the magnitude of the rise had been exaggerated in the historical literature, at least for the period up to 1830. After this date, by implication, ratios were much higher. The impact of this study, as another writer was to put it, was to reveal that, "One of the most important conclusions of the analysis of capital structure of firms (in the Industrial Revolution) is to show how small a proportion of their total assets, even for the most capital-intensive businesses such as large iron works or a London porter brewery, lay in fixed assets." [20]

This work may be criticised on two levels: first, does the quantitative evidence really say what the authors report; and second, do these concepts of fixed and circulating capital correspond to any particular paradigm of economic theory, so that we might evaluate their significance? The first query takes up the remainder of this section, while the second is postponed until the next section of this chapter.

As one might expect, most of these generalizations derive from a very small sample of evidence. For the period 1770-1830, Pollard only reports <u>one</u> ratio of fixed to circulating capital for a textile mill, and that appears to be a misprint. [21] For the metallurgical industry nine ratios are reported: seven ratios in Pollard's Table I and two in the body of his text. We reproduce all nine ratios below in our own Table I.

One begins to be suspicious of the quality of the evidence when, first, one sees the extent of the variance of this ratio when reported at two separate time periods for the same firm, and second, one sees that the ratios excluded from Pollard's table are appreciably higher than those included in the table. Are these ratios in fact "small," as Pollard contends? In order to pose that question properly, we must first <u>clarify "small" relative to which state of affairs</u>? If Pollard has in mind a conception of the importance of fixed capital growing through time, then he must mean <u>small relative to the modern situation</u>. Surprisingly, no one has been moved to test this hypothesis. In order to do so, we consulted the most recent issue of the British Department of Industry's <u>Business Monitor MA3</u>, the most likely source of data most comparable to Pollard's figures, which are derived from the balance sheets of individual firms. Pollard does not define precisely what he means by "fixed" or "circulating" capital; but from the context it seems his perception of fixed capital encompasses long-lived non-financial assets such as buildings and machinery, while circulating capital refers to stocks, inventories, and other tangible non-financial short-lived assets. As the closest possible approximation to these concepts, we identified "net tangible fixed assets" as fixed capital and "stocks and works in progress" as circulating capital. The aggregate of fixed capital in 1977 for the industry groups "Metal Manufacture" and "Metal Goods not elsewhere specified" comes to 1786.2 million pounds (HMSO, 1979, pp. 14 and 18), giving us a modern ratio of fixed to circulating capital for metallurgical industries of .863. Now, let us take the information provided by Pollard and reproduced in our Table I, only excluding the figure for the Mona Mine Co., because Pollard reports that those figures for fixed capital are incomplete. We can then perform a test of the null hypothesis that there is no difference between the ratio of fixed to circulating capital in Great Britain in 1977 and the mean ratio in Pollard's sample. The resulting t-statistic is equal to -1.38, which under conventional intervals is not sufficient to reject the null hypothesis. Therefore, Pollard's article does <u>not</u> provide adequate evidence that ratios of fixed to <u>circulating</u> capital were relatively smaller in the period conventionally designated "The Industrial Revolution."

Table I

POLLARD'S EVIDENCE CONCERNING THE PREVALENCE OF
FIXED AND CIRCULATING CAPITAL

Firm	Year	Fixed Cap. / Circ. Cap.
Mona Mine Co.*	1788	.219
	1829-30	.096
M. Boulton	1782	.417
Soho Foundry	1822	.096
	1830	.497
Nevill Copper Works	1806	.369
Pontrhydyrun Tin Mill	1832	.200
(Figures reported in Pollard's text, but not included in his Table I)		
Cyfartha	1812	.725
Carron Co.	1769	1.728

* fixed capital figures not complete

Source: S. Pollard, "Fixed Capital...", Ibid., pp. 149-150

As a _caveat_, one commonly expressed reservation with respect to the previous test is that accounting methods have substantially changed over long periods of time, and this might obviate any comparison. For now it should be pointed out that if accounts truly are not comparable over time, then Pollard's thesis founders in any event, since we then lack any standard of how to judge whether ratios of fixed to circulating capital were ever relatively "large" or "small."

What is perhaps even more curious is that the many economic historians who approvingly cite Pollard in the course of their archival work on business records rarely bother to calculate the historically contemporaneous fixed/circulating capital ratios they have unearthed, for if they did, they would be much more cautious in adopting his thesis. These ratios, calculated from the published work of Peter Mathias, Sidney Chapman and C.H. Lee, are presented below in Talbe II in order to illustrate this point.

TABLE II

FIXED/CIRCULATING CAPITAL RATIOS, VARIOUS FIRMS

Year	Truman Hanbury & Buxton	McConnel & Kennedy	Pleasley Mills
1759	2.335		
1760	2.408		
1761	2.071		
1762	1.609		
1763	1.482		
1764	1.912		
1765	1.662		
1766	1.810		
1767	1.292		
1768	1.730		
1769	.938		
1770	1.346		
1771	1.446		
1772	1.263		
1773	1.067		
1774	.768		
1775	.684		
1776	.844		
1777	.824		
1778	.791		
1779	.761		
1780	.794		
1781	.692		
1782	.803		

TABLE II - CONTINUED

Year	Truman Hanbury & Buxton	McConnel & Kennedy	Pleasley Mills
1783	.714		
1784	.878		
1785	.835		
1786	.811		5.811
1787	.661		2.206
1788	.709		2.671
1789	.571		2.472
1790	.557		1.888
1791	.629		1.882
1792	.584		1.966
1793	.539		
1794	.569		1.563
1795	.537		1.302
1796	.396		.907
1797	.314	.35	.978
1798	.304	3.50	1.574
1799	.267	8.67	1.584
1800	.327	2.45	
1801	.327	1.15	
1802	.240	.86	
1803	.253	1.60	
1804	.256		

SOURCES FOR TABLE II:

Truman, Hanbury & Buxton:
P. Mathias, The Brewing Industry in England, Cambridge Univ. Press, 1960; pp. 556-558. The appropriate definitions of fixed and circulating capital were taken from P. Mathias, The First Industrial Revolution, London: Methuen, 1967; p. 148.

McConnel & Kennedy:
C.H. Lee, A Cotton Enterprise, Manchester: Manchester Univ. Press, 1972; p. 166. Lee reports 'fixed capital' and 'liquid capital', which I presume correspond to Pollard's concepts of fixed and circulating capital.

Oldknow, Cowpe & Co. (Pleasley Mills):
S. Chapman, The Early Factory Masters, Newton Abbott: David & Charles, 1967; p. 126. Chapman presents 'stock plus net credit, i.e.,

> circulating capital' and 'fixed capital net of depreciation', which do not precisely represent Pollard's notions beacuse of the intrusion of financial assets. However, one would expect that this would bias the ratio downwards.

A number of things should become apparent from persual of these time-series. First, the variance of these ratios is large enough that by a process of judicious choice of years, one could prove either that the ratios were "small," or conversely, that they were "large" relative to modern experience. Thus Pollard's method of reporting ratios for a few randomly selected years is flawed. Second, there is a marked cyclical component to these ratios, which suggests we may be witnessing macroeconomic effects here. This does not correspond well with Pollard's conception of fixed and circulating capital as magnitudes determined primarily by fixed physical parameters of technology. Third, on the basis of this admittedly small sample, it seems that the ratio at the inception of a business was actually quite large, and only fell to a lower average after some years of operation. This directly contradicts Pollard's inference, echoed by many others, that it was comparatively easy to embark upon factory production, since at the firm level initial fixed capital requirements, and therefore requirements for long-term finance, were so small.

It seems that we are left with nothing but equivocal and ambiguous results as the fruits of these attempts to gain some empirical insight into the question of the role of fixed capital in history. I do not meant to suggest this is because of procedural inadequacies on the part of the various investigators, however. The problem is much more fundamental than that. It traces back to the fact that there is no one concept or definition of fixed capital in the history of economic thought.

AN ALTERNATIVE CONCEPTION OF THE FIXITY OF CAPITAL

The confusion which reigns in discussions of the economic history of capital are ultimately due to the tensions present between the alternate theoretical concepts of capital. It is quite clear, for instance, that Pollard was not aware of the differing meanings and relative importances for different schools of thought of the alternative definitions of fixed and circulating capital which we have surveyed above. To wit: Pollard cites Adam Smith as supporting his assertion that the fixed capital of manufacturers in the eighteenth century would be small; yet Smith does not share Pollard's definition of fixed capital which identifies fixed capital as duration of physical existence. In fact, Pollard's chosen definitions of fixed and circulating capital correspond closely to none of the schools of though we have surveyed, and therefore we possess no theoretical criteria with which to evaluate his work. His stress on the durability of physical goods would seem to place his work within the Marxian orbit; and yet numerous other statements in the same article concerning supply and demand suggest he perceives his framework as marginalist, but a marginalism of the outdated sort, such as that found in the writings of Jevons and the Austrians. Yet even this framework is not subscribed to with any conscientious rigor, since we have observed that the duration referred to in the early marginalist work identifies the first application of labor and the final consumption of the goods as endpoints.

The question which confronts the historian of capital of a particular empirical bent is, quite simply: what is the appropriate concept of capital to use when discussing <u>historical</u> trends? Recent debates on capital theory seem to agree that the passage of historical time is important and crucial to an understanding of capital--this as opposed to previous practice which operated in terms of timeless equilibria and so forth--but unfortunately, matters are generally left there, to the chagrin of our historian. Granted that historical time is important, how can one tell that history has occured when examining capital? What is the appropriate indicator of change?

Many historians such as Feinstein propose that the indicator simply be the aggregate amount of capital, whence the trajectory of history is traced by the progressive rise of this aggregate. Recent theoretical debates should cause us to view this option with skepticism. If by aggregate capital we mean a collection of physical objects aggregated at their prices, then both price Wicksell effects and real Wicksell effects can wreak havoc with any parable appealing to the simple accumulation of objects: that is, accumulation accompanied by a changing rate of profit and changing technologies can lead in an indiscriminate manner to "more" or "less" capital in these terms. Therefore the track record of this "aggregate capital" is merely a jumble of many effects, which tells us little about actual historical events. To put it bluntly, the accumulation of physical capital goods quite possibly may accompany a fall in the aggregate value of the capital stock. Incidentally, the same objection applies to attempts to see movement in history as an accumulation of objects <u>relative</u> to other "factors": say, for instance, a greater ratio of "capital" per person. These figures also fall prey to real and price Wicksell effects. Of course, we have ignored the other major problem with these concepts: the sheer impossibility of any reasonable precision in historical measurement. The evaluation of such attempts has consistently baffled historians, largely because those attempts were theoretically unjustified in the best of all possible worlds.

For all of these reasons, the physicalist conception of aggregate capital is probably impossible to implement in any coherent historical narrative. That leaves us with the other aspect of capital: its financial manifestation. Would it be instructive to attempt a measure of the stock or flow of finance present within a country in a particular historical epoch? Patently, the growth of the amount of legally recognized specie or currency, or for that matter, the growth of the volume of credit tells us little directly about the accumulation of capital over time. Another potential definition of capital would isolate its financial representation in the institutional units organized for the purpose of self-expansion: that is, firms. It is this candidate for historical benchmark of the accumulation of capital which we have argued for in previous chapters.

Unlike the other proposed measures, the financial or accounting structure of the firm is inherently an historical phenomenon, dependent and conditional upon the legal institutions of the organization of enterprise and the existing conventions of business accounting and record-keeping. In recent times both economic theorists and economic historians have been quick to discount the relevance of these business conventions to their studies, preferring instead to work in terms of abstract "real capital" and "economic profits," which are by their very nature a-temporal and a-historical. In opting to downplay business accounts, economists tend to forget that their own "pure" notions of capital and income themselves originally derive from pre-existing business practice: witness Keynes' admission in the General Theory that his definition of net income was very close to the practical definitions of Income Tax Commissioners. [22]

The identification of the changing financial structure of the firm as the historical record of the accumulation of capital can do much to clarify the preceding confusions in the existing historical narrative. To return to the concrete example of the work of Pollard, his attempt to resolve the accumulation of capital into relative movements of fixed and circulating capital fails logically for three major reasons: a) He continually confuses the factory, a locus of physical production, with the firm, a financial entity defined by its accounting records. One fixed/circulating capital ratio of his which we reproduced in Table I was for Soho Foundry, which was one production arm of the firm of Boulton and Watt. The financial accounts of one portion of a firm may not necessarily represent the physical capital intensity of that production process because the firm can and does regularly shift balance sheet entries between its component sub units. It is the firm which is the empirical unit of accumulation, not the factory. b) Pollard confuses stocks and flows by restricting his empiricism to the items on the balance sheet which have physical analogues. Financial assets are excluded in his ratios, and yet they share the key attribute of differential time duration with the physical assets. c) What Pollard seems to be getting at is the time structure of capital within the firm, but his chosen ratio is logically imcapable of capturing a phenomenon along the time axis. He chooses to divide the aggregate of fixed capital by the aggregate of circulating capital; that is

$$\frac{\sum_{i=k+1}^{n} p_i (x_i \cdot \tau_i)}{\sum_{i=1}^{k} p_i (x_i \cdot \tau_i)}$$

where p_i is the price of input i, x_i is the unit of flow of input i necessary for the production of one unit of output, and τ_i is the length of time x_i must be present in the production process in order to produce one unit of output. (Note that the product of x and τ is the required stock of the input, as was discussed in chapter six.) Further, if the inputs are arrayed in order of their associated τ's, then some arbitrary cutoff point "k" is indentified, such that goods one through k are defined as "circulating capital" and goods k+1 throught n are defined as "fixed capital." As one can observe in this ratio, the time dimensions cancel, and the outcome is a pure number with no time dimensionality. One would hope that any proposed index of the time structure of capital should itself have a time dimension.

When Marx shifted the definition of fixed capital, he still preserved elsewhere the Smithian notion of presence or absence of value within the boundaries of production as a significant theoretical variable. One can observe this in Volume II of Capital, which is entirely concerned with the circuit of capital: a clear elaboration of Smithian preoccupations. It is the fundamental importance of this circuit for economics that has been mislaid in more recent theoretical discussions. In particular, the later shift towards a preoccupation with the physical fixity of capital goods has led to the present historical confusion over how one should empirically measure that fixity. Since it involves an aggregation of the time structures of physical objects, it too falls prey to the objections of price Wicksell and real Wicksell effects. While physical fixity of production is an underlying determinant of the system, it is not an empirical manifestation of the system, since what ultimately circulates and grows is value. The work of

Veblen argues persuasively that what is ultimately important about the development of capital is the speed with which it can complete its circuit and therefore expand in value terms. This is the time structure of the financial accounts of the firm in money terms; it is the empirical aspect of capital tangible both to the contemporary capitalist and to the economic historian.

There are at least two potential measures of the circuit of capital to be found within the rudimentary records of most firms. The first is a familiar quantum, the rate of profit; i.e., profit/equity. The reciprocal of this ratio is a number capturing a pure time dimensionality: it is the length of time it takes the firm to recoup its investment in the form of accounting profits. The historical study of this ratio will be further discussed in the next section of this chapter.

The second potential measure of the time structure of capital is much less problematic theoretically: it is the ratio of flow of sales to the firm's stock of equity. This ratio also has a pure time dimension, in that its reciprocal represents the length of time it takes for the firm to recoup the magnitude of its investment in the form of cash sales. This ratio is much less problematic than the first because agreement can be achieved much more readily as to what precisely consititutes "sales." Further, it summarizes our interest in the time structure of capital: it is the partial result of the firm's physical capacity to bring forth output in a timely manner, expressed through the firm's speed of its circuit of capital.

It is this sense in which investment capital is "fixed"; that is, the size of required costs relative to cash flows. There is one more reason why we would like to suggest that economists and economic historians give some consideration to this variable. It might be that the ratio of sales to equity is the historical benchmark of capital accumulation which has eluded economic historians for so long.

In order to support this last statement, we have collected from various sources a sample of the ratios of total cash flow divided by book equity (called "cash turnover") and the ratios of total sales divided by book equity (called "sales turnover") for various eighteenth-century firms. This sample was collected for the period of the "Industrial Revolution" by the author both from published sources and archival recontruction of business ledgers. These ratios, which we will call "financial turnover," are displayed in Table III. They represent our best estimates of the "fixity" of capital during the birth of the business cycle.

TABLE III

EIGHTEENTH CENTURY RATES OF FINANCIAL TURNOVER

	Cash Turnover		Sales Turnover			
Year	East India	Hand-in-Hand	Spencer Stanhope	Sun Fire	East India	British Linen Co.
1721	.89	---	.46	---	---	---
1722	.83	---	---	---	---	---
1723	.66	---	.50	---	---	---
1724	.72	---	.54	---	---	---
1725	.72	.31	.52	---	---	---
1726	.72	.40	.61	---	---	---
1727	.66	.16	.70	---	---	---
1728	.83	.12	.63	---	---	---
1729	.67	.10	.63	---	---	---
1730	.70	.13	.73	---	---	---
1731	.73	---	.69	---	---	---
1732	.81	---	.72	---	---	---
1733	.58	---	.77	---	---	---
1734	.62	---	.83	---	---	---
1735	.73	---	.80	---	---	---
1736	1.23	---	.69	---	---	---
1737	1.21	---	.68	---	---	---
1738	.58	---	.63	---	---	---
1739	.56	---	.70	---	---	---
1740	.51	---	.68	---	---	---
1741	.66	---	.60	---	---	---
1742	.50	---	.51	---	---	---
1743	.75	---	.59	.36	---	---
1744	.89	---	.60	.36	---	---
1745	.59	---	.76	.36	---	---
1746	1.08	---	1.16	.36	---	---
1747	.81	---	1.20	.37	---	---
1748	.84	---	1.21	.38	---	---
1749	.93	---	.85	.42	---	.74
1750	2.77	---	.96	.42	---	.57
1751	1.70	---	---	.44	---	.55
1752	1.09	---	---	.32	---	.61
1753	.96	---	---	.34	---	.75
1754	.92	---	---	.36	---	.80
1755	.86	---	---	.38	---	.31
1756	.69	---	---	.40	---	.26
1757	.83	---	---	.40	---	.46
1758	.71	---	---	.41	---	.55
1759	.88	---	---	.43	---	.74
1760	.93	---	---	.47	---	.80
1761	.90	---	---	.46	---	.69
1762	.81	---	---	.51	.60	.54
1763	.92	---	---	.56	.74	---
1764	.97	---	---	.60	.87	---
1765	1.04	---	---	.66	.84	---

TABLE III - CONTINUED

	Cash Turnover		Sales Turnover				
Year	East India	Hand-in-Hand	East India	Boulton & Watt	Sun Fire	Carron	Hudson's Bay Co.
1766	1.02	---	.69	----	.70	----	---
1767	1.11	---	.93	----	.73	----	---
1768	1.38	.40	1.10	----	.76	----	---
1769	1.47	.46	1.12	----	.83	----	---
1770	1.70	.43	1.06	----	.89	----	---
1771	1.64	.35	1.06	----	.91	----	---
1772	1.75	.53	.96	----	.97	----	---
1773	1.33	.33	.96	----	.97	.28	---
1774	1.29	.34	1.06	----	1.03	.37	---
1775	1.23	.39	.98	----	1.07	.31	---
1776	1.14	.31	1.06	----	1.08	.36	---
1777	1.21	.29	.97	----	1.13	.36	---
1778	1.30	.31	1.00	----	1.14	.37	---
1779	1.10	.43	.75	----	1.18	.53	---
1780	1.30	.28	----	----	1.17	.38	---
1781	----	.37	----	----	1.23	.38	---
1782	----	.31	----	----	1.31	.43	---
1783	----	.41	----	----	1.14	.28	---
1784	----	.32	----	----	1.08	.28	---
1785	----	.31	----	----	1.11	.36	---
1786	----	.42	----	----	1.08	.43	---
1787	----	.26	----	----	1.10	.40	---
1788	----	.29	----	----	1.09	.46	---
1789	----	.29	----	----	1.09	.50	---
1790	----	.33	----	----	1.16	.45	---
1791	----	.35	----	----	1.19	.42	---
1792	----	.31	----	----	1.23	.51	---
1793	----	.24	----	----	1.29	.63	---
1794	----	.45	----	----	1.28	.78	---
1795	----	.32	----	----	1.38	.86	---
1796	----	.31	----	----	1.39	.80	---
1797	----	.23	----	----	1.40	.68	---
1798	----	.25	----	----	1.41	.87	---
1799	----	.24	----	----	1.42	.71	---
1800	----	.24	----	.84	1.39	.80	---
1801	----	.23	----	1.25	1.40	.79	---
1802	----	.28	----	1.28	1.41	.65	---
1803	----	.24	----	1.32	1.36	.76	---
1804	----	.21	----	1.16	1.30	1.19	.53
1805	----	.21	----	1.09	1.27	1.11	.56
1806	----	.24	----	1.17	1.37	.92	.57
1807	----	.24	----	1.08	1.04	.98	.21
1808	----	.25	----	.96	1.17	1.12	.38
1809	----	.27	----	.99	1.19	.99	.69
1810	----	.28	----	----	1.19	1.16	.60

SOURCES FOR TABLE III

East India Company:
    Indian Office Records Library
    ledgers L/AG/1/1/15-25
    financial summaries L/AG/18/2/1-7

Hand in Hand Company:
    Guildhall Library
    Mss. no. 8658-8660

Sun Fire Insurance:
    estimated from data in:
    Guildhall Library Mss. no. 11963
    and P.G.M. Dickson, Sun Fire Insurance Office, Oxford, 1960.

Spencer Stanhope:
    estimated from profit rates and profit margins in: A. Raistrick and A. Allen, "The South Yorkshire Ironmasters," Economic History Review, 1939.

British Linen Company:
    Alastair Durie, The Scottish Linen Industry, Edinburgh: John Donald, 1979, chap. 7.

Carron Company:
    R.H. Campbell, Carron Company, Edinburgh: Oliver & Boyd, 1961; Appendices.

Hudson's Bay Company:
    London Public Record Office
    balance sheets BH/1/334
    and Ann Carlos, "The Causes and Origins of the North American Fur Trade Rivalry," Journal of Economic History, Dec. 1981, p. 785.

Boulton & Watt:
    Birmingham City Library
    Boulton & Watt Collection: ledgers

Examination of the ratios in Table III reveals that financial turnover has a cyclical component, and that mean turnover is surprisingly stable over the period, with successful firms showing a small but persistent rise in trend over the course of the century. This confirms our expectations concerning the endogenous and exogenous components of financial turnover discussed in chapter six. It is only by the nineteenth century that average turnover seems to rise above one; at which time firms were recouping the magnitude of their investment in the form of flow sales in a little less than a year. Obviously, because the sample is so small the conclusions must remain tentative; and yet, the agreement of the independent bits of evidence is striking.

Is it possible to extrapolate this upward trend over an even longer period, say, up to the present? While the author has as yet been unable to construct continous samples of firms through the nineteenth century and into the twentieth century for Great Britain, it is relatively easy to examine the most recent experience, again employing the governmental survey Business Monitor MA3. In the most recent issues, comparable figures for the aggregate of sales and equity for a sample of over one thousand listed companies in the areas of manufacturing and distribution are provided for the years 1969 to 1976. In an effort to compare this data with our earlier evidence, we have divided what is termed in Business Monitor "turnover" (sales excluding inter-group sales but including sales by overseas subsidaries) by "shareholders interest" (ordinary and preference shares plus capital reserves) (HMSO, 1979, pp. 8 and 42-45). The results are presented in Table IV below.

TABLE IV

SALES/EQUITY IN CONTEMPORARY BRITISH FIRMS

Year	Number of Firms	Sales/Equity
1969	1366	2.68
1970	1308	2.82
1971	1239	2.78
1972	1168	2.78
1973	1116	3.01
1974	1084	3.35
1975	1044	3.51
1976	750	3.59

Source: HMSO, Business Monitor MA3, 1979, pp. 42-45, 8.

While it seems we still experience short-term cyclical fluctuations, the average level of contemporary turnover is apparently much higher than that of our sample taken from the eighteenth century. It appears now that an average firm recoups the magnitude of its investment in the form of sales in something less than four months. Tentatively, it seems that if there is any trend in the time structure of capital over the very long run, it is this continual relative acceleration of financial turnover which accompanies the accumulation of capital.

Here it becomes imperative, in order to assert the above generalization with conviction, to confront anew the problem of the comparability of business accounts over long stretches of time. The numerator of our proposed measure of turnover should cause no problems in this regard, since the definition of sales has not undergone appreciable alteration over the time horizon of this study. The denominator, however, is much less straightforward an issue. In the eighteenth as well as the twentieth century data in this chapter, firm equity is defined as the balance sheet aggregate valuation plus any surplus accounts or reserves held by the firm.

Most economic historians seem to believe that eighteenth-century accounting techniques did not generally show an understanding of "the notion of capital as generalized, depersonalized property, seeking the highest returns irrespective of its concrete embodiment." For the purposes of this chapter, it is important to note that none of the objections which are conventionally used to support this position can be applied to the accounting records studied here: periodic and regularized balances are cast, there is no striking instance of confusions between business expenses and personal expenses of the owners, and the techniques of the most advanced textbooks on double-entry accounting of the eighteenth century appear to be put into practice in the accounts examined by the author. Perhaps more importantly, historians of accountancy seem to differ from their counterparts in economic history in their assessment of the essential continuity of accounting practices with respect to equity, although that consistency may not itself conform to the neoclassical conception of capital. [23] If any major generalization can be made about the evolution of accounting procedures between the eighteenth and twentieth centuries, it is that early modern accounts viewed profits as the change in value of net assets over some specified time period, and therefore tended to stress the balance sheet, whereas present day accounts subtract expenses from sales first and make asset valuation a residual, thus stressing the role of the income statement. There is nothing inherent in this trend which would act in net to bias the turnover measure in either direction.

It is true, nonetheless, that the higher a firm's debt/equity ratio, <u>ceteris paribus</u>, the higher the turnover ratio. It is also true that there appears to have been a long-term trend in firm's capital structures towards an increasingly higher leverage ratio. One might be tempted to discount the quickening of turnover through time as an artifact of leverage ratios; but this would confuse the robustness of the measure of fixity with the underlying causes of its movement, as discussed in chapter six.

Finally, economists in the last quarter of the twentieth century are painfully aware that the impacts of inflation must not be overlooked in the process of analyzing financial indicators. One might be inclined to explain the rise in the turnover ratio by a rise in the price level: that is, sales prices react much more rapidly to inflation than do book values of equity and reserves, and so a persistent unexpected inflation would account for the apparent quickening of turnover. In order to test this hypothesis, I regressed the various measures of eighteenth-century financial turnover on both the Schumpeter-Gilboy price index and the Gayer-Rostow-Schwartz price index [24]. Of all the permutations of regressions, only two out of a total of twelve coefficients on the prices indicies were significant at the 5% level: the East India sales turnover on the Schumpeter-Gilboy producer's price index, where the coefficient was unexpectedly negative; and the Carron Company's sales turnover on the Gayer-Rostow-Schwartz price index, where the coefficient was positive but explained an insignificant amount of variance. In total, the regressions provide little evidence for the view that the long-term rise in turnover was simply an artifact of movements in the price level.

Accounting Past and Present

To state that eighteenth century accounting practices did not show "an understanding of the meaning of the concept of capital" presumes that there must exist some accounting practices which do approach that ideal. The problem with attempting such Platonist comparisons where accounting is concerned is that "accepted practice" in England has continually been in flux since Jan Ympyn's <u>Notable and very excellent Woorke</u> was published in 1547. A contemporary accounting monograph states that, "It is only in recent times that accountants have in financial accounting theory and practice concentrated primarily on income. Prior to the late 1920's, the main emphasis in financial reporting was on the balance sheet as a statement of financial soundness and solvency of a business entity." [25] The question then becomes; does this process evolve ever-nearer to the ideal concept of capital, or is it simply changing as expediency and historical circumstances warrant?

For the answer, we need to look no further than our sources of contemporary news. Recently, the president of the Institute of Chartered Accountants in England and Wales said publically: [26]

"There was a crisis of credibility which is a challenge to the profession's independence. We must recognize that the challenge is serious and will be of recurring nature. It is not confined to these shores alone. It is not confined to the auditing of large companies. It covers all aspects of the work of every public accountant."

What prompted the cries of this prominent public Cassandra? The threat obliquely referred to is an expressed desire to nationalize the English accounting profession in order to make it more 'accountable'. The occasion of this threat was the perceived inadequacy of English practice involving the treatment of depreciation, the valuation of inventories and equipment in place in a rapid inflation, and inadequate auditing checks on accounting firms which have close relationships with their clients. The Insititute's response to this threat was to draft guidelines. This process was not as straightforward as it may sound--as an example, the Institute had to retract SSAP11, the guidelines involving deferred tax liabilities, because businesses adopting the standard disliked the way this caused liabilities to accumulate. This incident and many others like it remind us that accounts are kept in the interests of a particular class, whost ability to shape the rules far outweighs any independent devotion to a clear, consistent interpretation of owners' equity. Further, the complaints of those who challenged the Institute are mainly criticisms of modes of matching costs and revenues over time, the same problem Pollard identified in interpreting eighteenth century accounts. When Pollard notes disapprovingly that the Carron Company accounts were juggled in the interests of one family for many years, or a present-day journalist blames the Penn Central bankruptcy on inadequate audits, it becomes hard to maintain that accountancy is asymptotically approaching some ideal notion of capital through time.

There is a variation on this theme which must also be considered. Instead of postulating as ideal economic definition of capital and then searching history to find a social imperative to approximate it, some economic historians would maintain, along with De Mandeville, that a laissez-faire market turns any businessperson's private vice into a functional public virtue. [27] This persuasion hold that odd and unusual accounting practices really do not matter on the whole, since an efficient market will transform an individual's erratic behavior into something that (in the aggregate) behaves like the economists's notion of capital. A specific accounting incarnation of this view is the Modigliani-Miller theorem, which states that the amount of leverage chosen by a firm will not affect the cost of capital to that firm, which then also translated into the rate of profit. Subsequent work has shown that reasoning depends crucially upon the following assumptions: perfect knowledge on the part of all concerned about the firm's accounting practices; no possibility of bankruptcy (really the perfect information assumption in a different guise); and the rate of interest must somehow be given previous to the discounted present value calculations by individuals. [28] The theoretical niceties of this position have already been discussed in Chapter Five. We might just repeat that it seems the only way that economic theory can ignore historical accounting practice and postulate an ideal "capital" is by abstracting away from everything that the accountant is paid to deal with, such as the failure of the entity, an uncertain future and its concomitant ex post income surprises, and the institutional constraints imposed upon the forms and uses of accounts.

If we are agreed that 'capital' as such does not exist independent of the modes of account employed by the owners of capital, what kind of capital theory is appropriate to an understanding of eighteenth century business experience? This question bears added poignancy when one considers that neoclassical capital theory has come under heavy fire recently on the grounds of its logical consistency. Pollard's answer is purely negative: classical theory is inappropriate, he maintains. The only functional analysis he offers is that interest is a separate return to disembodied capital, while "profits are distinct...depending upon skill, the concrete business situation or pure luck."

We instead propose to change our viewpoint and take the historical business records at their face value. This mode of understanding is supported by the institutional theory of the long-period rate of profit, which is more amenable to examination of phenomena that seem contradictory when peered at through neoclassical spectacles. This change of viewpoint does not demand any wrenching dislocations of consciousness. As a case in point, consider Pollard's contention that the interest accounts explicitly entered in eighteenth century books and the corresponding profit and loss accounts really represent returns to separate factors. Why, instead, could not such a division represent the imposed center of gravity of the long-period return (i.e., the proprietors' interest charges on their capital) and the unpredictable fluctuations around that long-period center (the profit and loss account)? This would explain why, although they are two components of the same profit stream, the actual rate of profit is never calculated explicitly for the record. Their target average rate of return was calculated and imposed (this being important, because it shows a real world case of distribution being imposed prior to pricing and investment) under the rubric of interest. The owners were undoubtedly aware that this rate was quite often exceeded by the average ex post rate of profit, but this was also a calculated move. If an average rate of 15% to 20% were actually recorded, the proprietors might have been liable to prosectution under the existing usury laws, not to mention the more mundane pressures from sleeping partners and, more importantly, the ever-present creditors. Finally, since an income tax existed for only a short duration during the Napoleonic wars as a last ditch financial scheme when the government was threatened with dissolution, there were no legal compunctions (nor any legal definitions) to report income to anyone. As a result, the owners of a concern could easily get a reasonable estimate of their rate of realized profit if they wanted it; but there were very good reasons for not spreading it around. In any event, they were always in possession of a proxy in the form of an imposed rate of interest which was an effective yardstick against which to judge the total rate of return (especially if the rule of thumb was transparently simple--twice the rate of interest.) The main purpose of the recorded accounts was to convince the appropriate outsiders of the firm's solvency, and to a lesser extent, to provide some managerial check on the costs of separate activities.

The other class of accounting 'errors', involving the confusion of the private person and business entity, becomes perhaps more comprehensibile when we consider that owners were held to unlimited liability in the event of business failure. The first glimmerings of limited liability, in the guise of preference shares, grew out of the financial embarrassments of the early canal and railroad joint stocks in the first half of the nineteenth century; the same time that historians of accountancy find a distinct movement to separate private and business accounts. Again we see capital being historically defined. If a creditor can seize your spoons in partial payment of a business debt, your spoons are part of your investment, by definition?d

The final class of 'errors' include all the many and varied machinations employed to alter the time distribution of costs and revenues. Some examples are the arbitrary posting of depreciation, posting expenditures on long-lived equipment in current expenditure accounts, posting interest on debt on an accrual basis, and so forth. We have already seen that similar practices still haunt the accounting profession, albeit in more and more sophisticated forms. Pollard's mistake in condemning these practices is his unwarranted assumption that owners wish their accounts to approximate the unvarnished truth in all matters of timing. First, what the truth is in the timing of accounts has never been settled. A recent accounting textbook poses the choice as a continuum rather than pure black or white: one moves from 'economic income' which can never be attained since it involves perfect knowledge and the proper ex ante apportioning of windfalls, to traditional 'accounting income' which overlooks all changes in the value of non-traded assets. [29] Secondly, even if there existed a true time distribution of accounts, certain theoretical reasons have already been outlined why individual owners would find it to their advantage to alter that distribution towrds the present through manipulation of their accounts. Basically, we assume entrepreneurs are strongly motivated to achieve a higher financial rate of profit or realize extraodinary paper capital gains if they see a suitable opportunity to do so. Both considerations add up to a 'rational' motivation for the seemingly haphazard nature of the timing of costs and revenues in eighteenth century accounts.

In this paricular instance, if eighteenth century businessmen had institutional motivations to keep the records which they actually did keep, it then makes sense to study those muniments as economic documents which can be instrumental in providing empirical evidence for economic theories. Moreover, in our case, the theoretical link is forged between the classical theorists' long period profit rate and the rate experienced by businesspeople who were their contemporaries. In the interest of furthering this connection, we move in the next section to sample some eigtheenth century business records.

The Construction of the Profit Index

There are seventeen firms which comprise the sample. Eleven came from published sources, while six were extracted from archival sources by the author. The criteria for the inclusion of a series were that it extend for at least twenty years; that the firm be a 'going concern' which was not approaching bankruptcy; and that enough supplemental material existed so that there could be external checks on the financial records. These very weak conditions screened out perhaps three times as many records as were finally included. The names of the firms, the dates of their inclusion, geographic location, product character and source are summarized in Table 5.

As far as possible, profits were defined as inclusive of interest paid to owners, but exclusive of interest paid on outside debt. The usual source of the information collected by the author was the profit and loss account from the firm's ledger, although in the case of the Sun Fire Assurance it was a closing account termed the 'Office Account'. The accounts were adjusted to exclude all rents on land, wherever applicable; all dividends paid out of such accounts were restored to final profits. As a rule, changes in the value of net worth were not included in profits, except where there was additional evidence that such changes were the result of investments in real assets which had occured prior to the period's casting up of profit income.

TABLE V

FIRMS INCLUDED IN PROFIT INDEX

Concern	Dates of Inclusion	Product or Service	Geographical Location	Source
London Assurance	1728-1826	insurance	London	SALI
Million Bank	1728-1782	investment trust	London	PRO C/114/10, ii
Scotch Mines	1755-1811	lead mining	Leadhills Scotland	GL/12033
Sun Fire	1729-1826	insurance	London	GL/11963, 11933, 15042
East India Co.	1728-1779	trade	London	IOR:L/AG/18/2/1,L/AG/1/1/16-24
Westminster Fire	1761-1794	insurance	London	CWPL/343/83-85
Whitbread	1762-1794	brewing	London	Mathias, p. 553
Carron Co.	1770-1826	mining & metal fab.	Prestonpans Scotland	Campbell, pp.330-2
Hull Docks Co.	1775-1805	transport	Kingston-on-Hull	Jackson, p. 426
Drummonds	1777-1826	banking	London	Bolitho & Peel, pp. 212-213
Spencer Stanhope Partnership	1728-1762	iron forge	S. Yorkshire	Raistrick & Allen, pp.179,184
Fordell Colliery	1772-1789 1800-1812	mining	Scotland	Duckham, pp.147,197
Marshall Partners'	1805-1826	flax spinning	Leeds	Rimmer, pp.319-21

TABLE V - CONTINUED

Concern	Dates of Inclusion	Product or Service	Geographical Location	Source
Clark	1805-1825	woolen trade	Wiltshire	Beckinsale, p. xxxi
Coalbrook-dale	1739-45 1799-1826	metal fabrication	Lancas.	Raistrick, pp.278,298
Bridgewater Trust	1806-1826	canal, transport	Lancas.	Mather, pp.358-9
Cowpe, Oldknowe, Siddon & Co.	1790-1813	cotton spinning	Notts.	Pigott, p. 89

FIRMS INCLUDED IN PROFIT INDEX

Key to sources in Table V:

SALI: Sun Alliance & Life Insurance, private muniments
PRO: Public Record Office
GL: Guildhall Library muniments
IOR: India Office Records Library
CWPL: City of Westminster Public Library
Mathias: *The Brewing Industry in England, 1700-1830*, Cambridge: Cambridge U. Press, 1959
Campbell: *Carron Company*, Edinburgh: Oliver & Boyd, 1961
Jackson: *Hull in the Eighteenth Century*, Oxford: Oxford U. Press, 1972
Bolitho & Peel: *The Drummonds of Charing Cross*, London: Allen & Unwin, 1967
Duckham: *History of Scottish Coal*, Newton Abbott: David & Charles, 1970
Rimmer: *Marshall of Leeds*, Cambridge, Cambridge U. Press, 1960
Beckinsale: *Trowbridge Woolen Industry*, Wiltshire Arch. & Nat. Hist. Transactions, 1951
Raistrick: *Dynasty of Iron Founders*, London: Longmans, 1953
Raistrick & Allen: "The South Yorkshire Ironmasters," *Economic History Review*, May 1939
Mather: *After the Canal Duke*, Oxford U. Press, 1970
Pigott: *Hollins*, Nottingham: Viyella, 1949

Since all the firms whose records are summarized by the author were quite large, no problems of the mixing of personal and business accounts were discovered. Obviously, in cases of published series, there is little or no way of assuring that the above definitions were employed by the relevant author; but wherever the components of owners' income were also published, the appropriate corrections were calculated by the author.

The numerator of the profit rate was defined as the book value of net worth, which was taken directly from balance sheets when possible, and in all other cases was replaced by the stated value of nominal net capital in company records or as reported by company historians.

In keeping with the spirit of our model and the discussion in the previous section, the time patterns of profit realization were preserved, with one exception. We have already mentioned in section one of this chapter how the Million Bank chose to depreciate its holdings of government annuities in a hurried and sporadic manner. This erratic behavior can be explained in the context of the Bank's history. In 1741-2 a number of the stockholders began to be concerned that the annuities on which the Bank's assets were based would expire in less than fifty years, and that the government had ceased issuing new annuities as a method of funding; they argued that the Bank should expand its investment horizons. For various reasons the opinion prevailed that the original charter had only allowed investment in annuities; thereafter the financial operations of the Bank entered a period of benign neglect. The annuities were depreciated as an afterthought since all parties concerned realized the decisions of 1741-2 tacitly admitted that the Bank was to self-destruct in parallel with the annuities. This in fact happened in 1796-9 when the affairs of the Bank were calmly wrapped up. For our purposes, the importance of the 'going concern' assumption outweighs our respect for the integrity of eighteenth century financial manipulations. Therefore, the author has calculated the rate of profit for the Million Bank that would have existed if the annuities remained unchanged in the asset structure. This involved reacalculating profit for the years 1764, 1765, 1773, 1774, 1776, 1778, 1779, and 1781.

Before proceeding to the construction of the annual index, we should consider the expected relations between the components. The institutionalist conception of the profit rate is a center of gravity towards which subsets of the economy are constantly moving. While it is true that the more integrated the economy, the less dispersion we expect about this rate, it is not true that more integration necessarily means greater correlation between subsets or firms. Examples of the latter sort are studies which examine the cross-spectra of timeseries of wheat prices or exchange rates for different geographical areas: greater coherence squared and less phase shift over time are interpreted as evidence of the spread of efficient market structures. Since institutional economics does not view the profit rate as a 'price' of capital, it would not predict that a more efficient market would necessarily involve quicker and higher correlations of profit rates of individual sectors of the economy. The dynamics of the financial sector in the model presented in chapter six gives us further reason to think that financial manipulations and therefore the rate of profit are not homogeneous througout the economy. Still, stability demands behavioral convergence to the center of gravity, so we do expect a certain amount of positive correlation between firms in any given period. The amount of correlation is an inverse indicator of the extent of sectoral disequilibrium in the economy: the closer to full tranquil equilibrium is the system, the greater is the correlation of profit rates between sectors.

The same-period correlation matrix of the component firms' profit series are presented in Table 6. If there were less than ten overlapping data points between any two timeseries, zero is entered in the appropriate cell. If the correlation, either positive or negative, was significant at the 10% (two-tailed) t-statistic level, a plus or minus is entered in the appropriate cell. Blank cells represent insignificant correlations. Of the 136 possible correlations, 52 had less than ten shared data points. Of the remaining 84, there were 14 significant positive correlations, or 16.6%; while there were 3 significant negative correlations, or 3.5%. The profit rate of the London Assurance was significantly positively correlated with the largest number of other series, while three firms had no same-period positive correlations: Scotch Mines, the Clark proprietorship and the Bridgewater Canal Trust.

Own-period correlation is not the only way any given firms or sectors may be related; there may also be leads and lags. A statistically complete description would be produced by cross-spectral analysis, but none of our series is long enough to approach the asymptotic requirements of spectral analysis. However, we can further approximate a dynamic description by a single period lagged correlation matrix, which is presented in Table 7. The notation is the same as Table 6. The diagonal presents the correlation between the series and its own lagged values; the rows represent lags, while the columns represent leads. Out of 272 possible non-diagonal cells, 103 have less than ten points in common. Of the remaining 169 cells, 25 have significant positive correlations. The Clark proprietorship and the East India Company are the only concerns which are not positively correlated with any other firm in the sample in Table 7. Combining this result with the information in Table 6, only the Clark proprietorship has no positive correlation with any other firm in the sample. It is

Table VI

Same period correlation matrix

	London Assr.	Million Bank	Scotch Mines	Whitbread	Carron	Sun Fire	Spencer	Westminster	East India	Hull Dock	Drummond	Cosco	Fordell	Marshall	Clark	Coalbrook	Bridgewater	Number of cols. +	Number of rows +
London Assr.	#					+	+		+	+			+					5	2
Million Bank		#	+	+		+				0	0	0		0	0	0	0	2	
Scotch Mines			#	−		−	0							0	0	0	0		
Whitbread				#		0					+	0						1	1
Carron					#	0					−	+						1	
Sun Fire						#	+											1	
Spencer							#	0	0	0	0	0	0	0	0	0	0		1
Westminster								#				0		0	0	0	0		1
East India									#	0	0	0	0	0	0	0	0		1
Hull Dock										#	+	+	+	0	0	0	0	2	1
Drummond											#	+	+					1	1
Cosco												#	0	0	0	0	0		2
Fordell													#	0	0	+	0	1	3
Marshall														#					
Clark															#	+			1
Coalbrook																#	#		
Bridgewater																			

TABLE VII

One-period lag correlation matrix

	London Assr	Million Bank	Scotch Mines	Whitbread	Carron	Sun Fire	Spencer	Westminster	East India	Hull Dock	Drummond	Cosco	Fordell	Marshall	Clark	Coalbrook	Bridgewater	Other firm + corr. Lead	Lag
London Assr																	+	1	3
Million Bank		+			+	+	+			0	0	0	0	0	0	0	0	3	2
Scotch Mines				−			0	+				0		0	0			1	1
Whitbread			+				0				0			0	0	0	0		1
Carron					+		0					−	+				+	2	2
Sun Fire	+	+				+					+						+	3	2
Spencer	+		0	0	0		+	0		0	0	0	0	0	0	0	0	1	1
Westminster							0					0		0	0	0	0		1
East India				0				−		0	0	0	0	0	0	0	0		
Hull Dock	+	0	+				0		0	+		+	+	0	0	0	0	4	1
Drummond		0					0		0				+	−				1	2
Cosco		0		0			0	0	0					0	0		0		1
Fordell		+		+	+	+	0		0	+	0	+		0	0	0	0	5	3
Marshall		0	0	0			0	0	0	0		0	0		+	+		1	1
Clark		0	0	0			0	0	0	0			0	−		−			
Coalbrook		0		0			0	0	0	0			0	+		+		1	1
Bridgewater		0	0	0			0	0	0	0	+	0	0				+	1	3

interesting to note that Clark has by far the smallest capital in the sample for 13 out of 21 years of inclusion, and is also unusual because it is the only firm whose records incorporate the 'starting up' period of growth: we have suggested in the previous section that there is much that is anomalous about the capital structure in the first few years of operation of a business. On the whole, the material presented in Table 6 and 7 is evidence of a fair amount of capital flows integration between the firms whose records remain for the eighteenth and early nineteenth centuries.

Given our information, we must now face the perennial economist's affliction, the aggregation problem. Theoretically, in order for aggregation to be neutral with respect to the results, each of the profit rates should be weighted by their equilibrium prices and levels of output as a percentage of total output. Such precision of information remains a chimera for eighteenth century history; and moreover, we do not have a random sample. We are thus inexorably driven to expedients. Various weighting schemes could be devised, the most obvious of which is to weight the profit rates by the size of their capitals, producing an index which is equivalent to the sum of all profits divided by the sum of all the capitals. The problem with this sort of index is that it places inordinate emphasis upon exceptionally large concerns: in our case, this means the East India Company, which had a nominal capital of three million two hundred thousand pounds, while the capitals of the other concerns range from one thousand to roughly nine hundred thousand pounds. There is no good reason to stress the experience of the East India Comapany so heavily, and there are a few good reasons why such stress is undesirable. The East India Company has always been a special case when it came to government policy and governmental interests, as readers of Lucy Sutherland's The East India Co. in Eighteenth Century Politics are well aware. Further, the magnitude of the accounting demands required of the India Company exceeded anything else in contemporary experience. Finally, fluctuations in the India trade were not very representative of English trade as a whole, domestic or foreign; so the India company cannot support the burden of representation implied by such a weighting. Therefore, we had to reject any weighting scheme proportional to capitals.

Since we possess no other *a priori* evidence as to the proper weighting scheme, the optimal strategy is a flat prior; that is, take the unweighted mean of the information embodied in our sample. Hence our profit index is the sum of the calculated profit rates divided by the number of firms in the sample at time t. The result is named 'mean profit' and is reported in Table 8.

Because the composition of the sample is changing over time, the differing means of firms which enter and leave the sample will cause flucutations in the index which are independent of the fluctuations in any of the series. Since

TABLE VIII

Profit indices 1728–1826

Year	Adjusted Profit	Mean Profit	Number of Firms
1728	.275	.65	4
1729	-.376	-2.24	5
1730	.765	6.20	5
1731	-.011	.78	5
1732	1.384	10.68	5
1733	2.187	16.20	5
1734	.955	7.64	5
1735	.705	6.16	5
1736	1.447	11.72	5
1737	.565	5.10	5
1738	1.467	11.06	5
1739	.873	7.48	6
1740	.731	6.38	6
1741	.966	8.21	6
1742	.870	5.58	5
1743	.702	6.50	6
1744	.650	8.10	6
1745	1.128	9.26	6
1746	.983	10.90	5
1747	.645	6.04	5
1748	1.002	11.48	5
1749	.530	5.64	5
1750	.902	9.72	5
1751	.942	11.14	5
1752	1.246	8.12	5
1753	.796	9.98	5
1754	1.250	13.58	5
1755	.982	10.96	6
1756	.919	10.48	6
1757	.669	9.75	6
1758	1.509	14.41	6
1759	1.128	11.53	6
1760	1.102	11.95	6
1761	.935	9.44	7
1762	.869	9.29	8
1763	1.164	11.28	7
1764	1.114	14.01	7
1765	1.050	11.22	7
1766	1.158	13.56	7
1767	1.180	12.41	7
1768	1.136	13.75	7
1769	.902	9.50	7
1770	1.204	15.70	8
1771	1.151	14.48	7
1772	.789	11.82	8
1773	.973	11.25	9
1774	.907	12.66	9
1775	1.077	12.16	10
1776	1.063	14.31	10
1777	.965	14.09	11
1778	.772	11.78	11
1779	.594	8.14	11
1780	.645	12.22	10

TABLE VIII - CONTINUED

—continued

Year	Adjusted Profit	Mean Profit	Number of Firms
1781	.726	9.00	9
1782	1.256	17.61	10
1783	.668	8.50	9
1784	.802	11.24	9
1785	.428	6.35	9
1786	.842	12.73	9
1787	.853	12.34	9
1788	1.222	15.70	9
1789	1.056	15.38	9
1790	.995	13.73	9
1791	1.263	17.56	9
1792	.825	15.86	9
1793	.617	9.42	9
1794	.859	8.04	9
1795	.828	14.81	7
1796	.907	16.05	7
1797	.916	16.11	7
1798	1.097	19.90	7
1799	1.297	18.96	8
1800	1.153	15.52	9
1801	1.688	24.17	9
1802	1.184	14.95	8
1803	1.526	21.18	8
1804	1.319	19.48	8
1805	1.453	21.12	11
1806	1.211	17.33	11
1807	1.252	20.70	11
1808	1.127	15.84	11
1809	1.215	16.66	11
1810	.766	19.00	10
1811	.977	14.79	10
1812	.924	16.98	10
1813	.850	13.94	9
1814	1.228	20.95	8
1815	.967	16.17	8
1816	.911	18.02	8
1817	1.215	20.53	8
1818	.926	17.12	8
1819	1.700	19.50	8
1820	1.161	20.55	8
1821	1.040	15.98	8
1822	1.089	17.45	8
1823	1.015	15.32	8
1824	1.235	18.61	8
1825	2.025	40.10	8
1826	.920	12.35	7

we are interested in fluctuations, we can adjust for this effect by dividing all of the series by their means, and then taking the sum of the results divided by the number of firms at time t. This adjusted index, named 'adjusted profit' is reported in Table 8, along with the number of firms at time t.

The first index is a heuristic device, denominated in actual percentage units of profit rate. From it, we see the average profit rate is somewhere between 9 and 18% and rising over the course of the eighteenth and early nineteenth centuries. The first index is thus useful for an impressionistic indication of trend. The second index, while not detrended, has been rotated somewhat in a clockwise direction by the mean adjustment process. Consequently it is a pure index, its main purpose being to identify fluctuations and turning points in the profit rate.

The Index and Some Independent Evidence

The writers of the eighteenth century were interested in profits, although perhaps not with the same drive for quantification that characterized twentieth century man (or twentieth century cliometricians, anyway). They were aware of two of its salient characteristics: its rough level, and its upper turning points, which contemporaries called 'crises'. In order to gain some independent support for confidence in our index, we shall briefly review this evidence.

One mode of corroboration for our series is found in comparing the upper turning points of the series to contemporaries' perceptions of crises. These crises were usually credit contractions brought on by monetary manipulations or adverse trade balances, which are not the sole causes of downturns of profit. Credit crises can happen during or after an intial fall in the profit rate: there is no particular presumption about their timing other than this. Still, many pamphleteers insisted that crises and upper turning points of activity coincided. Because of this we shall compare some dates identified by historians as crisis years with the relative movements of our mean adjusted series.

Table 9 summarizes the crises identified by four different authors: Phyllis Deane, T.S. Ashton, Mentor Bouniatian and Alvin Hansen. [30] 1745 is identified in the literature as the year Bonnie Prince Charlie invaded England and induced Jacobite doubts about the stability of the Whig settlement; 1763 seems to have been the end of a short-lived flurry of activity after the cessation of the Seven Year's War in 1761; 1783 was marked by a large external drain of coin and bullion which caused sharp falls in the prices of consols, Bank stock and East India stock. Whatever

TABLE IX

CRISES OR UPPER TURNING POINTS

Deane	Hansen	Ashton	Bouniatian
1720		1720	
		1726	
		1733	
1745		1745	1745
	1753		
		1761	
1763	1763	1763	
1772		1772	
	1773		
1776			
		1778	1778
1783	1783	1783	1783
		1788	
		1792	
1793	1793		1793
			1796
1797	1797	1797	
		1799	1799
	1810		1810
	1815		1815
			1819
	1825		1825

Periods covered: Deane, 1720-1800; Hansen, 1750-1825; Ashton, 1720-1800; Bouniatian, 1720-1825.

agreement amongst these authors that is revealed in the table does not appear to be due to the particular severity of the crises at these dates according to contemporary narratives; but that is difficult to say with confidence since there was the inevitable tendency for contemporaries to see every crisis as the worst ever. Speculation is doomed to remain at this superficial level unless explicit criteria are specified for the choice of dates.

A more careful examination of the previous point is provided by a comparison of the adjusted profit index with the dates identified by Ashton. His dates 1733, 1745, 1763, 1788 and 1799 agree with peaks in the series, while 1772, 1783 and 1792 are years of precipitious falls from appreciable peaks. The three years that do not fit his expectations are 1761, 1778 and 1797. The years 1778 and 1797 come in the midst of profound stagnations, as defined by the adjusted profit index being below one (the average by definition) for five or more consecutive years. Ashton's choice of 1761 is very questionable, since none of the other writers mention it as a crisis date, and its position so near the agreed-upon date of 1763 makes it doubtful that it deserves to be in the same class as the other years.

Since Ashton never defines his crises, or even commits himself to more than a vague causality, it is difficult to adequately assess the relation of his chronology to our proposed indicator. Notwithstanding this criticism, the agreement of half of his dates with peaks of the index and another three peaks by one period lagged is heartening. the historical uniqueness of each of these turning point will be discussed in the following chapter, and a commentary on Ashton's chronology will be provided. In the meantime, some independent evidence has been produced which lends a modicum of support to the profit indices here constructed.

CHAPTER NINE

A CHRONOLOGY OF EIGHTEENTH CENTURY BRITISH INSTABILITY

> "It must be allowed that a spirit of speculation had much to do in accelerating and increasing these disasters; but speculation may be virtuous or vicious....Like another South Sea Bubble, the present panic will cease, and be remembered only for the fearful truths which it has taught."
>
> --Anonymous, The Panic
> London: Harchard and Son, 1862

Previous Measures of Eighteenth Century Instability, and the New Evidence

The standard (and effectively only) reference on the eighteenth century English macroeconomy, T.S. Ashton's Economic Fluctuations in England, 1700-1800, begins on an ingenuous note: "The title of this book is forbidding: if the attention of the reader is to be held there must be good will from the start. It would be unwise to begin with a disquisition on economic theory--for the fruit of that tree too often turns out to be the apple of discord." The present work, which purports to treat the same subject, has chosen the bitter apple (instead of the sweetsop?), perhaps to the relative discomfort of the reader; but now the time has arrived to complete the marriage of theory and evidence in a narrative of early English macroeconomic fluctuations.

Macroeconomic history, when it has aspired to something more than the strict chronology of business annals, has been notoriously difficult to organize. Ashton chose to begin with the weather, and thence on to harvests; only later gradually working through foreign trade and construction to reach financial crises. Gayer, Rostow and Schwartz (GRS), in a much more sober and businesslike proceeding, presented the period 1790-1850 divided into small three to seven year units, which were further subdivided into the standardized headings of prices, foreign trade, investment, industry and agriculture, finance, and labor. One suspects that the encyclopaedic rather than narrative form of these two works, and those which imitate them, are due to the diffuse theories and motivations which underlie their composition. Ashton, for example, never commits himself as to what a business cycle consists of, and therefore any phenomenon which might admit of an economic interpretation, had regular fluctuations, and which was already well-documented historiographically, was fair game. [1] GRS consciously limit themselves to the six discrete yet disjoint categories, in that what happens under the heading of prices has no connection with what occurs under the headings of investment or finance. (One must admit this could be due to the exigencies of joint ownership.) GRS do, however, commit themselves to a specific definition of the cycle, and an odd definition it turns out to be. One must read through 350 pages of text and figures based on a puzzling "Business Cycle Pattern (Abstract Scale)" before one discovers that the 'index' for 1790-1826 is a weighted average of: [2]

Timeseries	Weight
Hoffman's index of total production	1
Kondratieff's index of textile production	2
Number of bankruptcies	2
Total value of inland bills of exchange created	2
Brick production (excise)	2
Index of share prices	2
Volume of domestic good exports	3

It would be difficult to argue such a hodgepodge of timeseries could represent any one thing or idea, especially without some theoretical rationale. It indiscriminately mixes financial and physical phenomena, domestic and foreign influences, quantities with prices, and objects with occurences. And to think it is then vested with a spurious air of numerical authority through the assignment of weights! The whole enterprise is further compromised by the authors' explicitly professed disrespect for certain components of the index--the Hoffman index is the most glaring example. (A word about this shortly.)

The serial history of eighteenth century England, in fact, is plagued by the overtaxing of a very few economic timeseries which are endowed, as a consequence, with excessive significance. In the realm of physical goods, the quantitative measures of overseas trade and timeseries of excise returns have had to bear the whole brunt of circumstantial evidence. The ever-increasing craving of twentieth century historians for numbers, whatever the cost of significance, has obscured the logistical and theoretical drawbacks of these aggregate statistics. In the case of the foreign trade data, there are the more conventional <u>caveats</u> concerning the weaknesses of the official figures: even though E.B. Schumpeter has made a great advance in attacking the index number problem by recalculating aggregate export and import values at a fixed set of prices [4], as aggregates they are poor indicators of fluctuations because of concomitant fluctuations in the internal composition of the basket of imported and exported goods. Some analysts avoid this problem by isolating the international trade of a few selected goods such as timber, woolens and iron as presumably sufficiently representative of aggregate activity. For imports, this ignores the high incidence of smuggling and customs evasion in the eighteenth century, which has been estimated being, at times, as high as one-quarter of official imports [5]; this renders them questionable as indicators of macro fluctuations. But more importantly, it is a mistake to select any particular good or goods as necessarily representative of the functioning of the whole economy because the author happens to believe the good in question is widely and extensively employed in manufacturing processes, or for some such other ad hoc reason. To see the reason this is so, consider, for a moment, the model developed in chapter six. Since we do not expect balanced growth to exist for any extended period of time, it follows that the real sector of the model will continually be in a state of disequilibrium: depending upon the spectral properties of the A and B matrices and the postulated investment behaviors, some sectors will be expanding while others are contracting, and all will be cycling about the potential long term growth rate of the entire economy, which may itself be changing due to altered relations of financial and physical turnover. The rate of production of any particular good will not necessarily provide a reasonable estimate of the rate of expansion of the economy. It is entirely possible that the macroeconomy may be in a tailspin due to a falling 'tranquil equilibrium' growth rate, while simultaneously a particular sector's production is expanding in relative and even absolute terms. More precisely, if we expand the closed model to include foreign trade by adding an extra row to the A and B matrices to represent imports as inputs into production and an extra column for exports [6], aggregate imports and exports will themselves assume this sectoral characteristic of non-representative fluctuation. So from a theoretical point of view, customs and excise statistics are seriously flawed as macroeconomic proxies. They could only perform that function if the economy were always experiencing balanced growth--a contradiction in terms in the context of a study of cycles.

A word should also be inserted about Hoffmann's 'indices of industrial production', an imposing set of figures stretching from 1700 to the twentieth century, which have been used indiscriminately by many economic historians. Unfortunately, these series for 'consumer goods' and 'producer goods' add little to our prior knowledge of eighteenth century Britain, and are admitted to be "an extremely dubious measure of the physical volume of production" [7] and "too narrowly based to be conclusive." [8] The reasons for these condemnations are threefold: first, they are constructed almost totally from the customs and excise data surveyed above; secondly, Hoffmann makes extensive use of 'representative series' (such as malt and paper charged for excise as the only components of the 'consumer good' series in the early years of the century); and third, Hoffmann unabashedly employs numerous interpolations to fill gaps in series. All of these practices persuade us to reject Hoffmann's indices as having any substantial explanatory power in a macroeconomic history of eighteenth century England. Hoffmann himself insists that his indices are useless for analyzing business fluctuations with a periodicity of less than ten years; some independent calculations reported below by the present author suggest that the minimum period should be even longer.

In the financial sphere, historians of the English macroeconomy tend to rely on statistics of the Bank of England, exchange rates between the pound sterling and other major currencies, bankruptcy statistics, and especially the implicit yield on 3% British consols. With regard to the Bank of England, it has been argued that the Bank precociously assumed the function of lender of last resort in eighteenth century crises, and therefore timeseries information of the Bank's income from discounts of notes and bills serves as an indicator of those crises. [9] A little reflection leads us to question any strict correlation, because a rise in income mixes price and quantity movements, and merely indicates an expansion of credit on the part of the Bank, which may happen both in a boom as part of a larger acceleration of financial turnover, and in the downturn as the Bank assumes the function of lender of last resort (that is, preventing financial turnover from slowing to a crawl for essentially political motives) to whatever degree it deemed necessary. Thus it can not be a trustworthy measure of the extent or the direction of the financial economy. The same generic problem is encountered in timeseries of business failures: although one might normally expect the number of failures to rise in a depression, empirically, they conventionally increase substantially during a business expansion; in part because they are not standardized relative to the rate of business formation, and in part because a serious depression wipes out practically all businesses possessing weak balance sheets, which later results in a rising failure rate per thousand as businesses attempt to regain pre-depression levels of financial turnover. Other difficulties, such as changes in bankruptcy laws, varying stringency in reporting rules (usually in the London Gazette), and changes in the local availability of credit instruments all act to render these quantities problematic, at best. Foreign exchange rates, because they are tied to export and import quantities, fall prey to many of the same criticisms we have already voiced with respect to foreign trade quantity statistics.

To supplant these existing indicators, previous chapters of this work have developed a theoretical framework within which to evaluate microeconomic instability. Employing this framework, one may identify certain key indicators which have been hitherto overlooked. Basically, these are the forms of information which are contained in business accounts and financial records. It is important to stress that these are not artificial post hoc constructs (unlike retrospective national income accounts or industrial production indices), but rather the indicators of economic well-being which the historical actors themselves deployed and depended upon. As a rule, eighteenth century business records are not, unlike most government statistics, conditional upon the vagaries of bureaucratic objectives; they are attempts of the economic units to gauge the buoyancy of their own particular vessels. The manuscript and archival work represented by this and previous chapters does not simply add more indifferent data to the historiographic heap, but combines theoretical guidance with an epistemological precept that respects contemporary choices of forms of information for their own sake. While it is true, as Defoe maintained early in the eighteenth century, that "the Merchant is no more to be followed in his adventures than a Maze or Labyrinth is to be traced without a Clue," it is also the case that an institutionalist economics is based upon the fact that financial (or, more appropriately, pecuniary) information is the primary perceptible evidence of capitalist economic activity. Business accounts are the skeletal relics of capitalist growth and evolution.

The macroeconomic history of eighteenth century England, employing the new data, will be presented chronologially in the section immediately following. After that, some consideration will be given to older explanations of eighteenth century cycles which were surveyed in previous chapters of this book. Finally, we shall present an alternative analysis of trends in eighteenth century macroeconomic instability. But first, in order to provide an overview of the eighteenth century experience, Table A displays quinquennial means of the share price index and the mean adjusted profit index. Also included are the quinquennial means of annual percentage population growth figures and the quinquennial means of the debit total of the cash flow accounts of the East India Company. The latter two series are included in the first quarter of the century when profit data is sparse, partially because in the theoretical hierarchy of cyclical indicators, these series occupy the second rank of as yet unexplored data. Ideally, one would like to supplement the profit rate information

Table A

QUINQUENNIAL MEANS OF ECONOMIC INDICATORS

Year	Share Price Index	Mean Adjusted Profit	E. India Cash Flow	Annual % Pop. Change
1700-04	75.9		2.59	.40
1705-09	72.9			.16
1710-14	71.6		2.65	.14
1715-19	96.6		2.40	.28
1720-24	107.4		2.56	.24
1725-29	95.6		2.30	-.60
1730-34	100.8	1.056	2.17	.52
1735-39	104.6	1.011	2.75	.34
1740-44	98.8	.828	2.11	.24
1745-49	93.0	.901	2.72	.40
1750-54	104.1	.980	4.73	.52
1755-59	90.7	.976	2.52	.28
1760-64	84.0	1.037	2.88	.30
1765-69	107.0	1.085	3.84	.36
1770-74	103.2	1.005	4.92	.54
1775-79	96.3	.894	3.80	.56
1780-84	75.2	.819	4.51	.42
1785-89	92.3	.880	6.88	.68
1790-94	105.4	.912	6.94	.60
1795-99	85.2	1.009	10.59	.66
1800-04	96.7	1.374		.86
1805-09	108.4	1.251		.84
1810-14	107.5	.949		1.00
1815-19	99.4	1.143		.96
1820-24	123.3	1.108		1.02

Sources: Share price index: Philip Mirowski, "The Rise (and Retreat) of a Market" Journal of Economic History Sept. 1981, p. 572.
Mean adjusted profit index: see chapter eight above.
East India Co. total cash debit: East India Company Ledgers, India Office Records Library, L/AG/1/1/9-18.
Population average annual percentage growth rates: courtesy of Ronald Lee, Univ. of Mich. Population Studies Ctr., from the Cambridge group for the history of population and social structure; preliminary figures.

with cash flow figures for a significant proportion of the economy in order to make precise statements about changes in financial turnover. While we shall explore this issue further below, the dealings of the East India Company may have some intrinsic interest in their own right as representing the largest eighteenth century trading concern. The population growth figures are germane to a work on historical business cycles because some earlier work done by the author suggests population movements can be viewed as ecological responses to changes in wage (and perhaps employment) conditions: that is, labor may be viewed as the most important of the produced goods of the system. [10] This would reverse the lines of causality now found in conventional historical explanations (such as those of the Annales school), where population movements essentially govern the early modern macroeconomy, and of neoclassical explanations, where the wage is the outcome of a constrained maximization problem having to do with factor payments. This earlier paper found a significant positive reaction to births to real wages with an average lag of 1.58 years and a significant negative reaction of deaths to real wages with an average lag of 3.53 years for England from the sixteenth to the eighteenth cenuturies. One might tentatively infer from these results that wage and employment expansion would make itself evident as a rise in population, with a varying lag. Therefore, it will be interesting to see if population movemements correlate with measures of aggregate economic activity.

Some periods stand out as extreme contractions from the evidence in Table A: the latter half of the 1720's shows a sharp decline of share prices and cash flow of the East India Company and the only sustained decline in population of the whole period; the first half of the 1740's shows a diminished rate of expansion across the board; and the first half of the 1780's displays a relative trough of share prices, profits and the expansion of population. Some periods of peak activity appear to have occured in the first half of the 1750's, the later 1760's, and the decade of the 1800's. To augment these impressions with more specific data, we now turn to a chronology of the business cycle from 1690 to 1825.

Eighteenth Century Syncopations; or the Clock Commences Its Ticking

1690-1720

"This was the age of interested projects, inspired by a venal spirit of adventure, the natural consequence of avarice, fraud and profligacy which the monied corporations had introduced. This of all others is the most unfavorable era for an historian. A reader of sentiment and imagination cannot be entertained or interested by a dry detail of such transactions as admit no warmth, no colouring, no embellishment..."

> --Tobias Smollet
> *History of England* (1791)

It is not surprising that the earliest period of modern capitalistic organization yields the scantiest evidence concerning movements of the macroeconomy. The techniques and institutions of the firm, financial turnover, the discipline of labor, the factory and organized labor were in their nascent stages, pockets of expansion in a landscape dominated by earlier practices of punitive trade and biological/agricultural rhythms of work. This is doubly unfortunate, because it would be interesting to see if our thesis concerning the qualitative rise of the modern macroeconomy might have some counterpart in qualitative measures of growth and fluctuation; but part of the rise of the modern macroeconomy is a heightened concern with the forms and institutions of quantitative record-keeping (vide the political arithmeticians), and so such an opportunity would probably not exist in any event. Further, it is not clear what quantitative alterations we would be searching for: as has been argued in chapter four, previous concerns with changes in the length of periodicities are largely irrelevant from the vantage point of an institutional theory of the cycle.

More specifically, continuous business records are difficult to find for this period, mainly because the first wave of English joint stock company formation only occurs in the years 1688 to 1695, and experiences a sharp reversal thereafter. Scott estimates 85% of the total joint stocks existing in 1695 were formed in that internal of years [11]; and it is no accident that Houghton's share price list originates in those same years. Most historians associate the end of the expansion with the Great Recoinage of 1695-6, which had the effect over a period of six months of reducing the stock of money and notes in circulation by an estimated 36%. [12] The contraction of the currency, along with the demands of the war effort upon the Bank of England, led to the suspension of cash payments on notes after a run on the Bank on May 4, 1696. These events might be taken as evidence that credit extension and financial innovation outran the expansion of physical production. Many fledgling businesses were swept aside in the general contraction of balance sheets and credit, which later commentators would perhaps unjustly (but with the benefit of hindsight) dub 'bubbles'. Approximately one hundred of these companies operating in 1695 were no longer functioning in 1703.

Table B

AVERAGE QUARTERLY SHARE PRICES, 1693-1703

Quarter	Bank of England	Hudson's Bay Co.	Old E. India	Royal Lustring	Royal African	Million Bank
1693.1	-----	183.6	138.3	30.0	----	----
.2	-----	175.3	105.0	30.0	----	----
.3	-----	164.2	92.6	28.3	----	----
.4	-----	208.0	93.0	29.0	----	----
1694.1	-----	195.5	92.0	28.1	----	----
.2	-----	165.8	75.4	26.4	----	----
.3	101.0	150.0	76.4	22.7	----	----
.4	77.6	175.3	88.7	21.3	----	----
1695.1	87.0	165.7	84.2	20.0	----	----
.2	92.3	202.3	80.0	20.4	----	----
.3	96.3	209.1	85.6	25.0	----	----
.4	95.7	151.5	60.0	29.3	----	----
1696.1	93.4	119.6	56.3	31.3	----	----
.2	81.4	100.8	60.0	30.9	----	----
.3	72.0	104.0	57.1	29.0	----	----
.4	70.5	101.9	54.4	27.0	----	----
1697.1	67.0	97.0	51.3	25.0	----	----
.2	70.3	95.0	47.1	25.0	----	----
.3	74.4	94.4	----	25.0	----	----
.4	----	----	----	----	----	----
1698.1	87.1	103.7	53.4	----	13.2	----
.2	91.5	-----	46.7	----	14.7	----
.3	95.0	-----	39.8	----	16.7	----
.4	98.5	-----	40.9	----	16.2	----
1699.1	102.4	-----	41.9	----	16.1	----
.2	104.3	105.0	41.7	----	16.0	----
.3	110.4	-----	45.9	----	15.1	----
.4	117.3	-----	57.7	----	15.0	----
1700.1	137.3	105.0	86.1	----	22.6	----
.2	140.7	106.6	123.2	----	22.6	----
.3	138.5	-----	126.3	----	22.8	----
.4	126.2	-----	120.5	----	22.8	----
1701.1	112.5	-----	87.5	----	17.5	64.1
.2	110.0	-----	83.6	----	17.0	62.3
.3	111.6	-----	78.6	----	15.7	62.9
.4	110.3	-----	79.3	----	13.6	59.0
1702.1	115.8	-----	82.7	----	12.1	58.8
.2	116.3	-----	82.0	----	11.5	60.2
.3	121.5	-----	103.2	----	14.0	66.8
.4	125.2	-----	109.6	----	13.4	72.3
1703.1	127.3	-----	112.8	----	14.0	74.6
.2	128.6	-----	112.4	----	17.8	80.6
.3	135.2	-----	128.8	----	21.0	89.2
.4	126.8	-----	122.3	----	18.8	90.2

Some quantitative evidence of the expansion of the mid-1690's and the subsequent reversal may be gleaned from Table B, which contains selected average quarterly share prices, calculated by the author from Houghton's Collections. The Bank and East India shares both peak in the third quarter of 1695; the Bank stock does not reattain this level until the fourth quarter of 1698, while the India stock does not surpass its peak until the first quarter of the year 1700. While profit data is scarce for this decade, the two surviving accounts collected by the author more or less substantiate these movements. [13]

Year	Old India Co. % Profit Rt.	Spencer Stan. % Profit Rt.	India Co. Cash Flow
1691	-2.8	3.1	825.7
1692	13.6	4.3	382.3
1693	-7.6	4.0	1373.4
1694	32.1	7.4	1060.7
1695	8.4	5.4	1890.5
1696	1.0	3.9	611.5
1697	-15.4	5.2	1050.5
1698	-2.4	6.4	1841.1
1699	-11.3	9.2	1704.9
1700	-6.8	9.0	2004.7

Here the profit rate peaks in 1694 in both cases, and then falls off dramatically for the Old East India Company, while full recovery comes in 1698-9 for the Spencer Stanhope partnership. Curiously enough, the remittance burden of waging the Nine Years' War under William II (1689-97) does not seem to have proved a severe drain upon the domestic economy, since the years of the heaviest overseas remittances for the war effort coincide with the years of the boom, as can be observed below.

Year	Remittances mill. pounds	Hallage receipts
1689	.17	1898
1690	.80	2081
1691	.61	2203
1692	.72	2164
1693	1.10	2028
1694	1.35	2051
1695	1.70	1931
1696	.90	1824
1697	.75	1859
1698	.57	2032
1699	----	2327

The hallage receipts of the London cloth market (denominated in pounds), a proxy for cloth production in the area, peak much earlier than the other indicies, in 1691, but also display the sharp downward trend of the crisis period of 1695-6. The change in employment in cloth production, as represented by the number of bound apprentices introduced into the Weaver's Company, also shows a sharp contraction during the crisis period. [14]

1694-5	284	1679-8	162
1695-6	318	1698-9	202
1696-7	168	1699-1700	269

Although the quantitative evidence is not at all conclusive for this decade, we might tentatively suggest that the emerging capitalist economy underwent a paroxysm in the period 1695-97.

Evidence on macroeconomic movements in the next decade are only marginally more abundant. Share prices recover in 1699 and rise rapidly in 1700, only to fall throughout 1701 and then commence a sustained rise to 1704. Much of the financial disruption of 1701 seems to have been caused by a concerted attack by the Old East India Company upon the New India Company, which involved as a flanking operation a consciously engineered run on the Bank of England. [15] The repercussions of this internecine warfare were probably felt in the hinterland: for example, the profit rate of the Spencer Stanhope partnership drops from 9% in 1700 to 6.2% in 1701 and 4.9% in 1702, and then afterwards rises to 12.5% in 1703, 9.2% in 1704 and 9.9% in 1705.

Some broader movements of the fortunes of trade might also be extracted from the surviving ledger of Charles Blunt, nephew of the South Sea Company projector John Blunt and himself paymaster of the Two Million Adventure. Blunt was one of the tyro wizards of finance in turn of the century London, whose daring deeds and exploits led to his demise by his own hand during the collapse of the South Sea Bubble. [16]

Table C

LEDGER SUMMARIES, ACCOUNTS OF
CHARLES BLUNT (pounds)

Jan. 1	Assets	Liabilities	Net Worth
1701	7523	991	6532
1702	8220	1720	6500
1703	10500	2660	7840
1704	11153	2539	8614
1705	12499	3819	8680
1706	12853	4171	8682

Table C - CONTINUED

LEDGER SUMMARIES, ACCOUNTS OF
CHARLES BLUNT (pounds)

Jan. 1	Assets	Liabilities	Net Worth
1707	14686	5608	9078
1708	14544	5579	8965
1709	12432	3406	9026
1710	17249	7586	9663
1711	19197	9119	10078
1712	18573	7312	11261
1713	22281	8072	14209
1714	24159	7850	16309
1715	29735	12197	17538
1716	24826	6668	18158
1717	24674	6326	18348
1718	24088	2059	22029
1719	41858	18532	23326

Blunt's net worth moves in consort with other trends in the first decade of the eighteenth century. There is relative stagnation during the calendar year 1701, after which accumulation proceeds apace from 1702 through 1704. The latter half of the decade appears to be a period of dormancy, with Blunt's finances showing little significant growth. This impression extends to the market for shares, where prices remain essentially stationary, and population growth, which slows appreciably relative to the previous period. The produce of the duties on stamped paper, which provide an indirect index of the number of financial transactions, reinforce this characterization: between 1704 and 1709 they fluctuate very little between 54000 and 56000 pounds. [17]

Ashton has written that "the two years from the summer of 1710 to that of 1712 must have been omong the worst in the century," [18] but the evidence is by no means unequivocal. Blunt's finances start to thrive in 1710 after five years of indifferent success; the Spencer Stanhope partnership enjoys a period of high profits, its rate rising from 6.4% in 1709 to 9.5% in 1710, 8.8% in 1711, and 10.6% in 1712. Both the East India Company and Spencer Stanhope experience peaks of cash flow in 1711. On the other hand, share prices exhibit a pronounced fall from a minor peak in 1708 to a trough in 1711, as Table D documents. A possible sign that there is distress in the countryside is the fact that population growth is nil in 1709 and negative in 1710 and 1711; this may be connected with the fact that the relative price of agricultural goods with respect to

Table D

QUARTERLY SHARE PRICES, 1708-1720

Year	Bank of England	United E. India	Million Bank	Royal Africa	Irish Lands	South Sea	Royal Exchange
1708.1	118.3	-----	82.4	8.4	57.0	-----	-----
.2	126.3	-----	79.0	5.9	53.0	-----	-----
.3	126.7	-----	79.4	6.4	53.5	-----	-----
.4	115.1	-----	76.0	4.9	54.1	-----	-----
1709.1	116.5	-----	75.6	3.9	55.2	-----	-----
.2	124.2	120.9	76.7	4.2	58.9	-----	-----
.3	128.7	130.6	80.1	4.1	66.0	-----	-----
.4	119.1	131.2	76.4	3.5	66.7	-----	-----
1710.1	120.8	134.1	75.6	3.3	66.5	-----	-----
.2	122.8	136.1	75.1	3.4	65.0	-----	-----
.3	112.4	125.4	71.9	3.1	62.6	-----	-----
.4	103.0	119.7	67.2	3.4	60.6	-----	-----
1711.1	103.4	120.7	65.9	3.5	60.0	-----	-----
.2	102.8	117.7	61.8	2.7	60.0	-----	-----
.3	103.5	115.3	60.1	2.3	54.0	-----	-----
.4	109.6	125.2	60.7	3.9	52.5	-----	-----
1712.1	110.6	119.9	61.2	4.1	56.5	-----	-----
.2	112.3	115.5	63.5	2.9	59.9	-----	-----
.3	114.5	112.3	67.3	3.2	60.0	-----	-----
.4	115.6	117.9	66.0	3.1	60.0	-----	-----
1713.1	121.9	122.5	68.2	54.2**	----	83.7	-----
.2	124.1	123.5	70.4	49.1	-----	91.7	-----
.3	128.0	124.9	77.7	48.1	----	93.7	-----
.4	124.1	124.4	84.2	46.6	----	92.8	-----
1714.1	121.6	119.9	81.4	42.9	----	87.2	-----
.2	120.4	122.1	82.1	39.5	----	87.1	-----
.3	127.7	129.3	86.4	31.1	----	91.0	-----
.4	128.2	136.4	91.5	24.4	----	96.3	-----
1715.1	132.2	134.4	92.3	23.4	----	95.0	-----
.2	130.8	140.0	97.6	22.7	----	99.4	-----
.3	129.9	135.8	95.2	15.6	----	96.2	-----
.4	123.4	134.0	92.6	16.6	----	93.4	-----
1716.1	128.1	135.3	94.0	17.0	----	94.6	-----
.2	132.2	144.9	100.3	16.3	----	100.7	-----
.3	137.4	147.3	100.7	18.8	----	98.0	-----
.4	138.4	170.1	109.0	25.8	----	104.3	-----
1717.1	136.4	166.8	106.5	19.6	----	102.1	-----
.2	137.6	179.3	110.0	20.3	----	105.7	-----
.3	149.8	193.9	119.5	19.8	----	111.2	-----
.4	147.0	198.2	121.1	20.1	----	114.5	-----
1718.1	157.1	211.2	125.0	18.2	----	117.5	-----
.2	149.0	209.5	123.6	16.2	----	115.1	-----
.3	149.7	199.6	121.0	15.6	----	111.2	-----
.4	144.6	194.3	119.5	15.3	----	108.9	-----
1719.1	154.2	206.5	121.0	15.2	----	115.7	6.7
.2	146.7	197.2	119.9	13.3	----	114.1	8.7
.3	146.7	193.0	118.3	14.7	----	115.1	13.9
.4	144.4	194.8	121.9	25.3	----	120.0	16.0
1720.1	151.4	210.9	135.1	34.9	----	166.1	23.6
.2	186.1	274.2	227.7	94.3	----	491.2	58.8
.3	227.0	326.9	400.7	117.7	----	724.2	134.8
.4	154.2	166.5	188.0	45.3	----	194.0	17.0

**A reorganization of the capital structure of the African Co.

'producers' goods (here employing the Schumpeter-Gilboy price indices) [19] reaches its highest point of the subsequent sixty-five years. This evidence must be balanced against the fact that company promotion regained momentum in this period, with the most notorious exemplar being the projection and organization of the South Sea Company.

The period from the Treaty of Utrecht to 1720 has been portrayed by some historians as an unchecked boom which ended dramatically with the South Sea Bubble. Existing profit data reveal a much less continuous expansion.

| | Profit Rates | | |
Year	E. India	Spencer	Million Bank
1714	65.6	7.9	8.5
1715	-21.7	3.7	6.0
1716	31.8	8.4	6.1
1717	4.9	6.6	6.3
1718	4.5	8.1	8.8
1719	5.0	8.4	8.9
1720	20.0	5.1	21.8

Domestic exports (Schumpeter series) from 1714 to 1716 were much higher than they were in the years 1717-20; the population growth rate peaks in 1717 and falls off thereafter to being slightly negative in 1720. From 1715 to 1717 Charles Blunt's acccumulation of assets slows appreciably; while stamp duties of official paper fall from a peak of 88,255 pounds in 1715 to 76,145 pounds in 1716 and 77,808 pounds in 1717. The movements of share prices is most often cited with respect to statements about the vigorousness of this expansion; but most statements have hitherto been based on the price of a single stock. Table D shows that, with the exception of failing companies like the Royal African, share prices in general did show a continuous rise between Utrecht and the Bubble.

Clement Juglar, and others, have made much of an organized attempt to produce a fall in the stocks and bring about a financial crisis in January of 1714: "One day towards the end of January a well-dressed man, having all the appearance of a person of importance, rode furiously down the Queen's Road, shouting the Queen was dead. It was known she had been ill, and the news was accepted without suspicion." [20] Since the question of succession was a potentially inflammatory issue, it apparently was thought that the uncertainty would cause a faltering of confidence and the desired disruption of the market. From Table D it is clear that many of the stocks did undergo a decline in the first and second quarters of the year, but the effect was transitory and immediately reversed. Somewhat more serious for the conduct of business was the actual death of Queen Anne in August 1714 and the raising of the Pretender's standard at Kirkmichael on September 6, 1715. The Pretender actually landed in Scotland in January 1716, but was forced to beat a hasty retreat in February, and the Jacobite Rebellion was essentially crushed by June. Profit rates in 1715 show a distinct dip, although losses are promptly made good in the next year.

We have observed in previous chapters that there is a marked predisposition among many economists and historians to consider the South Sea Bubble as 'merely' a financial crisis. This has happened, in part, because the story of the Bubble is largely a tale of crass deceit and baseless speculation on the part of a few unscrupulous characters; this element of human drama has made it a thrice-told tale. [21] For the purposes of our narrative, it is enough to know the South Sea Company was created in 1711-12 in order to incorporate the holders of nine million pounds of unsecured government debt, through the artifice of trading their debt, which was selling at a discount, for stock in the new company at par. The Company was nominally to have a monopoly of trade to Spanish South America, although its main purpose was to relieve the government of the responsibility of paying back the principal of the debt, and simultaneously to give the Tory rivals of the Whiggish Bank of England and East India Company some comparable financial power base. The pretentions to trading activity were merely pretentions and nothing more because, as constituted, the South Sea Company had no funds with which to purchase commodities, ships, etc.; since its initial capital consisted entirely of government debt. So from the start, the South Sea enterprise was a dubious proposition; to succeed at all, it was forced to resort to even more dubious financial machinations.

The South Sea Company financed what little trade it managed to prosecute by two means: borrowing money, and increasing its initial capital stock. The latter option was not simple nor straightforward: the government had in effect prohibited the Company from any further expansions of capital; to get the prohibition lifted, the Company would usually have to assume more government debt of the amount of the rise in capital, leading only to a vicious cycle. John Blunt and the other directors of the Company attempted to exercise their one degree of freedom: if the new shares could be issued for a price above the par amount of government debt assumed, the Company could accumulate some free cash. Unfortunately this realization came at the same time that the free cash could no longer be used in the designated trade: war was declared in 1718 with Spain, and South America was closed to British trade. "With trade at a full stop for all to see, the Campany became, from sheer necessity, a naked finance corporation." Since the only way the South Sea Company could make a profit was through the initial sale of its own stock, it was only a matter of time before the company overreached itself by offering to convert the whole of the English national debt into its own stock. To make a worthwhile amount of money in this transaction, the South Sea directors had to drive up the price of their own stock. They employed various illegitimate and semi-unscrupulous means to do so, such as issuing new stock before any conversions took place, and distributing the money obtained from these early sales as large dividends to the owners in order to boost the price of the shares; they also loaned money which had been received as premia over conversation at par to persons wishing to purchase South Sea stock, with the purchased stock as the only collateral for the loan.

Granted that this thrice-told tale is concerned with a very localized 'aberration' of finance; yet, what can it mean to say that the South Sea Bubble was 'merely' a financial crisis? Clearly it affected not only to price of South Sea Company shares, but all other financial placements listed in 1720. Consulting our long-term share price index, it was the highest point ever attained by the index over the years 1700-1825, and was not even approached in comparable magnitude of fluctuation until 1825. It has been estimated that more than one hundred companies were projected in the Bubble period alone, which does not include those generated in the longer period of preceding expansion. [22] Outside London, the impact of the boom has also been noted. Wadsworth and DeMann have written, "...in the great boom of 1719-20, commercial Lancashire was caught up in the wave of speculation that was sweeping the country...all things seemed attainable if only stock could be thrown on the market." [23] The projects undertaken in Lancashire included canals, port development and public works. Further, far from being restricted to the confines of England, the financial expansion of 1719-20 spread to much of Western Europe. The unfolding of John Law's "System" in France is almost as infamous there as the tortured machinations of the Bubble in England. L.M. Cullen suggests that the French and English credit expansions were felt in Ireland. [24] There is abundant evidence of business expansion in Amsterdam [25] and in the remainder of the Low Countries. [26] In fact, Johan Akerman has called 1720 the first international monetary crisis. [27]

If the South Sea Bubble was not an isolated event, but a representative instance of a larger European expansion, in what sense could it have been relatively insignificant, as many writers would have us believe? One suspects that there is the presumption that these various financial schemes had no impact upon the physical sphere of production, and therefore this incident belongs more naturally in histories of popular delusions and mass hysterias than in economic history proper. As we already know from our review of the existing data, information is inadequate to seriously test this hypothesis, but the new data does suggest a tentative interpretation: that there was appreciable real expansion from 1714 to 1720, but it may have been that the peak of this expansion had passed before the latter date in England. This scenario would imply a drastic divergence of physical and financial rates of expansion by 1720; a possibility we shall explore in the next subsection.

1720-1733

The period from 1720 to 1763 is the great unexplored region of English macroeconomic history. The years leading up to the South Sea Bubble have been the subject of both popular and scholarly analysis, while the era after the Seven Years' War has drawn much attention due to the various debates about the beginning of that _ignis fatuus_, the Industrial Revolution. In between, the dearth of effort and interest is evident when historians of English fluctuations identify only one 'crisis' in the forty year period, and that in the year 1745. We shall discover that this period has its own characteristic topography; and that there are some other reasons the terrain has languished unexplored until now.

The outlines of this period become more distinct when we consider surviving profit statistics and the population growth estimates. There was a very marked contraction of business after the South Sea Bubble burst (calling into question those historians who have insisted that the Bubble had no appreciable economic effects.) There was a weak recovery in 1723-4, but the information contained in the data is mixed. Conditions remain unsteady in the latter half of the decade following the Bubble, with a mixed business recovery combined with the worst mortality crisis of the century. In 1729 the indifferent recovery is halted in its tracks by another downturn, and a sustained expansion only gets underway in the early 1730's, building to a very high peak in 1733. The one contractionary movement, the fall

Year	E. India	Profit Rates Spencer	London Assur.
1720	20.6	5.1	-----
1721	-3.8	.6	-11.3
1722	1.3	-2.3	.6
1723	-16.8	.3	1.2
1724	-5.5	2.4	1.4
1725	9.3	2.2	4.7
1726	-8.9	4.7	.4

1727	14.1	4.1	3.2
1728	-17.7	4.4	7.8
1729	-25.5	4.6	.1
1730	8.6	7.1	3.5
1731	-15.3	4.4	2.3
1732	28.9	5.5	5.2
1733	46.1	11.7	8.2

of the rate of profit of the East India Company in 1731, was mostly due to an attack on the renewal of the company charter by rival trading groups. Manifestly, what we are contemplating in the 1720's is the worst decade of the century from the point of view of the economic actors. It was, if you will, the Great Depression of the eighteenth century: a decade following a massive financial crash in which there is only indifferent recovery punctuated by repeated downturns, leading to the great and grievous distress of the populace. This distress was not confined to the London area. Lands as far away as Ireland were crippled with the chilling palsy of the economic sclerosis: Cullen writes, "The constitutional furore (over Wood's halfpence) of the 1720's coincided with a decade of economic difficulties." [28] This is often associated with the 'famine' of 1728-29 in Ireland in the works of Irish historians; but we see from the English population data that the crisis was not a localized harvest failure, but a widespread rise in mortality associated with common economic upheavals.

One of the bits of evidence which may have obscured this Great Depression from the ken of earlier historians may have been the movements of one or two individual share prices. For this reason we direct the reader's attention to the quarterly share prices in Table E. Many commentators note that recovery in the prices of Bank and East India, and to a lesser extent, South Sea shares had started in 1723 and was effectively complete by 1724, which lead them to speculate that the Bubble was shortlived and superficial in its repercussions. But it is apparent from the table that recovery was itself unstable, and deteriorated in the course of 1726. The year 1727 again saw uncertain recovery, the momentum of which could not be sustained into 1728. It was only in late 1729- early 1730 that a sustained boom in share prices got underway, building up to a peak in early 1733. By concentrating overmuch on Bank, India and South Sea shares, and not extending the horizon of empiricism over the whole decade, there has been the tendency to exaggerate the strength and speed of the recovery after the Bubble.

If the 1720's truly were the Great Depression decade of the eighteenth century, why is this not more apparent from the writings of contemporaries? The answer to the question lies partly in its phrasing. We have seen in the first part

-233-

Table E

QUARTERLY SHARE PRICES, 1721-1733

Quarter	Bank	East India	South Sea	Million Bank	Royal Exchange	London Assur.	York Bld.
1721.1	139.2	152.4	170.0	153.0	7.6	7.5	----
.2	130.3	137.6	134.6	128.1	6.5	6.2	----
.3	133.2	142.5	133.9	116.8	8.7	7.2	30.7
.4	123.8	140.6	95.1	107.3	7.8	5.8	31.1
1722.1	120.5	140.4	96.1	104.4	7.2	4.2	27.4
.2	114.8	138.3	89.6	99.7	5.6	5.5	21.0
.3	116.6	135.8	90.7	94.3	5.2	5.6	16.7
.4	114.7	131.2	92.8	91.3	4.6	5.3	15.6
1723.1	117.0	127.0	98.1	91.7	4.2	5.5	14.5
.2	116.9	129.9	99.3	94.2	4.3	6.0	13.3
.3	120.2	131.9	106.4	99.0	4.2	5.6	9.2
.4	120.6	137.4	112.4	101.0	43.9**	5.9	12.9
1724.1	128.7	146.7	116.8	103.9	44.7	6.8	11.4
.2	128.1	148.7	119.1	104.7	47.3	7.1	10.3
.3	131.4	146.4	118.3	106.8	53.5	7.7	8.0
.4	130.5	150.9	119.9	108.6	54.0	7.8	12.6
1725.1	132.2	149.3	119.4	110.8	56.1	8.2	18.6
.2	133.1	162.2	121.9	113.6	74.0	11.3	36.2
.3	135.8	169.1	121.2	118.1	91.6	13.2	27.4
.4	131.8	166.3	120.9	117.2	90.0	13.0	23.6
1726.1	125.6	151.3	109.3	109.6	85.0	11.9	17.7
.2	123.5	149.4	103.4	104.3	78.6	10.7	17.7
.3	127.0	148.0	104.9	105.5	79.5	10.9	12.6
.4	120.8	134.9	99.6	101.3	72.2	10.0	8.2
1727.1	123.2	136.8	98.4	100.1	71.9	10.2	7.1
.2	128.5	157.7	107.6	103.2	84.0	11.8	8.0
.3	132.8	163.8	110.9	109.4	93.1	12.7	8.1
.4	130.2	161.1	108.1	104.0	88.5	12.1	10.5
1728.1	136.5	169.1	106.5	105.6	91.1	12.7	11.6
.2	136.2	173.2	106.6	107.0	91.5	12.6	13.7
.3	135.2	168.8	103.1	107.4	88.8	12.3	15.5
.4	133.5	167.8	101.0	106.5	86.3	11.7	15.3
1729.1	135.2	165.1	98.0	105.5	84.5	11.6	13.7
.2	135.9	170.3	99.2	105.1	85.9	11.6	14.2
.3	138.6	178.1	102.3	106.0	86.2	11.7	14.9
.4	137.8	181.7	102.9	105.7	86.0	11.6	14.8
1730.1	139.9	183.4	103.2	106.8	87.3	11.7	17.5
.2	141.6	188.8	102.9	106.6	92.8	12.1	17.4
.3	142.9	186.1	103.0	108.1	91.7	12.1	21.2
.4	143.2	189.7	103.6	107.9	93.9	12.3	31.0
1731.1	145.1	192.4	102.4	109.2	95.7	12.4	25.3
.2	146.2	197.2	102.8	108.5	99.1	12.5	23.1
.3	147.7	194.2	103.0	108.7	97.7	12.5	23.9
.4	147.4	179.7	102.7	108.3	98.0	12.6	13.8
1732.1	149.5	178.4	100.4	110.2	98.9	13.3	10.7
.2	148.2	176.2	98.4	110.9	100.8	13.1	7.1
.3	151.0	160.9	102.2	112.8	102.7	13.4	5.5
.4	149.9	154.9	104.3	114.5	104.5	13.4	3.6
1733.1	150.8	158.8	103.6	115.0	105.3	13.6	2.6
.2	150.0	162.5	103.7	115.2	107.1	13.5	----
.3	148.0	157.4	94.1	116.0	103.9	13.1	----
.4	133.6	139.5	74.0	110.8	92.3	11.4	----

**A reorganization of capital stock.

of book one how many eighteenth century writers on the economy essentially had no concept of the failure of the economy as a whole, but instead restricted their vision and consideration to the slackening of trade in a particular sector or two. As a consequence, the very idea of a wide-ranging 'depression' does not make an appearance in most of the writings of the proto-economists of the eighteenth century. Further, lacking aggregate measures and concepts, movements in trade had no dimensions of being 'worse' or 'better' in any coherent way. But to so accuse the theorists of the period is not to so accuse the economic protagonists in general. Pamphleteers, newspaper writers and businessmen did know when trade slackened or accelerated, and often said so. A perusal of surviving runs of newspapers from the period after the Bubble uncovers quotes like this one from March 17, 1722: "The Committee of Trade at the South Sea House have bought 12,000 broad cloths and prodigious Quantities of other Woolen Goods, which we hope will set the Wheels of Trade in our own Manufactures once more in motion." Or this, from 21 July of the same year: "Several Directors of the Bank conferred last week with the Treasury in relation to the Circulation of 1,900,000 pounds in Exchequer Bills, and we are told a considerable Progress is made in that Affair, which, tis hoped will be a Means to revive publick Credit." [29] Even in these sorts of instances, comparisons of the severity of the depression were absent, because with the exception of the crisis of 1695-6, there was no previous event to compare with it; and the comparison with 1695 would not be apt, as contemporaries knew, because of the earlier coincidence of the Great Recoinage, and the earlier lack of complicity of the government in the general credit expansion and corporate promotion which was present in the Bubble. After the Bubble, the situation changed: every financial crisis for one hundred years afterwards was compared and contrasted with the South Sea Bubble (as typified by the quote from an anonymous pamphlet of 1826 which prefaces this chapter), and the term 'Bubble' entered the English language as an epithet. In the same way that the economic fears of the 1970's focussed upon the Great Depression of the 1930's as an example of the worst that could conceivably happen, so too did the fears of the late eighteenth and early nineteenth centuries focus on the South Sea Bubble and its aftermath.

Recently, certain economic historians have become more aware of some sort of economic stagnation in the period; but they tend to expand the stagnation to occupy the three decades of 1720-50, and then take the position that the situation was all due to harvest fluctuations which produced the 'agricultural depression' of that time. [30] We have already examined the neoclassical theoretical underpinnings of a harvest-induced depression, and found them wanting in chapter four above. But further, the timing of this story is somewhat inconsistent, because if we accept the Schumpeter-Gilboy price indices, the agricultural terms of trade fell from 1711 to 1731, and rose thereafter until about 1740. The dating of the 'agricultural depression' from the later 1720's to 1750 does not coincide with the available price data. Moreover, the trough of this supposed depression came during one of the strongest expansions of the period, as measured by the rate of profit--the boom of 1730 to 1733.

This boom of the early 1730's, from evidence already presented, seems to have been quite a significant expansion on all economic fronts. Profits rose to an exceptional peak; population expanded appreciably and continuously; share prices rose from 1730 to 1732. The Bank of England apparently fuelled the incipient expansion with generous infusions of credit, as revealed by its large income from bills and notes discounted from 1729 to 1731. [31] It is interesting to note that this is the first pronounced boom of the century which is not directly linked to a war by virtue of its timing (no mean feat in the war-riddled eighteenth century: minor war preparations took place in 1727-29 and 1733-7, straddling the boom); there are certainly endogenous macroeconomic movements in the English economy by this date.

1733-1758

The preceding boom and crash of 1733-4 must have been perceived as almost as odious and dramatic as that of 1720. There is evidence of business failures and financial crises simultaneously in England, Scotland and Amsterdam. [32] One by product of this crisis in England was the hardening of an already ingrained institutional aversion to the easy manipulation of financial turnover: Sir John Barnard's Act (7 Geo. II c.2) was the capston of the legislative program implied by the previous Bubble Act; it was passed in reaction to the 'excesses' of 1733. It was drawn up to outlaw all stock market practices of puts and refuses, option buying, and any other forms of time bargains in shares then prevalent. While it is true that Barnard's Act was not doggedly enforced, it certainly did remove all legal redress for those making such bargains, and did effectively stunt the spread of 'stock-jobbing'. Like the Bubble Act, its main effect was to make it very difficult to maintain and manipulate balance sheets in order to exercise close control over financial turnover. This, we shall discover, had important implication for future macroeconomic stability.

Profit rates fell for two years after their peak in 1733; and in their wake came the search for a scapegoat. Accusations and recriminations concerning financial mismanagement filled the periodicals of the day. Shortly, the main target for reproach was resolved to be the Charitable Corporation. This unhappy hybrid of a desire to do good (in the form of making small loans to the poor at low rates of interest) and the drive to make a profit (as a private corporation, it was meant to pay a return on shares) came to grief for the most miserable of reasons, the absconding off of two officers with the corporate funds. Somehow, this rather mundane circumstances became the focal point of public dissatisfaction with the corporate form of organization and with 'high' finance in general.

Unlike the 1720's, the recovery set in relatively rapidly in 1737-8; but pulling back to the longer view, the trend of profits was downward from 1733 to a trough in 1749, which gave way to a rise until 1752-4, a sharp fall to 1757,

	Profit Rates				
Year	East India	Spencer	London Assur.	Million Bank	Average Profit
1733	46.1	11.7	8.2	5.9	16.2
1734	10.9	8.0	4.2	6.2	7.6
1735	10.0	5.3	2.1	4.5	6.1
1736	36.6	5.5	2.6	4.2	11.7
1737	7.1	1.3	3.9	4.4	5.1
1738	25.3	2.4	12.7	4.5	11.0
1739	17.7	2.9	3.2	4.8	7.4
1740	3.2	6.0	2.9	4.6	6.3
1741	14.7	5.9	3.6	4.8	8.2
1742	4.7	3.4	5.7	5.2	5.5
1743	1.4	4.1	4.3	5.0	6.5
1744	-.6	5.9	1.7	4.7	8.1
1745	11.7	7.0	4.3	5.4	9.2
1746	7.7	6.9	6.3	5.1	10.9

and a peak in 1758. One suspects that part of this temporal pattern could be accounted for by the influence of wars: war from 1739 to 1748 may have acted as a damper on trade, which when lifted, reversed the trend until the beginning of the Seven Years' War; but evidence is too thin to examine this temporal coincidence in much more detail. War probably cannot explain the earlier section of the downward trend from 1733 to 1739; nor can it explain the jagged fluctuations at either end of this period. In fact, there is a qualitative characteristic of the financial side of accumulation which transcends the usual economic historian's litany of wars and harvest fluctuations: both profit rates and share prices become more stable in their fluctuations in this period than previously. Some indication of this may be derived from a comparison of the ratios of standard

MEANS AND RATIOS OF STANDARD DEVIATIONS TO MEANS

Period	Profit Rates						Share Prices			
	Spencer		East India		London Ass.		Bank		Index	
	Mean	SD/M	Mean	SD/M	Mean	SD/M	Mean	SD/M	Mean	SD/M
1695-1720	7.64	.29	4.27	4.51	----	----	117.8	.20	85.1	.36
1720-1733	3.91	.81	2.55	7.58	2.10	2.20	137.0	.12	101.3	.31
1734-1758	6.37	.41	9.65	1.14	4.24	.56	135.8	.06	98.0	.06
(1740-50)	6.79	.30	4.63	1.72	3.50	.52	136.4	.05	95.8	.04

deviations to means of the various timeseries of profit rates and share prices for our chosen periodization. As the reader will observe, variances of a number of series from independent sources are markedly diminished in the period after 1733.

Share prices obey much the same pattern as profits, except that they tend to lead turning points by about a year. Shares fall abruptly in 1733-4 and then rise to a peak in 1737. After another drop in 1739, they are roughly stable until there is a quick fall in 1746. The trough of share prices in this sub-period is found in 1747-8, following which is a five year rise to the second peak in 1753. Share prices then slide until 1756, and then recover for the next two years. More generally, the trend of the share prices are downwards for the years 1754 to 1762.

As we have already reported, most English economic historians identify only one 'crisis' in the whole era from 1720 to 1763, and that they locate in the year 1745. The significance of that data is that it marks the landing in September of the Young Pretender in Scotland: in many ways, a re-enactment of the threat of 1715. The invasion reached Derby in January 1746, but the tide was unmistakably turned by the battle of Culloden in April of that year. Table F traces the course of quarterly share prices through 1753. The pattern of share prices in 1745-6 is what one would expect, given the politically disruptive events. In the last quarter of 1745 prices drop precipitously across the board. They continue to fall in the first quarter of 1746, but with the reversal of the Pretender's fortunes, they immediately recover in the second and third quarters. But the isolation of 1745 as a significant crisis year is not supported by the data, as examination of the rest of the table and the earlier profit statistics reveal. The slide in share prices is embedded in a longer term downward trend which stretches from 1744 to 1748-9, which cannot simply be attributed to the threat of the Pretender. As for profits, their trough had apparently occured before 1745, and were in the midst of a minor expansion during the invasion. This instance illuminates the previous historiographic predisposition to maintaining that all eighteenth century fluctuations were due solely to random shocks, such as wars and other readily identifiable historic events.

A different and perhaps more extreme 'shock' which occured in this period happened in the years 1740-41. According to modern work done on long-term temperature and precipitation trends, it seems 1740 saw the coldest harvest year of the century, while 1741 was included in the coldest 5% of the century. [33] Simultaneously, these years were also two of the driest years in the century. [34] The correlation of this extreme weather and the last two instances in the century when annual population change contracted in absolute terms is undoubtedly more than a

Table F

QUARTERLY SHARE PRICES, 1744-1753

Quarter	Bank	East India	South Sea	Million Bank	Royal Exchange	London Assur.
1744.1	147.0	188.9	109.9	118.0	77.6	11.5
.2	143.0	173.2	105.7	115.7	75.4	11.0
.3	146.7	177.8	108.8	115.6	79.7	11.0
.4	145.4	182.1	110.4	116.0	86.4	11.1
1745.1	145.5	181.3	107.9	115.4	86.7	11.1
.2	146.5	185.8	109.2	114.3	84.3	11.1
.3	144.4	178.1	105.5	114.9	82.9	11.0
.4	134.7	168.1	97.7	112.7	79.8	10.3
1746.1	122.4	157.2	92.2	110.0	77.5	9.7
.2	123.7	166.8	95.7	97.0	74.7	9.8
.3	133.7	180.0	104.3	104.5	76.4	10.8
.4	129.5	179.4	102.6	104.7	78.7	10.9
1747.1	128.3	176.6	102.2	103.6	75.5	10.5
.2	126.9	158.6	102.8	102.6	75.1	10.4
.3	125.4	158.8	102.4	102.4	73.2	10.2
.4	121.2	160.8	100.2	100.2	72.5	10.0
1748.1	118.4	158.6	93.2	99.2	70.9	9.9
.2	124.3	172.5	103.9	100.3	72.5	10.0
.3	127.5	179.5	106.9	102.5	77.5	10.1
.4	126.3	178.8	105.8	102.2	74.1	9.8
1749.1	128.7	175.1	106.5	104.1	69.0	10.0
.2	133.4	181.7	111.3	109.0	73.2	10.6
.3	138.3	188.4	115.8	115.0	77.3	11.6
.4	136.1	189.2	113.1	-----	75.7	11.6
1750.1	133.3	187.6	110.4	-----	76.8	11.8
.2	133.3	185.6	110.3	-----	78.6	12.2
.3	134.8	185.3	112.0	-----	76.5	12.2
.4	134.9	186.0	113.2	119.6	76.4	12.4
1751.1	136.7	189.6	111.5	120.0	76.2	12.5
.2	138.2	190.4	113.9	-----	78.5	12.7
.3	140.6	187.6	114.5	121.5	----	----
.4	140.9	188.6	115.9	120.0	80.0	----
1752.1	143.5	188.6	117.3	123.2	79.5	13.3
.2	145.8	188.9	118.9	-----	83.3	----
.3	147.2	189.2	120.9	-----	85.0	----
.4	144.1	193.5	122.6	-----	85.6	----
1753.1	143.5	194.0	122.7	-----	85.4	13.7
.2	141.0	195.0	120.9	-----	85.7	13.8
.3	137.8	194.0	120.9	-----	85.0	13.8
.4	137.2	191.7	119.6	-----	----	13.7

coincidence; it must have been a period of severe distress in the agricultural countryside. To disentangle the effect upon the 'modern' sector is more problematic, however; it seems profits were already falling in 1739, but the evidence is mostly mixed. At any rate, such a severe 'random shock' does not seem to have been responsible for any extreme dislocation in the pecuniary sector.

Finally, as some indirect evidence, we present the returns on stamp duties for ready money, which corroborates the broad outlines of our description of the period. [35]

Aug.-Aug. Year	Stamp Returns	Aug.-Aug. Year	Stamp Returns
1734	79,625	1747	86,065
1735	78,213	1748	84,942
1736	81,271	1749	81,795
1737	83,024	1750	80,190
1738	79,265	1751	78,111
1739	80,151	1752	------
1740	80,579	1753	77,061
1741	80,775	1754	------
1742	83,763	1755	80,148
1743	82,034	1756	------
1744	84,717	1757	------
1745	83,920	1758	142,096
1746	84,446	1759	125,098

1758-1775

If it in any way makes sense to look for an eighteenth century candidate for a 'silver age' (silver, because there is no age so sterling that it deserves to be dubbed 'golden', from the historian's viewpoint), then it would be this period. To justify this statement, let us consider the share and profit rate indices calculated over the 'epochs' delineated in this study.

This table reveals that there is a marked trend in the stability of the profit rate and finance in general over the course of our 'elongated' eighteenth century. The variance in profits falls to a trough in 1758-75, and rises thereafter. The same 'v' pattern is found in the share index, except that the trough of the variance leads that of the profit index by one 'epoch'. The pinnacle of stability of the system--relatively high rates of return with low variance--seems to have been enjoyed in the years running from the beginning of the Seven Years' War to the eve of the War of American Independence. (From the Table, one might expect that a close runner-up would be the Napoleonic war years, but we shall shortly find that there were extenuating circumstances which might act to raise questions about the character and desirability of macroeconomic patterns in that

MOVEMENTS IN VARIANCE

Period	Share Index			Mean Adj. Profit Index		
	Mean	Std. D.	SD/M	Mean	Std. D.	SD/M
1695-1720	85.1	30.90	.36	---	---	---
1720-33	101.3	32.37	.31	---	---	---
1734-58	98.0	6.22	.06	.93	.27	.29
1758-75	97.1	11.52	.11	1.07	.15	.14
1776-91	88.4	11.75	.13	.90	.24	.26
1791-1801	94.7	12.29	.12	1.05	.29	.27
1801-19	102.8	9.78	.09	1.18	.26	.22
1820-26	125.8	15.28	.12	1.27	.36	.28

period. We beg the reader's indulgence to postpone discussion of the causes of this silver age until later in this chapter.

Within the period 1758 to 1775, profits fell from the beginning of the period to a trough in 1762, and then underwent a stable recovery from 1763 to 1768. There was a steep fluctuation in 1769-70, and then a declivity in profits to a trough in 1771-2. The remainder of the period experienced a slow recovery. Some individual profit rates are presented below.

Year	London Assurance	Scotch Mines	East India	Bolton & Fothergill
1758	5.8	6.6	34.6	-----
1759	7.5	9.5	14.0	-----
1760	5.6	12.9	13.9	-----
1761	4.4	6.7	19.8	-----
1762	4.2	6.3	9.9	-----
1763	5.7	16.5	18.4	-----
1764	3.0	14.4	16.4	-28.0
1765	2.7	14.9	14.6	7.6
1766	1.2	15.5	12.5	17.0
1767	3.1	12.0	10.9	14.3
1768	6.1	11.9	12.8	2.5
1769	3.2	15.2	16.4	-3.0*
1770	3.3	3.2	19.6	-1.4*
1771	4.5	----	11.7	-1.1*
1772	3.7	----	6.0	- .8*
1773	5.2	8.6	10.2	-3.3*
1774	4.8	7.6	10.6	61.2
1775	4.8	10.6	7.8	4.9
Mean	4.3	10.7	14.4	6.0
Std.Dev.	1.4	3.8	6.1	19.7
SD/mean	.33	.36	.42	3.26

*Estimated by the author

Source of Bolton & Fothergill: unpublished M.Sc. thesis by J. Cule, Univ. of Birmingham, 1935, "The Financial Hisotory of Matthew Bolton & Co.".

It is instructive to compare the profit experiences of the first three stable and established companies with the wild gyrations of Matthew Bolton's first partnership, which as Cule documents, was having a torturous time finding a steady source of cash flow. It is also striking how close the mean standardized variances of the stable corporations are, given their various lines of endeavor.

Share prices, as we have now come to expect, follow the same broad patterns as profit rates. From 1758 to 1762 there is a fall, and then a continuous rise to 1768, broken by a sharp fluctuation in 1763-4. From the peak in 1768 to 1775 there are wide fluctuations about a declining trend. The quarterly data for the Seven Years' War and its aftermath, and the period of fall from 1770 on, are presented in Table G.

The coincidences of the declining trends in profits and share prices and the dates of the Seven Years' War are too close to be ignored. Other exogenous factors coming into play were a) the years from the battle of Plassey to 1763 were a period of internal struggle for the control of the East India Company, which shows up in our figures; and b) the agricultural terms of trade fell from 1758-1762, in part because 1757 and 1763 were two of the first years of large-scale English grain importation. But on the whole, it was the Seven Years' War that seems to have been increasingly a drain on the British economy as it progressed. Estimates have been made that the number of men in the Navy rose from 33,000 in 1755 to 85,000 in 1760, 80,000 in 1761 and 84,000 in 1762. The cost of the war was almost double the last military adventure, with expenditures on the War of the Austrian Succession estimated at roughly 43 million pounds, while the Seven Years' War cost Britain approximately 82 million pounds. [36] In many ways it is surprising that Great Britain was able to prosecute such a large war effort without more drastic strains being imposed upon the economy: the average profit index during the War of the Austrian Succession was .855, while during the Seven Years' War it stood at 1.036. Still, it is a mistake to make such a broad pronouncement as "No commercial crisis occured during the (Seven Years') war in England." [37] Between the second quarter of 1758 and the third quarter of 1759 Bank shares dropped ten pounds, East India shares dropped twenty-three pounds, the shares of the South Sea Co. fell thirteen pounds, and those of the London Assurance dropped two pounds. Share prices between the third quarter of 1761 and the first quarter of 1762 fell on average 18% of their initial levels. Profits in 1761 and 1762 were appreciably below long term averages, with the exception of that of the East India Company. The Bank of England's income from the discounting of notes and bills hits a short term peak in 1760/1, and then rises even higher in 1764. These new heights were partially due to the Bank's commitment to fund the war effort, but on these particular dates the Bank was exercising its function of lender of last resort. [38] While certainly neither of these instances was anywhere near as catastrophic as a 1720 or a 1733-4, they do show that Britain did not bear her wars effortlessly.

Table G

QUARTERLY SHARE PRICES, 1758-1765

Quarter	Bank	East India	South Sea	Royal Exchange	London Assur.
1758.1	119.3	143.0	103.7	----	----
.2	121.4	147.2	106.5	----	12.0
.3	119.6	136.8	103.3	73.0	----
.4	117.9	135.5	101.0	----	12.1
1759.1	116.6	134.0	98.3	72.0	----
.2	113.3	129.5	93.8	----	12.0
.3	111.3	124.2	93.1	67.5	10.0
.4	113.9	133.5	96.8	74.0	9.8
1760.1	111.2	136.8	92.3	----	----
.2	110.2	136.9	92.7	65.5	10.0
.3	111.0	138.4	93.6	66.5	10.6
.4	109.3	140.2	91.4	67.5	10.5
1761.1	105.4	136.8	87.6	60.0	----
.2	114.8	142.5	96.1	----	----
.3	112.9	138.5	92.3	----	----
.4	104.7	126.7	84.5	60.0	----
1762.1	93.8	113.5	74.6	----	----
.2	96.8	117.8	80.1	60.0	----
.3	104.9	129.0	89.8	----	10.0
.4	110.7	146.1	94.0	----	----
1763.1	124.2	164.5	102.7	----	12.0
.2	125.5	169.9	105.8	80.7	12.0
.3	119.1	164.8	97.6	----	----
.4	112.2	155.8	93.3	----	----
1764.1	114.8	151.2	95.4	----	10.8
.2	115.7	151.2	95.4	----	10.8
.3	113.0	146.1	93.4	70.0	11.5
.4	122.3	149.0	94.7	----	11.5
1765.1	127.8	152.6	97.0	81.0	11.7
.2	128.7	154.6	100.0	----	11.4
.3	133.7	159.0	103.2	----	11.5
.4	137.4	164.9	104.7	85.0	11.3

Quarterly Share Prices, 1770-75 Table

Quarter	Bank	East India	South Sea	London Assur.
1770.1	153.5	217.6	99.1	12.0
.2	153.0	226.8	99.5	- - - -
.3	150.7	218.6	98.8	12.1
.4	136.7	192.1	91.0	11.2
1771.1	144.2	210.4	93.5	12.0
.2	152.8	225.1	98.5	12.5
.3	155.7	219.9	100.0	- - - -
.4	148.2	216.1	99.5	12.0
1772.1	151.9	217.2	100.4	- - - -
.2	151.3	217.5	100.0	12.3
.3	149.1	212.2	97.4	- - - -
.4	145.2	179.0	96.6	- - - -
1773.1	142.6	161.5	93.9	- - - -
.2	141.1	148.2	93.4	- - - -
.3	142.5	150.1	93.6	- - - -
.4	142.0	145.5	94.3	12.2
1774.1	140.0	140.0	93.4	- - - -
.2	140.6	148.0	94.8	- - - -
.3	143.4	149.9	96.0	- - - -
.4	143.7	149.0	97.9	- - - -
1775.1	143.8	154.4	99.0	- - - -
.2	142.8	155.0	98.6	14.7
.3	142.4	154.2	97.5	14.8
.4	142.8	159.7	98.0	15.0

It is quite common among English economic historians (such as Phyllis Deane, W.W. Rostow, Clement Juglar, and others) to single out the year 1763 as a significant crisis year in England. The sources of data we have developed tend to belie that notion to a great extent. Profits generally rise in 1763; share prices do fall over the last three quarters of the year; but the extent of the fall is not of the magnitude of 1761-2, and is rapidly reversed. What has previously been identified as a major declivity in the topography of the eighteenth century was in reality a very small sinkhole, a ripple created by a much more grave situation on the continent. During the course of the Seven Years' War, Amsterdam had adopted the role of paymaster to the British allies, and in the process had extended much credit to all and sundry as a means of smoothing the process of international exchanges. The Dutch banking houses that undertook this expansion were fundamentally flawed, in that they performed most banking functions, such as bill brokerage and the issuance of loans, but in general they did not accept deposits. Reserves were dangerously low (and financial rates of profit unstably high); the combined jolt of the post-war contraction of remittances plus a fall in the price of many Dutch export goods (which these houses often held as collateral on loans) set off a wave of failures in August-October 1763. Many failing houses, such as De Neufville Bros., had previously built up a far-flung credit network, extending to such distant commercial centers as Sweden, Hamburg, and Prussia. [39] Both T.S. Ashton and Charles Wilson have suggested that this crisis was transmitted to London directly by the extensive forced sale of Dutch holdings of English funds in the course of their general scramble for liquidity; but Alice Carter has found little evidence of this in the Bank of England and various Dutch transfer books. [40] From our information, the timing of the fall in share prices is appropriate to the Ashton/Wilson hypothesis, but the rapid recovery belies any of the significance with which they wish to endow the fall.

The other widely recognized crisis in this period occured in the year 1772, and it seems this disturbance was much more substantial. Profits fell abruptly, and there is evidence in the business history literature that this crisis shocked many an entrepreneur previously lulled into complacency. As examples: the Carron Company underwent a major reorganization and instituted the accounting system it was to use for the next half-century, mainly as a consequence of this crisis. [41] Josiah Wedgewood discovered for himself the technique of unit cost accounting, as necessity and the wolf at the door became the mother of invention. [42] The downturn in 1772 was internally generated by a credit contraction, which is often traced to the failure of a major bank in Scotland, and, later in Amsterdam, to the collapse of a consortium trying to drive up the prices of English shares. [43] The press resorted to the usual breast-beating: "...the stoppage of every banker's house in London was looked for. The whole City was in an uproar; the whole City was in tears." [44] Since most of these failures happened from June to December of the year, and downturns in some of our indices preceded these months, they may have been effects rather than causes. Yet, however severe the contraction, recovery appears to have been complete by 1775.

1776-1791

If the period from 1758 to 1775 was a silver age, this era was largely one of depression and faltering trade. Profits are above average levels for only five out of fifteen years, and three of those years fall at the very end of the period. Inspection of Table A in this chapter informs us that the quinquennium of 1780-84 had the lowest quinquennial means of the century for both share prices and profits (excepting the very first years of the century, when information is sparse). This epoch had the lowest mean profit index of any of the periods developed in this chronology. The two stretches of depression within this period were 1777-81 and 1783-87, when activity hit new lows for the century. Sandwiched between these two chasms was an unlikely boom in 1782, and following them, a more sustained revival of activity from 1788 to 1791. Some aspects of the slowdowns are revealed in the following individual profit

Year	Lond. A.	Carron	Whitbread	Drummond	S. Mines
1776	4.6	14.0	20.7	----	6.7
1777	4.2	14.1	25.9	3.7	7.4
1778	2.6	22.1	22.4	3.3	1.5
1779	3.5	27.6	18.0	3.3	8.0
1780	1.8	11.3	32.7	4.4	7.3
1781	6.6	15.0	25.5	6.6	5.2
1782	2.1	12.8	30.7	16.3	5.6
1783	2.8	5.6	22.9	2.9	11.1
1784	3.2	6.7	19.1	3.7	6.5
1785	3.4	6.9	26.7	4.7	7.2
1786	5.0	13.5	26.8	5.9	6.3
1787	4.9	13.9	30.0	4.6	7.4
1788	4.3	23.2	20.9	4.7	14.5
1789	5.8	20.4	24.2	6.1	10.0
1790	4.0	15.9	29.1	6.0	13.3
1791	7.1	15.8	32.4	10.0	5.5

statistics. In their general outlines, the movements of share prices conform to those of the profit index. There is a long fall from 1777 to 1781, some recovery in 1782-3, a trough in 1784, and then a predominantly unbroken rise to 1791. We must present the caveat, however, that by this time share price reporting has degenerated to the point that most movements in the index are governed by only three stocks: the Bank of England, the East India Company and the South Sea Company.

We have made periodic reference to Ashton's work on eighteenth century fluctuations throughout this chronology; perhaps this is the appropriate place in which to reveal some of its drawbacks, using this period as an example. He writes, "The two fluctuations of the eighties--those of 1781-4 and 1786-9--were short and of limited amplitude. In both cases the crisis was relatively mild." [45] Of course, the first rule when making statements about amplitude is that one must identify some quantitative measure which is the object of one's attentions. Further, we read earlier in the book that the year 1788 experienced a "deep depression," [46] which diametrically contradicts his later dictum. From our data, it appears Aston was wrong both times: the eighties were a very depressed period, and yet the year 1788 was no crisis or depression year at all, but the early part of an expansion. Ashton was probably following some hints of one of his students, L. Pressnell, who cites that year as the first crisis in England which involved the activities of country banks. [17] It is true that the later eighties was a period of widespread credit expansion, both by country banks and the staid Bank of England, and this institutional predisposition did eventually affect macroeconomic instability; but this disturbance had a longer gestation period than either Ashton or Pressnell have allowed for.

A development contemporary with the expansion of credit was the return of the joint stock company, although initially it was mostly confined to such endeavors as the building of canals and turnpikes. The canal movement had been building steadily since the 1760's, spurred on by the obvious success of the Duke of Bridgewater's achievement. No adequate statistics exist which measure the extent of this early period of canal construction, although by the late 1780's a full scale boom in the projection of such schemes is evident. Even though the joint stock form needed either explicit Parlimentary or Royal sanction (because the Bubble Act was still nominally in force), we do have some estimate of the pecuniary size of the joint stocks being projected. From this evidence it appears that new canal company formation peaked in 1793, lagging the turn in general activity by a year or so.

River Navigation and Canal Investment
Authorized by Parliament
(thousands of pounds)

1788	115	1792	1064
1789	134	1793	3160
1790	377	1794	2589
1791	804	1795	385

The resuscitation of the joint stock company in the context of canal construction proved to be a fertile ground for institutional innovation, because the need of these projects for ever increasing amounts of cash flow induced the fabrication of the preference share, and various accounting techniques for dealing with time-phased investments. [48] The trading of shares again became a common activity, and because of their local character, the canal shares penetrated the countryside in a much more fundamental way than in the earlier joint stock boom of 1690-1720. Canal shares are not listed in the eighteenth century Course of the Exchange, suggesting that the main locus of trading activity was not London, but rather the provinces. The coincidence of the rise of country banking and the financial organization of canals paved the way for a unified organization of the whole English macroeconomy.

Because canal shares were a relatively provincial financial instrument, we may employ information from the older canal companies to gauge the financial climate outside London. Recently, timeseries data of the quantity of shares traded of a number of canal corporations has been published. [49] The peak of this activity in 1768-71 coincides, with a lag, with the peak in our share index; while the lesser peak of 1775-7 also agrees with a more minor bulge in the share price index. The upsurge of 'the canal mania' of 1785-93 is associated with a slower rise (at least until 1791-2) in the share price index. All in all, it seems that London and the provinces are financially synchronized by at least the last quarter of the century.

Some further corroborative evidence on the timing and severity of fluctuations in the eighties may be obtained from the statistics of the Bank of England. There are two periods of extreme movements of Bank credit expansion in these years: 1777-8, and 1783-5; both of which concur with our dating of the contractionary years. One presumes this again represents the Bank in its role of conscious interventionary in the credit market with a mandate to encourage stability. The Bank's income in pounds from bills and notes discounted and from private loans, from August 31 of the previous year to August 31 of the cited year, is presented below. [50]

Year	Bills & Notes	Private Loans
1776	40,621	7,003
1777	58,386	9,115
1778	102,729	12,096
1779	51,740	12,535
1780	55,414	4,992
1781	84,390	4,944
1782	106,100	5,276
1783	126,595	8,851
1784	139,661	6,563
1785	167,607	15,906
1786	130,481	16,282
1787	129,685	16,333
1788	141,070	13,643
1789	58,177	23,532
1790	35,090	39,670
1791	26,520	22,518

1791-1801

The relative stability of the third quarter of the century was not maintained as time passed. After a decade and a half of depression, the boom of the late 1780's and early 1790's was not sustained. The profit index peaks in 1791 and then falls to a trough in 1793. Recovery is very slow, and profits only rise above average in 1798; but afterwards, there occurs one of the strongest and sustained surges of the century to 1801-3. Below we present some profit rate data for individual firms, and the Shannon brick production index, which has been employed by Gayer, Rostow, Schwartz and Brinley, Thomas, and others as a proxy for a building and/or production index.

Year	London Assurance	Drummond	Scotch Mines	McConnell & Kennedy	Brick Prod.
1791	7.1	10.0	5.5	----	778
1792	5.2	6.7	6.3	----	858
1793	5.8	3.1	2.1	----	848
1794	4.1	5.0	10.0	----	673
1795	4.1	6.1	3.3	----	596
1796	8.4	1.9	-2.8	----	575
1797	7.1	3.5	-1.7	----	517
1798	5.8	4.8	7.6	16.7	469
1799	7.0	6.6	23.4	30.2	482
1800	4.7	7.4	4.8	30.3	608
1801	7.3	8.2	12.0	27.2	686

Sources: McConnell & Kennedy, from C.H. Lee, A Cotton Enterprise, Manchester: Manchester Univ. Press, 1972. Brick production (millions of bricks): originally from H. Shannon, "Bricks: A Trade Index," Economica, Aug. 1934; the version here reported has been smoothed to coincide with calendar year data by Gayer, Rostow & Schwartz, op. cit.

We note that the brick index practically reproduces the movements of the profit index, with a lag of one year at turning points. Share prices follow the other indicators in that they rise to a peak in 1792, fall almost continuously to 1798, and then undergo a very marked rise to 1802.

A superficial reading of the situation in the 1790's often holds that the beginning of the French wars in February 1793 ushered in the paralysis that gripped the economy for the succeeding four years; but the fall in share prices begins in late 1792, and profits decline in that year. One therefore suspects that the movements possessed more of an endogenous character than some historians are willing to admit: "The crisis of neither 1793, 1797 nor 1799 seemed to have resulted in prolonged setbacks to home or foreign trade." [51] If we shift our focus to a theoretically sanctioned measure of the cycle, we see how inadequate were previous methods of identifying historical instability. The first crisis year mentioned does herald a severe contraction which lasts until the second date, after which there is sustained recovery. The suspension of payments by the Bank of England in 1797 has often been attributed to the drain of gold to Paris after the disintegration of the French Assignats. While the subsequent events may have been detrimental to the Bank, they were most assuredly beneficial to England as a whole. This picture of the economy is borne out by Pitt's budget speech of 18 February 1801, wherein he stated that the present war had been attended by almost constant increase of commerce and revenue. [52] The growth of the issuance of Bank of England notes after 1797, the rise of country banking, and the attendant easing of credit and speeding of payments had a salutary effect on expansion on all fronts. [53]

Amidst the exuberance of trade, some omens threatening its reverse were largely ignored. The years 1799-1800 saw the passage of the Combination Acts, a clumsy (and many would add mostly ineffectual) reaction to a perceived increase in the obstreperousness of the labor force, partly encouraged by the egalitarian doctrines being espoused across the Channel. Peel's Factory Act, passed in 1802, presaged a willingness on the part of the government to occasionally intervene in the organization of the workplace on a side other than that of the factory master. And most importantly, although the Peace of Amiens (preliminarily agreed to on 30 September 1801 and signed April 1802) was greeted by the English initially as the dawn of a new era, it rapidly became apparent that while France had relinquished the formalities of war, she had not relinquished her plans to thwart the growth of English commercial power.

1801-1819

Tallyrand is reported to have said in 1806, "The Emperor (Napoleon) does not imagine that any particular article of the Treaty of Amiens produced the war. He is convinced that the true cause was the refusal to make a treaty of commerce, which would necessarily have been prejudicial to the manufactures and the industry of his subjects." [54] Napoleon, who held some of his own theories about macroeconomic stability, perceived in the Bank of England's Restriction Act a blatant sign of weakness; this partially because the previous Revolutionary experience with a much lesser absolute debt convinced many a Frenchmen that Britain's load of debt must necessarily make her falter. The impact of the Napoleonic Wars upon British trade has been a matter of contention ever since. Gayer, Rostow and Schwartz approvingly quote a Manchester operator on the subject: "In the summer of 1802 there were about twenty (cotton) factories under construction in or around Manchester. But the industry reacted sharply to the resumption of hostilities, with prices falling and bankruptcies increasing. One operator at the time expressed the view that the 'dullness of trade' would continue until 'Bonaparte was settled'." [55] Heckscher, restricting his examination to the Continental System proper, maintained that its effect upon domestic trade in Britain was minimal; although this broad pronouncement was based on the perusal of cotton imports and coals shipped from Newcastle over a brief period of years. [56] More recently, Mokyr and Savin have chosen to portray the war years as a period of 'stagflation', similar to that of the later 1970's. They justify calling the war years a depression by fitting all manner of trend lines to timeseries of cotton imports, the Hoffmann indices and the brick output index. [57] Criticisms of both their general technique and the variables employed have already been broached in this and previous chapters. As it turns out, our theoretically motivated measure of aggregate activity does identify the war years as unique in British macroeconomic experience, but in a manner much more subtle than some hasty comparison with present experience.

In the most marked medium-term trend for the whole one hundred years, the index of the profit rate falls continuously from a very high level in 1801 to a trough in 1810. The period 1811 to 1818 witnesses very unstable improvement of a minor sort with transitory peaks in 1814 and 1817. Only in 1819 is the level of activity of 1801 regained. Share prices do not reproduce this pattern, however: after a peak in 1802 the index declines until 1804; but thereafter it undergoes a tremendous rise to a peak in 1810, a peak only surpassed by the South Sea Bubble and the 'mania' of 1824-5. An equally sharp fall ensues (broken only by a weak rally in 1814) to a trough in 1816, and then there is a rapid recovery in 1818-19. The share price boom of 1805-10 is the only sustained example we have discovered of the share index pursuing a contrary secular movement to the profit index. Some further evidence with regards to profit rates of individual firms and the movement of brick production is presented below. The evidence of brick production presents a third potential scenario. There is agreement on the fall of activity from 1812 to 1816, and the subsequent peak in 1819; but levels of production remain relatively flat from 1805 to 1810, while the profit index is falling and the share price index is rising. It is no wonder that historians can differ as to the relative impact of the Napoleonic Wars upon the economy of Great Britain.

Part of the problem in interpreting the later Napoleonic period resides in the fact that there are many unusual economic events impinging upon the polity simultaneously, the repercussions of which are difficult to weigh and isolate. First, there is the Continental System: Napoleon's grab-bag of policies nominally designed to strangle British trade. The theoretical motivations behind the idea that Britain must necessarily suffer the most in a self-blockade of the Continent were obscure at that time (as Heckscher has shown), and remain so today. The two main rationales seem to have been: a) the anachronistic mercantilist doctrine that levels of foreign trade and its balance or lack thereof directly controlled the health of the domestic economy; and b) the idea that an abrupt stop of trade would undermine the British paper economy, or, as Napoleon wrote, "inasmuch as (continental) merchants never

PROFIT RATES

Year	McCon. & K	Boulton & W.	Lond. A.	Drummond	Carron	Bricks
1801	27.2	11.1	7.3	8.2	15.3	686
1802	26.5	7.6	4.5	6.6	15.6	770
1803	14.3	7.8	7.9	6.7	15.7	818
1804	30.1	----	2.5	6.4	20.1	820
1805	15.3	----	4.9	7.3	19.5	889
1806	10.6	5.4	4.5	6.3	17.0	882
1807	13.5	3.5	2.9	6.0	17.5	836
1808	9.9	----	3.6	8.0	17.3	810
1809	2.4	2.3	6.1	7.0	17.1	826
1810	----	5.3	5.9	7.2	17.5	912
1811	----	3.2	5.2	6.7	17.4	945
1812	----	7.6	4.1	7.0	16.8	925
1813	----	-1.6	5.5	7.2	17.4	835
1814	----	5.3	5.1	9.8	17.5	768
1815	----	----	5.3	6.1	17.6	778
1816	----	----	5.2	7.6	16.2	673
1817	----	3.2	4.9	15.6	15.9	701
1818	----	----	.5	8.3	15.6	952
1819	----	----	34.8	7.0	16.5	1106

Sources: see previous tables, &
Boulton & Watt: profit rate estimated by the author from ledgers, Boulton & Watt collection, Birmingham City Library, and information in E. Roll, An Early Experiment, op. cit., p. 314.

buy except on credit, it is a fact that no goods are ever paid for..." and therefore are all traded on the basis of English credit. Their confiscation would mean "...a backhanded blow for England which is terrific." [58] Secondly, the war caused a well-documented shift in the channels of trade, away from northwestern Europe (and temporarily the United States due to the War of 1812) and towards the further reaches of the Mediterranean and to South and Central America, a shift which was further encouraged by the Spanish revolution of 1808. Most certainly it was this experience which led Ricardo to attribute all instability to 'sudden changes in the channels of trade' and its attendant confusions, which McCulloch further documented in his story of British speculators mindlessly sending ice skates to be sold in Rio de Janiero. These wartime shifts in the channels of trade caused temporary dislocations in the supply of crucial raw materials which plagued the British in this period. For example, American cotton imported at Lancashire fell from 143,700 bags in 1807 to 25,400 bags in 1808, and again fell from 79,500 bags in 1812 to 18,600 bags in 1813. Other unpleasant surprises included the fact that the process of taxation attained new heights of ingenuity of exaction with the levying of the Income Tax. Superimposed upon (and perhaps due to) this near-chaos in trade was the final internal breakdown of strictures restraining the spread of the joint-stock form of organization: it seems 1807-8 witnessed the first generalized rash of joint stock promotions since 1720. Tooke lists forty-two projections in the space of two years, including banks, mines, breweries, and companies for the purveyance of insurance, wine, liquor, vinegar and textiles. Finally, there was a pan-European credit crisis in 1810, the causes of which are still quite obscure. [59]

Although the evidence is not very strong nor consistent, it appears that real economic growth was formidable in the first few years of the Napoleonic wars, but the pressure of various circumstances forced a reversal in the later years, which was partially counteracted by an expansion of finance. After 1810 contraction set in slowly but persistently. The short-lived exhiliration over Napoleon's downfall and the gloom induced by the Hundred Days is clearly revealed in the profit index, which rises abruptly in 1814 and falls back down in 1815; but, more strikingly, the contraction outlasts the war. Signs of reduced circumstances are abundant throughout the latter period. The Luddite movement becomes a national bogey man in 1811 with riots in the North; Smart's Annals for the decade of the teens are peppered with the word 'distress'. The government, alarmed by the sharp rise of the poor rates, tried to relieve part of that burden by such ill-conceived legislation as the Bastardy Act, which forced the reputed father to indemnify the parish, and the Suspension of Habeas Corpus Act. Political economy, most assuredly a dismal science, becomes a prominent and popular topic of debate. To contemporaries, it must have seemed as if heavan and earth were in league with the devil to lay waste to mighty Albion. It was only by 1819 that redemption appeared shining on the horizon.

1820-1825

Gayer, Rostow and Schwartz call the period leading up to 1825 "the first truly modern boom in British economic history," [60] because, they stress, of the large role played by financial capital market flotations. Akerman, as we have mentioned earlier, called 1825 the first international economic crisis. As we have tried to argue in this section, neither statement is true. What the boom of 1822-25 was, was the most extreme expansion and contraction within a limited time period in the British economy since the South Sea Bubble.

All of our chosen theoretical indicators agree on this verdict. Profits fall from the peak in 1819 to an above-average trough in 1821, and then rise rapidly in 1824 and 1825 to the all-time peak of the century index at more than twice the average rate of profit. The share price index, which is exclusive of mining shares, reaches the second-highest peak of the whole series in 1824-5, smaller only than that of 1720. Since South American mining shares were one of the favored vehicles of speculation in this era, the share index, if anything, understates the extent of the actual rise. Some evidence for individual firms' profit rates, and the brick production index, is presented below.

Year	London Assurance	Carron	Drummond	Bridge Canal	Coal-brookdale	Bricks
1820	8.8	16.8	8.0	10.6	5.1	949
1821	7.3	17.3	9.9	14.5	3.0	899
1822	6.2	16.2	9.5	14.5	4.0	1019
1823	5.1	16.9	9.8	17.9	4.8	1244
1824	6.2	18.3	14.0	22.7	4.7	1463
1825	23.4	21.8	3.9	15.0	9.8	1948

Since, conventionally, historians have not been able to link this obvious disturbance with any random shock, such as a war or a harvest failure, attention has usually been focused on the psychology of speculation and credit expansion as the 'causes' of this headlong rush to riches. For example, Thorold Rogers wrote, "Is it not a little instructive that the same region gave occasion to the Bubble of 1720 and that of 1825." [61] Few have followed him in identifying some mysterious and tragic flaw in the British psyche which involves a morbid fascination with things Latino. Other historians have located the disturbance in the expansion of credit in the early 1820's. In 1822, 150 million pounds of government consols were converted from 5% to 4% interest, and in 1824 there was further conversion of 70 million pounds of debt to 3%. In June 1822, the Bank Rate was reduced to 4%, which Clapham suggests was done to attract more business to the Bank. The years 1823 to 1825 saw a rapid extension of note issue, both by the country banks and by the Bank of England. In the course of the expansion, Bank policy became much more daring, with the lending of money on mortgages (May 1823) and the lending of money on its own stock for collateral (Sept. 1823), both being practices which had not been seen since the South Sea Bubble. Further, certain legal changes, such as the Bank of England's Resumption of Cash Payments (1819), and the legal opinion which held that country banks must pay their noteholders in gold upon demand, made the banking system much more institutionally vulnerable to attack.

At the same time, the breakdown of inhibitions against joint stock promotions in 1807-8 came to fruition in the 1820's. In the two years 1824-5, 379 joint stock companies were projected, when there had previously been only 156 functioning joint stocks in existence. Some of these promotions were ill-disguised attempts to take the money and run, and only 127 of the new companies survived to the year 1827. [62] Yet, in the interests of verisimilitude one must not downplay the seriousness of many of the new ventures: Thomas notes, for example, that a large number of the projected companies proposed to apply the newly developed steam power to energize various industrial projects. [63] Irrespective of this fact, contemporaries knew that the object of the game was not necessarily a forwarding of physical production, but merely the capture of a pecuniary gain. As the *Times*, the bastion and repository of British morality, wrote on August 19, 1825: "Fresh projects and speculations break out, if we may say so, every day....It has now ceased to astonish, but not disgust us, to observe how little British capitalists are governed by moral principles in the disposal and employment of their money."

The third phenomenon often cited to explain this boom was the recent independence of various South American states, and the close political ties which they developed with Britain. One of the consequences was a series of loans to the governments of these nations floated on Exchange Alley. Thomas provides the following estimates of the amounts of these loans in the two major boom years: [64]

(Millions of Pounds)

1824		1825	
Brazil	3.6	Brazil	2.0
Mexico	3.2	Mexico	3.2
Peru	.7	Peru	.6
Columbia	4.7	Guatemala	1.4
Buenos Aries	1.0	Gudalaxaca	.6

Within two years, all of these states except Brazil were in default. These loans accompanied a longer term influx of British goods, a flow which had begun during the Continental Blockade years, much of which failed to provide the anticipated levels of return.

Of course, the frenzy had to come to a halt, and did so, beginning in December 1825. The Bank reversed its credit policy and a wave of failures of country banks ensued; a downturn in share prices started a snowballing of bankruptcies of those trading on margin; the South American governments went into default; and the repeal of the Combination Laws in 1824 was followed by a rash of strikes and labor intransigence. But the story of this massive contraction would take us beyond the bounds of our narrative.

However, before we delve a little deeper into the causes of eighteenth century fluctuations in the subsequent sections, it may do us well to compare the periods following our appointed 'silver age' with the previous conditions. To do so, we reproduce some of the information on Means and Standard Deviations with some further information below. Examination of the table shows that, in general, the variance of the profit rates and the share index manifest an increasing trend from the low point around 1758-75. Making appropriate allowances for company histories and other idiosyncracies, this seems to have been true whether the trend in the firm's profit rate was upward, as in the case of the London Assurance Company, or downward, as was the case of the Scotch Mines Company. These are the main outlines of the trends in instability which we shall explore in the final sections of this chapter.

Was It All Just Random Shocks?

In chapter one of book two we took note of the fact that many historians and economists tend to remove eighteenth century fluctuations from the realm of their consideration by writing them off as merely due to wars and harvest fluctuations. As we have explained, this in and of itself is an insufficient case for characterizing such fluctuations as pre-modern; but, even so, is there not still a germ of truth in their supposition? After all, the strict chronology of fluctuations in the previous section can be read as a catalog of shocks and disturbances: independent historical instances of wars, governmental changes, and so forth.

Interestingly enough, William Stanley Jevons's weather theory is not totally repudiated by economic theorists and economic historians: it is merely exiled to a period characterized by premodern or preindustrial economic structures. Some of the illustrious names associated with this position include Welsley Clair Mitchell, Michael Tugan-Baranowski, Joseph Schumpeter, Peter Mathias, T.S.

MEANS, AND STANDARD DEVIATIONS/MEANS

Period	Lond. A. Mean	SD/M	Scotch M. Mean	SD/M	Share Index Mean	SD/M	Profit Index Mean	SD/M
1695-1720	----	----	----	----	85.1	.36	----	----
1720-33	2.10	2.20	----	----	101.3	.31	----	----
1734-58	4.24	.56	----	----	98.0	.06	.93	.27
1758-75	4.29	.34	11.03	.34	97.1	.11	1.07	.15
1776-91	4.11	.35	7.71	.40	88.4	.13	.90	.24
1791-1801	6.05	.22	6.40	1.07	94.7	.12	1.05	.29
1801-19	8.17	1.23	4.63	2.55	102.8	.09	1.18	.26
1820-26	8.87	.68	----	----	125.8	.12	1.27	.36

Ashton, and W.W. Rostow. [65] This thesis has attracted little scrutiny, either in the way of empirical test or rational criticism. It is more interesting for what it implies than for its narrative value: that there either exists or did once exist a "natural economy," exhibiting market structures but lacking other structures--precisely which structures is a matter for disagreement among the cited authors. In this natural economy, breakdown, crises, and coordination failures were caused by largely exogenous shocks, such as weather fluctuations causing harvest failures, and so forth. Of course, this is precisely Jevon's theory: the substratum of market relations works well naturally and can only be undermined by external natural shocks.

One means by which to begin a reevaluation of our basic perception of macroeconomic fluctuations is to confront Jevons's thesis about the eighteenth and nineteenth centuries directly, using the historical evidence we have at our disposal. This is possible for two aspects of his theory: one, to review the possibility of a fixed decennial periodicity of fluctuations in that period; and two, to examine the likelihood that his particular exogenous shocks "caused" macroeconomic fluctuations in early modern England. Because most of the above characterizations of the "modern" English macroeconomy tend to cite 1825 as the first "modern" crisis, we shall restrict our intial quantitative inquiry to the period 1740 to 1825.

An impressionistic notion of economic fluctuations from 1740 to 1825 may be obtained from the table below. The index of a sample of profit rates was culled from the business accounts of various eighteenth- and nineteenth-century British firms. This compares Jevons's crisis dates with the peaks and troughs of the profit index, the Wolf sunspot numbers, and a share price index I constructed from <u>The Course of the Exchange</u>. If one merely calculates the mean peak-to-peak durations, one finds them to be 11.4 years for sunspots, 13.6 years for the share price index, and 10.4 years for the profit index. Evidence of this nature has undoubtedly fostered the impression of a rough decennial periodicity. It would be an error, however, to infer that Jevons's characterization has been vindicated by historical research.

More than the improved and augmented historical record, another advantage we have over Jevons is a much-improved understanding of the theoretical relationship between stochastic shocks and regular cycles in time series analysis. Because of the work of Slutzky and Yule, we know that periodicity in a time series may indeed be due to deterministic cycles in the underlying structural process (for example, a sine curve), but it also may be due to random or autocorrelated shocks impinging upon a stable structure, producing an output exhibiting nondeterministic cycles of stable periodicity. [66] Most economic time

PEAKS AND TROUGHS OF SUNSPOTS, SHARE PRICES, AND PROFIT RATES COMPARED WITH JEVONS'S "CRISES"

Jevons's "Crises"	Wolf Sunspot Numbers		Share Price Index		Profit Index	
	Peak	Trough	Peak	Trough	Peak	Trough
1742			1743	1747-8		
1752	1750	1755	1753	1762	1752	1757
1763	1761	1766			1758	1762
			1768		1763-7	1772
1772-3	1769	1775				
					1775	1780-5
1783	1778	1784		1784		
					1788-91	1793
1793	1787	1798	1792	1798	1799-1801	
1804-5	1804	1810	1802	1804		
						1810
1815	1816	1823	1810	1816	1819	1823
1825	1830	1833	1825		1825	

Sources: Wolf sunspot numbers: Harlan Stetson, Sunspots and their Effects (New York, 1937), pp. 197-99. Share price index: Philip Mirowski, "The Rise (and Retreat) of a Market," The Journal of Economic History, 41 (Sept. 1981), 559-77. Profit index: Philip Mirowski, "Adam Smith, Empiricism, and the Rate of Profit in 18th Century England," History of Political Economy, 14, no. 2 (1982); with additions.

series do not exhibit sine-wave-like deterministic cycles; the present series is no exception. The existence of stable nondeterministic periodicities is an open question, however, and there are many techniques available to provide an answer. The predominant technique is spectral analysis, but it requires inordinately large numbers of data points in order to identify periodicities with any reasonable certainty. An alternative (though less precise) technique is to fit parsimonious Box-Jenkins-style models to individual time series, and then use the estimated coefficients to calculate the theoretical spectrum peak. [67]

Using this method we find that from 1749 to 1826 the Wolf sunspot numbers have a significant frequency at 10.5 years (thus supporting Jevons's revised information), whereas first differences of the profit index have an insignificant frequency peak at 9.7 years, and first differences of the logarithm of the share price index have no significant discernible frequency peak. In other words, only the sunspots can be said to have a regular identifiable periodicity.

The second aspect of Jevons's theory that can be reevaluated is the assertion that exogenous natural shocks "caused" economic fluctuations in the period 1749-1826. One major problem is his characterizations of the crises. First, because of the absence of fixed periodicities, peak-to-peak durations vary from a minimum of 8 years to a maximum of 24 years for the share prices, and from 6 to 19 years for the profit index. Second, the leads and lags relative to his crisis dates are unstable. Peaks in the share price index tend to lead his crisis dates prior to the 1780's, and lag them thereafter until 1825. Profit index peaks lead his crisis dates by between 3 and 7 years, except for the years 1752, 1763, and 1825 as widespread credit crisis seems fairly well grounded, whereas the identification of 1763, 1783, 1804-05, and 1815 do not.

The question of leads and lags can be broached with somewhat more sophistication. Econometricians have recently developed a technique called "causality testing." Though incapable of solving age-old philosophical problems concerning the nature of causality, it is well suited to answer the question posed by Jevons: once we account for as much of the variance as possible of a time series variable by using as explanatory variables its own past values, how much more variance can be explained by the addition of a second explanatory variable? If the amount of additional variance accounted for is substantial according to conventionally accepted statistical criteria, the second variable is said to "cause" the first in a Granger sense. Many versions of Granger causality test have been proposed and implemented by economists, but recent theoretical and simulation work has suggested that the variant known as the "Granger-Wald" test has the most desirable statistical properties. [68] The value of this test is asymptotically distributed as chi-square, with the degrees of freedom equal to the number of lagged values of the potentially "causal" variable.

The table below displays the values of the Granger-Wald test for pairwise comparisons between the following variables: the Wolf sunspot numbers, the value of British exports to Asia, the index of British share prices, the British profit index, and the mean temperature of England by harvest year. If the series exhibited a trend, the test required that it be removed. The columns represent the variables as potential causal agents, whereas the rows represent the variables as being the resultant of the other variables. For example, the entry of 4.23 at the top of the first column is the value of the chi-square test that sunspots "Granger cause" fluctuations in British exports to Asia. At conventional statistical levels, the null hypothesis of no causation is not rejected. All of the tests in the table are performed with four annual lags of the "causal" variable for the period from 1753 to 1822. The endpoints of this analysis are determined by data availability.

GRANGER-WALD CHI-SQUARE CAUSALITY TEST, 1755-1826

	(1) Sunspots	(2) Exports to Asia	(3) Share Prices	(4) Profit Index	(5) Temp.
1. Sunspots	----	9.38	5.21	1.35	2.69
2. Exports to Asia	4.23	----	8.82	3.19	7.60
3. Share Prices	4.50	13.85*	----	2.68	4.43
4. Profit Index	0.84	2.07	5.24	----	2.58
5. Temperature	4.63	8.94	4.33	2.41	----

*Significant at 1 percent level.

Note: Some tests use truncated sample periods because of data availability.

Sources: Sunspots: Linearly detrended, see previous table. Exports: first difference of natural logarithms, from Brian R. Mitchell and Phyllis Deane, Abstract of British Historical Statistics (Cambridge, 1962), pp. 309-10. Share Prices: First difference of natural logarithms, see previous table. Profit Index: First differences, see previous table. Temperature: No detrend, harvest-year mean temperature of Britain, from G. Manley, "Mean Temperature of England, 1698-1952," Quarterly Journal of the Royal Meteorological Society, 42 (1953), 256-58.

According to the Jevons hypothesis, fluctuations in sunspots should cause fluctuations in temperature, which should in turn cause fluctuations in exports to Asia, triggering fluctuations in finance (the share price index) and finally in macroeconomic expansions and contractions (the profit index). As can be observed in the above table, the only link in this chain of reasoning that passes the Granger-Wald test is the relationship between exports to Asia and the share price index, which is significant at the 1 percent confidence interval in the direction of exports causing fluctuations in share prices. The result is not surprising, given that the shares of the East India Company compromise an important part of the share index. More importantly, the table shows there is no significant relationship between sunspots and any economic variable; nor, indeed, is there a significant relationship in the Granger-Wald sense between any of the "natural" shocks and any of the economic time series.

Finally, we can briefly examine the larger issue of the existence of a "macroeconomic watershed" between the premodern economy and the fully industrialized economy. The following table presents the Granger-Wald causality tests for the same set of variables as the above table, with the single exception of the replacement of the profit index with Deane's and Feinstein's national income estimates for the period 1830-1875, as an indicator of macroeconomic fluctuations. We observe that the pattern of results is very much the same, with no significant causal relations running from the "natural" shocks to economic fluctuations. Because the share index no longer weights the East India Company so heavily, there is not a strong connection between exports to Asia and share prices in this period. Share prices, however, do seem to be influenced by changes in aggregate income.

GRANGER-WALD CHI-SQUARE CAUSALITY TEST, 1755-1826

	(1) Sunspots	(2) Exports to Asia	(3) Share Prices	(4) GNP	(5) Temp.
1. Sunspots	----	0.93	4.28	1.57	7.74
2. Exports to Asia	1.77	----	1.91	4.57	9.05
3. Share Prices	2.31	1.50	----	12.00*	4.57
4. GNP	9.13	6.10	8.83	----	7.22
5. Temperature	9.14	3.94	4.02	2.49	----

* Significant at 5 percent level.
Note: Some tests use truncated sample periods because of data availability.
Sources: Sunspots, Exports, and Temperature: See previous table. Share Prices: Hayek's Index, in A. Gayer, W. Rostow, and A. Schwartz, The Growth and Fluctuation of the British Economy (Oxford, 1953), p. 456: first differences of natural logarithms. GNP: B.R. Mitchell, European Historical Statistics (New York, 1976), pp. 797, 782: splice Deane and Feinstein's estimates at constant prices, first differences of natural logarithms.

The conception of a premodern "natural" economy that fluctuates because of shocks external to social and market processes does not hold up well under scrutiny. The problem resides in the widespread notion of a premodern economy as a baseline against which to measure industrial development. It is a form of conjectural anthropology not so very far removed from Adam Smith's "early and rude state." But after a little critical examination, we are left neither with an Eden before the advent of markets, nor a Paradise of markets "before the Fall."

Can anything be said about the influence of wars upon macroeconomic fluctuations using a less restrictive procedure? First, we can simply split the sample into the two subsamples of war years and peace years: the average value of the mean adjusted profit index for the war years was .968 with a standard deviation of .248; while the mean and standard deviation for the peace years was 1.035 and .425 respectively. Interestingly enough, it was the peace years which experienced the greater variance (instability) in the eighteenth century. The question of whether war was 'good' or 'bad' for the economy as a whole is largely rendered inconsequential by posing it in this manner: a test of the hypothesis that the means of the two samples are not significantly different from each other does not reject the null hypothesis (t-statistic = .94).

So far we have only considered a uni-directional causality running from the war to the economy, but there is some precedent for considering causality in the other direction. A. MacFie, in an article written in the 1930's [69], suggested that European wars had tended to break out in the upswing of business cycles in the nineteenth century. His evidence was actually quite slim, considering the fact that he did not even have at his disposal all those retrospective national income accounts which we have come to take for granted. At any rate, from time to time generalizations have been made concerning the macroeconomic motivations for wars; here it is possible to address the question in a preliminary manner through examination of profits in the eighteenth century. Table H shows the magnitude of changes in the profit index for the year in which the war broke out, the year in which it ended, and the immediate surrounding years.

There are no substantial regularities of experience preceding the beginning or end of wars, as revealed in this table. The first year of a war tends to be accompanied by a fall in the rate of profit, but for two of the wars the effect is so small as to be hardly significant. Surprisingly enough, the year of the end of the war exhibits no consistent pattern.

Overall, we must conclude provisionally that the evidence does not support any statement that eighteenth century wars, and to a lesser extent harvest failures, had any consistently significant impact on British profit rates. This does not rule out the possibility that an individual war or harvest failure may have had a very specific historical impact; but such a statement must presume an articulated structure of economic theory which can impose meaning on the isolated event.

In chapter six, we divided up movements in accumulation and growth into four broad categories: the margin, financial turnover, the physical technology, and physical turnover. Unfortunately, it has proved impossible to collect much data at all concerning physical technology or physical turnover as we have defined them. The main reason this data is unavailable is because <u>it was unavailable to the historical actors themselves</u>: that is, the physical economy was not planned, but governed indirectly by movements in pecuniary quantities, which <u>were</u> observable by the contemporary actors. This state of affairs persists to a preponderant extent even today. A rigorous assessment of physical technology and physical turnover would mean possession of the information represented by the 'A' and 'B' matrices: phyiscal industry <u>flow</u> coefficients (and <u>not</u> the conventional Leontief input/output coefficients, which have the drawbacks of being calculated from pecuniary data, and confuse stocks and flows), and the time patterns of inputs

PROFIT MOVEMENTS AROUND WARS (FIRST DIFFERENCES)

	1739-48		1756-63		1776-85		1793-1815	
	Begin	End	Begin	End	Begin	End	Begin	End
Year$_{-2}$	-.88	-.14	+.45	-.16	-.06	-.58	+.26	-.07
Previous yr.	+.90	-.33	-.26	-.06	+.17	+.13	-.43	-.37
Begin/End	-.59	+.35	-.06	+.29	-.01	-.37	-.20	-.26
Subseq. yr.	-.14	-.47	-.57	-.05	-.09	+.41	+.24	-.05

Table H

in the production process. The concerted collection of such information would justify what has been up till now the opinion on the part of economists that the 'production function' should be the envelope function of a book engineering blueprints. Since we do not possess this information for either the past or the present, let us make some educated guesses in the interim. 'Technological progress' is both an idea and a faith which we in the west have all been nurtured upon; so let us presume to a first approximation that there has been, over the course of two hundred years, an increase in net flow output per unit flow input, defined in the manner of chapter six. Secondly, let us recall that the organization of human work has undergone vast changes in the last two hundred years: the development of round-the-clock work, Taylorism, the assembly line, the destruction of frequent folk holidays (and the 'rationalization' of the remaining holidays so that they always fall on Monday), the conversion of religious persuasion to a self-policed regularity, the rise of a class of managers who monitor the speed of production, etc. Let us _presume_ that the prepoderance of social innovations has acted over the long term to speed physical turnover, on average. If these two parables or presumptions (and that is all they are at this stage) are correct, then the equilibrium rate of physical growth of capitalistically organized economies has tended to rise over the long run.

Fortunately, for the financial side of the macroeconomy, we have more evidence. Chapter eight collects together the timeseries evidence I have been able to extract from various business records with regard to eighteenth century markups. Margins are defined as net profit divided by either total sales or else debit total cash flow of the business. The first that captures our attention is that in most cases the margin is quite high, although it may go negative if the firm in question is either just starting up or approaching bankruptcy. Rates of margin of twenty to thirty percent are not all that uncommon; in the particular cases of the Sun Fire Assurance Company and the Carron Company they even rise above 50% for extended periods of time. While this is extremely slim evidence upon which to base a generalization--many of the firms for which we could reconstruct profit rates had kept their cash accounts in separate books which were not available, and business histories almost never report such basic information as sales and cash flow--it may have been the case that average margins were well above 15% in eighteenth century businesses, and probably rarely went below 10%. This is to be compared with an average markup which is rarely above 10% in the U.S. in modern times and much lower in other countries, such as Japan. Again, remembering we are forced for the present to make comparisons across countries across 200 years, there is some evidence to suggest that the average margin has fallen over the long term in capitalistically orgainzed economies. One suspects it was this phenomenon which eighteenth and nineteenth century actors noticed in the course of their own business experience, and translated into the concern of a 'falling rate of profit' in the literature of economic history. [70] This trend in the margin can be explained within the context of an institutional theory: in a regime of ever increasing competition due to the penetrationof capitalist organization into most aspects of economic life, it is to be expected that profits per unit sales would be secularly forced downward from some arbitrarily high starting point.

Now we turn to the last category, the financial rate of turnover. Chapter eight presents the available data on the rate of financial turnover per year for various eighteenth century businesses. The rate of cash turnover is here defined as the debit total of the cash account divided by net equity; while the rate of sales turnover is defined as total sales divided by net equity. Cash turnover is by definition always greater than or equal to sales turnover for the identical firm. Three things revealed therein are worthy of note: a) the stability of financial turnover relative to the markup, a characteristic of modern times; b) the correspondence between firms over the level of turnover within a relatively narrow band of values; and c) a secular trend for all corporations of rise in the rate of financial turnover. All three points agree quite well with the theoretical expectations developed in chapter six. If the average level of financial turnover is a function of existing financial institutions--that is, not the outcome of some individual constrained maximization decision--then it should generally be more stable (in the sense of possessing more inertia) than the markup over time, and should vary within a relatively small band as between individual businesses. The upper bound of this band will be set by those businesses on the forefront of institutional innovation: innovations in accounting techniques, or the subtle use of leverage, or the art of merger, and so forth. Other firms will either copy these innovations, thus converging to best-practice technique, or else satisfice, stagnating at some low but sufficient level of financial turnover, which would have to be offset by an inordinately high markup to maintain some parity in profit rates. (Thus, 'stagnation' may still be characterized by a high pecuniary rate of profit.) A clear example of the former case of convergence to best practice technique, is provided in the next figure. Plotted on the graph are the financial turnover rates of the East India Company and the Spencer Stanhope partnership over the first half of the eighteenth century. In this era, it has been repeatedly acknowledged that the East India Company was a leader in accounting practices: "In bookkeeping it had from the beginning been advanced (perhaps, as has been suggested, because of the Mediterranean associations of its earliest members). Well

rates of financial turnover 1690-1750

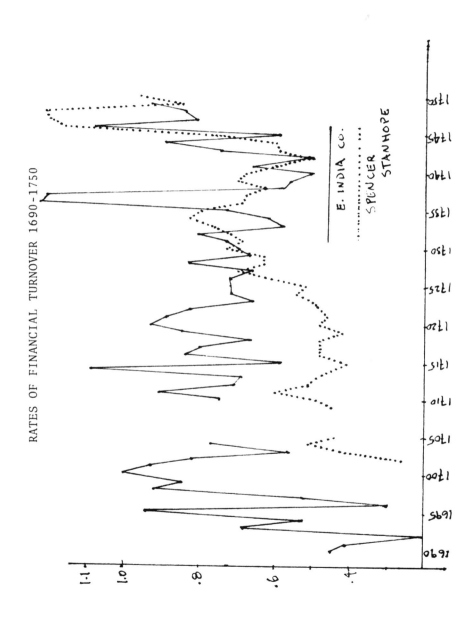

before the end (of the seventeenth century) the concept of shares as the profit (sic) on a proprietor's capital, of bonds as capital (sic again) borrowed at interest for limited periods, and of book credit, was fully developed and clearly differentiated." [71] While a more knowledgable assessment (that is, one that did not confuse equity with loans and flows with stock) would date the Company's innovations closer to the turn of the century [72], agreement is general that by that time the Company was in the forefront of creative accountancy, if only by virtue of necessity. The Spencer Stanhope partnership, on the other hand, was a rapidly growing iron forge business. In pursuit of best-practice technique, one might expect the latter's turnover to converge to the former's, and that is what happens from 1700 to circa 1730.

If we are correct in identifying the East India Company as a financial 'best-practice' firm, then certain other implications immediately follow, the primary one being that a turnover rate of under unity was institutional best practice in the first half of the eighteenth century. By the turn of the nineteenth century, institutional best practice has risen to over one, but with an upper bound of 1.5 or so. This can be compared to present-day U.S. experience, where average practice hovers about 2.3-2.6, and contemporary Japan, where from 1958 to 1974 the rate of financial turnover has risen from 2.8 to 6.0. Again, remembering that we are comparing situations across countries and over time, there is some tentative cause to believe that institutional innovation over time has led to a secularly rising rate of financial turnover. This discovery reinforces the theoretical expectations developed in chapter six. We would expect there to be continual institutional innovation to speed financial turnover because, of all of the components of the profit rate, there are located the smallest set of interests and the least set of conditions which would oppose or obstruct such innovation. Increases in the markup are constrained by conditions of competition; secular increases in physical turnover are opposed by the workers, who bear the brunt of such changes; and technology is assumed to be constrained by the known relations of physics, etc. Increases in financial turnover are private, easily hidden or disguised from the general purview, and might only be opposed by creditors or shareholders--if they ever found out--in fear of the possible consequences of failure; but in general, it is realized by the shareholders and creditors that it is they who reap where they do not sow: the benefits are solely pecuniary, and they belong to the rentier. Therefore in a majority of situations, speeding financial turnover will be the preferred means for secularly increasing the profit rate.

The conjunction of these last two findings explain the earlier, somewhat anomalous result that the financial rate of profit seems neither to have risen or fallen secularly over the last 200 years. To a first approximation, the reason is that a secularly falling margin has been offset by a secularly rising rate of financial turnover, with the outcome being a relatively stationary rate of profit. This conjuction of events, which is somewhat circumstantial, has important implications for the future of the western macroeconomies.

In the long run, the rate of financial turnover is unbounded, but the margin has a very real institutional lower bound at the value of zero. In actuality, this lower bound will never be reached, because it presumes a form of competition so intense and so effective, that the repercussions of this competition would threaten the underpinnings of society itself. [73] Therefore, if the present secular trend of rising rates of financial turnover continues, the secular fall of the markup slows or comes to a halt, and if technological change and the rate of physical turnover are unable to keep pace (and we have no <u>a priori</u> reason for believing that they will keep pace, and some reason to believe that the politically sanctioned obstreperousness of workers organized in unions can slow financial turnover), the western economies are secularly unstable: In simple terms, finance will increasingly outrun physical capabilities to a greater and greater degree, making the processes of adjustment more and more difficult. The rise of Keynesian interventionism, far from helping us understand and control these intrinsic incompatibilities, actually acts to exacerbate them. The two aspects of the same economy, the financial and real spheres, cannot help but diverge in their institutional paths, given present modes of organizing production.

But, for the time being, let us restrict our attention to macroeconomic movements in the eighteenth and early nineteenth centuries. We have taken note of a singular trend in the variance of profit rates and share prices over the period: variance falls until the 'silver age' of 1758-75, and then rises thereafter. Is this merely a fluke, or can it be linked to some theoretical causation? In fact, we have already collected all the elements of an explanation in the previous chapters.

The Joint Stock Company in Eclipse 1720-1807

The theory of business cycles developed in chapter six has stressed as one of its main components the significance of finance within the institutional context of the corporation. Expressly, financial data are the tangible evidences of fluctuations in the macroeconomy, both for the contemporary participants and the economic historian. In the process of attempting to extract this information form the historical record, we have stumbled upon (and some might add over) a specific historical anomaly: most of the institutions of finance which we deem 'modern'--balance sheet accountancy, an active marketplace for corporate shares, publications supplying timely and accurate price information, futures markets--existing concurrently with an absolute dearth of corporate shares to be traded in eighteenth century England. [74] A sample of portfolios has demonstrated that large blocks of investment were tied up either in direct government instruments or in the instruments of the three big quasi-governmental corporations: the Bank of England, the South Sea Company and the East India Company. Why were fully private corporations generally denied access to the stock market?

One thing is clear: it was not part and parcel of a smooth historical progression from inchoate premodern conditions to the 'rational' stock exchange of today. Prior to 1689 there were extant fifteen functioning joint stocks in Great Britain, with an aggregate nominal capital of over 850,000 pounds. [75] After the Glorious Revolution, there was a great burst of company formation, with approximately 140 joint stocks in existence in 1695, having an estimated nominal capital of 4,250,083 pounds. [76] Approximately sixty percent of these companies did not survive to the end of the century. Yet joint-stock formation continued, in fits and starts, up to the year of the South Sea Bubble, 1720. The number of joint stocks existing in 1720 is not known precisely, but to all accounts it was quite substantial: Scott estimates that 190 companies were formed between September 1719 and August 1720 alone, with a total nominal capital of more than 220 million pounds. [77] Then in May/June 1720 Parliament, in reaction to the frenzy of speculation, passed "An Act for better securing certain Powers and Privileges, intended to be granted by His Majesty by Two Charters, for Assurance of Ships and Merchandises at Sea, and for lending money upon Bottomry; and for restraining several extravagant and unwarrantable Practices therein mentioned" (6 Geo. I c.18), known as the Bubble Act. It is law which, as Maitland put it, "even when we now read it, seems to scream at us from the Statute Book." The Act was intended to outlaw all groups of persons who purported to "act as if they were corporate bodies" and had "pretended to make their shares transferable" without a charter either from the crown or from Parliament. The guilty were subject to the penalty of <u>praemunire</u> (the forfeit of all property rights) and brokers dealing in shares of these counterfeit companies were liable to a fine of 500 pounds. Many historians trace the collapse of share prices in 1720 from the writ of <u>scire facias</u> issued at the instigation of the South Sea Company under the authority of this Act. [78]

After 1720, joint stock company formation became a rarity. Although the history of British joint stock companies from 1720 to 1840 remains to be written, it seems there is little evidence of legal incorporation from 1720 to the 1760's. Afterwards, with the exception of canal and turnpike acts, there were only random few incorporations until the nineteenth century: the English Linen Company in 1764, the British Plate Glass Company in 1773, the Sierre Leone Co. in 1791. Note that even though these were legally constituted joint stocks, they were not included in the share price lists of the period. This was likewise true for the canal companies, of which there were more than one hundred incorporated between 1766 and 1800.

It is only 1807 and 1808 that we find anything like the generalized surge of joint stock promotions in the period of the 1690's to 1720, which was not linked to any particular field of endeavor, such as canal construction. [79] One result of this renaissance in finance was the expansion of share list reporting in 1811. Subsequent years saw fluctuations of company formation around an increasing trend, until the years 1824-5, when "bubble schemes came out in shoals like herring from the Polar Seas." Irrespective of the ghost of 1720, the Bubble Act was repealed in June 1825 (6 Geo. IV c.91), although provisions remained for governemental regulation of the degree of liability incident to incorporation.

Three-quarters of a century ago, the connection between the Bubble Act and the dearth of company formation in England seemed obvious to both historians and economists. Alfred Marshall in his Industry and Trade suggested that a counterfactual England without the Bubble Act would have seen the spread of joint stock organization in the eighteenth century. Both Scott and Hunt saw the Bubble Act as stunting eighteenth century financial organization; Hunt particularly stressing the absence of limited liability. Present-day authors, on the other hand, tend to view the Bubble Act as inconsequential, and in replacement of the previous interpretation they proffer weak arguments about eighteenth century psychology, or the supposed lack of a need for a placement market. [80] All and sundry cite one author, A.B. DuBois, as their sole justification for taking the position that the Act was less of an obstacle to joint stock companies than had been previously supposed.

One wonders whether any of these authors have acutally read DuBois. [81] As part of the endless seesaw of historical revisionism, DuBois was particularly interested in correcting Hunt's emphasis on the stifling of limited liability as the main deterrent effect of the Bubble Act. He showed that the link between limited liability and incorporation was neither explicit nor ambiguous in early joint stock corporations, and that the first comprehensive recognition of the limited liability motive in incorporation was only to be found in 1768. DuBois then asked what it was that proprietors sought when they applied for charters, and compiled a list of motivations from those petitions. The reasons given were: [82]

i) prohibition by the Bubble Act of raising a transferable stock;
ii) increasing supervision of officers and managers through the ability to sue and be sued in the name of the corporation;
iii) ability to hold property in the name of the corporation;
iv) the need to delegate power in a large organization to a small number of individuals;
v) difficulties of continuity with the death of a partner;
vi) to facilitate the borrowing of funds.

DuBois admits that, although there were potential legal mechanisms for circumventing these problems, the Bubble Act was a real obstacle with respect to these matters. The extent of the impediment was an issue concerning which DuBois declined to make any firm statement. The complexity of the issue is best summarized by his statement, "When difficulties of internal operation arose in the case of the unincorporated association, the only possible forum where adequate relief could be obtained was the Chancellor's court. Since the unincorporated company was definitely not 'the creature of the state', the state in its turn was less accessible to such a unit." [83]

One reason for Dubois' equivocal statment was that conventional economic theory had little to add in the way of clarifying the issue. Previous chapters have outlined the ways in which neoclassical theory is ahistorical and a-institutional; the absence of state guidelines in the case of the unicorporated enterprise would probably be viewed as salutary and even beneficial from within the neoclassical context. But in the context of an institutional theory which recognizes the potential for both growth and instability inherent in capitalist finance, the hiatus of joint stocks in the eighteenth century assumes a more complex character and set of motivations. The rapid development of financial institutions from the Glorious Revolution to 1720 was disturbing to contemporaries, especially, as they described it, when thye witnessed the extremes of deception and frenzy which men were driven to in the pursuit of purely paper financial gain. This unease was more significant than a rash of complacent moralizing; 'stock-jobbing' threatened to rend the social fabric. It undermined the fledgling work ethic; the aristocrat and the valet might be jostling each other in the 'democracy' of Exchange Alley in the same pursuit; and the economy suffered from the periodic failures of paper expansion. The Bubble Act was but one in a long series of eighteenth century British governmental actions which identified the buying and selling of placements with palpable sabotage of the economic process--not so very different a view from the Veblen of The Theory of Business Enterprise. The bills attacking aspects of Doctor Johnson's "politico-peripatetic school of Exchange Alley" usually were passed after a financial crisis. In

1697, two acts were passed (8 & 9 Wm. III, c.20 & c.32) to register all sales of stock at the Bank of England and to regulate and limit the number of stockholders to the fanciful figure of one hundred individuals. In 1734, Barnard's Act (10 Geo. II c. 8) outlawed puts and refusals and heavily curtailed dealings on margin. This list does not include the dates of those bills which were proposed but did not pass a vote of Commons in 1745, 1756 and 1773. It was not until the late 1780's that an ideology of laissez-faire was both articulated and extended to apply to the transferability of shares. It was not the Bubble Act alone, but open hostility to transferable share ownership and financial manipulation on many institutional fronts which explains the paucity of joint stock formation and share listings in the eighteenth century, and also, therefore, the peculiar pattern of the variance of share prices and profit rates discussed above.

In the terms of our macroeconomic theory, the history of the English corporation in the eighteenth century is the tale of the vicissitudes of an institution which embodied the threatening potential for the divergence of the physical and financial spheres of production and reproduction, and therefore was the object of many punitive measures meant to force the two spheres of coincide. The prohibition of transferable shares was part of this program: to inextricably tie the owner to the physical process of production and restrict the possibilities of the manipulation of capital gains in balance sheets. the prohibitions against margin sales and time bargains are perhaps the most obvious attempts to contain the extention of leverage and to consciously lengthen financial turnover times. This is also clear in the instances of impedimenta and institututional nuisances imposed upon the issuance of corporate debt. Corporations were placed in extra jeopardy by the Bubble Act and by difficulties with the legal discipline of its own officers because they were the main vehicles for financial manipulation. Indeed, "It is more than a coincidence that the Bubble Act, inhibiting corporate activity, and the first suppressive legislation against workers' organizations were enacted in the same decade." [84] This legislation was a concerted program which aimed to lengthen financial turnover and thus reduce the financial profit rate, and at the same time to place the state on the side of the employer in the struggle for discipline in the workplace in order to speed up physical turnover and therefore raise the physical rate of growth. The corporation, the locus of control over financial turnover, came under attack.

Therefore, in the historical context of the situation--partially defined by the unique and extreme fluctuation of the share price index herein constructed--the Bubble Act, Barnard's Act and the hundreds of pamphlets villifying 'stock-jobbing' are not some anachronistic holdovers from an ignorant and ill-tutored age, but a 'rational' attempt to bring financial expansion into line with perceived real expansion. An evidence of this rationality is the fact that as the rate of physical expansion increases in the last quarter of the eighteenth century, the institutional restraints on finance start to recede. One question which remains is whether the restraints, when in force, were actually effective. To a certain extent we have already answered this question. Finance in the eighteenth century was channelled either into land, government securities, a very few chartered companies or into the balance sheet (that is, the liabilities and assets) of a circumscribed partnership. Up until the late eighteenth century, the shares listed in <u>The Course of the Exchange</u> are very nearly the only corporate financial instruments to be found in the portfolios of the period. In that respect, the curbs on finance were very effective.

The Business Cycle as an Endogenous Phenomenon

The birth of the modern macroeconomy in England was accompanied by two periods of hyperactive financial innovation: 1688 to 1695-6, and the years immediately preceding 1720 and the South Sea Bubble. The extremes of expansion and contraction which resulted from these innovations were, understandably, viewed with fear and trepidation by many in the polity, and the uneasiness which was not assuaged by finding individual scapegoats and making them suffer openly was channelled into the suppression of the financial institutions themselves: the Bubble Act prevented the spread of the business corporation; Barnard's Act and numerous other lesser Acts legislated against the 'stock-jobbers' and institutions allowing the issuance of time bargains in general. In the parlance of the theory in chapter six, the initial innovations acted to appreciably speed financial turnover, which increased the variance about the equilibrium rate of growth relative to anything that had been experienced previously. Perceiving this increased variance as threatening to the larger social order (which it was in late Stuart and early Hanoverian England), the government, in consort with the larger culture, adopted a hostile attitude to such innovations. Insofar as these laws, strictures and nasty insinuations had an effect, they acted to reduce, or prevent the further increase of, the rate of financial turnover in the whole economy. We can observe the subsequent lowered variance in the share and profit indicies, and the absence of any appreciable trend in financial turnover from 1720 to roughly 1760. After circa 1760, the situation is reversed. Finance has been moribund, while the spread of the factory has instituted routinized work as a way of life for the mass of the populace. Strict supervisory control over the work activity became associated with breaking processes down into sequences which identified different tasks with different working individuals, and it was then a short step to applying motive force from a centralized power source to these sequential tasks. This paradigmatic innovation, in its various physical forms (the mill, the power loom, etc.) increased physical turnover and perhaps (the evidence is certainly not in on this yet) the flow technology coefficient, in either case raising the potential physical rate of growth. In fact, it is this phenomenon of rise in physical volume of production per time unit in certain lines of endeavor between 1760 and 1780 or so which led earlier economic historians to postulate the existence of an 'Industrial Revolution'.

As physical expansion accelerated, the demands of growth also resumed institutional pressure to speed the rate of financial turnover. Chapter eight shows a pronounced acceleration in the course of the 1760's of financial turnover in differing firms. But institutional barriers, once in place, cannot just be wished away effortlessly. The spread of the joint stock form was still shackled by legal and practical contraints; in the 1760's and 1770's their spread was limited to canal construction and a few other forms of quasi-public endeavor. Organized pressure to free the firm of institutional constraints on financial turnover became apparent in the 1770's: the repeal of the law which forced firms to pay 'interest' on paid up capital, the development of the nascent 'preference share', and other legal manoeuvres. Notwithstanding this assault, the demands of expansion could not yet prevail against the social presumption against the firm as an autonomous sum of money (witness Adam Smith's disparaging remarks in the Wealth of Nations), and we are left with the paradoxical situation of the 1780's, often cited as the first full decade of the 'Industrial Revolution', being a decade of capitalist depression. The resolution of the paradox is dialectical: physical production was expanding more rapidly than before, but existing financial organization could not keep pace, and therefore became a drag on the economy, increasing macroeconomic instability. This pressure to accelerate finance leads to the 'canal mania' of the early 1790's (partially because the canal companies take the lead in being the most financially innovative of the period), and the generalized revival of the joint-stock form in 1807-8. As finance accomodates itself to the rise in physical production, Britain experiences an above-average rate of expansion from 1799 to roughly 1808, when the Continental System and the attendant disruption of the Napoleonic wars temporarily prevented the further untrammelled growth in the physical sphere. (Napoleon may also have been partially correct about the impact of confiscations on British credit.) By 1819 physical production again accelerates, but by this time so many insitutional barriers have been broached that finance is more than able to accomodate. Joint stock promotions and Ponzi-style schemes proliferate, and financial turnover accelerates to the point where the pecuniary rate of profit overshoots the potential physical growth rate, eventuating in the great crash of 1825-6.

To summarize: the variance of the British macroeconomy was high in the first years of 'modern' fluctuation because of a low physical rate of growth coupled with a period of intense financial innovation leading to a high pecuniary rate of profit. In reaction to the South Sea Bubble and the ensuing decade of depression, institutional constraints were imposed on the capitalist firm and finance, which did act to reduce instability in the economy. Later in the century, these institutional constraints themselves became binding when institutional innovation in physical production led to accelerating rates of output. The subsequent evolution of finance and the firm first acted as a drag on accumulation, and then outstripped it, causing an increase in variance and instability which culminated in the other great crash of the era in 1825-6.

Some Further Thoughts on Periodization in Economic History

If this work has accomplished anything, the author hopes it has contributed to an increased awareness of how theory and history can conceivable interact fruitfully. What at first blush seems to be an incredibly prosaic idea has become novel because of the impact of neoclassical economics on the practice of economic histroy in the twentieth century. It was no accident that Toybee's "Industrial Revolution" follows hot on the heels of the "marginalist revolution": that division of history into two epochs divided by "a wave of gadgets." In the Walrasian world-view there are only three classes of phenomena exogenous to the economy's operation: tastes, technologies, and the endowments of individuals. Since economists have generally shied away from Weberian schemes of changes in 'tastes' (broadly defined) as ushering in the modern era, one of the other two classes had to be isolated as the initial cause of the quantitatively altered growth and as the historical boundary between we moderns and traditional antiquity. Some historians have opted for the 'endowments' route (e.g., England had abundant coal resources while France did not, or western Europe 'already had enjoyed high standards of living while eastern Europe did not), but it is clear that the existence of a certain configuration of endowments cannot provide a division between the two historical epochs, since any configuration would not be strictly exogenous: that is, the endowments themselves would have historical antecedents which would demand further specification. (As a sidelight, this is exactly the Achilles heel of neoclassical capital theory.)

Therefore, it was a forgone conclusion that the theoretically sanctioned story of the Great Divide, the Industrial Revolution, would have to be a wave of gadgets which appear out of nowhere and transform the structure of the economy and its ability to expand. If one feels that this may be too grandiose a generalization, let them consider the title of the most popular textbook of European economic history in the early postwar period: The Unbound Prometheus. The gods, having given men fire, now release them to subdue the earth. As economic historians have come to be trained increasingly within the confines of economics departments, they are also coming to realize the sheer theoretical necessity of this conception of history, given their framework. [85]

This necessity ultimately arises out of the ideological corner into which neoclassical economics has painted itself at the very inception of its research program. We have observed in chapter five that the notion of laissez-faire and all its attendant baggage effectively exiled social and economic institutions from economic theory from Walras onwards. The 'naturalness' of the market precludes other forms of social organization (including those that prop up the market) from entering into the determination of economic variables, and thus denies them any historical coordinate referents, except for some vain search for an approximation to 'laissez faire' in the past. The Promethean metaphor is misleading because the new technologies did not enable the subduing of the earth, but rather facilitated the subduing of people by other people. Government, social relations, religious mores, wars, communal actitives—everything that is interesting in history—are all obscured by this procedure, all reduced to mere snags or nuisances in the path of the Juggernaut.

The only way to elevate these institutions to positions of historical relevance and importance is to alter the underlying theoretical conception of the economy. This involves a redefinition of terms, and of the idea of causality, as explained in chapters five and six. It leads to a periodization of history in which the 'wave of gadgets' is relegated to a place of more minor importance, and to a certain extent made endogenous. Relations between people, no longer 'white noise' which creates frictions in the smooth operation of the market, become instead the criteria by which we set off one historical epoch from another, as suggested in chapter four. Again, the exogenous becomes endogenous.

In this vision, the early modern period is punctuated by two major convulsions in 1720 and 1825-6; the latter date provides us with a convenient and sensible stopping point for this work. The latter date is not only significant because of the crash which punctuates a long wave of expansion in the English macroeconomy, but also because many innovations in turnover enter a new phase at that date. The

Bubble Act, which has played a significant role in our narrative, is repealed in 1825. This action explicitly recognized that the firm as a distinct sum of money was here to stay; which meant the polity had to try to tame this growth and make it into a symbiotic rather than a parasitic organism. Further, the Combination Acts were repealed in 1824. This involved a recognition that the polity must somehow create a balance of forces out of the inevitable tensions in the hierarchically structured workplace. And finally, the Stockton and Darlington railway was completed in 1825, introducing a technology which surpassed anything previous to it in the employment of massive units of long-lived physical inputs. All of these certainly changed the relations of physical and financial turnover which followed. These changes would justify a separate study in and of themselves.

FOOTNOTES TO CHAPTER I

[1] T. Sowell, Say's Law, Princeton, NJ: Princeton U. Pr., 1972.
P.M. Sweezy, The Theory of Capitalist Development, New York: Monthly Review Pr., 1941, part III.
R. Link, English Theories of Economic Fluctuations 1815-1848, New York: Columbia U. Pr., 1959.
M. Bleaney, Underconsumption Theories, London: Lawrence & Wishart, 1976.
J. Schumpeter, History of Economic Analysis, Oxford: Oxford U. Pr., 1954, pp. 688-753, 1074-1139.

[2] Version one: Alvin Hansen, Business Cycle Theory, Boston: Ginn and Co., 1927.
Version two: Alvin Hansen, Business Cycles and National Income, New York: Norton, 1964.

[3] J.M. Keynes, Essays and Sketches in Biography, New York: Meridan, 1956, pp. 32, 36.

[4] J.M. Keynes General Theory of Employment, Income and Money, New York: Harcourt, Brace, 1964, p. 213 et seq.
T.R. Malthus, Principles of Political Economy, Ricardo's Works, Sraffa Edition, Cambridge: Cambridge U. Pr., 1966, p. 38 et seq.
See also L. Pasinetti on "The Ricardian Features of Keynes's Analysis" in his Growth and Income Distribution, Camb. U. Pr., 1974, pp. 42-5 and B. Corry, Money, Saving and Investment In English Economics, London: St. Martin's, 1962, pp. 125-128.

[5] G. Haberler, Prosperity and Depression, 3rd ed., Geneva: League of Nations, 1941.

[6] Harberler, op. cit., p. 235.

[7] J.M. Keynes, Collected Works, ed. D. Moggridge, Cambridge: Cambridge U. Pr., vol. XIV, 1973, p. 106.

[8] This discussion of 'incommensurability' has been heavily influenced by Paul Feyerabend, Against Method, London: New Left Books, 1975; especially chapter 7.

[9] These examples are from Feyerabend, ibid., pp. 274-275.

[10] Keynes, Collected Works, vol. 13, p. 243.

[11] Keynes, Collected Works, vol. 13, p. 265.

[12] Friedrich van Hayek, Profits, Interest and Investment, London: Routledge, 1939, p. 13 fn. and Hayek, "The Ricardo Effect" Economica, May 1942. See also: Hayek, Tiger by the Tail, ed. by S. Shenoy, p. 103: "(Keynes) alleged, with only parital justification, that the classics had based their argument on the assumption of full employment, and he based his own argument on what may be called the assumption of full employment, i.e., the assumption that there normally existed 'unused 'reserves of all factors and commodities...An analysis on the assumption of full employment even if the assumption is only paritally valid, at least helps us to understand the functioning of the price mechanism, the significance of the relations between different prices and of the factors which lead to a change in these relations. But the assumption that all goods and factors are available in excess makes the whole prices system redundant, undetermined and unintelligible."

[13] Keynes Collected Works, vol. 14, p. 486.

[14] G. Mehta, The Structure of the Keynesian Revolution, New York: St. Martins, 1978, p. 164. See also G. O'Driscoll Economics as a Coordination Problem, Kansas City: Sheed Andrews & McMeel 1977, p. 136.

[15] It must be stressed that Say's Law, as it is now understood, is predominently a neoclassical concept, irrespective of the fact that it is attributed to J.B. Say. This is because it is merely some form of an expression of a neoclassical condition that 'quantity supplied' must equal 'quantity demanded' in all markets. Therefore, attempts to attribute some modern form of Say's Law to Ricardo or Marx is often inappropriate, because the 'quantity demanded' plays a totally passive role in their systems, and is not a primary determinant of equilibrium.

[16] T. Sowell, Say's Law, op. cit., pp. 34-36.

[17] See for example, M. Feldstein, J. Green, & E. Sheshinski, "Corporate Financial Policy", Quarterly Journal of Economics, Aug. 1979.

[18] R. Frisch "Propagation & Impulse Problems" in Economic Essays in Honor of Gustav Cassel, London: Cass 1933.

[19] Joseph Schumpeter Business Cycles, New York: McGraw Hill, 1939.

[20] L. Pasinetti "Cyclical Fluctuations and Economic Growth" especially pp. 72-75 in Growth and Income Distribution, op. cit.

FOOTNOTES TO CHAPTER II

[1] B. Supple, Commercial Crisis and Change in England, Cambridge: Cambridge U. Pr., 1959, p. 198. The theoretical writings of the mercantilists are discussed in Chapter 9 of that work.

[2] C. Hull, ed., The Economic Writings of Sir William Petty, Cambridge: Cambridge U. Pr., vol. 1, pp. 50-51.

[3] British Museum, Sloane MSS no. 2902.

[4] The London Journal, A bound copy of many of the issues is perserved in the Goldsmith's Library, Senate House, University of London.

[5] This trend in economic thought is amply documented in G.S.L. Tucker, Progress and Profits in British Economic Thought, Cambridge: Cambridge U. Pr., 1960.

[6] Debate on the Salt Excise in the House of Commons, reported in the Historical Register, 1732, p. 239.

[7] See Tucker, op. cit., p. 63 et seq., and Michael Bleaney, Underconsumption Theories, London: Lawrence and Wishart, 1976; p. 91 et seq.

[8] Adam Smith, Wealth of Nations, Cannan Ed., Mod. Lib., 1937, p. 406.

[9] The Correspondence of Adam Smith, ed. E. Mossner and I. Ross, Oxford U. Pr., 1977; p. 162.

[10] For example, B. Corry, Money, Saving and Investment in English Economic 1800-1850, London: St. Matin's, 1962, p. 3.

[11] D. Ricardo, Notes on Malthus' Principles, Sraffa edition, Works, vol. II, pp. 304-5.

[12] D. Ricardo, quoted in B. Corry, op. cit., p. 29.

[13] D. Ricardo, quoted in B. Corry, op. cit., p. 59.

[14] Barry Gordon, Political Economy in Parliament, London: Macmillan, 1976, Chapt. 4.

[15] Malthus in Sraffa edit., Ricardo's Works, vol. II, pp. 302-3.

[16] In a letter to Malthus, Ricardo wrote: "If you think that with an increase of capital men become indifferent both to consumption and accumulation, then you are correct in opposing Mr. Mill's idea, that in reference to a nation, supply can never exceed demand....Tho' it appears natural that the desire of accumulation should decrease with an increase of capital, and diminished profits, it appears equally probable that consumption will increase in the same ratio." --Quoted in B. Corry, op. cit., p. 37.

[17] Ricardo, Works, vol. II, p. 308.

[18] T. Sowell, Say's Law, op. cit., pp. 51 & 76.

[19] Quoted in Rosa Luxemburg, The Accumulation of Capital, New York: Monthly Reviews Press, 1968, pp. 213-4.

[20] Quoted in Sowell, op. cit., p. 77.

[21] Elie Halevy, "Sismondi" in H. Spiegel, ed, The Development of Economic Science, New York: Wiley, 1952, p. 266.

[22] B. Corry, op. cit., p. 106: T. Sowell, op. cit., p. 149.

[23] John Lalor, quoted in Corry, op. cit., p. 107.

[24] Karl Marx, Theories of Surplus Value, vol II; Moscow: Progress Publishers, pp. 504, 506.
For further elaboration on the interaction of money and Say' Law in Marx, see Suzanne de Brunhoff, Marx and Money, New York: Urizen Books, 1975.

[25] P. Wicksteed, The Common Sense of Political Economy (1910), vol. I, New York: Augustus Kelley, 1967, p. 460.

[26] W. Stanley Jevons, Investigations in Currency and Finance (1884), New York: Kelley, 1964, p. 204.

[27] See, for examples, R. Hawtrey, "The Trade Cycle" in H. Ellis, ed. Readings in Business Cycle Theory, Philadelphia: Blakiston.
Irving Fisher, "Gold Depreciation and Interest Rates," Moody's Magazine, Feb. 1909, and
"The Business Cycle Largely a Dance of the Dollar," Journal of the American Statistical Association, Dec. 1923.

[28] Knut Wicksell, <u>Lectures on Political Economy</u>, 2 Vols., London: Routledge, 1936.
For and extended criticism of Wicksell's interest theory, see F. Lutz, <u>The Theory of Interest</u>, Chicago: Aldine, 1968, Chapter 2.

FOOTNOTES TO CHAPTER III

[1] T. Veblen, <u>The Theory of the Leisure Class</u>, New York: Mentor, 1953; pp. 133-4. Veblen had perhaps more exposure to the utility school's views than most of his contemporaries, not only reading the Austrians in the original German but also through studying under J.B. Clark as an undergraduate, when Clark was forming his marginal productivity doctrine.

[2] T. Veblen, "Professor Clark's Economics" in E.K. Hunt and J. Schwartz, <u>Critique of Economic Theory</u>, Baltimore: Penquin, 1972. Parenthetically, Veblen anticipated much of the spirit if not the substantive points of the capital theory debates of the 60's in this short review.
If the reader thinks that the connection between J.B. Clark-style parables and Say's Law is a bit overdrawn, he/she need only read Clark's introduction to the English translation of Karl Rodbertus' <u>Overproduction and Crises</u>: "That universal overproduction is impossible has been considered axiomatic and certainly it is not possible that more of every kind of article should be created than is wanted by the entire public...In a world of reality we have insatiable wants to deal with, and an unsaleable surplus of all things can never be produced. An unsaleable surplus of <u>many</u> things can be produced. Overproduction is practically misdirected production...If the productivity theory of wages is true,--if natural law tends to give to the worker what he specifically creates, and if that amount is an increasing one--the major premise of Rodbertus' reasoning about crises [that increasingly workmen cannot purchase the goods produced for them] must be reconsidered." (pp. 2-3, 9)

[3] T. Veblen, <u>Theory of Business Enterprise</u>, New York: Mentor, 1932, p. 20.

[4] T. Veblen, <u>Theory of Business</u>, op. cit., p. 58 et seq.

[5] T. Veblen, <u>Theory of Business Enterprise</u>, op. cit., p. 50.

[6] "Therfore such loans cannot, at least not directly, swell the aggregate industrial equipment or enhance the aggregate productivity of industry, for the

items which serve as collateral are already previously in use in industry to the extent that they can be used." Veblen, Theory of Business Enterprise, op. cit., p. 54.

[7] If he was mentioned at all, it was as the butt of ridicule. For example, see Frank Knight:
"Perhaps it had been neglected unduly by economists, but Veblen's allegation that such stealing though production of disturbances in business arrangements is the usual or characteristic activity of modern economic life is of course merely humorous." Risk, Uncertainty and Profit, New York: Harper & Row, 1965; p. 335.
It seems the reason that Knight thought it humorous was because, writing in 1915-16, he thought "Economic progress under real conditions shows similar advance and recession, proceeding in cycles of a character now fairly well understood."

[8] Quoted in Arthur Burns, "Wesley Clair Mitchell," in H. Speigel, ed., The Development of Economic Thought; New York: Wiley, 1952.

[9] W.C. Mitchell, Types of Economic Theory, ed. by J. Dorfman; New York: Augustus Kelley, 1969; p. 677.

[10] A. Burns, op. cit., p. 424.

[11] J. Dorfman, The Economic Mind in American Civilization, vol. III, New York: Viking, 1949, pp. 470-71.

[12] W.C. MItchell, quoted in Burns, op. cit., p. 425.

[13] W.C. Mitchell, Business Cycles, Berkeley: U. of Cal. Pr., 1913, 1963, p. xi, p. 149.

[14] Evidence in this paragraph is taken from Appendix VI, pp. 825-7, Types of Economic Theory, op. cit.

[15] The only reference I have come across which stresses Mitchell's crucial role in the discussions of instability in the 20's and 30's is William Stoneman, A History of the Economic Analysis of the Great Depression In America, New York; Garland, 1979.

[16] Joan Robinson has written, "Keynes' identities, $Y=C+I=C+S$; $S+I$ have the great advantage that they correspond to columns in the national accounts: income, consumption, investment and saving." Economic Heresies, New York: Basic Books, 1973, p. 77. Another 'great advantage' was that Keynes himself did not have to explain too precisely what he meant by his definitions and identities, as we shall see in the next chapter.

[17] See, for example, Mitchell, Types of Economic Theory, op. cit., pp. 676 et seq.

[18] J. Ronnie Davis, The New Economics and the Old Economists, Ames, Iowa: Iowa State U. Pr., 1971. Susan Howson & Donald Winch, The Economic Advisory Council, Cambridge: Camb. U. Pr., 1977.

[19] "Until the appearance of the mathematical models of Meade, Lange, Hicks and Harrod there is reason to believe that Keynes himself did not truly understand his own analysis..., the Keynesian savings-investment-income cross is not formally different from the 'Marshallian supply-demand-price cross'." Paul Samuelson, "On Keynes", in H. Spiegel, ed., The Development of Economic Thought, New York: Wiley, pp. 765 and 777.

[20] D.H. Robertson to Keynes, 5 Dec. 1919, in The Collected Works, vol. XIII, p. 118.

[21] J.M. Keynes, The General Theory of Employment, Income and Money, New York: Harcourt, Brace, 1964, p. 135.

[22] See J.M. Keynes, "The Theory of Unemployment", Quarterly Journal of Economics, Feb. 1937, p. 218; and The General Theory, op. cit., pp. 199-201.

[23] J.M. Keynes, General Theory, op. cit., p. 75.

[24] J.M. Keynes, Quarterly Journal of Economics, Feb. 1937, op. cit., p. 220.

[25] See H. Minsky, John Maynard Keynes, New York: Columbia U. Pr., 1975, p. 40 et seq.

[26] J.M. Keynes, The General Theory, op. cit., p. 295.

[27] J.M. Keynes, The General Theory, op. cit., p. 313.

[28] J.M. Keynes, Collected Works, vol. XIII, p. 615.

[29] J.M. Keynes, "Theory of Unemployment", op. cit., p. 222.

[30] Harrod to Keynes, letter of 1 Aug. 1935: "The notion that price is determined by supply and demand always rests on a cet. par. assumption: e.g., that there are no price changes of other things or that they are irrelevant. What you seem to me to have shown is that there are changes in other things which are so relevant and of

such overpowering importance, that the old s. and d. analysis had better be put away." in Keynes, Collected Works, vol. XIII, p. 531

[31] J.M. Keynes, General Theory, op. cit., p. 317.

[32] P. Sraffa, "The Law of Returns Under Competitive Conditions," Economic Journal, 1926. See also David Levine, Contributions to the Critique of Economic Theory, vol. I, London: Routledge & Kegan Paul, 1977; ch. 8, and Nina Shapiro, "The Revolutionary Character of Post-Keynesian Economics," Journal of Economic Issues, Sept. 1977.
Joan Robinson was aware in 1932 that Sraffa's criticism may have implications for Keynes' analysis. See Keynes, Collected Works, vol. XIII, P. 378.

[33] J.M. Keynes, The General Theory, op. cit., p. 213.

[34] J.M. Keynes, Collected Works, vol. XIII, pp. 533-34.

[35] This controversy started while Keynes was alive. See Harrod's letter to Keynes of 15 April 1937: "I want to bring level-of-output theory into relation with the system of cost and utility equations on which orthodox general theory has--in a way rightly--rested. The level of output ought prima facie to depend on the desire for goods, for leisure, etc.," J.M. Keynes, Collected Works, vol. XIV, p. 176.

[36] Ohlin in Keynes, Collected Works, vol. XIV, p. 195.

[37] D.H. Robertson to Keynes, 3 Feb. 1935: "I never liked Kahn's [short period] method in his public works article: but it did at least allow time (though unspecified in amount) for the 'savings' corresponing to an act of investment financed by new bank money, to be elicited: whereas now, since there is no limit to the shortness of time over which we are at liberty to apply your equations, they are simultaneous and identical."
J.M. Keynes, Collected Works, vol. XIII, p. 497.
See also Collected Works, vol. XIII, p. 432.

[38] J.M. Keynes, Collected Works, vol. XIII, p. 438.

[39] J.M. Keynes, Collected Works, vol. XIV, p. 180. See also, Collected Works, vol. XIII, p. 432, and G. Mehta, The Structure of the Keynesian Revolution, New York: St. Martin's, 1978, p. 153.

[40] J.M. Keynes, Collected Works, vol. XIII, p. 517.

[41] Ohlin in Keynes, Collected Works, vol. XIV, p. 198 FN.

[42] For a further explication of the checkered history of time-phased processes in economic theory, see chapter eight below.

[43] For a summary of this literature, see Mehta, op. cit.

[44] J.M. Keynes, Collected Works, vol. XIV, p. 209.

[45] J.M. Keynes, Collected Works, vol. XIV, pp. 11-12.

[46] Paul A. Samuelson, "The Interaction Between Multiplier Analysis and the Principle of Acceleration," in Haberler, ed., Readings in Business Cycle Theory, Homewood, IL: Irwin, 1951.

[47] It must be stressed, in all fairness, that the Harrod/Fellner equation of the accelerator and a marginal capital/output ratio is acutally arbitrary, and that some neoclassical economists have recognized that fact. Ott [Ott, Review of Economic Studies, June 1958] seems to have been the first to see that the problem had to do with the conception of time in economic analysis; he has also concisely shown in which discrete cases the accelerator coefficient and the marginal capital coefficient are one and the same. Let induced investment be

$$I = B(Y_{t-p} - Y_{t-p-1})$$

Here 'p' is the behavioral lag between the time new income is realized and when investment, as derived demand, takes place. Further, we have a relation which translates units of investment into new units of national income

$$Y_{t+q} - Y_{t+q-1} = I_t/v$$

Ott interprets this as a technological relation, with 'v' as the marginal capital/output coefficient, but here he is on shaky ground, since he has collapsed the whole sequence

>   investment--increased physical inputs--
>   increased physical outputs--increased sales--
>   increased incomes

into one equivalence, which surely makes more hidden equilibrium assumptions than are tenable in a Keynesian system (except perhaps in golden age growth, which would preclude the existence of cycles anyway). At any rate, only if the lags p=q=0 will the acceleration coefficient equal the marginal capital/output coefficient. Thus, Harrod's statements depend crucially upon the time patterns inherent in the anaylsis, something which his exposition has suppressed.

It would also be mentioned that Samuelson himself did not want to appeal to a technological relation as Harrod did, but only a behavioral relation, on the same analytic level as the consumption function.

[48] See, for example:
N. Rau, _The Trade Cycle: Theory and Evidence_, New York: Wiley, 1974;
A. Hansen, _Business Cycles and National Income_, New York: Norton, 1964;
J. van Doorn, _Disequilibrium Economics_, New York: Wiley, 1975;
R.C.O. Matthews, _The Business Cycle_, Cambridge: Cambridge U. Pr., 1959.

[49] J.R. Hicks, _A Contribution to the Theory of the Trade Cycle_, Oxford: Oxford U. Pr., 1950, p. 4: Ragnar Frisch, "Propagation and Impulse Problems in Dynamic Economics" in R. Gordon & L. Klein, eds., _Readings in Business Cycles_, Homewood, IL: Irwin, 1965.
Rutledge Vining succinctly summarized the state of the art by 1949 in writing, "I should feel much safer in bringing my little work before the Commissar of Research if that chair were occupied by Burns or Mitchell than if Koopmans were the occupant. I would feel that the final question put by Commissar Koopmans would be, 'Where are your difference equations?'"
("Koopmans on the Choice of Variables to be Studied and of Methods of Measurement" in Klein and Gordon, eds., op. cit., p.216.)

[50] R.N. Goodwin, "The Nonlinear Accelerator and the Persistence of Business Cycles," _Econometrica_ Jan. 1951; Goodwin, "The Problem of Trend and Cycle," _Yorks Bulletin of Econ. and Soc. Research_, Aug. 1953.

[51]   E. Slutsky, "The Summation of Random Causes as the Source of Cyclical Processes," Econometrica, 1937.

[52]   For a concise description of this reversed theoretical sequence see Minsky, op. cit., pp. 32-54; see also Hicks, "Mr. Keynes and the Classics," Econometrica, 1937. The textbook authority of the early 70's was William Branson, Macroeconomic Theory and Policy, New York: Harper & Row, 1972. Branson only managed to mention business cycles once in the whole book, and that is in the context of the specification of the consumption function.

[53]   I. & F. Adelman, "The Dynamic Properties of the Klein-Goldberger Model," Econometrica, 1959.

[54]   P. Naylor, T. Wertz, & P. Wonnacott, "Spectral Analysis of Data Generated by Simulation Experiments," Econometrica, Apr. 1969, and other articles cited therein; E.P. Howrey, "Stochastic Properties of the Klein-Goldberger Model," Econometrica, Jan. 1971.

[55]   E.P. Howrey, "Dynamic Properties of Stochastic Linear Econometric Models," unpublished Princeton Econometric Program Research memo no. 87, June 1967.

[56]   B. Hickman, ed., Econometric Models of Cyclical Behavior, New York: Columbia U. Pr., 1967.

[57]   E.P. Howrey, "Dynamic Properties of a Condensed Version of The Wharton Model," in Hickman, ed., op. cit.

[58]   B. Hickman, op. cit., p. 11.

[59]   G. Harcourt, "The Theoretical and Social Significance of The Cambridge Controversies," in J. Schwartz, ed., The Subtle Anatomy of Capitalism, Santa Monica, CA: Goodyear, 1977; and
G. Harcourt, Some Cambridge Controversies in the Theory of Capital, Cambridge: Camb. U. Pr., 1972.

[60]   Minsky, Keynes, op. cit., p. 53.
See also Clower and Leijonhufvud:
"Is the existing economic system, in any significant sense, self-adjusting? The standard Keynesian model does not address this central question."
"The Co-ordination of Economic Activites: A Keynesian Perspective," American Economic Review, March 1975, p. 182.
See also Alan Coddington's characterization of the ISLM model as promoting "the indespensable method of analyzing cyclical movements by ignoring the fact that there is a cycle" in his review of Malinvaud, Journal of Economic Literature, Sept. 1978, pp. 1012-18.

FOOTNOTES TO CHAPTER IV

[1] Karl Marx, quoted in E.P. Thompson, The Making of the English Working Class, New York: Pantheon, 1963, p. 552. See also Marx, Capital, vol. I, New York: International Publishers, 1967, p. 283.

[2] Less frequently do we find admissions of theories being tailor-made by the theorists themselves, which makes the following anecdote related by Von Hayek all the more interesting:
"Later a turn in the conversation made me ask him (Keynes) whether he was not concerned about what some of his disciples were making of his theories. After a not very complementary remark about the persons concerned, he proceeded to reassure me: those ideas had been badly needed at the time he had launched them. But I need not be alarmed; if they should ever become dangerous I could rely upon him that he would again quickly swing round public opinion--indicating by a quick movement of his hand how rapidly that would be done. But three months later he was dead..."
F.A. Von Hayek's review of Roy Harrod's Life of Keynes reprinted in his Studies In Philosophy, Politics and Economics, New York: Simon & Schuster, 1967, p. 348.

[3] See May Brodbeck, "Explanation, Prediction and Imperfect Knowledge" in Minnesota Studies in the Philosophy of Science, vol. III, ed. by H. Feigl and M. Maxwell, Minneapolis: U. of Minnesota Pr., 1962. For a critique, see Terrence Ball, "On Historical Explanation," Philosophy of the Social Science, Sept. 1972.

[4] Peter Temin, Did Monetary Forces Cause the Great Depression? New York: Norton, 1976, pp. 174 et seq.

[5] Otto Lightener, A History of Business Depressions, New York: Burt Franklin, 1970 (1922).

[6] E.M. Carus-Wilson and O. Coleman, England's Export Trade 1275-1547, Oxford: Oxford U. Pr., 1963, pp. 122-23, 138-9. See also H. Miskimin, The Economy of Early Rennaissance Europe, Englewood Cliffs, NJ: Prentice Hall, 1969, p. 130.

[7] H. Hauser, "The European Financial Crisis of 1559," Journal of Economic and Business History, Feb. 1930.

[8] Irving Fisher, "Our Unstable Dollar and Our So-Called Business Cycles," Journal of the American Stat. Assn., June 1925, pp. 191-2.

[9] R. Heilbroner, The Worldly Philosophers, 3rd ed. New York: Simon and Schuster, 1972, p. 70.

[10] H. Dennison, "Management and the Business Cycle," Journal of the American Stat. Assn., March 1922, p. 20.

[11] D. Aldcroft and P. Fearson, British Economic Fluctuations 1790-1939, London: Macmillan, 1972, p. 3.

[12] M. Tugan-Baranowski, Les Crises Industrielles en Angleterre, Paris: M. Giard and E. Briere, 1913, p. 6.

[13] B. Supple, Commercial Crisis and Change in England, 1600-1642, Cambridge: Camb. U. Pr., 1959, p. 8; see also J.G. Van Dillen, "Economic Fluctuations and Trade in the Netherlands 1650-1750" in P. Earle, ed., Essays In European Economic History, Oxford: Oxford U. Pr., 1974, p. 199.

[14] This is a revised and shortened version of: Philip Mirowski, "Some Parables in the Theory and History of Fixed and Circulating Capital." Tufts Univ. discussion paper, 1981.

[15] "Between 1660 and 1719 some 54 major joint stock companies were given charters....There is a temptation to see this as a boom in real economic activity. The reality was less attractive. It was the first big performance in England by that familiar and dangerous commedian of the capitalist stage: the company promoter." D.C. Coleman, The Economy of England 1450-1750, Oxford: Oxford U. Pr., 1977, pp. 169-70.
"...the tulip craze in Holland, the South Sea Bubble in England, the Law schemes in France, show only a superficial similarity to the later expansion-crisis-depression cycle, on the one hand because they were purely local in character, and on the other because they were purely financial affairs." Emlyn Thomas, The Crisis of 1825, MSC thesis, unpublished, Univ. of London, 1938, p. 12.
"Before 1870 there were crises due to ignorance in the handling of coinage and note issues; misuse of state credit; speculative manipulation in the early days of joint stock companies." Alvin Hansen, Business Cycle Theory, Boston: Ginn and Co., 1927, p. 73.

[16] Karl Marx, Theories of Surplus Value, Vol. III, Moscow: Progress Pub., 1968, p. 525.

[17] W.C. Mitchell, Business Cycles and Their Causes, Berkeley: U. of Cal. Pr., 1941 (1913), p. 169.

[18] J. Schumpeter, Business Cycles, Vol. I, New York: McGraw Hill, 1939, pp. 223, 249.

[19] See, for example, Peter Mathias, The First Industrial Nation, London: Meuthen, 1969, Chapter 7.

[20] "Neglect of the instability of credit (by economic theory) began by and large with the depression of the 1930's." Charles Kindelberger, Manias, Panics and Crashes, New York: Basic Books, 1978, p. 70. This is not surprising, as we have seen in chapter three, since the adoption of Keynesian economics encompassed Keynes' attitudes towards finance. Present day neglect is bound up with the idea that market speculation could not be destabilizing. See L. Telser, "A Theory of Speculation Relating Profitability and Stability," Review of Economic and Statistics, Aug. 1959.

[21] See, for examples, T.S. Ashton, Economic Fluctuations in the Eighteenth Century. Oxford: Oxford U. Pr., 1959, p. 173 et seq.; A. Gayer, W.W. Rostow and A. Schwartz, The Growth and Fluctuation of the British Economy, Oxford: Oxford U. Pr., 1955; W.W. Rostow, The World Economy, Austin: U. of Texas Pr., 1978, Chapter 21, Joseph Schumpeter, obviously, also was a proponent of this view.

[22] "En Depit des multiples theories des crises il n'existe un fond que quatre categories de crises et de depressions pre-industrielles: celles qui sont provoquées par des catastrophes, par une mauvaise recolté, par une inflation de guerre et par une speculation capitaliste." J. Akerman, Structures et Cycles Economiques, second volume, Paris: Presses Universitaires de France, 1957, p. 249.

[23] See 'Some Theorists in Search of an Auctioneer, below.

[24] W.S. Jevons, Investigations in Currency and Finance, New York: Kelley, 1964, p. 209 et seq. See also Philip Mirowski, "Macroeconomic Fluctuations and Natural Distrubances," Journal of Economic History, June 1984, and chapter nine below.

[25] R.C.O. Matthews, A Study in Trade Cycle History, Oxford: Oxford U. Pr., 1954, p. 28. See also J.M. Keynes, General Theory, op. cit., pp. 329-32.

[26] T.S. Ashton, Economic Fluctuations, op. cit., Chapter 2, and A.H. John, "Agricultural Productivity and Economic Growth in England," Journal of Economic History, 1962.

[27] G. Mingay, "The Agricultural Depression," Economic History Review, 1956, and J.D. Chambers, The Vale of Trent, Cambridge: Camb. U. Pr., 1956.

[28] V. Timoshenko, "The Role of Agricultural Fluctuations in the Business Cycle," *Michigan Business Studies*, June 1930, p. 1.

[29] R. Ippolito, "The Effect of the Agricultural Depression on the Industrial Revolution in England," *Economica*, Aug. 1975.

[30] This is also true of Keynes' characterization of early trade cycles in his *General Theory*, op. cit., pp. 329-32.

[31] A.H. John, "War and the English Economy, 1700-1763," *Economic History Review*, 1954-5 and P. Deane, "War and Industrialization" in J. Winter, ed., *War and Economic Development*, Cambridge: Camb. U. Pr., 1975.

[32] For an extreme, and therefore clear example of this contradiction, see Glen Huckel, "War and the British Economy, 1793-1815," *Explorations in Economic History*, Summer, 1973.

[33] M. Dobb, *Studies in the Development of Capitalism*, New York: International Pub., Chapter 1, is an early statement of this position.

[34] J.R. Hicks, *A Theory of Economic History*, Oxford: Oxford U. Pr., 1969, p. 7.

[35] J.R. Hicks, *Theory*, op. cit., p. 28.

[36] R. Clower and A. Leijonhufvud, "The Coordination of Economic Acitivity: A Keynesian Perspective," *American Economic Review*, May 1975, p. 178. This section is also based on: R. Clower, "Anatomy of Monetary Theory," *American Economic Review*, Feb. 1977; R. Clower, "Snarks, Quarks and Other Fiction," in L. Cain and P. Uselding, eds., *Business Enterprise and Economic Change*, Kent State U. Pr., 1973.

[37] See E. Furbotn and S. Pejovich, "Property Rights and Economic Theory: A Survey," *Journal of Economic Literature*, Dec. 1972; Martin Shubik, "The General Equilibrium Model Is Incomplete and Not Adequate for the Reconciliation of Macro and Micro Theory," *Kyklos*, 1975; and Douglas North, "Structure and Performance: The Task of Economic History," *Journal of Economic Literature*, Sept. 1978.

[38] The argument of the last paragraph is made in much greater detail in Philip Mirowski, "Is there a Neo-Insitutional Mathematical Economics?" *Journal of Economic Issues*, Sept. 1981.

FOOTNOTES TO CHAPTER V

[1] Quoted in Gunnar Myrdal, The Political Element in the Development of Economic Theory, New York: Simon & Schuster, 1969, ppp. 57-8.

[2] R.M. Rauner, Samuel Baily and the Classical Theory of Value, London: Bell, 1961, Chapter One.

[3] P. Garegnani, "On a Change in the Notion of Equilibrium in Recent Work on Value and Distribution" in Brown, Sato and Zarembka, eds., Essays in Modern Capital Theory, North-Holland, 1976.

[4] For a fascinating modern elaboration of this premise, see Michael Thompson, Rubbish Theory, New York: Oxforrd U. Pr., 1979.

[5] See Thorstein in Veblen, The Place of Science in Modern Civilization, New York: Heubsch, pp. 280-85; and Martin Shubik, "The General Equilibrium Model Is Incomplete and Not Adequate for the Reconciliation of Micro and Macroeconomic Theory," Kyklos, 1975; Philip Mirowski, "The Rule of Conservation Principles in 20th Century Economic Theory," Philosophy of the Social Sciences, Dec. 1984.

[6] John R. Commons, The Legal Foundations of Capitalism, Madison Univ. of Wisconsin Press, 1968, Chapter Two.

[7] C. Bliss, Capital Theory and the Distribution of Income, New York: North Holland, 1975, p. 44.

[8] Gary Becker, "A Theory of the Allocation of Time," Economic Journal, Sept. 1965.

[9] Nicholas Georgeescu-Roegen, The Entropy Law and the Economic Process, Harvard University Press, 1971, p. 134.

[10] J.R. Hicks, Captial and Time, Oxford: Oxford U. Pr., 1973.

[11] R.C.O. Matthews, The Business Cycle, Cambridge Univ. Pr., 1959, p. 13. For a more extended discussion of the problems mentioned in the next paragraph, see H.B. Malingren, "Information and Period Analysis in Economic Decisions," in J.N. Wolfe, ed., Value, Capital and Growth, Edinbrugh Univ. Pr., 1968.

[12] Matthews, Business Cycle, op. cit., p. 14.

[13] Alfred Ott, "The Relation Between the Accelerator and the Capital Output Ratios," Review of Economic Studies, June 1958.

[14] C. Kennedy, "Time, Interest and the Production Function," in J.N. Wolfe, ed., Value, Capital and Growth, op. cit.; see also G.S.L. Shackle, A Scheme of Economic Theory, Cambridge: Camb. Univ. Pr., 1965.

[15] P.W. Bridgman, The Logic of Modern Physics, New York: MacMillan, 1961, p. 72.

The striking parallel between Von Neumann's work in physics and in economics may become more pointed if we consider the verdict of a contemporary philosopher of science:

..."in order to achieve this miracle (of mathematical structures of great generality) all the existing troubles had to be pushed into the relation between theory and fact, and had to be concealed, by ad hoc approximations and other failures...Von Neumann's work in quantum mechanics is an especially instructive example of this procedure. In order to arrive at a satisfactory proof of the expansion theorem in Hilbert space, Von Neumann replaces the quasi-intuitive notions of Dirac and Bohr by more complex notions of his own. The theoretical relations between these notions are accessible to a more rigorous treatment than the theoretical relations between the notions that precede them ('more rigorous' from the point of view of Von Neumann and his followers). It is different with their relation to experimental procedures. No measuring instruments can be specified for the great majority of observables, and where specification is possible it becomes necessary to modify well known and unrefuted laws in an arbitrary way or else to admit that some quite ordinary problems of quantum mechanics, such as the scattering problem do not have a solution. Thus the theory of becomes a veritable monster of rigor and precision while its relation to experience is more obscure than ever."

--P. Feyerabend, Against Method, London: New Left Books, 1975, p. 64.

The parallels with his work in economics are so strong and striking, that one wonders whether it was the epistemological program of Von Neumann's life work which gained it its popularity. Quoting him in his own words:

Indeed, in classical mechanics there are two absolutely equivalent ways to state the same theory, and one of them is causal and the other is teleological. Both describe the same thing...Newton's description is causal and d"Alembert's description is teleological...This is very important, since it proves that if one has really technically penetrated a subject, things that previously seemed in complete contrast, might be purely mathematical transformations of one another. Things which appear to represent deep differences of principle and of interpretation in this way may turn our to not affect any significant statements and any predictions. They mean nothing to the context of the theory."

[16] G. Debreu, The Theory of Value, New Haven: Yale U. Pr., 1959, pp. 29-30.

[17] "Our model has all the time in the world, for we are concerned with actions each of which is neither preceded or followed, in any effective sense, by any other action. These actions are not embedded in any history, and there is really, in our model, no means of measuring the length of a time interval." G.S.L. Shackle, ibid., p. 15.

[18] See J.M. Blatt, "the Utility of Being Hanged on the Gallows," Journal of Post Keynesian Economics, Winter 1979-80.

[19] A.D. Knox, "The Acceleration Principle and the Theory of Investment," Economica, Aug. 1952, p. 46.

[20] T.J. Sargent and C. Sims, "Business Cycle Modelling Without Pretending to Have Too Much A Priori Theory," in Sims, ed., New..., op. cit., p. 46.

[21] For a summary see Harcourt, op. cit., pp. 63 et seq.

[22] The best introduction to and summary of this literature is G. Winston, "The Theory of Capacity Utilization and Idleness," Journal of Economic Literature, Dec. 1974.

[23] "The neo-Ricardians, by means of the neoclassical theory of the choice of technique, have established that capital aggregation is theoretically unsound. Fine. Let us give them an alpha for this."
--F. Hahn, "The Winter of Our Discontent," Economica, 1973, p.363.
"Economists have looked for this simple relationship, one of the main propositions of neoclassical economics, for a century; but now it is generally recognized that the property (sic) did not always hold...Cambridge UK has been right on this point."
--E. Malinvaud, "Discussion," in Harcourt, ed., The Microeconomic Foundations of Macroeconomics, London: Macmillan, 1977, pp. 40-41.

[24] J.M. Keynes, General Theory, op. cit., pp. 136, 140. See also above, Chapter Three.

[25] Harcourt, Controversies, op. cit., p. 99 et seq.

[26] See for instance, M.N. Buechner, "Frank Knight or Capital as the Only Factor of Production," Journal of Economic Issues, Sept. 1976.

[27] See A. Brody, Proportions, Prices and Planning, New York: Elsevier, 1974.

[28] See J.O Winjum, The Role of Accounting in the Economic Development of England 1500-1750, Champaign, IL: CIERA, p. 80 et seq.

[29] For elaborations on the history of this tax, see A. Hope-Jones, The Income Tax in the Napoleonic Wars, Cambridge: Camb. U. Pr., 1939; and E.R.A. Seligman, The Income Tax, New York: MacMillan, 1914.

[30] P.H. Wueller, "Concepts of Taxable Income," in G. Harcourt and R. Parker, eds., Readings in the Concept and Measurement of Income, Cambridge: Camb. U. Pr., 1969, p. 142.

[31] I. Fisher, "Income and Capital," in Harcourt and Parker, eds., op. cit., p. 34. All subsequent quotes are from this article.

[32] J. Hicks, in Harcourt and Parker, eds., op. cit., p. 74.

[33] H.C. Simons, "The Definition of Income," in Harcourt and Parker, eds., op. cit., p. 67.

[34] J.M Keynes, General Theory, op. cit., pp. 40-41.

[35] For this see Brian Tew, "Keynesian Accountancy," Yorkshire Bulletin of Economic and Social Research, Aug. 1953.

[36] Keynes, General Theory, op. cit., p. 61.

[37] Simon Kuznets, National Income and Its Composition, New York: NBER, 1954, p. 35, p. 5. For a description of Smith's adding-up theory of value, see M. Dobb, Theories of Value and Distribution Since Adam Smith, Chapter 2.

[38] John Commons, Institutional Economics, New York: MacMillan, 1934, p. 254.

[39] A. Sen, "the Concept of Efficiency," in Parkin and Nobay, eds., Contemporary Issues in Economics, Manchester: Man. U. Pr., 1975, p. 198-9.

[40] L. Walras, Elements of Pure Economics, London: George Allen and Unwin, 1969, p. 225.

[41] F.H. Knight, Risk, Uncertainty and Profit, New York: Houghton Mifflin, 1921, p. 22.

[42] For elaboration, see M.N. Buechner, "Frank Knight on Capital as the Only Factor of Production," Journal of Economic Issues, Sept. 1976.

[43] If this were true, it would take a rather baroque social theory to explain why anyone would rationally opt for garnishing an inherently unknowable and unfathomable stream of returns rather than a nice, steady contractual wage. In fact, this objection to Walrasian theory was voiced quite early by as eminent a neoclassical theorist as Edgeworth. See J. Schumpeter, History of Economic Analysis, Oxford: Oxford U. Pr., p. 1049 et seq., especially Schumpeter's wriggling reply, in which he can only reassert his belief in the Walrasian creed.

[44] I think I am safe in taking Samuelson's text as representative (Economics eighth ed., New York: McGraw Hill, 1970). Chapter 31 revels in down-home prose, a change of pace for Samuelson, but necessary because of the obvious differential in level of rigor between this and other chapters. "Profits are the report card of the past, the incentive gold star of the future, and also the grubstake for new ventures." (p. 602) "Much of what is ordinarily called profit is really nothing but interest, rent and wages under a different name," (p. 594). "A factual examination of the great fortunes of the past shows a strong luck element in many of them." (p. 595) "Economic activities that involve much uncertainty and risk will be forced by competitive entry and exit of risk takers to pay a positive profit premium to compensate for aversion to risk." (p. 596)
It is entertaining to note that all of these 'explanations' of profit can be found in the pre-neoclassical works of William Ellis (1826) and G.P. Scrope (1813). See D.M. Lmaberton, "Information and Profit," in C. Carter and J. Ford, eds., Uncertainty and Expectation in Economics, A. Kelley, 1972.

[45] R. Schramm and R. Sherman, "Profit Risk, Management and the Theory of the Firm," Southern Economic Journal, Jan. 1974.

[46] J. Eatwell, "The Long-Period Method and the Intertemporal Method in the Neoclassical Theory of the Rate of Profit," unpublished manuscript, Cambridge: March 1976, and M. Milgate, "A Change in the Notion of Equilibirum," Economica, 1979.

[47] Joan Robinson, quoted in J.A. Clifton, "Competition and the Evolution of the Capitalist mode of Production," Cambridge Journal of Economics, June 1977, p. 145.

[48] See J. Clifton, "Competition," ibid.

[49] Oscar Morganstern, On the Accuracy of Economic Observations, 2nd edit., Princeton, NJ: Princeton U. Pr., 1963, p. 70 et seq.

[50] P.A. Samuelson, "Proof That Properly Anticipated Prices Fluctuate Randomly," Industrial Management Review, Spring, 1965.

[51] For a summary of this evidence see Michael Firth, The Valuation of Shares and the Efficient Markets Theory, London: MacMillan, 1977, Chap. 7. One point in this literature which has been ignored until the present is how crucially these test rest on the choice of the appropriate time period, which is arbitrary.

[52] F. Modigliani and M. Miller, "Some Estimates of the Cost of Capital to the Electric Utility Industry," American Economic Reivew, June 1966, pp. 338-9. See also, _____, "Cost of Capital, Corporation Finance and the Theory of Investment," in E. Solomon, ed., The Management of Corporate Capital, NY: Free Press, 1959, and Burton Malkiel, The Debt-Equity Combination of the Firm and the Cost of Capital, Princeton: General Learning Corp., 1971.

[53] Malkiel, ibid., p. 18.

[54] J. Stiglitz, "A Re-examination of the Modigliani-Miller Theorem," American Economic Review, Dec. 1969; James Scott, "Bankruptcy, Secured Debt, and Optional Capital Structure," Journal of Finance, Mar. 1977.

[55] J.M. Blatt, "The Utility of Being Hanged on the Gallows," ibid.

[56] Douglas Vickers, Financial Markets in the Capitalist Process, Univ. of Pennsylvania Press, 1978, p. 8 et seq.

[57] Vickers, Financial..., ibid., p. 40.

[58] Christopher Sims, "Macroeconomics and Reality," *Econometrica*, Jan. 1980, p. 4.

[59] See R. Marris and D. Mueller, "The Corporation and Competition," *Journal of Economic Literature*, March 1980; and R. Marris, *The Corporate Economy*, Cambridge: Harvard U. Pr., 1971, p. 23.

[60] See Victor Goldberg, "Institutional Change and the Quasi-Invisible Hand," *Journal of Law and Economics*, Oct. 1974.

FOOTNOTES TO CHAPTER VI

[1] See John R. Commons, *The Legal Foundations of Capitalism*, Madison: Univ. Wisconsin Press, 1968, ch. 5; and his *Institutional Economics*, New York: MacMillan, 1934, Chaps. 2 and 9.

[2] See Piero Sraffa, "The Laws of Returns Under Competitive Conditions," *Economic Journal*, 1926.

[3] Nicholas Kaldor, "The Equilibrium of the Firm," in his *Essays in Value and Distribution*, Glencoe: Free Press, 1960. Sraffa was the first to examine the arbitrary character of this distinction:
"...increasing and decreasing costs are nothing other than different aspects of one and the same thing that can occur at the same time, for the same industry, so that an industry can be classified arbitrarily in one or the other category according to the definition of 'industry' that is considered preferable for each particular problem, and according to whether short or long periods are considered."
--Quoted in A. Roncagalia, *Sraffa and the Theory Prices*, New York: Wiley, 1978, pp. 19-20.

[4] Much of the mathematics of our physical production model is discussed in: Michio Morishima, *Equilibrium, Stability and Growth*, Oxford: Oxford U. Pr., 1964, chapter 4; Andras Brody, *Proportions, Prices and Planning*, New York: American Elsevier, 1974; and A. Brody, "A Linearized Model of the Cycle," *Acta Oeconomica*, 1978.

[5] See, for example, Donald Harris, *Capital Accumulation and Increase Distribution*, Stanford Univ. Press, 1978, pp. 90-95 et seq.

[6] A. Takayama, *Mathematical Economics*, Hinsdale, IL: Dryden, 1974, p. 383, Thm. 4.c.4.

[7]   Takayama, op. cit., p. 372, Thm. 4.b.1.

[8]   See E. Burmeister & R. Dobell, Mathematical Theories of Economic Growth, New York: Macmillan, 1970; and Morishima, op. cit.

[9]   David Levine, "Aspects of the Classical Theory of Markets," Australian Economic Papers, June 1980.

[10] Levine, op. cit., pp. 11-12.

[11] Cf. Axel Leijonhufvud, Information and Coordination, Oxford: Oxford U. Pr., 1972.

[13] C.K. Wilbur & R.S. Harrison, "The Methodological Bssis of Institutional Economics," Journal of Economic Issues, 12, March 1978; William Dugger, "Methodological Differences Between Institutional and Neoclassical Economics," Journal of Economic Issues, 13, June 1979; Philip Mirowski, "Is There a Mathematical Neoinstitutional Economics?" Journal of Economic Issues, 15, Sept. 1981.

[14] Nicholas Georgeescu-Roegen, The Entropy Law and the Economic Process, Cambridge: Harvard U. Pr., 1972; Philip Mirowski, "Institutions as Solutions in a Game Theory Context," in Larry Samuelson, ed., Advances in Microeconomic Theory, Boston: Kluwer-Nijhoff, 1985.

[15] Douglas Reid, "The Decline of Saint Monday," Past and Present, May 1976.

[16] An excellent example of the type of historical work which reconceptualizes the conventional explanation is Avi Cohen, "Technological Change as an Historical Process," Journal of Economic History, vol. 44, Sept. 1984.

[17] J.M. Keynes, "Alternative Theories of the Rate of Interest," Economic Journal, June 1937, p. 666.

[18] As John Commons wrote in his textbook Institutional Economics (New York: Macmillan, 1937, p. 72): "It is from the field of corporation finance, with its changeable assets and liabilities, rather than from the field of individual wants and labor, or pains and pleasures, or wealth and happiness, or utility and disutility, that institutional economics derives a large part of its data and methodology. Institutional economics is concerned with the Assets and Liabilities of concerns contrasted with Adam Smith's Wealth of Nations."

[19] A short survey of the institutional structure is provided by the Bank of Japan, The Japanese Financial System, Toyko, 1972.
The Japanese financial structure was completely reorganized after the Occupation, with a stress on commercial banks rather than bond issue as the primary source of funds for the industrial sector. Since Japanese commercial banks are chronically 'over-loaned' (and this is the Bank of Japan's choice of wording), financial turnover is higher than under many other Western regimes. Something on the order of 90% of funds for the corporate business sector are provided by direct arrangements with banks or crypto-banks. Quoting the Bank of Japan publication, p. 18, "Japanese enterprises are financially unbalanced, with the relative inadequacy of net worth on one hand and the excessive liabilities on the other."

FOOTNOTES TO CHAPTER VII

[1] Calculated from Table I, p. 6 in D.C. Coleman, Economy, op. cit.

[2] "By the end of the (Seventeenth) century, at least, life-long wage laborers may well have been a majority of the population." Christopher Hill, "Pottage for Freeborn Englishman," in C. Feinstein, ed., Socialism, Capitalism and Growth, Cambridge: Camb. U. Pr., 1969, p. 347. See also C.B. MacPherson, The Political Theory of Possissive Individualism, Oxford: Oxford U. Pr., 1962, pp. 286-90.

[3] T. Veblen, The Theory of Business Enterpise, New York: Mentor, p. 43, et seq. See also John Commons, Institutional Economics, New York: Macmillan, 1934, pp. 42-43.

[4] T. Veblen, Theory, op. cit., p. 46.

[5] See C. MacPherson, The Political Theory, op. cit., p. 206 et seq.

[6] J.O. Appleby, Economic Thought and Ideology in Seventeenth Century England, Princeton: Princeton U. Pr., 1978, pp. 175-76.

[7] See K. Thomas, "Work and Leisure in Pre-Industrial Society," Past and Present, no. 29. It is important that the reader does not detect a Rousseauvian 'natural state' lurking somewhere in this statement. The existence of biological rhythms has been accepted by the biological and psychological scientific communities for

quite some time now: as examples, see A. Sollberger, "Biological Measurements in Time with Particular Reference to Synchronization Mechanisms" in R. Fisher, ed., Interdisciplinary Perspectives on Time, Annals of the New York Academy of Sciences, vol. 138, art. 2, pp. 561-99; and Sollberger, Biological Rhythm Research, Amsterdam: Elsevier, 1965; and S. Binkley, "A Timekeeping Enzyme in the Pineal Gland," Scientific American, April 1979. The simple point is, in the absence of Western measured time, these temporal and chronological rhythms must have predominated.

[8] T. Veblen, The Theory of the Leisure Class, New York: Macmillan, 1899, especially Chapter 3.
Henry Fielding, in his Increase of Robberies (1751) wrote: "To the upper part of mankind, time is an enemy and (as they themselves often confess) their chief labor is to kill it; whereas with the other, time and money are almost synonymous..."
Abraham Crowley admitted in 1702 that "...the workmen's time is their livelihood." Quoted in M. Flinn, Men of Iron, Edinburgh: Edinburgh U. Pr., 1962, p. 211.

[9] A.P. Usher, A History of Mechanical Inventions, Boston: Beacon Press, 1954, p. 211.

[10] C. Cippola, Clocks and Culture, New York: Norton, 1967, pp. 139, 69.

[11] E.P. Thompson, "Time, Work-Discipline and Industrial Capitalism," Past and Present, no. 38.

[12] Thompson, op. cit., pp. 81-2; Flinn, Men of Iron, op. cit.

[13] N. McKendrick, "Josiah Wedgewood and Factory Discipline," Historical Journal, 1961, p. 41. For an example of a factory which failed due to, among other things, a lack of supervision, see J.V. Backett, "The Eighteenth Century Origins of the Factory System," Business History, January 1977.

[14] E. Roll, An Early Experiment in Industrial Organization, London: Cass, 1930, p. 204.
T.S. Ashton, normally an apologist when confronting these matters, admits that by the Eighteenth century all that was left of the apprenticeship system was thinly disguised ploy for the binding of cheap labor to the workplace. See Ashton, Peter Stubs: An Eighteenth Century Industrialist, Manchester: Manchester U. Pr., 1939, p. 28.
Subcontracting drove out regular day wages in Scottish lead mining in the course of the Eighteenth century. See T.C. Smout, "Lead Mining in Scotland," in P. Payne, ed., Studies in Scottish Business History, London: Cass, 1967.

Subcontracting children was prevalent in the cotton spinning industry in the later Eighteenth century. See S. Pollard, The Genesis of Modern Management, Baltimore, MD: Penguin, 1965, p. 57 et seq.

[15] R. Baxter, A Christian Directory (1673), pp. 274-77, quoted in Thompson, op. cit., p. 87. See also reading 38 (1675) in J. Thirsk and J. Cooper, eds., Seventeenth Century Economic Documents, Oxford: Oxford U. Pr., 1972, pp. 97-99.

[16] O. Heywood, Youth's Mentor (1689), quoted in Thompson, op. cit. See also Christopher Hill, Society and Puritanism, New York: Schocken, 1967, Chapters 4 and 5.

[17] Quoted in R.H. Campbell, Carron Company, Edinburgh: Oliver and Boyd, 1961, p. 61.

[18] Quoted in N. McKendrick, "Cost Accounting in the Industrial Revolution," Economic History Review, 1970, p. 55.

[19] P. Mantoux, The Industrial Revolution in the Eighteenth Century, New York: Harper & Row, 1961, p. 78 et seq.

[20] For examples and further references, see S. Pollard, Genesis, op. cit., p. 220 et seq.; Flinn, Men of Iron, op. cit., pp. 40-41, 194 et seq.; R. Campbell, Carron, op. cit., pp. 68-69; McKendrick, "Factory Discipline," op. cit.; A. Aspinall, Early English Trade Unions, London: Batchworth, 1949; S. and B. Webb, History of Trade Unionism, London: Macmillan, 1920.

[21] M.M. Postan, Medieval Trade and Finance, Cambridge: Camb. U. Pr., 1973, Chapter 3.

[22] For some of the problems with viewing the Sixteenth century joint stock as modern, see Carole Shammas, "Invisible Merchants and Property Rights," Business History, July 1975.

[23] G. Parker, "The Emergence of Modern Finance in Europe, 1500-1730," in C. Cipolla, ed., The Fontana Economic History of Europe, London: Fontana, vol. II, pp. 555-56.

[24] See Lucy Sutherland, The East India Company in Eighteenth Century Politics, Oxford: Oxford U. Pr., 1952, p. 10, and P. Dickson, The Financial Revolution in England, London: Macmillan, 1967, p. 460 et seq.

[25] For elaboration, see Philip Mirowski, "The Rise and Retreat of a Market," *Journal of Economic History*, Sept. 1981.

[26] C. Carr, *Select Charters of Trading Companies*, New York: Burt Franklin, 1970 (1913), p. xvi.

[27] Pollard, *Genesis*, op. cit., pp. 24-5. For those familiar with the Coase Theorem, this opinion very nearly characterizes the orthodox theoretical opinion of the neoclassical firm.

[28] Shammas, "Invisible Merchants," op. cit., p. 104. See also Violet Barbour, *Capitalism in Amsterdam in the Seventeenth Century*, Ann Arbor, Mich.: U. of Mich. Pr., 1963, p. 79.

[29] C. Wilson, *Anglo-Dutch Commerce and Finance in the Eighteenth Century*, Cambridge: Camb. U. Pr., 1941, p. 14.

[30] P. Dickson, *Financial Revolution*, op. cit., p. 500 et seq. See also evidence from Houghton's *Collections* in Mirowski, "Rise...," op. cit.

[31] M.M. Postan, *Medieval*, op. cit., Chapter 1.

[32] L. Stone, *The Crisis of the Aristocracy*, Oxford: Oxford U. Pr., 1966, p. 529. Also, "The general attitude of medieval law to assignment of debts, and the special requirements which the transfers had to satisfy in order to be legally valid made the emergence of fully negotiable paper impossible." M. Postan, *Medieval*, op. cit., p. 42.

[33] Appleby, *Economic*, op. cit., pp. 214-15.

[34] Parker, "Emergence," op. cit., p. 545. See also J. Holden, *A History of Negotiable Instruments*, op. cit.

[35] S. Pollard, *Genesis*, op. cit., pp. 67, 76-77.

[36] S. Marglin, "What Do Bosses Do?" Part I, *Review of Radical Political Economics*, vol. 6, no. 2, Summer 1974.

[37] MacPherson makes a compelling case that wage labor was associated with slavery in the minds of turn of the century freeborn Englishmen. C. MacPherson, *Political*, op. cit., and Hill, "Freeborn," op. cit.

[38] See Flinn, <u>Men</u>, op. cit., p. 213; Ashton, <u>Peter Stubs</u>, op. cit., p. 33; T.C. Smout, "Lead Mining," op. cit., p. 122.

[39] "The adoption of regular, periodic returns in place of the <u>ad hoc</u>, waste book or journal type of bookkeeping, the forcing of the natural rhythm of work into a strait-jacket of comparable sections of time," (Pollard, <u>Genesis</u>, op. cit., p. 252) was the intrusion of the clock into the firm as well as into the factory. At the point where finance must also obey the rules of the measured hour, we see the capitalist relinquish the keeping of the books to a new type of worker: the accountant. The indulgence in biological rhythms which separates the nonworker from the worker must be maintained, even at the risk of less direct control over financial turnover.

[40] B. Supple, <u>Crisis and Change</u>, op. cit.

[41] W. Scott, <u>The Constitution and Finance of English, Scottish and Irish Joint Stock Companies</u>, vol. I, New York: Peter Smith, 1951 (1912), p. 317.

[42] E. Morgan and W. Thomas, <u>The Stock Exchange</u>, 2nd ed., New York: St. Martins, 1969, p. 16 and Scott, op. cit., Chapter xvii.

FOOTNOTES TO CHAPTER VIII

[1] G.S.L. Tucker, <u>Progress and Profits in British Thought</u>, Cambridge: Camb. U. Pr., 1960.

[2] A. Smith, <u>Wealth of Nations</u>, Cannan ed., Encyc. Brittanica, p. 37.

[3] Quoted in J.O Winjum, <u>The Role of Accounting in the Economic Devlopement of England 1500-1750</u>, Urbana, IL: Ctr. for Internat. Educ. & Res. in Accounting, 1972, p. 22.

[4] B.S. Yamey, "Sceintific Bookkeeping and the Rise of Capitalism," <u>Economic History Review</u>, 1949.
_____, "Accounting and the Rise of Capitalism: Further Notes on a Theme by Sombart," <u>Journal of Accounting Res.</u>, 2 #2, Autumn 1964.

[5] Richard Grassby, "The Rate of Profit in Seventeenth Century England," <u>English Historical Review</u>, October 1969.
G.E. Lee, "The Concept of Profit in British Accounting

1760-1900," <u>Business History Review</u>, vol. XLIX no. 1, Spring 1975.
Sidney Pollard, <u>The Genesis of Modern Management</u>, Baltimore, MD: Penguin, 1965, chap. 6.

[6] J.O. Winjum, op. cit., p. 196.

[7] Public Record Office, C/114/9,10,11.

[8] R.H. Campbell, <u>Carron Company</u>, Edinburgh: Oliver & Boyd, 1961, pp. 165-6.

[9] Sidney Pollard, "Capital Accounting in the Industrial Revolution," in Francois Crouzet, ed., <u>Capital Formation in the Industrial Revolution</u>, London: Meuthen, 1972, pp. 126, 144.

[10] S. Pollard, "Capital Formation in the Industrial Revolution," in Crouzet, op. cit.

[11] Karl Marx, <u>Capital</u> vol. II, New York: International Pub., 1967, p. 158.

[12] Marx, op. cit., p. 185.

[13] W.S. Jevons, <u>The Theory of Political Economy</u>, London: Penguin, 1970, p. 229.

[14] Eugen von Bohm-Bawerk, <u>Capital and Interest</u>, Libertarian Press, 1959, vol. I, pp. 169-70. The fact that Bohm-Bawerk dealt mainly with point-input point-output processes allowed him to ignore the implied paradox.

[15] Bohm-Bawerk, op. cit., vol. II, pp. 110-11.

[16] J.R. Hicks, <u>Theory of Economic History</u>, Oxford: Oxford U. Pr., 1964, pp. 315 and 311.

[17] Frank Fetter, <u>Capital, Interest and Rent</u>, Kansas City: Sheed, Andrews & McMeel, 1977, p. 148.

[18] J.R. Commons, <u>Legal Foundations of Capitalism</u>, Madison: Univ. of Wisconsin, 1968, pp. 168-9.

[19] Pollard, "Capital Accounting," op. cit., pp. 147-8.

[20] Peter Mathias, "Capital, Credit and Enterprise in the Industrial Revolution," <u>Journal of European Economic History</u>, Spring 1973, p. 126.
Mathias is actually in error here, because Pollard is not concerned with the ratio of fixed capital to <u>total</u>

assets, since he ignores all financial assets, as we shall see below.

A similar contention is made by Charles Feinstein in "Capital Formation in Great Britain" in P. Mathias and M.M. Postan, eds., The Cambridge Economic History of Europe (New York: Cambridge U. Pr., 1978, pp. 66-68). Feinstein uses a national income accounts methodology (the perpetual inventory method) to estimate the magnitude of fixed capital in the aggregate of four points in time: 1760, 1800, 1830 and 1860. He then makes some assumptions about the ratio of circulating capital (for which he has no data) to output, and suggests that fixity rose appreciably around 1830 or thereabouts. In this book we shall not directly address aggregative attempts to empiricism with regard to physical fixity, for reasons discussed in chapter 5.

[21] "At Gott's, the first Large integrated woolen mill, fixed capital was valued at 28,000, circulating capital at 65,400 in 1801" (Pollard, op. cit., 1972, p. 149). This gives a ratio of .428; but examination of the reference (W.B. Crump, The Leeds Woolen Industry, 1931, p. 257) reveals the following balance sheet for 1901:

B. Ing. Stock	43,575
Build'g & Machin.	23,000
Estate at B. Ing.	3,000
debt owed by P.W.A. Pottgeiser	2,625
Total	73,000
less debts	18,324
	54,676

The only ratio of fixed to circulating capital which I can derive is the ratio of plant and machinery to stock, or 26,000/43,575 = .596.

[22] J.M. Keynes, The General Theory, New York: Harcourt, Brace, 1964, p. 59.

[23] Richard Brief, Nineteenth Century Capital Accounting, NY: Arno, 1976, pp. 19 et seq; and J.O. Winjum, The Role of Accounting in the Development of England, Urbana: CIERA, pp. 61-63.

[24] The price indicies were taken from P. Deane & B. Mitchell, Abstract of British Historical Statistics, Cambridge: Camb. U. Pr., 1962, pp. 468-70.

[25] T.A. Lee, Income and Value Measurement: Theory and Practice, London: Nelson, 1974, p. 18.

[26] Stanley Kitchen, quoted in the London Financial Times, June 30, 1977.

[27] Joyce Appleby, in an unpublished lecture to the 1977 Anglo-American Historians Conference at the University of London, shared the insight that De Mandeville's private vices were only the province of the leisured aristocratic class whoe consumption kept the whole system functioning. From examples of laissez-faire theory like the Modigliani-Miller theorem, it is not clear that contemporarily allowable private vices are all that much more democratically based.

[28] F. Modigliani and M. Miller, "The Cost of Capital...," American Economic Review, June 1958; J. Stiglitz, "A Re-examination of the Modigliani-Miller Hypothesis," American Economic Review, December 1969.

[29] T.A. Lee, Income, op. cit.

[30] Phyllis Deane, The First Industrial Revolution, Cambridge: Camb. U. Pr., 1967, p. 226. T.S. Ashton, op. cit., pp. 172-3; Mentor Bouniatian, Geschichte Der Handeldrisen in England, 1640-1840, Munich: Ernst Reinhardt, 1908; Alvin Hansen, Business Cycles and National Income, New York: Norton, 1964, p. 214.

FOOTNOTES TO CHAPTER IX

[1] In fact, Ashton's motivation was hardly theoretical at all as can be judged from his summary chapter:
"(Historians)...have observed that, over the century, there was a growth of income and capital, but they have also observed that much indicated extreme poverty and distress; and they have sought to explain this conjunction by all sorts of misty theories. The paradox disappears, or at least loses its sharpness, when it is realized that the upward slope was not continuous by was broken throughout by declivities, and that it was at these points that most of the instances of misery were concentrated."
--T.S. Ashton, Economic Fluctuations in England 1700-1800, Oxford: Clarendon Press, 1959, p. 177.

[2] A. Gayer, W.W. Rostow & A. Schwartz, The Growth and Fluctuations of the British Economy 1790-1850, Oxford: Oxford U. Pr., 1953, p. 354, vol. I.

[3] See P. Deane & W. Cole, British Economic Growth 1688-1959, 2nd ed., Cambridge: Camb. U. Pr., 1969; chap. 2 and esp. pp. 76-79; also B. Thomas, "The Rhythm of Growth in the Atlantic Economy of the 18th Century," Research in Economic History, vol. 3, 1978.

[4] E.B. Schumpeter, English Overseas Trade Statistics, Oxford: Oxford U. Pr., 1960.

[5] W. Cole, "Trends in 18th Century Smuggling," Economic History Review, 1958.

[6] This is a common methodological procedure in the construction of Leontief input/output talbes. Cf. W. Leontief, Input Output Economics, New York: Oxford U. Pr., 1966, pp. 18-19.

[7] Gayer, Rostow & Schwartz, microfilm appendix to Growth, op. cit., p. 846.

[8] Deane & Cole, British, op. cit., p. 41; and P. Deane, book review, Economic Journal, 1956.

[9] Cf. M.C. Lovell, "The Role of the Bank of England as a Lender of Last Resort in 18th Century Crises," Explorations in Entrepreneurial History, X, 1957; the source of the data is J. Clapham, The Bank of England, Cambridge: Camb. U. Pr., 1945, vol. I, app. E.

[10] P. Mirowski, "The Plague and the Penny Loaf," unpub. man., 1976; presented to the 1976 Cliometrics conference, Madison, Wisc.

[11] Scott, Constitution & Finance, op. cit., vol. I p. 328.

[12] J. Horsefield, British Monetary Experiments, Cambridge, MA: Harvard U. Pr., 1960, p. 14.

[13] East India Company data from home ledgers, India Office Records Library, L/AG/1/1/9-10. The Profit rate is the balance of the profit and loss account, corrected for dividends, divided by nominal equity. Cash flow is cash account debit total, in thousands of pounds. Spencer Stanhope partnership information calculated from information, mostly concerning Colnbridge forge, in A. Raistrick & E. Allen, "The South Yorkshire Ironmasters, 1690-1750," Economic History Review, May 1939. War Remittances and hallage receipts were taken from D.W. Jones, "London Merchants and the Crisis of the 1690's" in P. Clark and P. Slack, eds., Crisis and Order in English Towns, Toronto: U. of Toronto Press, 1972, p. 323.

[14] British Museum, Sloane Mss., no. 2902; p. 285.

[15] Scott, Constitution & Finance, op. cit., vol. I; p. 367.

[16] For some biographical information, see J. Carswell, The South Sea Bubble, London: Cresset Press, 1961, p. 52 and p. 275. The ledger data was collected by the author from Public Record Office C/114/164.

[17] PRO AO/3/950.

[18] Ashton, Economic Fluctuations, op. cit., p. 141.

[19] See Deane & Mitchell, Abstract of British Historical Statistics, Cambridge: Camb. U. Pr., 1962, p. 468.

[20] J. Francis, Chronicles and Characters of the Stock Exchange, London, 1948, p. 47.

[21] The best versions of the tale are J. Carswell, South Sea Bubble, op. cit.; and P. Dickson, Financial Revolution, op. cit.

[22] Adam Anderson, The Origins of Commerce, London, 1801, vol. III, pp. 108-112.

[23] A. Wadsworth & J. deLacy Mann, The Cotton Trade and Industrial Lancashire, Manchester: Manchester U. Pr., 1931, p. 214.

[24] L.M. Cullen, An Economic History of Ireland Since 1660, London: Batsford, 1972, p. 46.

[25] F. Groeneveld, De Economische Crisis Van het Jaar 1720, Groningen, Batavia: Noordhoff, 1940.

[26] A. Sayous, "Les Repercussions de l'Affaire de Law," Bijdragen Voor Vaterlandsche Geschiednis en Oudheitkunde, vii, 2.

[27] J. Akerman, Structures et Cycles Economiques, Paris: Presses Univ. de France, 1957, tome 2, pt. 1, p. 255.

[28] L.M. Cullen, Economic History, op. cit., p. 36.

[29] London Journal, issues for dates given in the text. A bound copy of a complete run of issues of the Journal was found in the Goldsmith's Library, Senate House, University of London, which ranged from 1721 to 1722; there was also a shorter run of issues from January 28 to May 15, 1726. Unfortunately, the author was unable to find complete runs of any other newspaper for any other period of the 1720's, which might have provided contemporary evidence of the depression.

[30] G. Mingay, "The Agricultural Depression," Economic History Review, 1956.

[31] the levels of income from August to August of the year were: 1729: 13,225; 1730: 15,992; 1731: 12,483; 1732: 8,249; 1733: 7,845. The data is from J. Clapham, The Bank of England, op. cit., appendix E.

[32] C. Wilson, Anglo-Dutch Commerce, Cambridge: Camb. U. Pr., 1941, pp. 169-71.

[33] G. Manley, "The Mean Temperature of England, 1698-1952," Quarterly Journal of the Royal Meteorological Society, 1953.

[34] J. Glasspoole, "Two Centuries of Rain," Meteorological Magazine, Feb. 1928.

[35] PRO AO/3/951-954.

[36] L. Neal, "Increasing Power and Profit in Economic History," Journal of Economic History, March 1977.

[37] L. Neal, "Increasing," op. cit., p. 34.

[38] The figures, in pounds, from Aug. of the previous year until Aug. of the quoted year were:
1758 12,224   1761 30,319   1764 101,746
1759 17,747   1762 61,090   1765 61,308
1760 14,942   1763 79,166

Cf. Clapham, op. cit., p. 301.

[39] See E.E. de Jong-Keesing, De Economische Crisis van 1763 te Amsterdam, Ph.D. dissertation, Univ. of Amsterdam, 1939.

[40] Ashton, Economic, op. cit., p. 126; C. Wilson, Anglo-Dutch Commerce, op. cit.; Alice Carter, Getting, Spending and Investing in Early Modern Times, Assen: Van Gorcum, 1975, p. 63.

[41] R. Campbell, Carron Company, op. cit., pp. 136 et seq.

[42] N. McKendrick, "Cost Accounting...," op. cit.

[43] H. Hamilton, "The Failure of the Ayr Bank, 1772," Economic History Review, 1959; also Ashton, op. cit., pp. 127-29.

[44] London Chronicle, quoted in Clapham, Bank, op. cit., p. 247.

[45] Ashton, Economic, op. cit., p. 166.

[46] Ashton, op. cit., p. 132. There may have been a serious crisis in France, however. See C. Schmidt, "Les Crise Industrielle en France de 1788," Revue Historique, Jan.-Feb. 1908.

[47] L. Pressnell, Country Banking in the Industrial Revolution, Oxford: Oxford U. Pr., 1958, p. 454.

[48] G. H. Evans, British Corporate Finance, 1775-1850, Baltimore, MD: Johns Hopkins Univ. Pr., 1936. Page 4: "To induce investors to subscribe to projects which could not in the immediate future earn dividends, interest on all outstanding shares was frequently paid out of capital. Later, under stress of circumstances, this parctice was modified and preference shares were developed." See also p. 76: from 1696 to 1775, Parliament required corporations to pay interest on paid-up calls, which meant that dividends were, in a sense, obligatory. The repeal of this statute gave great incentive to the resuscitation of the corporate form of organization.

[49] J.R. Ward, The Finance of Canal Building in the Eighteenth Century, Oxford: Oxford U. Pr., 1974.

[50] J.H. Clapham, Bank, op. cit., p. 302.

[51] Gayer, Rostow & Schwartz, Growth, op. cit., vol. I, p. 44.

[52] William Smart, Economic Annals of the Nineteenth Century, vol. I, New York: Kelley, 1964, p. 42.

[53] The figures for Bank of England notes in circulation were: (in millions of pounds)
1769 10.7   1798 13.1   1800 16.8
1797   9.7   1799 13.0   1801 16.2

[54] Quoted in Smart, Annals, op. cit., vol. I, p. 65.

[55] Gayer, Rostow & Schwartz, op. cit., vol. I, p. 71.

[56] E. Heckscher, The Continental System, Oxford: Oxford U. Pr., 1922, p. 328.

[57] J. Mokyr and N. Savin, "Stagflation in Historical Perspective," paper presented to Cliometrics Conference, Madison, 1976, revised version published in vol. I, Research in Economic History.

[58] Quoted in Heckscher, op. cit., p. 157.

[59] Cf. Heckscher, op. cit., pp. 238-46. Gayer, Rostow & Schwartz, op. cit., p. 92, attribute the crisis in England entirely to a tightening of the Blockade and speculation in South America, but this explanation would hardly account for the crisis in New York, and it is only a weak explanation for its occurence in Paris and Switzerland.

[60] Gayer, Rostow & Schwartz, op. cit., p. 171.

[61] J. Thorold Rogers, Industrial and Commercial History of England, London, 1892, p. 83.

[62] Gayer, Rostow & Schwartz, op. cit., p. 186; data taken from H. English, A Complete View of the Joint Stock Companies Formed During the Years 1824 and 1825, London, 1827.

[63] Emlyn Thomas, The Crisis of 1825, unpublished M.Sc. thesis, University of London, 1938, p. 125.

[64] E. Thomas, op. cit., p. 173.

[65] W.C. Mitchell, Business Cycles and Their Causes, op. cit., p. 167; M. Tugan-Baranowski, Les Crises Industrielles, op. cit., p. 6; J. Akerman, Structures et Cycles Economiques, op. cit., tome 2, p. 249; J. Schumpeter, Business Cycles, op. cit., vol. 2, pp. 223, 249; Peter Mathias, The First Industrial Nation, op. cit., pp. 228-31; W.W. Rostow, The World Economy, op. cit., chapter 21.

[66] John Gorman, Time Series Analysis, Cambridge: Camb. U. Pr., 1981, part I.

[67] Ibid, p. 223.

[68] John Geweke, "Inference and Causality in Economic Time Series Models," in Z. Griliches & M. Intrilligator, eds., Handbook of Econometrics, North Holland, 1982.

[69] A.L. McFie, "The Outbreak of War and the Trade Cycle," Economic History, Feb. 1938.

[70] Thus it would have been the classical economic theorists, and not the businessmen (as Pollard contends) who were confused about stocks and flows. Some support for this reading of the situation can be found in G. Tucker, Progress and Profits in British Economic Thought, op. cit., pp. 59 and 87.

[71] L. Sutherland, The East India Company in 18th Century Politics, Oxford: Oxford U. Pr., 1952, p. 9.

[72] In this respect see J.O. Winjum, The Role of Accounting in the Economic Development of England, op. cit., chap. X.

[73] The inherent contradictions between an effective market competition and other social institutions is the subject of Karl Polanyi's The Great Transformation, Boston: Beacon Press, 1944.

[74] Philip Mirowshi, "The Rise (and Retreat) of a Market," Journal of Economic History, Sept. 1981.

[75] W.R. Scott, The Constitution and Finance of English, Scotch and Irish Joint Stock Companies, New York: Peter Smith, 1951, vol. I, p. 324.

[76] Scott, Constitution, op. cit., vol. I, p. 336.

[77] Scott, Constitution, op. cit, vol. III, pp. 445-8.

[78] B.C. Hunt, The Development of the Business Corporation in England, 1800-1867, New York: Russell and Russell, 1969, p. 8; and Dickson, Financial, op. cit., p. 184 et seq. Alice Carter, in Getting, Spending and Investing in Early Modern Times, (Assen: Van Gorcum, 1975, p. 20) suggests that this is a myth, but cites an article in Law Quarterly Review which I have been unable to find.

[79] Hunt, op. cit., p. 15 et seq.; T. Tooke, History of Prices, London, 1838, vol. I, p. 277.

[80] Morgan and Thomas, op. cit., p. 125; Dickson, Financial Revolution, op. cit., p. 489.

[81] A.B. Dubois, The English Business Company After the Bubble Act, New York: Commonwealth Fund, 1938.

[82] DuBois, *English*, op. cit., p. 91.

[83] DuBois, op. cit., p. 227.

[84] Abram Chayes, "Introduction" to John P. Davis, Corporations: *A Study of the Origin and Development of Great Business Combinations and their Relation to the Authority of the State*, New York: Capricorn, 1961, p. iv.

[85] J. Mokyr, "Demand vs. Supply in the Industrial Revolution," *Journal of Economic History*, Dec. 1977, is an example. It seems few historians, including Mokyr himself, has realized the full implications of this article.

UNPUBLISHED WORKS CONSULTED

MANUSCRIPT COLLECTIONS

Birmingham City Library, Boulton and Watt Collection

British Museum
    Add. Mss. #17477, papers of Adam Anderson
    Add. Mss. #38739-41, 38759, stamp revenue returns
    Sloane Mss. #2902, papers of Abraham Hill

Guildhall Library
    Mss. #12033, Scotch Mines Co. ledgers
    Mss. #8658-8688, Hand-in-Hand Co. records
    Mss. #15042,11933,11963, Sun Assurance accounts and ledgers
    Mss. #8749-50, London Assurance records
    Mss. #10188, reconstructed ledger of Sir Charles Peers

Indian Office Records Library
    L/AG/1/1/9-28, home ledgers of the East India Co.
    L/AG/18/1/45-48
    L/AG/18/2/1-7, various financial summaries of the East India Co.

Public Record Office
    C/114/5-23, ledgers and accounts of the Million Bank
    C/114/164, account books of Charles Blunt
    BH/1/231-235,334-337, accounts of the Hudson's Bay Co.
    T/70/607-621, ledgers of the Royal African Co.
    AO/3/950-958, stamp duties, general accounts

Sun Alliance & London Assurance Group
    muniments of the London Assurance Co.

Westminster City Library
    Mss. #343/83-89, accounts of the Westminster Fire Office
    Mss. #344/50-56, accounts of Gillow & Sons, cabinet makers

UNPUBLISHED WORKS

Cule, J.E. *The Financial History of Matthew Boulton & Co., 1759-1800.* M.A. thesis, University of Birmingham, 1935.

Hartridge, R.J. *Development of Industries in London South of the Thames, 1750-1850.* M.Sc. thesis, University of London, 1955.

Runyon, Herbert. *The Economics of Irving Fisher.* Ph.D. thesis, University of Michigan 1959.

SEVENTEENTH AND EIGHTEENTH CENTURY PERIODICALS

Course of the Exchange

Gentleman's Magazine

Historical Register

Houghton's Collection for the Improvement of Husbandry and Trade

London Journal

Proctor's Price Courant

The Times